P9-AGG-494

International Terrorism

edited by
Yonah Alexander

foreword by
Arthur J. Goldberg

Published in cooperation with
the Ralph Bunche Institute
on the United Nations,
the City University of New York

The Praeger Special Studies program—
utilizing the most modern and efficient book
production techniques and a selective
worldwide distribution network—makes
available to the academic, government, and
business communities significant, timely
research in U.S. and international economic, social, and political development.

International Terrorism
National, Regional, and Global Perspectives

PRAEGER SPECIAL STUDIES IN INTERNATIONAL POLITICS AND GOVERNMENT

Praeger Publishers   New York   Washington   London

Library of Congress Cataloging in Publication Data
Main entry under title:

International terrorism.

   (Praeger special studies in international politics and
government)
   Bibliography: p.
   Includes index.
   1. Terrorism--Addresses, essays, lectures.
I. Alexander, Yonah.
HV6431.I57   364.1   75-8396
ISBN 0-275-09480-4

PRAEGER PUBLISHERS
111 Fourth Avenue, New York, N.Y. 10003, U.S.A.

Published in the United States of America in 1976
by Praeger Publishers, Inc.

Second printing, 1976

All rights reserved

© 1976 by Praeger Publishers, Inc.

Printed in the United States of America

Be not afraid of sudden terror!

Proverbs 3: 25

A poor man, finding a dried date on the road, said
to it: "Where should I go to eat you in peace?"

An Arabic proverb

The only real victory is one in which all are
equally victorious and there is defeat for no one.

Buddha

WITHDRAWN

761627

Although acts of individual and collective terrorism committed in the name of supposedly "higher" ideological and political principles date from time immemorial, the world has been plagued during the past decade by an alarming and unprecedented expansion of such phenomena. The wave of hijackings, kidnappings, bombings, and murders around the globe, the cycle of terrorism against Israel, and violence in Northern Ireland are cases in point.

This epidemic of threats to and sacrifices of human lives imperils both the growth and functioning of our system of international law. Indeed modern terrorism, with sophisticated technological means at its disposal and the future possibility of access to biological and nuclear weapons, presents a clear and present danger to the very existence of civilization itself.

This volume represents the first serious effort by a group of scholars to write a comprehensive account of national, regional, and global perspectives of international terrorism. It makes a commendable start toward filling a gap in contemporary scholarship by analyzing and interpreting, with objectivity and clarity, the many aspects of this serious problem, which is of importance to all who are deeply concerned with the maintenance of peace and justice both home and abroad.

CONTENTS

INTRODUCTION
Yonah Alexander

Human relations on all levels have been characterized by decisions demonstrating the Lasswellian formula, "who gets what, when
and how," often accompanied by the threat and use of force. Political and ideological violence, which sometimes arises from and con-
tributes to such conflict, includes what is commonly known as "terrorism."

Despite its history as a symbol, tool, method, or process of
force—taking the form of random and systematic intimidation, coercion, repression, or destruction of human lives and property—used
intentionally by an organized group to create a climate of extreme
fear in order to obtain avowed realistic or imaginary goals, terrorism has evaded a universally acceptable definition. What constitutes
"terrorism" is highly controversial. Some feel that the validity of
their cause, such as the right of self-determination and the resistance to an oppressive totalitarian regime, justifies the resort to
terrorism, viewing it as an acceptable alternative to the exercise of
legitimate power. To others, the use of this type of violence, regardless of motivation, is considered a negative and even criminal
act, outside the realm of what is tolerable, which therefore necessarily must be punished in accordance with the relevant law applicable.

While the controversy over the permissibility or impermissi-
bility of terrorism will probably persist, most observers agree that
nearly every political and ideological group has, under certain circumstances, resorted to both governmental and nongovernmental terrorism. Such violence has been, in the first place, from time immemorial, the "normal" and "rational" strategy of the strong utilized
in the perpetual struggle for power within and among nations. Thus,
governments wishing to secure and maintain a desired degree of obedience and loyalty have frequently directed institutionalized violence
against their own citizenry, as well as against other communities under their control. The tyranny of fear instituted and the terror policy employed by revolutionary France in the eighteenth century have
been duplicated manifoldly in contemporary history. The shocking
events in Nazi-occupied Europe, in Japan-dominated Asia, and in
the Soviet Union under Stalin; in war-torn Algeria, the Congo, Cyprus, Nigeria, Pakistan, and Vietnam; in dictatorially ruled Chile,

Greece, Spain, and Uganda; and in democratically blighted India and the Philippines provide dramatic illustrations of the proliferation and severity of official violence in times of war and peace.

Whenever outside forces—national, transnational, and private bodies—have attempted to modify, if not eliminate, the manifestations of terror in countries where it has occurred, governments have tended to resist external interference in their domestic affairs. South Africa's consistent refusal to accept numerous UN resolutions dealing with the apartheid system and the future of Southwest Africa, and the stubborn unwillingness of Rhodesia's white minority to relinquish its power to the black majority in the country, are cases in point.

Indeed, governments have gone further than that. They have resorted to the most extreme kind of terrorism, namely, aggressive wars. The surprise attacks by Germany on Russia and Japan on the United States during World War II, and by North Korea on South Korea, are classic examples of such policy.

The second major manifestation of terrorism, which is the main concern of this volume, is the use of sporadic and relentless "extra-normal" nongovernmental violence, principally, but not exclusively, as part of a parochial or transnational revolutionary strategy. Epitomizing the state of anarchy of contemporary life and increasingly becoming a universal nightmare, it includes acts such as the kidnapping of American and British diplomats in Brazil, Canada, Haiti, Mexico, and Uruguay, of the mayoral candidate of the Christian Democratic Party in West Berlin, of foreign companies' executives in Argentina, of Soviet Jews in Austria, and of American and Dutch students in Tanzania; the assassination of Spanish and Jordanian premiers in Madrid and Cairo, of a Quebec minister in Canada, of Belgian, American, and West German ambassadors in Guatemala and the Sudan, of Israeli diplomats in Istanbul, London, and Washington, of a Bolivian consul in Hamburg, of American army advisers in Iran, of an Italian director of a Fiat plant in Argentina, and of an Oakland school superintendent in California; the murder of a black civil rights leader in Mississippi, of passers-by in San Francisco streets, of FBI agents in South Dakota, of Israeli athletes at the Munich Olympic games, of Jewish schoolchildren at Maalot, of Christian travelers at Lod Airport, of Greek and Turkish civilians in Cyprus, of Maronites and Moslems in Lebanon, of rich landlords in West Bengal, of policemen in northern Spain, and of multinational passengers on a Pan Am plane at Rome; the bomb explosions in the business and financial districts of Chicago, New York, Paris, and Tokyo, in Catholic and Protestant areas in Belfast and Dublin, in railroad stations and mailboxes in London, in a Basque bookstore in southern France, in the British Embassy in Washington, and in Birmingham pubs; the hijacking of American, Belgian, British, Bulgarian, Ethiopian, Israeli, Russian, and West German commercial aircraft; and the destruction on the ground and in mid-air of Japanese, Lebanese, Swiss, American, and Yugoslavian airlines.

Such spectacular acts of terror have been planned and executed by subnational groups, including, on the one hand, marginal antisocial elements, conspiratorial adventurers, underground fanatics, pseudo-ideological extremists, political hallucinationists, religious enthusiasts, and racial bigots and, on the other hand, more institutionalized opposition movements such as banned political parties and paramilitary resistance organizations. Thriving on frustration and desperation, unresolved grievances, and feelings of injustices, these "have not" bodies are concerned with and dedicated to the achievement of a wide variety of ends. Anarchist groups, exemplified by Japan's Rengo Sekigun (United Red Army), are in opposition to all forms of government, law, and order. The Baader-Meinhoff group, an urban guerrilla group in West Germany, wishes to overthrow capitalism and the present parliamentary system in the country. In India, the Naxalites, who owe allegiance to Peking, wage a militant form of agrarian struggle, which they hope will lead ultimately to economic and social justice. A militant Catholic nationalist movement, the Irish Republican Army (IRA), is campaigning for the unification of the predominantly Protestant province of Northern Ireland—Ulster—now under British rule, with the Irish Republic. The Black Panther Party for Self Defense, an extreme antiwhite organization, has challenged the American system. The Marxist People's Revolutionary Party is determined to destroy the Government of Zaire, headed by President Mobotu. Euzkadi ta Azkatasuna (Basque Nation and Freedom), a clandestine militant group, is seeking a separate homeland in Spain. The Armed Forces of the National Liberation (FALN) is fighting the independence of Puerto Rico. In the Philippines, the Muslim Independence Movement is engaged in a rebellion against the Manila government. Al-Fatah, a radical nationalist group, aims to establish a "secular" Palestine in the former British mandated territory and present-day Israel. Argentina's Montoneros is a left-wing Peronist guerrilla movement challenging capitalism. An eclectic, subversive group known as Siakhal is attempting to overthrow the Shah of Iran. Moslem bands in Thailand seek equal rights in the Buddhist-dominated Thai society. Italy's Partito Communista Revoluzionario, a Trotskyist group, is working for the furtherance of international communism. The Maoist tactic of armed peasant warfare is followed by the Malayan National

Liberation Army. And, finally, Rhodesia's Zimbabine People's Union, a Moscow-oriented Marxist group, fights both capitalism and imperialism.

Although they are nourished by various cultural roots and sustained by ideologies ranging from Franz Fanon to Che Guevara, these groups have, nevertheless, a common disposition, namely, contempt for the establishment's legal and moral norms and glorification of violent deeds for the sake of the cause. They regard themselves as beyond the limits of any society and system of government and, consequently, not bound by any obligations and constraints, except those they have imposed upon themselves.

In their view, since changes in the status quo and balance of power (both domestic and international) can be achieved by violence, then the end justifies the means, and terrorism becomes enlightened heroism, constituting a supreme act of unselfish commitment and sacrifice. The National Liberation Front (FLN) therefore insisted that they were not "terrorists" but "fedayeen," freedom fighters, engaged in a struggle for the liberation of Algeria from the French. Yasir Arafat, chairman of the Palestine Liberation Organization (PLO), in an address at the United Nations explained, "whoever stands by a just cause . . . cannot possibly be called a terrorist." A spokesman for the Basque aspirations asserted, "We are not terrorists. We are soldiers." And Carlos Marighela wrote that to be labeled a terrorist in Brazil is "an honour" because he is fighting "the monstrosity of the present dictatorship." (For the Liberation of Brazil, Penguin, 1971.)

Significantly, the strategy of political and ideological violence in the context of internal and transnational revolution and warfare does not prescribe instant victories over established regimes or states. On the contrary, the struggle for fundamental political, economic, and social change is seen as complicated and protracted. Terrorist groups, by their very nature, are too small and too weak to achieve an upper hand in an open struggle for sheer power. Violence can therefore accomplish nothing in terms of immediate goals. Because of this realization, terrorists aim at psychological rather than physical results. That is, the purpose of terrorism is to create an emotional state of extreme fear in specific groups and, thereby, to ultimately alter their behavior and dispositions, or bring about a general or particular change in the structure of society and government. For example, the aim of the Palestinian terrorist attack in Jerusalem in the summer of 1975, in which 14 Israelis were killed and 72 wounded, was not only to disrupt the delicate diplomatic negotiations for a new interim agreement between Israel and Egypt. It was also directed at inflaming Jewish passions and provoking brutal police and military measures against the Arab residents of the united city so that the prerequisite conditions for a popular revolution would be created. Recognizing, therefore, that Arab violence will win only if Jews respond to it in the way that the Palestinian Movement wanted them to, Teddy Kollek, the mayor of Jerusalem, urging the two communities to display "mutual tolerance," warned over Israeli radio, "I can understand the desire for revenge, but violence now will play only into the hands of those who want to divide the city again." (The New York Times, July 5, 1975.)

To be sure, terrorism is not aimed only at the establishment. Subnational groups, some of them even officially recognized, also use violence against each other. Sufficient to mention the factional miniwar between Catholics and Protestants in northern Ireland; the hostilities between the right-wing Christians of the Phalangist Party and the left-wing Socialist Moslems and Druzes in Lebanon; and the fighting between three rival Angolan nationalist movements with tribal and racial overtones.

But whatever the rationale of violence advanced by these subnational groups to justify their challenges to particular public or private bodies, the essential fact is that modern terrorism, in contradistinction to its older precedents, has introduced a new breed of warfare in terms of technology, victimization, threat, and response. More specifically, whereas in the past weapons at the disposal of terrorists were basically knives, pistols, or grenades capable of inflicting limited suffering on intended targets, today's opposition forces possess highly sophisticated and portable instruments of destruction and death. The capture of a Palestinian group outside Rome planning to shoot down an Israeli passenger plane with a Soviet-built Strella shoulder-fired antiaircraft missile is a chilling instance of this development. Potential accessibility by terrorist groups to even more technologically advanced and threatening weaponry is not unlikely. The most alarming possibilities are situations where terrorists would obtain and use nuclear devices to intimidate, blackmail, and even devastate entire cities and countries. The proliferation of tactical nuclear weapons and the laxness of security conditions under which they are often kept make such possibilities real. Moreover, as the world is shrinking through intercommunications and swift transportation, terrorists are able to obtain an unprecedented amount of publicity for their struggles. For instance, the kidnapping of Patricia Hearst was used as a form of propaganda for the revolution of the Symbionese Liberation Army (SLA). Similarly, the extensive media coverage of the destruction of three airliners in the Jordan desert by Arab guerrillas in September 1970 has given the Palestine cause a worldwide exposure.

Modern technology has also provided terrorist groups with a facility that did not exist in the past, that is, intensified interconnection among them across national boundaries. Collaboration among ideologically linked bodies and even among those without a common philosophy or political interest has increased rapidly and substantially. Japanese anarchists were recruited to execute the Lod airport operation on behalf of the Palestine Liberation Movement. Joint training programs and transfers of arms have been carried out between the Turkish People's Army and Black September. And the People's Revolutionary Army of Argentina cooperated with the Tupamaros of Uruguay in attacking Uruguayan targets in Argentina.

The sanctification of violence, coupled with the new opportunities offered by the advances in technology, has raised the magnitude and brutality of modern terrorism to a level unknown previously. Unlike past experiences, the intended targets of attack are not restricted to individuals and property with direct involvement in a particular struggle. Current violence has also expanded to embrace neutral countries as well as citizens of uninvolved states during the past decade has spread like a contagious disease from which no society is immune. Now terrorism is no longer waged in some distant land but is brought closer to home, affecting innocent people and institutions. For example, the deliberate carnage at the Athens airport on August 5, 1973, undertaken on behalf of an Arab Palestine, resulted in a heavy toll of multinational passengers who were not personally involved in and concerned with the Arab-Israeli conflict. Their only crime was that they happened to be present at the wrong place at the wrong time.

The globalization of this new plague is matched only by its brutalization. Since, in the course of the struggle, every action is tolerated and no violence is too excessive, the level of barbarism has risen. The sadistic resort to "knee capping" in the sectarian strife in northern Ireland is a case in point. Practiced by both the Irish Republican Army (IRA) and Protestant guerrillas, it consists of punishment by shooting out that sensitive and vital joint. Through such and other cruelties, these groups hope to produce the desired effects of intimidation in order that the fear resulting will ultimately lead to satisfactory consequences.

Also, the lives of a growing number of defenseless victims are being tragically touched. For instance, diplomats, formerly regarded as enjoying protection and immunity, are kidnapped in countries to which they have been accredited by terrorists seeking to achieve goals which are internal. Often, when guerrillas' demands are rejected, their hostages are murdered in cold blood. Thus, terrorists slew a commercial attache and blew up parts of the West German Embassy in Stockholm when Bonn refused to release jailed Baader-Meinhoff members.

The emergence of this unprecedented, unpredictable, and most frightening method of warfare, whereby unrestricted and indiscriminate acts of violence turn the whole world into a battlefield without frontiers, illustrates the extreme vulnerabilities of all peoples and governments, regardless of their ideological persuasions or political dispositions. For example, flying in an airliner holds constant danger, and opening one's mail is a risk of life and limb. Indeed, the more materially developed a modern society is and the more technologically complex it becomes, the more susceptible to attack it is likely to be. Terrorism, then, has become more feasible and more profitable a weapon at a lesser risk to its perpetrator than ever before.

Moreover, with the proliferation and sophistication of modern technology, coupled with the probability that more "have not" groups will emerge with the increase of world population, the danger of terrorism will become unbearable. At that point in time, practically all targets will be extremely vulnerable and victims of violence totally defenseless. Ultimately, then, terrorism will become more than a sporadic disruption to law and order; it will menace the very survival of civilization itself.

In spite of this predicted eventuality, the current national and transnational attitude toward terrorism is not based on a universal revulsion, nor is the response to it uniform. Whereas, in the past, establishments have condemned political and ideological violence, today, voices rejecting it are somewhat muted. Moreover, no adequate juridicial, social, and physical means of protection have been developed unilaterally and multilaterally. In fact, many states tend to tolerate, appease, and, frequently, even support the use of terrorism as an acceptable legitimate tool in achieving certain desirable goals.

Western liberal democracies, for instance, have in general been reluctant to adopt strong measures to control it, fearing that extreme use of official violence in such cases may be counter productive. A case in point is Uruguay. Here the repressive response of the government against the Tupamoro terrorists transformed the country from a democracy into a military dictatorship.

Laxness toward terrorism is also nourished by a philosophical trend that places greater value on human life. This explains the prevailing practice of some governments to surrender readily to ransom demands or requests for release of political prisoners, as well as their unwillingness to punish harshly terrorists whom they apprehend. West Germany, for example, delivered $5 million cash ransom to Palestinian hijackers who had taken over an Athens-bound Lufthansa 747 with 186 passengers and crew members and diverted the plane to Aden. Brazil's military rulers have flown some 130 jailed leftists out of the country in order to free four kidnapped diplomats. And, in India, the government has deferred the hanging of two Naxalites who were sentenced to death for the murder of landlords because of the pressure of public opinion for compassion for the terrorists.

Interestingly, private bodies following such practices also succumb to terrorist demands. For instance, the Bunge and Born Company, a multinational corporation in Argentina, paid a reported sum of $60 million for the release of two executives kidnapped by left-wing guerrillas.

But terrorism is tolerated much further than that. The Third World countries of Asia, Africa, and the Middle East have accepted opposition violence as an expression of "self-determination"; to them force used by oppressed peoples to fight "tyranny," "colonialism," and "imperialism" is completely justified. Arab states, for example, have provided the Palestinian guerrillas with financial, diplomatic, and military assistance; have trained Palestinians in guerrilla warfare methods; have permitted their territories to be used as bases for attack, and their embassies abroad to function as recruiting offices for volunteers to Palestinian groups; and have maintained close liaisons with them, offering their members freedom of movement and places of refuge.

Similarly, socialist states have been supporting insurgent and revolutionary activities in cases where the struggle followed a strict party line and was tightly centralized. The overwhelming Sino-Soviet political, economic, and military aid to North Vietnam and the Viet Cong is a case in point. Although the emphasis here has been placed on the participation of organized masses in popular revolutions rather than individual terrorism, socialist countries have also provided help in even less ideologically based situations. For instance, Communist China, Cuba, and North Korea trained Mexican, Palestinian, and Puerto Rican guerrillas.

While the borderline between "sanctified" violence and plain terrorism is blurred, thus resulting in confusing and half-hearted responses as well as in outright support, evidence also indicates that, under certain circumstances, national and transnational bodies have formulated general and specific policies on this issue. This has occurred whenever states have determined that either violence is too outrageous on moral grounds to be tolerated, or that their national self-interests have demanded that prompt action be undertaken. Following the Munich killings, the United States embarked on a diplomatic campaign to curb international terrorism. It has taken the initiative of introducing in the United Nations a draft convention for the prevention and punishment of certain acts of international terrorism. The United States has also concluded a bilateral agreement with Cuba for the expressed purpose of the extradition and punishment of hijackers. Domestically, the government instituted electronic surveillance devices at airports to prevent hijacking and has required visas for anyone who visits the country in transit in order to clamp down on terrorists. In response to a series of successive bombings in England, the government has passed an antiterrorist bill that outlawed the Irish Republican Army. Jordan put an end to Palestinian activities in that country when King Hussein's control was seriously threatened. And Israel, concerned with its survival, has adopted numerous strategies including stricter safety measures, sealing off its borders against infiltrators, police crackdowns on terrorists at home, and military reprisals against Palestinian bases in neighboring countries.

At times, governments react to acts of terror against them with clandestine counterterrorism. Portugal's secret police sent a letter-bomb that killed Eduardo Chivambo Mondlane, a founder of the Mozambique Liberation Front, popularly known as Frelimo. Spain dispatched policemen across the border into France to break up the Basque Movement. And Israeli agents have carried out assassinations of Arab guerrilla leaders and have mounted rocket attacks on Palestinian headquarters in Beirut.

On the international level, the response of multilateral organizations has been far less effective than unilateral national reactions. For example, despite the plea of the UN Secretary General that the world body cannot remain a "mute spectator" to acts of violence that are plaguing society, member states have been concerning themselves with exploring the underlying causes of terrorism rather than stemming the acts themselves. The discussions at the United Nations have been inconclusive, and it is unlikely that the organization will forge a coordinated policy on the matter because of the polarization of many viewpoints. Similarly, the International Civil Aviation Organization, which has been successful in enacting antihijacking treaties, has no means of enforcing its decisions.

Also, regional agreements such as the Convention to Prevent and Punish Acts of Terrorism Taking the Form of Crimes Against Persons and Related Extortions That Are of International Significance, approved by the Organization of American States on January 2, 1971, are limited in their scope and application. Moreover, acts of terrorism are on the increase in other areas (the use of letter-bombs, for instance) where normative measures on an international scale have not been formulated and implemented.

The implications of these facts are indeed distressing, for they obviously indicate that society, thus far at least, is unwilling to take maximum concerted action to stamp out this serious threat to its very existence. But even if a high degree of transnational consensus regarding the future danger of the scourge of terrorism had existed, and strategies to cope with it were prepared and executed, it would be folly to expect the total elimination of political and ideological violence from human relations. All that can be done is to make terrorism less inviting and more costly to its precipitators and supporters.

It is out of these realizations that this volume grew. Deeply concerned with the upsurge of terrorism throughout the world, particularly during the last decade, and with the assessment that its meaning and dangers are not fully appreciated, a group of academicians teaching in U.S. and Canadian universities have decided to join forces in order to present a general overview of the problem. The result of this collaboration is this collection of original essays on national, regional, and international perspectives of terrorism. The main questions to which we have sought to address ourselves are which acts constitute terrorism, what are the underlying causes for this alarming phenomenon, and how society can and should deal with it.

Although discussions and consultations have been held by the participants over the past two years, each contributor bears sole responsibility for his findings and views. Similarly, the Ralph Bunche Institute on the United Nations, City University of New York, gave valuable assistance to the project and this is gratefully acknowledged, but the Institute bears no responsibility for the views expressed herein.

It is hoped that this book will stimulate further study and research in the field of international terrorism, with a view to advancing the cause of peace and justice.

TERRORISM—THE
CANADIAN PERSPECTIVE
L. C. Green

TERRORISM DEFINED

According to the Oxford English Dictionary, terrorism has two primary meanings. First, it is "government by intimidation as directed and carried out by the party in power in France during the Revolution of 1789-1794: the system of the Terror (1793-4)." Second, it connotes "a policy intended to strike with terror those against whom it is adopted: the employment of methods of intimidation: the fact of terrorizing or condition of being terrorized." Inherent in both meanings is the concept of fear, with the consequence that the term automatically acquires an emotive meaning. If one takes the first and peculiarly political meaning in its historical context, it is easy to see why the term has this emotive impact, given the reaction that was adopted by England and the rest of Europe to the French Terror. Moreover, extension of the term to cover the sort of activities undertaken by the secret police in Nazi Germany or Stalinist Russia and emulated later in other countries that do not pursue the "democratic" way of life makes it easy to employ it for any ideological purpose that the user may desire. Despite the trend in modern international politics to maintain that the protection of human rights everywhere is a matter of international concern and the resulting embodiment of a pledge of self-determination or self-government, even by way of the ballot box, in various international declarations and covenants, governments still fall back on the plea of noninterference in domestic affairs when confronted with demands that they take action against this type of terror. For this reason, terror by government as a means of pursuing policy aims is outside the scope of this chapter.

Insofar as the less specific meaning is concerned, this has come to mean any activity that involves some measure of threat directed at those beyond the scope of the immediate act that has been perpetrated. Thus, it would cover any action associated with political blackmail whereby the actor seeks to secure ends not necessarily directly involved with the victim of his act. As a result, the term has acquired an extensive meaning that tends to embrace all acts of which one does not approve and in which some element of either horror or threat independent of the act itself is involved. At some levels, therefore, it would include the activities of a Jack the Ripper or a Manson family, the agitation of groups like the Black Panthers, and campus riots and Kent State. On other levels, activities such as these would tend to be excluded, and the idea would be confined to acts like the kidnappings of leading business figures in South America, which are associated with demands for ransoms that are allegedly supposed to contribute to changes in the political or economic framework of the country in which the kidnapping has taken place. For this reason, kidnappings for purely private ends, though associated with ransom demands, would not be included. Political assassination directed at alleged tyrants will be considered terrorism only by those who sympathize with the policy and establishment represented by that tyrant; for others, it may well amount to a high act of patriotism. It is this consideration that has become of extreme importance in recent years, when political terrorism has become more common than it was in the first half of the twentieth century, even though the League of Nations, representing the established order of its time, promulgated, as a result of the 1934 murder of Alexander of Yugoslavia at Marseilles, its Convention Against Terrorism in 1937, which, however, never came into force, having been ratified only by India.[1] Today we have become accustomed to acts that would normally and formerly have been described as terrorist, such as the destruction of villages inhabited by sympathizers of either the government or the rebels, being described as legitimate activities since they are part of wars of national liberation, although the sympathizers of the "liberationists" are prone to describe such acts by the government forces as genocidal.

THE PROTECTION OF DIPLOMATS

In addition to this type of "legitimate" terrorism there is a new development whereby diplomats, formerly regarded as enjoying protection and immunity, become victims of kidnappings by rebel movements in the countries to which they have been accredited, the purpose of these kidnappings being to embarrass the host country into meeting the demands of the kidnappers or to anticipate that the diplomat's coun-

try will pressure the host country into meeting the demands in order
to ensure the diplomat's safe release. This new development in what
is sometimes described as "urban guerrilla warfare" has taken place
at the same time as a realization that holding the citizenry hostage can
also impose political pressure upon a government, and there have recently been kidnappings of ordinary citizens who are held hostage for
the release of revolutionary leaders or to secure arms or funds for
the revolutionary cause. This has influenced escaped criminals to
seek the release of fellow convicts or the wherewithal to guarantee
their own escape in safety.

An associated development on the part of certain Arab movements and their supporters in the Middle East has arisen. As part
of their struggle against Israel these activists have indulged in a variety of acts of terror ranging from mass killings at the Olympic Games
in Munich to murders within Israel to attacks on Israeli and other diplomats abroad—either to secure publicity for the Arab cause, to obtain the release of Arabs arrested during other terrorist activities,
to attempt to force third countries into changing their policies in the
Arab-Israeli confrontation, or to impose direct pressure and incon-
venience on Israel, although these last acts may be considered as part
of the hostilities still going on between the Israelis and the Arabs and
as such not terrorism in the ordinary sense of the word. But it must
not be forgotten that many of the acts committed in time of war are
essentially terrorist in the classic meaning of the term.

One of the most common recent forms of terrorism is the hijacking of aircraft during scheduled flights. On occasion, this has
been accompanied by gun and grenade assaults on passengers in international airports. For the main part, these attacks have been associated with the Arab campaign against Israel, although there have
been other similar attacks, for example, in Japan. There is, however,
some evidence to suggest that these Japanese attacks, or at least the
organizations setting them in motion, have been associated ideologically with the Arab movement. It is not possible to say with any conviction whether this association is based on sympathy for the Arab
cause or is a manifestation of a new and violent outburst of anarchism
and is thus based on terrorism for terrorism's sake.

So far no reference has been made to acts of terror alleged to
have taken place, whether or not intended as part of an international
policy of terrorism, against the populations of Vietnam, Cyprus,
Uganda, Burundi, Brazil (against the aborigines), or northern Ireland. Using the simplest definition, there can be no doubt that each
of these falls within the concept of terrorism. However, in some
cases the acts were committed during hostilities, in some by way of
genocide, and in others to put down a civil uprising. Whatever the
cause, they are either within the rubric of some other accepted con-

cept or are a matter of "private" concern in the sense that the interests of some third and neutral party are not directly affected. For
our purposes, therefore, they may be ignored.

What concerns us in this chapter are those acts that, whatever
their motivation, involve terrorist violence against innocent individuals and private institutions or that involve the interests of third
states not involved in the activities of the actors vis-a-vis the entity
against which their act is really directed. That is to say, the concept
of terrorism should be victim oriented and the higher ideals of the
terrorists ignored.

While there has been an increase in interest in terrorism and
its control in recent years,[2] it should not be thought that municipal
systems of law have not been confronted with questions relating to
this offense in the past. From the point of view of Canada, the law in
this field is still very much the common law as interpreted by the English courts, so that it becomes necessary to see how, and on what basis, the Canadian courts have acted when confronted with requests for
extradition, for by and large Canada has been free of terrorist acts
of the kind described above on its own territory, of fugitives present
within Canada and accused of some violent act that he maintains is
political and exempt from extradition. As long ago as 1891 an English
court held that murder committed during a political disturbance was
nonextraditable as long as it could

> at least be shown that the act is done in furtherance
> of, done with the intention of assistance, as a sort
> of overt act in the course of acting in a political
> manner, a political rising, or a dispute between two
> parties in the State as to which is to have the govern-
> ment in its hands. . . . The question really is,
> whether, upon the facts, it is clear that the man was
> acting as one of a number of persons engaged in acts
> of violence of a political character with a political
> object, and as part of the political movement and
> rising in which he was taking part.[3]

On the other hand, acts of violence, although they might have been
politically motivated, would not be covered by the concept of political
crime from the point of view of granting protection against extradition
if they were not part of an organized attempt to seize the reins of government. Thus, an anarchist who perpetrated his acts by causing explosions in a cafe and at military barracks was held not to be so protected, for

> to constitute an offence of a political character,
> there must be two or more parties in the State, each

> seeking to impose the Government of their own
> choice on the other, and that, if the offence is com-
> mitted by one side or the other in pursuance of that
> object, it is a political offence, otherwise not. In
> the present case there are not two parties in the
> State, each seeking to impose the Government of
> their own choice on the other; for the party with
> whom the accused is identified . . . namely, the
> party of anarchy, is the enemy of all Governments.
> Their efforts are directed against the general body
> of citizens. They may, secondarily and inciden-
> tally, commit offences against some particular
> Government; but anarchist offences are mainly di-
> rected against private citizens . . . the crime
> charged was not a political offence within the mean-
> ing of the Extradition Act. [4]

In both these instances there is no doubt that the countries in
which the crimes were committed—Switzerland and France, respectively—would have described them as the acts of terrorists, and their
purpose was broadly to terrorize the authorities. If, however, the
courts of the country from which the extradition has been requested
classify the offense as political in character, this will suffice to remove from it the stigma of terror and make it sufficiently respectable
for the offender to receive at least temporary asylum from the country
of his refuge. But the fact that the offense may be described as political in the country in which it was committed does not bind the courts
of the refuge country in any way. They may acknowledge that there
is a political aura about the offense, they may even acknowledge that
the offense in question should be tried by a special tribunal, but unless they recognize the offense as political in the sense understood by
themselves—and in the common-law countries this is as just enunciated—extradition will nevertheless be granted.

Canadian courts, when faced with this problem, have applied
the same principles. Thus, in Re Federenko[5] a member of the Russian Social Democratic Party was charged with murder and in response
to the extradition request had submitted that his offense was in fact
political. Chief Justice Mathers, King's Bench, Manitoba, cited the
Castioni definition and inquired,

> Was the crime of the accused committed in the
> furtherance of a political object? He belonged to
> the social democratic party, whose object was not
> only to alter the form of government, but also to
> do away with private ownership of property. A

propaganda was carried on by them throughout the
country and numerous revolutionary outrages were
perpetrated by them. . . . Can it be said that this
[particular] killing was in furtherance of a political object? I think not. Nor do I think the fact
that the crime of the accused would, in the demanding State, be called a political crime and be tried
by a special tribunal make it a crime of a political
character within the meaning of the [Treaty]. The
crime of killing a policeman by a person in no way
identified with any political movement would in Russia be so described, and would be tried by the same
tribunal.

While this decision is in accordance with the established concepts
of the time, it raises the question of whether it has not been overrun
by events, since cases concerning crimes committed in the course of
escaping from Eastern Europe have been held by Lord Chief Justice
Goddard of England as being political, even though they did not fall
within the classical concept.[6] Recent events in the United States,
such as the murders of police officers and others by members of the
Black Panthers or the Symbionese Liberation Army, might well be
thought to be political in character, even though they were not committed during an organized attempt by an organized political party to
take over the government.

The English courts have recently tended to cut back the liberalism introduced by the Lord Chief Justice and to revert to the Castioni
rule,[7] and it would appear that this is the line that would be adopted
by the Canadian courts. Thus, in Re Commonwealth of Puerto Rico
and Hernandez[8] it was held that the killing of a police officer during
riots by members of a Puerto Rican independence movement directed
against the activities of the Reserve Officers' Training Corps (ROTC)
on a university campus, as distinct from the government as such, was
not "political," for

the question in issue should be determined by look-
ing primarily at the events of the day and not the actual circumstances of the murder. The actual political climate of Puerto Rico at that time is of a secondary interest. It is important only if it is a predominant factor in the circumstances of the murder. It
is not relevant that the act subsequently became a
major political issue if it was not of a predominantly
political character at the time of the act. . . . What
took place . . . was not to overthrow the government

but rather to force the university authorities to divorce the R.O.T.C. from the campus. . . . One
cannot deny that political considerations were involved in the antagonism towards the cadets, but I
cannot feel persuaded that this could be considered
a political uprising against the government or that
the murder . . . should be considered an act in
furtherance of a political uprising.

To the same effect was <u>Re State of Wisconsin and Armstrong</u>,[9] which
arose from a charge of murder and arson during campus rioting connected with the draft and U.S. operations in Vietnam, in which it was
held, moreover, that the burden of proof was upon the fugitive. Applying the principles in <u>Castioni</u>, <u>Federenko</u>, and <u>Schtraks</u> (in which
the English court returned to <u>Castioni</u>), this burden was found not to
be discharged, so that "the offences . . . are not of a political character and the proceedings are not taken with a view to prosecute or
punish the respondent for an offence of a political character."

In light of these decisions (although one should not ignore the
fact that there had been a number of similar campus riots in Canada
culminating in the destruction of computers at George Williams University and that this may have unconsciously had an effect on the attitude of the judges involved), it would appear that any terrorist whose
offense, except for the political motivation of his terrorism, fall
within the normal rubric of extraditable crimes as understood in Canada,[10] would be unable to plead before the Canadian courts that his
act was political in character so as to exempt him from extradition.
As yet, however, there has been no case to test this assumption. The
only case of a clearly terrorist character in the modern usage of the
term arose in 1970 when Pierre Laporte, a provincial cabinet minister in Quebec, was kidnapped and murdered by members of the Front
de Liberation du Quebec (FLQ) who, at the same time, kidnapped
James Cross, British trade commissioner in Montreal. While this
was obviously a case of political terrorism it presents two distinct
questions. The actions against Laporte were rightly considered as
internal matters of concern to the Canadian government and the provincial administration alone and were to be dealt with either adminis-
tratively or in accordance with the Criminal Code. In the Cross affair, international problems of real substance were involved. First,
it raised issues of Canada's liability in connection with the protection
of diplomats while, at the same time, regardless of whether the Canadian government was in default in any way (and it is submitted that
it was not), settlement of the problem depended on the policy that the
Canadian government decided to adopt toward the kidnappers and the
extent to which the British government was prepared to cooperate.

Kidnapping is an offense under section 247 of the Criminal Code, and section 51 provides that "every one who does an act of violence in order to intimidate the Parliament of Canada or the legislature of a province . . . is liable to imprisonment for fourteen years." Although this was clearly the purpose of the FLQ, the government of Canada decided, in order to ensure Cross's safety, to offer immunity from prosecution to the kidnappers, provided they left Canada and undertook not to return. As a result, they were allowed to depart for Havana under the protection of the Cuban ambassador. When it was rumored in mid-1974 that some or all of them had arrived in Paris and were hinting that they might return to Canada, the authorities reminded them that, were they to do so, criminal proceedings under the Criminal Code would be instituted.

Although it is clear that Canadian criminal law provides the means for dealing with attacks directed against diplomats, Canada has considered the frequency of kidnappings and other acts of violence directed against diplomatic personnel to be sufficient to warrant the adoption of an international convention on the matter, taking as its point of departure the 1971 "Report of the International Law Commission," which expressed the commission's willingness to prepare draft articles if requested to do so by the General Assembly.[11] Not only has it advocated action to this end in the United Nations but it closely followed the developments taking place in the Organization of American States (OAS) and the Council of Europe and has "been in contact with the OAS and other governments so that Canadian views and interests will be taken into account."[12] By Resolution 2780 (XXVI), the commission received the necessary instructions and member states were invited to submit comments. In the course of its comments, Canada stated:

> The attacks of a new kind against diplomatic and
> consular inviolability which we have been witnes-
> sing in recent years must be countered in every
> appropriate way. It is the Canadian government's
> opinion that an international convention to ensure
> inviolability traditionally accorded by international
> law to those professionally engaged in international
> relations is highly desirable. . . . The deterrent
> effect is the most important feature of any conven-
> tion intended to ensure the security of international
> relations through better protection of diplomats.[13]

In April 1972, the Canadian government issued a statement commenting on the draft being considered by the International Law Commission[14] in which it proclaimed its belief in the vital importance of dissuasion but also declared that it felt the convention should be as simple and limited in scope as possible. It pointed out that a convention of this kind would inevitably touch upon a number of issues on which the rules of international law were controversial and on which the commission would eventually have to do further work, such as political asylum, state responsibility, and extraterritorial penal jurisdiction. Every incursion into these fields risked raising controversy that would make the convention unacceptable to some states, and since wide support was desirable, difficulties of this kind should be avoided as far as possible. The Canadian government was aware of the fact that in recent years the number of people who might be able to claim that they represented their governments had grown to an enormous extent, and it feared that careless wording in the convention as to the persons to be protected could easily result in abuse. For this reason it believed that protection should be limited to those whose official status might be said to involve state dignity—that is to say, the head of state, the prime minister, ministers, diplomatic and consular officers enjoying inviolability under the Vienna Conventions of 1961[15] and 1963,[16] and the most senior officials of the most important international organizations and the national delegates accredited to those organizations. Since the members of special missions change frequently, it was not considered that they were exposed to the same dangers, and therefore the Canadian government did not consider that they needed the same protection. Moreover, most of the foreign and international officials not included in the above classifications were already sufficiently protected by the normal responsibility of a state in respect of resident foreigners. At the same time, aware of the emotion and publicity that is associated with crimes against dignitaries and the manner in which such offenses are treated by the media, Canada was of the opinion that the convention should be concerned only with the most serious crimes, such as murder, kidnapping, illegal detention, and grave acts of violence, thus avoiding any necessity for the parties to introduce new offenses into their criminal codes. On the other hand, it favored heavy penalties for the offenses concerned and was opposed to any of the parties' being able to classify them as political, thus rendering them extraditable and ineligible for any grant of political asylum. On the other hand, Canada was aware of the fact that some members of the United Nations were wedded to the idea of political asylum but emphasized that there is a great difference between an offense against the representative of a foreign state and one committed by a national against the security or government of his own state. It was also argued that, since international law recognizes the right to disregard even conventional obligations when state security or self-defense is concerned, there was no need to make express provision to this effect in the convention.

Clearly reflecting the problems with which Canada had itself been confronted at the time of the Quebec kidnappings, it was pointed out that the Vienna conventions merely require the host state to take all appropriate steps for the protection of diplomatic and consular representatives without attempting to define what these are. In Canada's view, although the conventions were silent as to state responsibility if a diplomat's rights were impinged upon, the host state was obliged to take action to restore the inviolability and seek out those responsible for the infringement. However, it had to be recognized that the state concerned could well find itself in a dilemma. In the event of a kidnapping, the easiest way to restore full immunity would probably be to concede to the demands of the kidnappers, although this might endanger the maintenance of internal order, state security, or other national interests. On the other hand, to refuse such concessions might result in physical harm and even death to the victim. In Canada's view, the fact that international law made no specific provision for such matters might be advantageous since it left to the host state freedom of action depending on the circumstances, the risks, and the various interests involved. However, it could not be denied that, in the interest of international relations, there must be some guarantee of equitable reparation, although the problems in determining such responsibility were probably insurmountable. In Canada's view the basis for such reparations should not be responsibility as much as concepts of hospitality and courtesy.

The Canadian view may be seen from the terms of its extradition agreement of 1971 with the United States.[17] While this treaty reaffirms the immunity from extradition of those charged with political offenses, it provides in Article 4 that

> a kidnapping, murder or other assault against the life or physical integrity of a person to whom a Contracting Party has the duty according to international law to give special protection, or any attempt to commit such an offence with respect to any such person, shall not be regarded as of a political character.

The importance of the political offense and asylum issues for Canada was made clear during the General Assembly debate that led to the adoption of the "Convention on the Prevention and Punishment of Crimes against Internationally Protected Persons, including Diplomatic Agents."[18] The Latin American delegations had introduced an amendment with regard to asylum and this was opposed by Canada, whose delegate was, in the first place, unwilling to see a regional concept that would make it easy to evade the general provisions of the

document introduced into a universal convention. The amendment was
also considered to be contrary to the aim of the proposed convention,
which was to protect foreign diplomats and the like from all attacks,
and therefore there should be no provision that might enable an alleged
offender to escape, and any reference to the concept of asylum was
bound to draw the attention of such an offender to a possible route of
nonliability. Moreover, the Latin Americans were reminded that
there was no asylum provision in the Hague and Montreal conventions
on offenses relating to aircraft, and Canada regarded the offense of
air piracy as being sufficiently similar to offenses against diplomats
to justify similar treatment in this particular area. In addition, Canada believed that the very fact that there was general support for a
convention indicated that such an act was regarded not as a political
offense but as an offense against the unrestricted operation of institutions, universally and traditionally recognized, enabling states to
communicate among themselves—that is to say, not as political offenses traditionally are, as crimes against national law, but as crimes
against the law of nations. Canada did, however, recognize that the
proponents of the amendment regarded asylum as a rule of regional
international law and had worded it to apply only to treaties guaran-
teeing asylum already in force and between the parties to those treaties. Nevertheless, Canadian objections were sufficiently strong
that its delegate announced that he would abstain from voting on it,
but despite its presence in the convention, Canada did not abstain
from or oppose the convention, which was adopted by consensus.

HIJACKING AND SABOTAGE

Despite the attitude of the Canadian government toward unlawful attacks upon diplomats, it appears that the peculiar political circumstances surrounding the events in Quebec and the absence of any
further attack on a diplomat in Canada have made this an issue that
no longer excites the Canadian public. The media in Canada seemed
far more concerned with hijackings, which carry a glamor of their
own and arouse much more public interest, possibly because of the
number of persons at risk and the large-scale violence threatened in
each case, with the likelihood of each private citizen's recognizing
that he could easily be on a hijacked plane. The government, on the
other hand, was as concerned with the need for international measures
of control in this field as in any other. When the International Civil
Aviation Organization (ICAO) established its Legal Sub-Committee at
the end of 1968 to draft an international convention on hijacking, Canada was a member, and it later supported the request put forward by
a number of European states in the aftermath of the Swissair and Aus-

trian Airlines explosions for study on the need for a special convention
directed against sabotage and armed attacks against aircraft. As to
the latter, however, Canada was not overly enthusiastic insofar as a
convention was concerned. It was more inclined to advocate uniform
parallel legislation, for a convention would take at least 12 to 24
months to prepare and probably longer to secure the necessary ratifications. Moreover, since the problem was, for many countries, one
of seeking to specify a new offense in criminal law, it would almost
certainly require municipal legislation in any case, which would come
after the convention had been drafted. In the same way that it was
concerned with ensuring recognition of the fact that attacks against
diplomats should not be regarded as political offenses, Canada was
equally convinced that "acts of unlawful interference with aircraft
should, in all cases, be considered a non-political offence, subject to
the contrary being proved in a court of law. In our view, this principle would not detract from the sovereign right to grant political asylum
but would merely put the burden of proof where it really belongs."[19]
It can, of course, be argued that this statement is merely an expression of the existing law with regard to political offenses and the extent
to which the political character of a charge may be raised as a defense
in an extradition hearing.[20] On the other hand, it recognizes the
practical fact that too often hijackers and their sympathizers tend to
argue facilely that the offense is political in character, an argument
that is often made on only the slightest evidence.

There have been many suggestions to the effect that countries
that harbor hijackers and give assistance to them in any way should
be subjected to sanctions, perhaps including severance of air traffic
with them. This seems to have been in the minds of Canadian government officials in 1970 when they stated that "the Government has under
consideration a proposal which would link bilateral air agreements to
ICAO unlawful interference conventions and provide a legal basis for
suspension of operation of the air agreements in the event of failure
to implement international obligations set out in the convention."[21]
Such a policy was in fact put forward by the Canadian delegate in the
Legal Committee of the ICAO at its Montreal session in June 1970,
with the intention that

> in the event that a State refused or failed to imple-
> ment its international obligation under the special
> clause . . . setting out the appropriate provisions
> of the Tokyo Convention and any other relevant
> ICAO Convention in force at the time in question,
> which dealt with unlawful interference, and of the
> insertion of a similar special clause in all future
> bilateral air agreements . . . any other State which

has a bilateral air agreement with the offending State
would have the right, notwithstanding any other provision respecting termination or suspension in the agreement itself, to suspend operation of the bilateral air
agreement at short notice. Such suspension—to have
maximum effect—would likely be exercised only after
appropriate consultations with other States having bilateral agreements with the offending State.

Canada has entered a bilateral agreement with Cuba concerning
hijacking that did not require ratification but came into force on signature.[22] While this provided for the trial or extradition of hijackers,
it made no provision for the sort of sanction just mentioned, but it
might be argued that, since there is an assumption that the parties will
carry out their obligations in good faith, it would be improper to include a provision envisaging the opposite possibility. In keeping with
the Canadian view that hijackers should not be able to plead that their
offense was political, the agreement makes no reference to an exemp-
tion for political offenders, but it does go part of the way toward recognizing that this may in fact still be a possibility. The agreement provides that the state of refuge

may take into consideration any extenuating or mitigating circumstances in those cases in which the persons responsible for the acts were in real and imminent danger of death without a viable alternative for
leaving the country, provided there was no financial
extortion or physical injury to the crew, passengers
or other persons in connection with the hijacking.

As worded, this leaves open an interesting issue with regard to a
repetition of a crime like the killing of Laporte. It is quite possible
that any country to which the killers might have fled, as distinct from
being transported under cover of safe conduct with the permission of
the Canadian authorities, would have regarded the offense as political
in character and denied extradition. But what if the killers had hijacked an aircraft in order to effect their escape to Cuba, having made
no demand for ransom nor having in any way injured any member of
the crew, any passenger, or any other person "in connection with the
hijacking?"

The problem of air piracy has been proved in practice to be of
universal significance in that there appears to be no limit on the variety of countries whose aircraft may be affected or whose nationals
might be involved. In addition, not all the countries participating in
international air transport are members of the ICAO, and therefore it

is not enough that this organization has been concerned in coping with
the problem. On the other hand, all these states are members of the
United Nations and Canada has been one of the leading proponents of
securing UN action on this matter, having been one of the proposers
of what eventually became the 1970 "Resolution of the General Assembly on Aerial Hijacking or Interference with Civil Air Traffic."[23]

Canada did not feel that the UN resolution or the Hague and Montreal conventions went far enough and was in any case disappointed by
the apparent lack of willingness on the part of governments to put into
effect even these international documents. After the Lod airport massacre Canada became even more convinced of the need to introduce
some measure that would include real sanctions. It sought, therefore,
in conjunction with the United States, to secure the adoption of a convention that would impose joint action involving severance of services.
In this it was blocked by the opposition of such countries as the Soviet
Union and France, which maintained that any form of enforcement action was the prerogative of the Security Council, and the Arab countries, which sympathized with, or feared to appear critical of, any
hijackers or activists employing violence against aircraft or airports
allegedly on behalf of the Palestinian movement. The two countries
were, however, able to persuade the ICAO council to establish a legal
subcommittee "to work on the preparation of an international convention to establish appropriate multilateral procedures within the ICAO
framework for determining whether there is a need for a joint action."
Although the subcommittee was able to agree that the time was "ripe"
for such a consideration, when the assembly met to consider a variety
of drafts, all that the ICAO assembly could achieve at its Rome meeting at the end of 1973 was a resolution that

> condemns all acts of unlawful interference with civil
> aviation and any failure by a contracting State to fulfil its obligations to return an aircraft which is being illegally detained or to extradite or submit to
> prosecuting authorities the case of any person accused
> of an act of unlawful interference with civil aviation;
>
> Appeals to all States which have not already become
> parties to the Tokyo, Hague and Montreal Conventions
> to give urgent consideration to the possibility of so doing;
>
> Reaffirms the important role of the International
> Civil Aviation Organization to facilitate the resolution
> of questions which may arise between contracting
> States in relation to matters affecting the safe and orderly operation of civil aviation throughout the world.[24]

From this it is clear that not only were Canada and the United States unable to secure support for their proposal for sanctions against any state implicated in hijacking, whether a contracting party or not,[25] but the majority of the members of the ICAO were unwilling to see any form of sanction provided for recourse in the event of the offender being a member of the ICAO or a contracting party to any antihijacking treaty. It can hardly be said that the achievements of the ICAO in this field so far have been impressive. One is in fact inclined to sum them up with the comment from Horace, "Parturient montes, nascetur ridiculus mus."[26]

While Canada has not been able to achieve its aims in regard to hijacking on an international level other than by the bilateral agreement with Cuba, it has taken the necessary steps to carry out its aims internally, as far as this is possible. In 1972, section 76 of the Criminal Code relating to ship stealing and mutiny was amended so that now

> Everyone who unlawfully by force or threat thereof or by any other form of intimidation seizes or exercises control of an aircraft with intent
> (a) to cause any person on board the aircraft to be confined or imprisoned against his will [this would include holding a crew member, passenger, or other person as a hostage],
> (b) to cause any person on board the aircraft to be transported against his will to any place other than the next scheduled place of landing of the aircraft,
> (c) to hold any person on board the aircraft or to service against his will [which could also be considered unlawful confinement under section b], or
> (d) to cause the aircraft to deviate in a material respect from its flight plan, is guilty of an indictable offence and is liable to imprisonment for life.[27]

This is important in view of the fact that the Hague and Montreal conventions declare that hijacking is an extraditable offense by virtue of these agreements, even in the absence of special extradition agreements. Moreover, Part II of Canada's Extradition Act makes it possible for the governor general in council to extend the act by proclamation to any foreign state, even if Canada has no extradition treaty with that state.[28]

Deviations of aircraft have often been indulged in for national political purposes, as has a variety of acts that fall within the concept of terrorism, especially in its popular sense. While Canada has played a major role in promoting human rights,[29] it has not been prepared to issue blanket condemnations of every act of internal terrorism

that may occur, although it has been willing to make its views known
with regard to some terrorist acts directed by a government against
its own citizens. This has happened, for example, in the case of Soviet pressures upon dissidents and Ukrainians, but in the case of the
latter it must be borne in mind that the government of Canada is subject to internal pressures from its own large Ukrainian population.
It also made its views known at the time of the coup that overthrew
President Allende in Chile and offered asylum to a number of refugees
from that country, as it has done on a number of other occasions.
Similarly, representations have been made to the government of South
Vietnam in connection with the treatment and continued imprisonment
of political opponents. For many people, the exercise of terror by a
government against a segment of its population is nothing but an act
of genocide, even though the acts in question do not fall within that
concept as defined in the Genocide Convention. Canada ratified that
convention in 1952 and amended its Criminal Code in 1970 to make
genocide an offense under Canadian law.[30]

TERRORISM AT LARGE

While efforts have been made to deal with specific types of
act of terrorism, efforts have also been made to secure a general
ban on terrorism as such, and Canada has also played its part in this
endeavor. The United Nations first became interested in the problem
of terrorism in 1972, when the secretary general requested the General Assembly to place on its agenda the problem of "measures to
prevent terrorism and other forms of violence which endanger or take
innocent human lives or jeopardize fundamental freedoms." Drafted
this widely, many issues that could be regarded as matters of domestic jurisdiction might be included, for in the event of any civil disturbance or period of emergency it is almost certain that innocent
lives would be endangered and fundamental freedoms jeopardized by
the acts of the dissidents or rebels or by the governmental authorities
seeking to cope with the threat against their rule. An example of this
is northern Ireland. Since the United Nations is not, was not intended
to be, and does not purport to be a world government or policeman
entitled to maintain or restore internal peace and order wherever it
might be threatened, it is not surprising that, when issues like that
of Northern Ireland occur, neither the powers responsible nor the
members of the United Nations are anxious to have the matter discussed out in the open. The allegations against Britain brought by the
government of Ireland or the Irish internees before the European Commission of Human Rights are somewhat exceptional and could only
arise because of the special character of the regional arrangements

concerning human rights that prevail in Europe. The attitude of the former Greek government when accused of similar activities demonstrates how exceptional the Anglo-Irish situation is. Another difficulty that confronts us when faced with acts of terror of the kind envisaged in the dictionary definition quoted earlier is that such acts frequently occur in the course of what have become known as "wars of national liberation"—an ideological and often jaundiced title applied to any dissident movement of which one happens to approve. The complexities are increased, however, by virtue of the fact that the struggles for independence by the inhabitants of the few colonial territories still remaining and, more seriously, by the black population of South Africa, a member of the United Nations, have been acclaimed with glee by the Third World and its partisans and received support from the Organization of African Unity and the blessings of the United Nations, while the so-called right of self-determination has been embodied and sanctified in the first article of each of the two UN covenants on human rights.[31]

When the General Assembly took up the secretary general's suggestion in 1972, Canada was one of the members that voted to replace the phrase "terrorism and other forms of violence" with "international terrorism" and was against the Saudi Arabian proposal to include causes of, as well as measures against, such activities, which would open the door to an interminable debate of a political and chicken-and-egg character. Both amendments were in fact adopted and the matter was referred to the Legal Committee, where the political undertones of the whole question soon became clear. The United States, supported by Canada and others, sought to have this issue placed at the head of the agenda, while the Arabs and some African delegations sought to relegate it to the bottom. As a way out of this impasse, Canada proposed that it be considered fourth, and eventually a Mauretanian amendment to give it sixth place was adopted. Canada's view was that the matter should be dealt with as one of high priority by the International Law Commission (ILC) but when this proposal was rejected Canada agreed to serve on an ad hoc committee to prepare "recommendations for the speedy elimination of the problem." The efforts of countries like Canada to obtain anything practical from the committee were nullified since discussion soon shifted from the question of terrorist acts by individuals or groups to acts of "state terrorism" and the legitimacy of the struggles being waged by national liberation movements and oppressed or occupied peoples. It is not surprising that this occurred, since the resolution setting up the committee, while

> (1) express[ing] deep concern over increasing
> acts of violence which endanger or take innocent human lives or jeopardize fundamental freedoms [and]

(2) urg[ing] States to devote their immediate attention to finding just and peaceful solutions to the underlying causes which give rise to such acts of violence;

(3) reaffirms the inalienable right to self-determination and independence of all peoples under colonial and racist regimes and other forms of alien domination and upholds the legitimacy of their struggle, in particular the struggle of national liberation movements, . . .

(4) Condemns the continuation of repressive and terrorist acts by colonial, racist and alien regimes in denying peoples their legitimate right to self-determination and independence and other human rights and fundamental freedoms; . . .

(10) Requests the Ad Hoc Committee to . . . submit its report with recommendations for the speedy elimination of the problem, bearing in mind the provisions of paragraph 3. [32]

A casual glance at the identities of the 35 members comprising the Ad Hoc Committee may indicate why this particular emphasis was present. [33]

The attitude of Canada toward terrorism may be seen from some of the statements made by its delegates when the subject has come up in the United Nations. In the first place, Canada has always maintained that any resolution or convention must be specific in its condemnation of acts of international terrorism that result in the loss of innocent lives. While recognizing the difficulty facing some states in agreeing to any blanket or general condemnation, Canada was convinced that the right to self-determination was irrelevant in a document condemning terrorism, even though it could see the advantage of referring to the principles of equal rights and self-determination as embodied in the UN Charter and as elaborated in the General Assembly's "Declaration of Principles of International Law Concerning Friendly Relations and Cooperation Among States in Accordance with the Charter of the United Nations." [34] Perhaps most important has been Canada's desire to keep the political and legal aspects of the problem distinct, requiring a severance through recognition of the causes and the acts. As seen by Canada, there was no reason to delay taking action to control and suppress acts of international terrorism, which are merely an aspect of violence, while struggling with the basic causes of those violent acts. After all,

> We do not wait for solutions to complex underlying
> causes of violence and crime in our societies before
> adopting laws and penal systems to combat individ-
> ual acts of violence and crime. In the international
> field, as in the national, measures to prevent such
> acts must go hand-in-hand with efforts to remove
> underlying conditions which breed violence.[35]

In view of the divisions that separate the various groups insofar as
the political aspects of this matter are concerned, to adopt any other
approach would be to postpone measures to control terrorism to the
Greek calends.

The statement just quoted is only a reiteration of that made by
the Canadian representative during the debate in the Sixth Committee:

> It is only necessary to recall what has long been a
> universally agreed legal principle, that the intent to
> commit the act and not the reasons that led to its
> commission is the governing factor . . . the legiti-
> macy of a cause does not itself legitimize the use of
> certain forms of violence, especially against the in-
> nocent. And it is the protection of the innocent that
> we must keep firmly in mind at all times during this
> debate; especially the protection of those individuals
> who are in no way connected with the issues of con-
> cern to the terrorist.
>
> Moreover . . . a formally agreed definition of
> international terrorism in the abstract is not a nec-
> essary prerequisite to international action against
> its various international manifestations.
>
> Surely, all we have to be clear upon at this
> point is that our mandate is restricted to those acts
> of terrorism which have a definite international ele-
> ment. My Delegation considers that, in the case of
> politically motivated acts, this international element
> would be present when acts of terrorism are carried
> out in states which are not parties to a dispute, or
> are directed against the innocent citizens of non-in-
> volved states within the area of conflict. . . .
>
> In the view of the Canadian Government, no op-
> pression can be so severe as to excuse the cold-
> blooded murder of innocent persons. The common
> human goals of freedom, justice and self-fulfillment
> are not advanced by terror. History provides no
> cases where terrorism by itself has been success-
> ful in achieving a major political aim.

Acts of international terrorism must be dealt
with by the international community acting in con-
cert. Obviously we should not minimize the difficulties nor perhaps expect positive results, but equally
we cannot ignore the problem because of its inherent
complexities. . . .

Canada is of the opinion that it is necessary to aug-
ment existing conventional international law through
a new instrument on terrorism having the broadest
possible coverage and application in cases of violent
attack having international characteristics or effects
and directed against innocent persons wherever they
may be and regardless of the motives or objectives
involved—a convention which will enjoy the principle
of universality as the basis for the assertion of jurisdiction in respect of such acts, and a convention
which will provide for the punishment of these crimes
by severe penalties which take account of the aggra-
vated nature of the offences, and will call for the extradition or prosecution by the competent authorities
of the state in which the perpetrators of the terrorist
act are found—in short a new instrument patterned
on the Hague and Montreal Conventions and on the
ILC Draft Articles on the Protection of Diplomats
under International Law.[36]

Perhaps the most comprehensive statement and clearest indication of Canada's perspective of what must be done with regard to international terrorism is to be found in the statement made by Mitchell
Sharp, the Minister of External Affairs, before the General Assembly
in September 1972:

First, we must strongly condemn all acts of international terrorism, direct or indirect, involving innocent persons.

Second, we should recall and be guided by the past
efforts of the international community to deal with
terrorism and the progressive development of relevant principles of international law.

Third, we should seek to strengthen the worldwide
network for the collection and dissemination of information, through INTERPOL, and by other means, multilateral or bilateral, about terrorists, individuals and
groups, as part of a concerted and coordinated plan of
preventative action to stop terrorist acts from occur-
ring.

Fourth, we should reaffirm and where necessary strengthen existing international instruments which govern crimes found shocking to the conscience of mankind: piracy, slavery, trafficking in narcotics and more recently aerial hijacking and sabotage and acts against internationally protected persons, all of which instruments are directed against the crime, regardless of motive or cause. We should encourage all states to become parties to these conventions, which prescribed special treatment for these abhorrent acts. . . .

Fifth and finally, we must act quickly to develop such additional legal instruments as we deem to be desirable to deal with the international elements involved in acts of terrorism . . . we should concentrate on the need to protect the innocent and to create instruments which will be victim oriented and will deal effectively with the problem. We must be clear also about what is being done in different fora about the different aspects of international terrorism and then concentrate on what remains to be done. [37]

Sharp's reference to different fora for different aspects of terrorism is important, for it is easy for overlapping or conflicting action to ensue, whereas it would be more useful to have a general convention on terrorism as such, without worrying whether every type of terroristic act has been adequately described and brought within the ambit of the convention. In any case, recent activities have proved that the inventiveness of terrorists is broader than the imagination and expectations of politicians and lawyers. While it is important, therefore, to be specific when one can, it must be recognized that some states will be prepared to enter into conventions relating to specific acts but perhaps not to enter into a general convention. At the same time, it is necessary to include in the general convention a catch-all clause to include potential acts of a character similar to those mentioned by the secretary of state. Moreover, some aspects of terrorist control are exceedingly specialized in character because the acts in question are only likely to arise under special circumstances, such as in time of war. For this reason a convention on terrorism should not deal with those aspects of humanitarian law that are really only of concern in a war situation. This aspect of the problem is already under consideration by the International Committee of the Red Cross, and here too Canada is playing an active role.

AGGRESSION

There are some who maintain that war, and particularly aggressive war, is the worst terrorist act of all. Since the days of the League of Nations, efforts have been made to secure an adequate definition of aggression, and the United Nations has been concerned with this problem virtually since its creation. Many states have feared that to define aggression is really to undertake a retrograde step, for they fear that states may be able to argue that, if the action in which they are indulging does not actually fall within the definition, then it cannot possibly be aggression. This fear has been somewhat mitigated by the realization that whether or not it is given a definition, the decision as to what is to be done about an alleged act of aggression will be made in the Security Council, and the definition adopted by the members in deciding their vote will depend upon political subjectivity. Regardless of the difficulties, however, it has always been recognized that to encourage acts of infiltration or to lend support to rebel bands constitutes a breach of international law, and most attempts at defining aggression agree on the need to include this manifestation. This is clear from the declaration on friendly relations, but the attitudes of both the United Nations and the OAS toward wars of national liberation and their willingness to look kindly on assistance being given from outside to rebels engaged in such activity raise problems. It is this type of violence that has frequently been resorted to by Arab activists in their campaign against Israel and which is partly responsible for the difficulties that have been encountered in securing agreement on conventions against hijacking and terrorism.

By April 1974, the UN Special Committee on the Question of Defining Aggression finally reached a consensus and was able to draw up a draft definition.[38] As with other recent UN efforts at dealing with politically dynamic situations crossing the ideological interests of the UN members, this definition reflects the clash between the new states and the old and acknowledges the strength of the conviction that self-determination is now a principle of international law. In the preamble there is a reaffirmation of "the duty of States not to use armed force to deprive peoples of their rights to self-determination, freedom and independence, or to disrupt territorial integrity," but Article 3(g) of the actual definition condemns as aggression

> the sending by or on behalf of a State of armed bands, groups, irregulars or mercenaries, which carry out acts of armed force against another State of such gravity as to amount to the acts listed above, or its substantial involvement therein,

while Article 5 states that

> no consideration of whatever nature, whether political,
> economic, military or otherwise, may serve as a jus-
> tification for aggression.

An explanatory note states that the term "State" "is used without prejudice to questions of recognition or to whether a State is a member of
the United Nations." Far more important than this, however, is Article 7:

> Nothing in this definition, and in particular Article 3
> [defining acts of aggression], could in any way pre-
> judice the right to self-determination, freedom and
> independence, as derived from the Charter, of peo-
> ples forcibly deprived of that right and referred to
> in the Declaration on Principles of International Law
> concerning Friendly Relations and Cooperation among
> States in accordance with the Charter of the United
> Nations, particularly peoples under colonial and ra-
> cist regimes or other forms of alien domination;
> nor the right of these people to struggle to that end
> and to seek and receive support, in accordance with
> the principles of the Charter and in conformity with
> the above-mentioned Declaration.

It would appear that the special committee was oblivious to the
contradictions inherent in its own definition. In view of the pledges
regarding friendly relations and peaceful coexistence in the Charter
and in a multitude of declarations since, the commitment against non-
intervention in the declaration on friendly relations, and the customary
law ban on aiding and stimulating rebellion, it is surprising to find
Article 7, which in itself is a blatant contradiction of the definition
embodied in Article 3. The principle of equality of states based on
sovereignty, which has been recognized since the system of international law developed and which is embodied in the Charter as a fundamental principle, must give way before the all-powerful and overwhelming influence of the newly discovered principle of self-determination—for others, of course, and not for one's own minorities.

The attitude of Canada toward this self-contradictory manifesto
is made clear in the statement of the Canadian delegate after the consensus had been achieved:

> On the question of article 3(g) relating to armed
> bands, my Delegation is satisfied that this article re-

flects general acceptance of the thesis that the distinction between direct and indirect aggression is an
artificial distinction; the determining criteria must
be whether or not a sufficient degree of armed force
has been used so as to amount to an act of aggression
by the state to which such acts can be attributed.

As regards article 7, relating to self-determination, my Delegation shares the view that nothing in
the definition should result in an inference that its
application could impede the right of peoples under
colonial rule to self-determination in accordance
with the provisions of the Charter. However, I believe that it is important to state once again at this
time that the Government of Canada does not support
the use of violence as a means of settling political
conflicts or differences. Canada does support the
efforts of those engaged in a struggle to achieve
self-determination and human dignity. Accordingly,
the Canadian Government would interpret the reference to "struggle" in article 7 of this definition to
mean struggle by peaceful means, and we do not in
any way regard this formulation as condoning the use
of force in situations other than in self-defence or
other than in accordance with the Charter.

The delegate also found consolation in the fact that the definition
recognized the supreme authority of the Security Council in deciding
when aggression had occurred and what action to take. Unfortunately,
history has shown that the members of the Security Council pay little
attention to the legal interpretation of terms in the Charter or elsewhere. Their representatives are politicians, deciding political questions in accordance with the political instructions they receive from
their governments. Moreover, since the definition leaves the decision as to statehood, as well as to whether acts of violence are part
of a war of national liberation on a discretionary basis, to be made
subjectively on political grounds, the definition is wide enough to ensure that acts of international terrorism of the kind to which the world
has become accustomed of late are not heinous, unconscionable, terrorist, or criminal, but part and parcel of the necessary activities of
a group seeking its national liberation. Acceptance of this definition
will have the effect of rendering all the conventions on the various aspects of terrorism just so much wastepaper.

CANADA'S AIM

Since international terrorism became a problem, Canada has been active in its endeavors to secure satisfactory measures of control. It is for this reason that it sought to secure agreement on the need to deal with terrorist acts as such, viewing the problem from a victim oriented angle and seeking agreement that the motives for such acts must be considered irrelevant, except perhaps by way of mitigating punishment. Canada is aware that in the present bipolarized world—bipolarized between political activists among the new countries and their partisan friends on the one hand and the rest of the world, particularly the Western democracies, on the other—achieving agreement on the treatment necessary to remove the causes of terrorism is well-nigh impossible. It is aware that if attention is directed to control of terrorism at the same time as the causes are dealt with, nothing is likely to be achieved in any measurable period of time. Canada's aim, therefore, is to support to whatever extent possible the adoption of conventions aimed at defining terrorism and providing measures for its control. Aware of the fact that any such effort will prove tedious, Canada is prepared to move on a bilateral basis insofar as this may prove feasible, hoping that such bilateral action may prove contagious. The record of the international society in the field of human rights suggests that concrete achievement on a universal basis is likely to prove impossible or artificial. The same seems to be true of measures to control terrorism in any of its forms. Just as Canada set an example in the field of maritime pollution control,[39] so it might yet be able to set an example in the area of terrorism. The agreement with Cuba on hijacking came into force immediately upon signature. Canada's delegates at each international conference operating in this field have shown dissatisfaction with the way in which political ideology has prevented the achievement of real concrete progress. As a realist, however, Canada has been willing to go along with compromises, acknowledging that half a loaf is better than none. Perhaps we may yet see in the near future Canada's announcing that it is prepared to put into effect unilaterally all those measures of control that she has been advocating multilaterally and on an international level. Insofar as international agreements are concerned, perhaps Canada will extend the policy adopted in the Cuban case and announce that, if not willing to put into effect an agreement of a near universal character immediately upon signature, it will be prepared to operate it fully between itself and any other country ratifying it, even though, as tends to be the case, the agreement provides for a minimum number of ratifications in order to put it into effect.

NOTES

1. M. O. Hudson, ed., International Legislation, vol. 7 (Washington, D.C.: Carnegie Endowment for International Peace, 1931-1950), p. 862.

2. See, for example, Leslie C. Green, The Nature and Control of International Terrorism, University of Alberta, Department of Political Science, Occasional Paper no. 1 (Edmonton, Alberta, 1974).

3. Re Castioni [1891] 1 Q.B. 149, 156, 159 (per Denman J.).

4. Re Meunier [1894] 2 Q.B. 415, 419 (per Cave J.).

5. (No. 1) (1910) 17 C.C.C. 268, 270-71.

6. R. v. Governor of Brixton Prison, ex p. Kolczynski [1955] 1 Q.B. 540.

7. See, for example, Schtraks v. Government of Israel [1964] A.C. 556.

8. (1972) 30 D.L.R. (3d) 260, 268 (per Honeywell, Co. Ct. J., Ont.).

9. (1972) 28 D.L.R. (3d) 513, 520 (per Weisberg, Co. Ct. J., Ont.).

10. See, for example, G. V. LaForest, Extradition To and From Canada (New Orleans: Hauser Press, 1961); and Leslie C. Green, "Immigration, Extradition and Asylum in Canadian Law and Practice," in MacDonald et al., Canadian Perspectives on International Law and Organization (Toronto: University of Toronto Press, 1974), p. 244.

11. I.L.C. Yearbook, 1971, vol. 2, Part 1, p. 352.

12. Speech by Mitchell Sharp, Secretary of State for External Affairs, "Canadian Foreign Policy and International Law," External Affairs 23 (March 1971): 175, at p. 179.

13. Department of External Affairs, Bureau of Legal Affairs, Some Examples of Current Issues of International Law of Particular Importance to Canada, October 1973, p. 21.

14. April 12, 1972, Doc. FLA-272.

15. Diplomats, 500 U.N.T.S. 95 (ratified by Canada in 1966).

16. Consuls, 596 U.N.T.S. 261 (not signed or ratified by Canada).

17. Canadian Department of External Affairs, Canada Communique No. 92, December 3, 1971; and U.S. Department of State, Press Release No. 282, December 3, 1971.

18. Res. 3166 (XXVIII), December 14, 1973.

19. Department of External Affairs, Bureau of Legal Affairs, Some Examples of Current Issues of International Law of Particular Importance to Canada, June 10, 1970.

20. See Leslie C. Green, "The Nature of Political Offences," The Solicitor Quarterly 3 (1964): 213; "Hijacking and the Right of Asylum," in McWhinney, Aerial Piracy and International Law, 1971,

p. 124; "Hijacking, Extradition and Asylum," Chitty's Law Journal 22 (1974): 135.

21. Some Examples of Current Issues of International Law, op. cit.

22. Department of External Affairs, Communique No. 19, February 15, 1973.

23. Res. 2645 (XXV), November 25, 1970.

24. International Legal Materials 12 (1973): 1536.

25. See draft articles on air security proposed by Australia, Canada, Italy, the Netherlands, New Zealand, Nicaragua, the United Kingdom, and the United States, December 8, 1972, "Article on Joint Action," ibid., p. 1 at pp. 6-8.

26. Ars Poetica 139 (the mountains labor to bring forth a laughable mouse).

27. 1972, c.13, s.6.

28. Extradition Act, R.S.C. 1970, E-31; see Green, in MacDonald et al., op. cit., p. 277.

29. See papers in Allan Gotlieb, ed., Human Rights, Federalism and Minorities (Toronto: Canadian Institute of International Affairs, 1970).

30. Criminal Code Amendment Act, R.S.C. 1970, 1st Supp., c.11.

31. See, on this right, Whiteman, Digest of International Law 6 (1965), ch. 18, s.4; Nawaz, "The Meaning and Range of the Principle of Self-Determination," Duke Law Journal, 1965, p. 82; Johnson, Self-Determination Within the Community of Nations, 1967; Green, "Self-Determination and Settlement of the Arab-Israeli Conflict," 65 A.J.I.L. Procs. 1971, p. 40; and "Canada's Indians and Trusteeship," Osgoode Hall Law Journal 13 (1974).

32. Res. 3034 (XXVII), December 18, 1972.

33. International Legal Materials 13 (1973): 734.

34. Res. 2625 (XXV), October 24, 1970.

35. Speech by Ambassador Saul Rae in Plenary Session, December 15, 1972, explaining Canada's vote.

36. Canada, Delegation to the United Nations, Press Release no. 21, November 16, 1972.

37. Canada, Department of External Affairs, Statements and Speeches, no. 72/20.

38. International Legal Materials 13 (April 12, 1974): 712.

39. See Green, "International Law and Canada's Oil Pollution Legislation," Oregon Law Review 50 (1971): 462.

2

PERSPECTIVES ON
POLITICAL TERRORISM
IN THE UNITED STATES
Bernard K. Johnpoll

Political terrorism and violence are not—revolutionary rhetoricians to the contrary—as American as apple pie. There have been occasional outbreaks of political terrorism in the United States during the past 200 years, but most of these have been local and limited in scope. None of the terrorist movements succeeded in achieving its aims; most resulted in repression and an increase in the power of the very institutions that the terrorists were attacking. In those few cases in which terrorist activity had been credited with effectuating radical change—particularly in the case of the Ku Klux Klan of the post-Civil War period—closer examination has revealed that the change occurred in spite of, rather than due to, the terrorists' activities.

Few of the terrorist groups have been revolutionary. During the past 150 years, only one small, short-lived, imported group of revolutionaries preached the use of terror. Most revolutionary groups during the first two-thirds of this century opposed the use of terror, although some preached organized, violent revolution. It has only been during the past decade that small groups of alienated, elitist, would-be revolutionaries have turned to terrorism as a means for radical change.

THE KLAN AND THE "MOLLIES"

Terrorist movements have almost invariably been pawns in the hands of political and social elites, whose interests rarely reflected those of the movements' members. The earliest terrorist groups in the United States—the vigilantes—were originally organized to keep law and order in the lawless frontier West. These uniquely American bands came into being because there was no law enforcement in that underpopulated area. But they were soon controlled by the frontier elites, whose interests were served by terror. In San Francisco, for example, the vigilantes were "dominated lock, stock, and barrel by the leading merchants of the city."[1] The Ku Klux Klan, another early terrorist group, helped the former slaveholding Democratic political establishment of the old Confederacy regain its power from the black-Republican coalition that had control of the South during the post-Civil War period. The Klan weakened black and Republican morale, thus making it possible for the planter elite of the Southern Democratic Party to reassert itself.[2] But the Klansmen, most of whom were poor whites, gained nothing for their efforts.

Even when the establishment did not directly control the terrorist groups it was able to use them for its own purposes by creating the myth that the terrorists, who were invariably feared and hated by a majority of the populace, were the progeny of antagonistic organizations, thus destroying political and economic opponents and maintaining its own dominance. The classic example of this use of terrorism occurred in the anthracite fields of northeastern Pennsylvania during the 1870s. The Molly Maguires (a pseudonym given to some of the members of the Ancient Order of Hibernians in that region) were involved in organized terror. Some of the "Mollies" were miners and belonged to the Miners' National Association, their trade union; most of the leaders were tavern owners with little interest in the conditions under which miners worked. Moreover, the primary interest of the Mollies was vengeance against the anti-Irish-Catholic Scotch, Ulster, Welsh, and English Protestants of the region, whom they accused of unfriendly acts or slights. The Mollies murdered at least 15 of their enemies. Although none of the murders were strike connected and there was no relation between the terrorists and the union, a fortuitous coincidence enabled the anthracite barons to use the hatred that the Mollies engendered to destroy the labor organization.

A major strike had closed the anthracite fields at the very time that the Molly Maguires were being arrested and tried for their depredations. Franklin Gowen, president of the Philadelphia and Reading Railroad Company, the largest coal operator in the region, took advantage of the coincidence and had himself named a prosecuting attorney. He then used his position to create the false impression—broadcast throughout the country by a basically antilabor press—that the miners' union was the gray eminence behind the murders in the hard-coal fields. The fact that the miners' union leaders had publicly assailed the terror tactics and that James McPartlan, a Pinkerton spy and agent provocateur employed by Gowen, helped incite the Mollies, was ignored. The union was destroyed by the libel created by Gowen. He thus saved the political, social, and economic hegemony of the anthracite barons with the unwitting aid of the Molly Maguires.[3] As one historian wrote, "It has been revealed that the operators themselves instigated some of these attacks in order to provide an excuse for moving in, not only to crush the Molly Maguires but also all union organization."[4]

LABOR AND TERROR

The United States has had the "bloodiest and most violent labor history of any industrial nation in the world," but the terror has generally been directed against the unions. Violence in labor disputes has almost always been harmful to the labor unions by giving employers an excuse to ask for police or national guard aid in fighting against the unions. Moreover, labor violence has created the illusion that union men are irresponsible desperadoes.

Regardless of the evidence, labor unions have invariably been accused of instigating terror and violence, particularly during strikes. No union organization has been more maligned on this account than the Industrial Workers of the World (IWW). It is true that the "Wobblies"—as members of the IWW were commonly called—spoke of "direct action" and sabotage as tools for "emancipating the working class." But by "direct action" they meant nonviolent economic action, and sabotage was a more militant synonym for direct action in their lexicon. The IWW virtually never employed violence; its members were often the victims of shootings, assaults, kidnappings, and lynchings.[5]

There is only one major authenticated case of the use of terror by trade unionists. The McNamara brothers, James and John, who were officials of the Bridge and Structural Steel Workers Union, a conservative affiliate of the American Federation of Labor, bombed the building of the antiunion Los Angeles Times, killing 21 persons. They were arrested, tried, and convicted. As a result, the prolabor Socialist candidate for mayor, Job Harriman, was defeated; the iron workers' union was made impotent for more than a decade; and Los Angeles remained an antiunion bastion for the next 30 years.[6]

JOHANN MOST

There has been little theoretical defense of terrorism and individual acts of violence in the United States. Occasional ex post facto rationalizations for such acts have been made. The minority members of the Joint Select Committee to Inquire into the Late Insurrectionary States defended the Ku Klux Klan for rebelling against "the tyrannical, corrupt carpetbagger or scalawag rule."[7] Nor has there been any

theoretical explanation of the terrorism employed by the vigilantes or
the Molly Maguires. The only philosophic appeal for the use of terror
in the United States came from the Anarcho-Communists, particularly
Johann Most, during the 1880s.

Most, a native of Germany, came to the United States in 1882 at
the age of 36 from a London prison, to which he had been committed
for hailing the murder of Czar Alexander II. Given a hero's welcome
by American Socialists, he soon alienated the more moderate among
them by arguing that it was necessary to destroy the personal representatives of the capitalist system as well as the system itself. This
call for personal terror was repugnant to the American Marxists, but
Most argued that the slaughter was necessary because it would create
fear and demoralization in the ruling class while at the same time
raise the morale of the masses, thus leading to a successful uprising. [8]
In his American writings and speeches he called for the use of dynamite; he even wrote a pamphlet entitled "Revolutionare Kriegswissenschaft," which was a manual that included instructions on the use of
dynamite. Most's infatuation with dynamite spread like a prairie fire
among American radicals, few of whom were Marxists. Within a year
after Most's arrival in the United States, revolutionary Socialists and
Anarchists formed the International Working People's Association
(IWPA) at a convention in Pittsburgh. Most and his creed of terror
was the dominating force at the meeting. The delegates heard innum-
erable calls for arming the proletariat and educating the workers in
the "new scientific developments, especially chemistry." The manifesto that resulted called for terror and revolution, and the organization that was born at the convention had as its rallying cry: "gunpowder and dynamite will set you free."[9]

Most, personally, had no intention of ever using dynamite, but
his rhetoric (which one scholar has compared to the "sinister enthusiasm of a malevolent and utterly irresponsible child") did inflame
most opponents of capitalism in the United States. "Dynamite! Of
all the good stuff, that is the stuff," an Anarchist newspaper screamed.
"Stuff several pounds of this sublime stuff into an inch pipe . . . plug
up both ends, insert a cap with a fuse attached, place this in the vicinity of a lot of rich loafers who live by the sweat of other peoples'
brows and light the fuse. A most cheerful and gratifying result will
follow. . . . A pound of the good stuff beats a bushel of ballots hol-
low—and don't you forget it!" And August Spies, who was to die on
the gallows in Chicago in 1887, argued that, since capitalists would
not listen to reason and because they were prepared to use force to
maintain their power, the workers had no alternative but to use dynamite to oust them. His fellow victim of the 1887 hangings, Albert
Parsons, viewing the starvation among workingmen in Chicago in
1885, wrote, "It is clearly more humane to blow ten men into eternity

than to make ten men starve to death." And his wife, Lucy, wrote in the Denver <u>Labor Enquirer</u> that "dynamite is the voice of force, the only voice tyranny has been able to understand."[10]

The theoretical basis for the use of terror developed by Most and his followers was thus the argument that the only means available for overthrowing the oppressive system and making the new Utopia secure was individual terror. They assumed that the threat to the revolution came from those individuals who had held power under the old system and their destruction was a prerequisite for a successful revolution. Peripherally, Most and his followers argued that terror was essentially less oppressive than the continuation of the present system, that at least as many persons had died under the present system as would die during a period of terror, and that death from privation under the present system was far worse than death by assassination. This was to remain, with some modification, the basic philosophic argument for terror in the United States.

The violent rhetoric spawned by this theory was to be the weapon used by the capitalist state to destroy the Anarcho-Communists themselves. Given the first opportunity, the state used its power to erase what it perceived to be a threat to its power. That opportunity came in May 1886, when a demonstration was held in Chicago's Haymarket to protest the slaying of six strikers at the McCormick agricultural implements factory the day before. Their peaceful meeting was ordered disbanded by a police captain, who was acting illegally. The Anarcho-Communists attempted to argue that their meeting was legal and orderly. The police began to disperse the crowd with needless brutality. Suddenly, someone—probably an agent provocateur—threw a bomb. Seven policemen and four demonstrators were killed and 60 policemen and 50 demonstrators and bystanders were injured, some seriously. Eight Anarchists were tried for the crime. None were linked with the throwing of the bomb. The only charge proved was that they had at some time in the past called for the use of terror. Most's "Revolutionare Kriegswissenschaft" and the calls for the use of dynamite by Spies and the Parsons were the chief witnesses against them. Four of the eight were executed, one committed suicide, and three were sentenced to long prison terms. The rhetoric of terror played bloody havoc with the Anarchist movement and did irreparable harm to the labor movement that the Anarcho-Communists had claimed to be supporting. The bomb, Samuel Gompers told Henry Demarest Lloyd, "has killed the eight-hour movement."[11] By 1892 even Most was discouraged and condemned terrorism, although nine years later he served a year in jail for incitement after the assassination of President McKinley. Most had nothing to do with the assassination nor was he genuinely guilty of incitement. But a filler article, accidentally placed in his newspaper, was used as evidence against him.[12]

"SUPERSENSITIVE"

The people who were attracted to terrorism rarely belonged to
the class for which they claimed to be fighting. Most, Spies, and Parsons, for example, were editors. Of the three only Most had a working-class background. Spies was of upper-middle-class German origin, and Parsons' family—New Englanders who migrated to the South
—had been well off. The same was true of the quixotic Burnette G.
Haskell, the leader of the ephemeral antipolitical and quasi-terrorist
International Workingmen's Association in San Francisco between
1883 and 1887. He came from an upper-class family in the Sierra
region of northeastern California, had attended Oberlin College (from
which he withdrew after only one year), and had been an attorney and
an editor before devoting 10 years of his life to revolutions of various
sorts. The same is true of the so-called revolutionary terrorists of
today. Few if any workingmen have ever been involved in such movements.

Emma Goldman, the leading Anarchist thinker of the twentieth
century, argued that ideological terrorists were supersensitive "to
the wrong and injustice surrounding them" and this led them "to pay
the toll of our social crimes." She denied that even Leon Czolgosz,
the assassin of President McKinley, was a depraved creature of low
instincts. He and others like him were "in reality supersensitive be-
ings unable to bear up under too great social stress. They are driven
to some violent expression, even at the sacrifice of their own lives,
because they cannot supinely witness the misery and suffering of their
fellows." She called them martyrs and believed them to be "the forerunners of a better and nobler life."[13] While it is probably true that
most terrorists were supersensitive, the fact that they were invariably romantics, alienated from society, and elitists is of greater significance. Goldman's closest collaborator during her long career,
Alexander Berkman, who had attempted to kill Henry Clay Frick after
he had broken the 1892 strike of the steel workers in his Homestead,
Pennsylvania, plant, was a typical terrorist-revolutionary. A romantic who argued that a life "uninspired by revolutionary ideals" has
no value, he was alienated from society. He argued at his trial that
the real defendant was "society—the system of injustice, of the organized exploitation of the people." He was an elitist who considered
his deed to be an act of lese majeste for which the Homestead workers
should have been grateful. When one of the strikers, himself facing
trial for murder in connection with the strike, told Berkman that his
action could only hurt the strikers, Berkman was angered. The worker, he wrote, was "a cowardly overgrown boy . . . concerned only
with his own safety . . . a veritable Judas . . . the traitor," unwilling to die for a cause (in which, by the way, the worker did not be-

lieve). Because the strikers did not accept the great "truth" that
Berkman had found, he held them in contempt. There was no attempt
by Berkman to empathize with or understand the common worker. To
Berkman, "mere human sentiment is unworthy of the real revolution-
ist."[14]

Thirty-seven years after his attempt against Frick, Berkman
had changed his mind. He no longer believed that terror was a legitimate revolutionary tactic, but he still argued that in "every land, in
all ages there have been tyrannicides" carried out by "men and women who loved their country well enough to sacrifice even their own
lives for it."[15]

Just as the philosophical rationalization of terror as a political
tactic that was first enunciated in the United States by Most and his
cohorts has remained intact over the past 95 years, so has the personality profile of the revolutionary who employs individual violence.
And the results of the tactic have shown little if any change.

THE WEATHERMEN

There have been two major and a few minor organized terrorist
groups over the past two decades in the United States. Their effect
has been minimal, except for some temporary and localized disloca-
tion and governmental repression. Besides these small terrorist
groups there have been some localized acts of individual political violence in defense of the status quo, but such cases as the murder of
three civil rights workers in Mississippi and the slaughter of black
students at Jackson State College and white students at Kent State
University are beyond the scope of this chapter. It might be well to
notice, however, that, except for the covert official sanction given
the perpetrators by federal, state, or local government officials,
these depradations do not vary significantly from the vigilantes and
the Ku Klux Klan of the last century. The assaults in Mississippi
were generally perpetrated by poor whites, but their aim was to
eradicate a threat to the dominance of the white political elite. At
Kent State the shots were fired on the assumption that they would
somehow quiet antiwar sentiment. They had the reverse effect.

In none of these pro-status quo ante assaults was there a considered intellectual rationale for the use of terror. The two major
revolutionary terrorist groups of the past two decades—the Weatherman faction of the Students for a Democratic Society (SDS) and the
Symbionese Liberation Army (SLA)—on the contrary claimed to represent a utopia that, their members argued, required murder and
bombing to attain. Unlike the perpetrators of the Mississippi and
Ohio murders, these groups, which were composed of educated,

literate, articulate young people, claimed to have well-developed
philosophic rationalizations for their actions.

The Weatherman faction was a splinter group of the SDS, a campus organization originally affiliated with the Democratic Socialist
League for Industrial Democracy. The SDS was far more rhetorically
militant than its parent organization, from which it withdrew in 1963.
Almost immediately, the SDS, emulating its left-wing antecedents,
developed into a "federation of warring factions." Some were democratic and Socialist in outlook; others were admitted followers of
Most and the Russian Nihilist, Nachaev. The feuding within the SDS
reached its climax at the 1969 convention in Chicago, at which the organization split into the Maoist Progressive Labor faction and the terrorist Weatherman faction.[16] The membership of the SDS had by this
time declined to about 10 percent of what it had been two years earlier.

The Weathermen considered terror to be essential to revolution,
and they believed that revolution was urgently needed. But there was
one impediment—the Weathermen had no mass base. Most of them
were students, and revolutionary students, according to one of their
own spokesmen, were "the privileged" struggling "for more privi-
leges." There were thus many potential leaders but few followers.
Even the Weathermen recognized that a revolution required a mass
base. But earlier SDS attempts at recruiting nonstudents had invariably ended in failure. To solve this dilemma the Weathermen proposed
a unique solution—the organization of the "first revolutionary street
gang in history," which would win to its ranks "disfranchised and
alienated" youth. In this manner, the young people who composed the
criminal street gangs of the urban ghettos could be attracted to the
revolution. Once they had been won over, the Weathermen would become a major organization and the vanguard of the revolution. How
could they attract these potential revolutionaries? By organizing a
series of daylight escapades that would, by their audacity "against the
hated system," win support from street gang members. The Weathermen were soon disappointed; they had called a revolution to which no
one came.[17]

The failure of the Weathermen to win a following led to intense,
long-winded debate within the faction. But it did not lead to any dimi-
nution of their commitment to the use of violence and terror or the
rhetoric of violence and terror. Thus, when President Nixon and
S. I. Hayakawa, then president of San Francisco State University,
attended a dinner in October 1969, the Weathermen proclaimed that
their troops would be out to assure that "the streets of Amerika are
no longer safe for enemies of the people. . . . Kick Ass!" Violent
demonstrations followed, at which police and Weathermen were injured. Violence became an aim in itself: "When I beat up the pig
Friday afternoon, it helped define what Saturday [the day of the riot]
was all about."[18]

The Weathermen insisted that they were not nihilists who believed in revolt for its own sake but revolutionary idealists struggling for a better world. True, the Black Panthers, who had a temporary alliance with the Weatherman faction during the 1969 SDS convention, had published the Anarchist-Nihilist <u>Catechism</u> of Sergei Nachaev, whom the Panthers' leader, Eldridge Cleaver, had lauded.[19] But as Mark Rudd, a Weatherman leader, pointed out: "We do have a vision of the way things could be: How the tremendous resources of our economy could be used to eliminate want . . . how men could be free to keep what they produce, to enjoy peaceful lives, to create. . . . We will have to destroy at times, even violently, in order to end your [capitalist system]."[20]

Unfortunately, Rudd and his fellow Weathermen were more imbued with their dedication to violence, often for its own sake, than with their vision of a utopia. As John Jacobs, another leader of the faction, told his associates: "We're against everything that's good and decent." And Bernardine Dohrn hailed the depraved killer Charles Manson and his followers: "Dig it!" she told a Weatherman caucus. "First they killed the pigs, then they even shoved a fork in the victim's stomach! Wild!"[21]

For about a year the Weathermen sought a rationalization for their commitment to terrorism. In a long and rambling statement, 11 of the faction's leaders argued that

> the struggle activity, the actions of the movement,
> demonstrates our existence and strength to people
> in a material way. Seeing it happen, people give
> it more weight in their thinking. For the partici-
> pants, involvement in struggle is the best educa-
> tion about the movement, the enemy, and the class
> struggle. In a neighborhood or whole city the exis-
> tence of some struggle is a catalyst for other strug-
> gles—it pushes people to see the movement as more
> important and urgent, and, as an example and prec-
> edent, makes it easier for them to follow.[22]

With the war then raging in Indochina, the Weathermen argued even more vehemently for the use of terror. It was necessary, they argued, to "bring the war home! Turn New York into Saigon!" The revolutionary terrorists insisted that

> when General Electric is bombed, or the offices of
> the First National Bank are gutted . . . or when pro-
> fessors and researchers sell their brains to the De-
> fense Department and are attacked physically for it,

what is behind those actions is the attempt to bring
home to meatballs involved in the abstract plotting
of death that death and violence <u>really</u> exist, and to
make them . . . aware and accountable for their
acts.

But all did not go as anticipated. Despite a well-publicized confrontation with the Chicago police called "Days of Rage," at which an
assistant district attorney was seriously injured and most of the leading Weathermen were arrested, they failed to attract a following.
They were more isolated than ever. And then there was a blast in a
Greenwich Village townhouse. Some Weathermen were building antipersonnel dynamite bombs wrapped with nails and bits of shrapnel.
Someone made an error, the house was wrecked, and three of the
"revolutionaries" were blown to bits. The leadership, most of whom
were free on bail, vanished. Except for occasional messages to the
New York <u>Times</u> from Bernardine Dohrn, announcing that she had
given up on terror and violence, and occasional bombings attributed
to an ephemeral Weather Underground, whose connection with the
Weathermen is questionable, the group vanished. It had gone the way
of all revolutionary terrorists: it had accomplished nothing and had
in fact been counterproductive.

The collapse of the Weathermen followed the normal pattern for
they had ignored the lessons of history. Faced with the assumed oppressive nature of the state, they assumed that there was no way open
to the revolutionary except terror. They were convinced that there
were only two alternatives open to them, "the state or resistance,"
by which they meant terrorism or acquiescence. Destruction, as an
act of resistance, was thus a positive action, and "to destroy is to
feel free." Moreover, the Weathermen assumed that political repression—particularly fascism—would speed the revolution. Fascism, they
argued, would force the people to rebel. Ted Gold, theoretician of
the Weathermen, who died in the Greenwich Village bomb explosion,
told his followers shortly before his death: "If it will take fascism,
we'll have to have fascism [to achieve the revolution]."[23] They ignored the German and Italian experiences that indicated that fascism
had little to fear from internal opposition.

The Weathermen even failed to "win" fascism for the United
States. There was some minor repression following the Chicago confrontation, but the public was generally hostile or apathetic. The war
in Indochina ground to a halt and eventually ended because of disenchantment within the established political forces in the United States
and the superiority of the North Vietnamese forces and their allies.
Except for the deaths of three of their leaders in the Greenwich Village
explosion and the crippling of one assistant district attorney, the Wea-

thermen accomplished nothing. They merely proved that a tiny revolutionary elite could not lead an unwilling mass into a "heavenly Utopia" by terrorism. A revolution, to be successful, requires a mass indigenous base. Terrorists are doomed because they assume that a small dedicated cadre can create a revolution, and this is the chief lesson of the Weathermen.

THE SYMBIONESE LIBERATION ARMY

The failure of the short-lived Weatherman movement left many would-be "revolutionary leaders" without a base of operations. Most expected the Weathermen to rise from the ashes of the Greenwich Village blast and move to Berkeley, home of the University of California's main campus and historically the nation's leading site for militant antiestablishmentarian activity. There was also in the early 1970s a restlessness in the nation's dehumanizing, inhumane, and poorly staffed prisons. A mating of these two phenomena led to the formation of the most recent of the "revolutionary" terrorist movements, the SLA.

The SLA was a small 10- or 12-member organization composed of idealistic, educated, and frustrated would-be revolutionaries and semiliterate convicts. They had first met when the educated young people, all of whom were white and middle-class, turned their idealism to what seemed to them to be a pragmatic use: they established small groups that went into the San Francisco Bay area prisons as teachers. They found some of the convicts to be "perfect revolutionists"—totally alienated, dehumanized by the prison system, experts in violence, and unhampered by moral scruples. As soon as the convicts left prison (legally or illegally), they joined their teachers to form the terrorist "army" based, consciously or unconsciously, on Most's prescription for revolution.

Who were the "soldiers" of the SLA? Angel de Angelis Atwood was an ex-cheerleader from suburban North Haldon, New Jersey, whose father was a conservative trade union official. A devout Catholic in her younger days and a sorority girl of limited intellectual capacity at Indiana University, she turned Trotskyite for a short time but found it too confining and then turned to militant revolutionary terrorism. She refused to "stain her world with doubts or questions." Nancy Ling Perry, the daughter of conservative Californians had in 1964 been a Goldwater booster. Radicalized at Berkeley, where she obtained a degree in English, she sold fruit juice from a stand near the university campus in order that she would never take "the first steps up a bourgeois career ladder." Patricia Soltysik, the daughter of a California pharmacist, also turned radical at the university.

Camilla Hall, the daughter of a Lutheran minister, was a graduate of the University of Minnesota and had for a time been a social worker. Russell Little dropped out of the University of Florida and came to Berkeley where he "expected things to blow up . . . but they didn't. . . . The era of riots and demonstrations had passed. . . . People started talking about educating the people. Bull—— to that."

Of the criminals who joined the SLA, the leader was Donald DeFreeze, an escapee from the notorious Soledad prison with a long record of petty crimes and mental illness. One atypical recruit was Joe Remiro, a Vietnam veteran with a working knowledge of firearms.

The SLA was miniscule and thus almost impenetrable by informers. Its discipline was absolute. Its aim was absolute revolution, although the ultimate purpose of the revolution was never stated. Its tactic was to be organized terror, and its first act was murder—the slaying of Oakland's newly appointed black school superintendent, Marcus Foster. He was slain by the SLA because he had a month earlier given some consideration to the possibility of issuing identification cards to students and placing guards in the schools to keep disruptive nonstudents from the school buildings. This proposal roused the ire of the SLA leadership because it saw the black high school students as ostensible recruits, and such a regulation would keep them off the campus.

A few months after Foster had been shot to death with cyanide bullets and two SLA members were arrested in connection with the slaying, the terrorists made their next move. They ostensibly kidnapped Patricia Hearst, daughter of a wealthy San Francisco publisher. After a bizarre series of negotiations, millions of dollars of food was distributed under conditions of near-pandemonium as ransom. But the supposed victim cast her lot with her abductors, joined the SLA, and participated in a bank holdup in which a bystander was shot.

The story of the SLA reached a fiery conclusion in the Los Angeles black ghetto in May 1974, when almost 150 Los Angeles policemen and 100 FBI agents surrounded the group's hideout. In the gun battle and fire that ensued, six members of the SLA died. Only Patricia Hearst and two others escaped alive.

The movement was not dead, but Remiro romanticized from his jail cell: "The S.L.A. ain't nothing, man. The revolution is on with or without the S.L.A. . . . . I think a revolutionary underground is growing. . . . If the entire S.L.A. and everybody who relates to the S.L.A. would be killed tomorrow, the next day they'd have to kill a lot more."[24]

Perhaps, but for the time being the SLA is dead. And the history of other revolutionary terrorist groups indicates that they are never resurrected, nor do they ever make a revolution.

THE FUTILITY OF TERROR

An exhaustive study of all the terrorist movements in the United States would require the discussion of the agrarian movements immediately following the American Revolution, John Brown and his activities in Kansas, lynch violence in the South and the West, police terror in Selma and Chicago, the antialien depradations of the last century, the murder of black Sunday schoolchildren by segregationists, and the race riots of the past half-century. But the study of the selected movements of organized political terrorism covered in this chapter does indicate a pattern from which the following lessons can be drawn:

1. Terrorist movements have never accomplished the stated aims of their founders. The vigilantes hardly brought law and order to the West; the rhetoric of terror espoused by Most and his IWPA did nothing to advance their hoped-for revolution; the bombings and confrontations of the Weathermen had little effect on the social order; and the SLA was a passing moment of fright and terror.

2. Almost all political terror has been counterproductive. The vigilantes unloosed lawless violence that made the crimes they had been organized to fight pale by comparison; the IWPA and its leaders died on the gallows in Chicago; the Weathermen died in a Greenwich Village blast; and the SLA was destroyed "in a blaze of glory" in Los Angeles. In each of these cases the state temporarily became more repressive when faced with their threats, and movements aimed at genuine change were stymied by public antagonism engendered by the terrorists.

3. Terrorist groups serve the interests of the ruling elite. The merchants of the West were served by the vigilantes, the planter political elite of the South by the Klan, the anthracite barons by the Mollie Maguires, and the advocates of a police state by the Anarcho-Communists, the Weathermen, and the SLA.

4. Terror is not a revolutionary instrument. It attracts romantics, and a revolution, to be successful, requires pragmatic idealists.

5. The state has at its disposal far more effective instruments of counterterror than any weapons the terrorists may possess.

6. Violence has an unfortunate tendency to lead to more violence. Once terror has become the chief tactic, it invariably replaces ideals as the primary aim of a movement.

The terrorist who assumes "that what one really believes in is what will come to pass"[25] ignores the lessons of history. Romantic posturing is no substitute for reality. In sum, terrorism is the politics of futility.

NOTES

1. Richard Maxwell Brown, "Historical Patterns of Violence in America," in Violence in America: Historical and Comparative Perspectives, ed. Hugh Davis Graham and Ted Robert Gurr (New York: Bantam Books, 1970), p. 67.

2. Allen W. Trelease, White Terror: The Ku Klux Klan Conspiracy and Southern Reconstruction (New York: Harper & Row, 1971), p. 419. Trelease's book is the finest work on the Ku Klux Klan.

3. Wayne G. Broehl, The Molly Maguires (Cambridge, Mass.: Harvard University Press, 1964), is the best book on the Molly Maguires. Anthony Bimba, The Molly Maguires (New York: International Publishers, 1932), is a Communist book replete with minor and major errors of fact. Even Bimba concedes that labor leaders and labor papers were unsympathetic to the Mollies (see p. 127, for example).

4. Foster Rhea Dulles, Labor in America: A History (New York: Thomas Y. Crowell Co., 1966), pp. 117-18.

5. Philip Taft and Robert Ross, "American Labor Violence: Its Causes, Character, and Outcome," in Graham and Gurr, op. cit., pp. 281, 285, 381.

6. See, for example, Helen Marot, American Labor Unions (New York: Henry Holt & Co., 1914), pp. 190-98. See also Louis Adamic, Dynamite: The Story of Class Violence in America (New York: Viking Press, 1934), pp. 179-253; Daniel Bell, "The Background and Development of Marxian Socialism in the United States," in Socialism and American Life, ed. Donald Drew Egbert and Stow Persons (Princeton, N.J.: Princeton University Press, 1952), p. 285.

7. Quoted in Stanley F. Horn, Invisible Empire: The Story of the Ku Klux Klan, 1866-1871 (Boston: Houghton Mifflin Co., 1939), p. 2.

8. See, for example, John [Johann] Most, The Beast of Property (New Haven, Conn.: International Workingmen's Association Group, 1883).

9. Johann Most, Science of Revolutionary War: Manual for Instruction in the Use and Preparation of Nitro-Glycerine, Dynamite, Gun-Cotton, Fulminating Mercury, Bombs, Fuses, and Poisons, etc., etc. (New York: International Zeitung Verein, 1884), also reprinted in Northeast Reporter 12:894-901; George Woodcock, Anarchism (New York: World Publishing Co., 1971), pp. 461-52; Freiheit (New York), October 20, 1883; J. S. Hertz, Di Idishe Sotsialistishe Bavegung in Amerika (New York: Der Wecker, 1954), p. 59.

10. Woodcock, op. cit., pp. 461-62; quoted in James Joll, The Anarchists (New York: Grossett and Dunlop, 1964), p. 48; August

Spies, Autobiography (Chicago: Nina Van Zandt, 1887), pp. 51-52; Labor Enquirer, April 4, 1885; Northeast Reporter 12:879-80, 884-85, 887.

11. See the Chicago Tribune, May 5, 1886; Dyer D. Lum, A Concise History of the Great Trial of the Chicago Anarchists (Chicago: Socialistic Publishing Co., 1887), pp. 13, 29, 37-48, 150; Workmen's Advocate, May 12, 1888; Caro Lloyd, Henry Demarist Lloyd, 1847-1903: A Biography (New York: G. P. Putnam's Sons, 1912), pp. I, 99; Woodcock, op. cit., p. 465.

12. Joll, op. cit., pp. 144-45; "People v. Most," New York Reporter 128:109-11; Emma Goldman, Living My Life (New York: Alfred A. Knopf, 1931), pp. I, 105. For interesting and humorous details on Most and the assassination of McKinley, see Morris Hillquit, Loose Leaves from a Busy Life (New York: Macmillan Co., 1934), pp. 120-29.

13. Emma Goldman, "The Psychology of Political Violence," in Red Emma Speaks, ed. Alix K. Shulman (New York: Random House, 1972), p. 211; Goldman, op. cit., pp. I, 312.

14. Alexander Berkman, Prison Memoirs of an Anarchist (New York: Schocken Books, 1970), pp. 54-55, 73-75, 91 (originally published in 1912).

15. Alexander Berkman, Now and After: The ABC of Communist Anarchism (New York: Vanguard Press, 1929), pp. 174-75, 177.

16. No serious study has as yet been completed on the SDS. Kirkpatrick Sale, SDS (New York: Random House, 1973), is a reasonably accurate account. But see Wilson (Carey) McWilliams' review in the New York Times Book Review, May 6, 1973, p. 3. Alan Adelson, SDS: A Profile (New York: Charles Scribner's Sons, 1972), is a generally inaccurate work of pseudo-history. It is important only where it gives details of the 1969 convention. The early SDS can best be examined in the Student League for Industrial Democracy papers at the Tamiment Collection, Bobst Library, New York University.

17. Adelson, op. cit., pp. 233, 245.

18. Peter Clapp, "Columbia," New Left Notes, April 17, 1969, p. 5; Marion Delgado, "S.D.S. N.C., December 26-31," Fire, November 21, 1969, p. 1; "Enemies of the People: Dick Nixon and S. I. Hayakawa Will Be Dining at the Hotel Hilton," SDS handbill, October 1969, Tamiment Collection, Bobst Library, New York University.

19. See Paul Avrich's review, "Bakunin and His Circle," Nation, February 15, 1975, p. 181.

20. Quoted in Adelson, op. cit., p. 122.

21. Quoted in ibid., p. 247.

22. Karen Ashley, Bill Ayers, Bernardine Dohrn, John Jacobs, Jeff Jones, Gerry Long, Howie Machbinger, Jim Mellen, Terry Rob-

bins, Mark Rudd, and Steve Tappis, "You Don't Need a Weatherman
to Tell You Which Way the Wind Blows," in Debate Within SDS: RYM
II vs. Weatherman (Detroit: Radical Education Project, 1970), p. 29
(microfilm copy at Boston University Library, Special Collections).

   23. Dotson Rader, "On Revolutionary Violence," Defiance, no.
1 (New York: Paperback Library, 1970), pp. 201, 206-07, 210-11.
The Gold quotation is in Adelson, op. cit., p. 247.

   24. Michael Wolf, "Cheerleader for the Revolution," New York
Times Magazine, July 21, 1974, pp. 11-20; Sam Davidson, "Notes
from the Land of the Cobra," New York Times Magazine, June 2,
1974, pp. 36-46. Quotations are from the San Francisco Chronicle,
Newsweek, and Time, all of which covered the SLA, beginning in October 1973.

   25. SLA member quoted in Davidson, op. cit., p. 38.

3

Events in Latin America transpire with such rapidity that even the most current research is soon dated. Two cases in point are the recent $14.2 million ransom paid by Exxon for the release of a kidnapped company official and the death of Juan Peron, who was seen by some as the last hope for unity in Argentina.

AN OVERVIEW

In order to comprehend the problems of terrorism in Latin America, the background of economic and political stability must be understood, as well as the spread of armed insurgency since the Cuban revolution. Latin American peasants are moving from the country to the cities at a rate of about 8 percent per year. Currently about half of the inhabitants of Latin America live in urban areas.[1] It is not difficult to visualize the effect this surge to the cities has had on the economies of these countries. Slums and shantytowns such as the favelas of Brazil abound on the edges of urban areas, and with them come unemployment, hunger, sickness, and hopelessness. The award-winning poetic drama Morte e Vida Severina portrays the hope of the retirantes, peasants who move from Brazil's parched backlands to the urban areas, expecting to find good land and employment opportunities. Instead they end up living under conditions far worse than those they left. They do encounter fertile lands but they are all owned by a few rich fazendiros. Inasmuch as Latin America is not highly industrialized, the influx of people seeking employment in industry into urban areas does not correspond to the number of employment opportunities. In this part of the world, the urban revolution is preceding any industrial revolution. In their impoverished state, these

large transient masses have a great potential for unstable social and
political conditions.

Latin American culture naturally lends itself to the spectacular
and the daring. My own research on the cultural traditions of Latin
America, particularly Brazil, indicates a penchant for folk heroes
of action, such as Fidel Castro in Cuba and Pele in Brazil. Culture
has linked this identification to Latin American machismo. Brazil's
President Medici grasped the opportunity to capitalize on this phenomenon when he hosted the World Cup Soccer winners in Brazilia in
1970. The resulting publicity instilled a direct connection in the minds
of the Brazilians between their country's victory, an unequaled display of machismo, and the government. Acts of terrorism excite the
Latin Americans' machismo through their appeal to adventure and
daring. This is a definite plus for terrorists who seek to capture their
countrymen's imagination with their spectacular feats.

The Cuban revolution and the firm establishment of "Fidelismo"
provided a political and philosophical base in Latin America for the
spread of a doctrine that could take advantage of their social and economic conditions. Indeed, Castro has repeatedly voiced his support
for guerrilla warfare in Latin America. His assistance and supervi-
sion of guerrilla activities in Bolivia with Che Guevara is a case in
point. Castro even denounced Latin American Communists who opposed guerrilla warfare, blaming them for Guevara's defeat.[2] Until
recent times, aircraft hijackers were assured refuge in Cuba, which
assisted in fostering the image of that country as a protector of terrorists. In a nationwide radio and television statement in 1969, Castro pledged his full support of "any true revolution" in Latin America,
thus quashing speculation that he was ready to adopt a more moderate
policy. Although little evidence exists linking more recent Latin
American terrorist and guerrilla incidents to Cuba, that country has
nevertheless in times past given direct support and encouragement
to those activities. With a few exceptions guerrilla movements have
had little help from the established Communist parties since the early
1960s. Initially, Cuban support was somewhat limited, as Castro
seemed to prefer his own brand of diplomacy by conferring with bourgeois leaders in several Latin American and North American capitals.
This was eventually replaced in the early 1960s with a more revolutionary spirit when it appeared that Cuba's survival was not to come
through normal diplomatic relations with its neighbors. The last
chapter on the extent to which Castro has been involved in the guerrilla movement in Latin America has yet to be written.

Without question, the best-known proponent of rural guerrilla
activity in South America was Che Guevara. His diary and other
papers reveal that Guevara and Castro worked closely, viewing Bolivia as the nucleus of a revolution that would eventually embrace the

entire continent. Their plan included the establishment of impenetrable zones of operations, principally in the Andes, in which they would
train guerrillas for use in other parts of South America. But Guevara encountered several problems. His band was not familiar with
the extremely rugged terrain and received little support from the local
Communist Party, especially after 1967, thus giving them no political
base. Also, Guevara failed to win local and urban support, principally owing to his belief that revolution comes from the top down. In
1968 Cuban support began to wane, and the guerrillas began to encounter armies that were well trained in counterinsurgency operations.[3]
Guevara failed in his bid to establish a South American base for a
rural revolution, but he did establish guerrilla warfare as a fact of
life there. Moises Moleiro, a former guerrilla leader in Venezuela,
concluded that a rural revolution will never succeed in Latin America:
"It is just not possible to start a rural uprising that will end with the
countryside encircling the town. The rural areas are marginal to the
life of the country. . . . A peasant revolt is impossible, in the last
analysis, because we are not a peasant people."[4]

Following the Cuban revolution, two unsuccessful attempts at
guerrilla warfare in 1959 copied the Cuban pattern. In June there
was a poorly planned effort to overthrow Trujillo through an attempt
at invasion of the Dominican Republic. The second, a group of guerrillas entering Paraguay from Brazil in November, was aborted when
most of its members were captured within a week.[5] The leaders of
these missions had oversimplified the Cuban example, believing that
their meager efforts would bring similar results. Nevertheless, most
revolutionaries still dreamed of a future struggle for "independence"
having its genesis in Castro's example. The resultant shift of the
revolution to the cities transpired not through the failure of the rural
guerrillas' efforts but primarily as a move to take advantage of the
large revolutionary reservoir available for exploitation in the urban
areas. The transition was assisted by the mounting pressures of an
alarming population growth, massive foreign ownership of resources
and industry, and repressive regimes. Although industry had brought
great wealth to Latin America, the vast majority of the masses had
not benefited from it. Urban guerrillas need little manpower and few
resources to produce their desired results—confusion, apprehension,
and publicity. In contrast to the rural areas, the urban areas offered
an abundance of arms, funds, food, medical supplies, and intelligence.
Whereas the idealistic guerrillas in the country often adapted poorly
to the environment and found it difficult to identify with the peasantry,
these problems disappeared in the city. Arms were easy to obtain
from the police and the army, and bank robberies and kidnappings offered an inexhaustible source of funds.

Not until the revolution had moved from the countryside to the
urban areas did terrorist activities begin their explosive proliferation.

These began snowballing in the latter part of the 1960s with the murder of Colonel Houser, chief of the U.S. military mission in Guatemala, early in 1965, followed by several kidnappings that same year.[6] Colonel Houser's death was a response to the "criminal acts" commited by the United States in Vietnam.[7] On the second anniversary of the death of the Colombian guerrilla revolutionary Torres Restrepo in 1968, terrorists exploded a bomb at the U.S. Embassy in Bogota, and three weeks later they hijacked a Colombian airliner to Cuba. Shortly thereafter terrorists exploded a bomb in the U.S. Consulate in Santiago, which was followed by the bombing of the U.S. Consulate in Sao Paulo. In January of that same year, two U.S. military attaches were shot to death in Guatemala City, apparently in retaliation for the murder of an ex-beauty queen. The culmination of terrorist attacks in Guatemala came with the shooting of U.S. Ambassador Mein during a kidnapping attempt in retaliation for the arrest of a guerrilla leader. During 1969 bombings continued at the U.S. Embassy in Lima as U.S.-Peruvian relations deteriorated to the point that Peru signed its first trade agreement with the Soviet Union. Terrorists in Brazil finished out the 1960s with the spectacular kidnapping of U.S. Ambassador Elbrick, demanding as ransom the release of 15 unnamed political prisoners and the dissemination of the full text of an antigovernment manifesto by the press, television, and radio. Remembering the Guatemalan experience, Brazil accepted the demand and flew the 15 prisoners to Mexico, which had granted them asylum. Elbrick was later released unharmed. No small furor arose among the military in Brazil, who felt that the government should have taken a tougher stance. Forty Brazilian paratroopers seized a radio station and verbally assaulted the government for releasing the prisoners, and 200 Navy men attempted to block the departure of the plane. Some officers wanted to discredit the government junta in order to force either tougher internal policies or a change in government.

Although Communists have held positions in the Chilean government prior to 1970, the election of Allende marked the first time in the West that a Communist had become president through a bona fide election. This feat has caused some to speculate that legitimate elections may be an alternative route to violence and to revolution.[8] One must not forget that the September 1970 election of Allende was preceded by numerous outbreaks of violence caused mainly by guerrillas who were determined to prevent the elections. Nevertheless, Allende stated that, while not approving of the terrorists' tactics, he would ask for amnesty for them. Since his election, guerrillas from many parts of Latin America have found refuge in Chile.[9] Allende did not step into a vacuum inasmuch as in 1967 the ruling Christian Democrat Party had declared its support of guerrilla warfare as a legitimate means for achieving social change in unresponsive

governments.[10] It had even permitted the existence of the Cuban-
Latin American Solidarity Organization in Chile in exchange for this
organization's promise not to support insurgency. Only under pressure from extremist elements in his loose Popular Unity Coalition
did Allende condone urban guerrillas in Chile. At least two training
camps for these guerrillas were known to have existed in Chile during
his term as president.[11] There can be no doubt that the official position of the Allende government was a boon to terrorists in Latin America, since they could count on Chile as a refuge and a base for continental operations. Inasmuch as Chile became a virtual sanctuary for
political prisoners from Latin America's right-wing regimes, profes-
sionals, students, and professors also came, which gave the revolutionaries a cosmopolitan look.

LATIN AMERICAN TERRORIST PHILOSOPHY

"The terrorist has a political tool; the urban guerrilla has a
strategy for revolution," says Robert Moss, but to understand the
mind of the terrorist one must examine the philosophical background
of the urban guerrilla.[12] Terrorism in Latin America is the back-
bone of the urban guerrilla movement and its most frequent manifestation.
    The philosophy of the guerrilla in Latin America was formed
primarily by Che Guevara, the philosopher par excellence of the rural
revolution, and Abraham Guillen, the most far-reaching of the urban
philosophers. The latter's Theory of Violence (1965) and Strategy of
the Urban Guerrilla (1966) are bibles for the urban guerrilla. The
later work helped mold the foundation of guerrilla movements in Uruguay, Brazil, and Argentina. In comparison with Carlos Marighella's
well-known Minimanual of the Urban Guerrilla, Donald C. Hodges
calls Strategy the "maximanual of the urban guerrilla."[13] Marighella's
strategy has been the basis of operations in Guatemala, Colombia,
Venezuela, and Bolivia.[14] In his introduction to Philosophy of the Urban Guerrilla, Hodges compares Guevara's philosophy with that of
Guillen to show that he actually anticipated Guevara in his continental
strategy responding to the U.S. blockade of Cuba.[15] Guillen believed
that the decisive factor is the man, not the terrain, and that the mass
character of the urban guerrilla movement is preferable to the elite
foco favored in the rural revolution. He believed that an international,
heroic sense must replace the narrow nationalism that then existed in
Latin America. He envisioned war between the United States and
Latin America as a possibility, whereby the United States would face
a deterioration in its standard of living once it lost the cheap labor
and resources of Latin America. This in turn would lead to a revolu-

tion in the United States as the workers defended their standards and established a Socialist order. This second Latin American war of independence would come about as a result of the military dictatorships supported by the United States and the lengthy economic and political crises in Latin America, among other things. Guillen believed that a series of Vietnams in Latin America could bring about a unification of the people. The guerrilla groups assume that, under pressure, the United States will always support the repressive right-wing governments to ultimately protect their holdings in Latin America. Indeed, the United States, they theorize, can be counted on to intervene wherever guerrilla uprisings threaten. This intervention would be advantageous to the guerrillas because the presence of U.S. troops would arouse the masses against both the United States and the government in power. They reason that the kidnapping or assassination of prominent Americans may also prompt the United States into sending troops into Latin America.

The use of terrorism in Latin America has as an objective the alienation of popular support for the government through acts of terror, which in turn will cause the government to respond with progressively more repressive measures. This is in keeping with Marighella's strategy: "It is necessary to turn political crisis into armed conflict by performing violent actions that will force those in power to transform the political situation of the country into a military situation. That will alienate the masses, who, from then on, will revolt against the army and the police and blame them for this state of things."[16] To do this, he states, "the principal task of the urban guerrilla is to distract, to wear out, to demoralize the militarists, the military dictatorships and its repressive forces, and also to attack and destroy the wealth and property of the North Americans, the foreign managers, and the Brazilian upper class."[17] Unfortunately, the lofty ideals of terrorism may be replaced by a certain sense of adventure that makes any philosophical base suspect. Moss also notes that terrorism "is also characteristic both of the early and the declining phases of an insurgency: when a rebel movement is gathering strength, or when it has suffered heavy reverses."[18] The results of these objectives are well documented. Antigovernment terrorist attacks in Argentina in 1969 intensified with the visit of Nelson Rockefeller to the point that the government declared a nationwide state of siege. Calling the terrorism a "Communist Chinese-Castroite plot," authorities arrested several hundred people. The government had responded as the terrorists had hoped. In September of that same year, terrorists caused the government of Colombia to declare a state of siege in the face of a wave of kidnappings that netted $60,000 in ransom. The state of siege declared in Bolivia in July 1970 followed the kidnapping of two West German technicians. President Ovando of Bolivia was forced by

radicals into taking an increasingly repressive line, which resulted in
violent antigovernment demonstrations. His resignation in October
1970 touched off power struggles between militant leftists and rightists.
The resultant confusion satisfied the terrorists' immediate goals.

Marighella, in his Minimanual, gives his followers a list of
possible acts for the guerrilla to accomplish his goal. It includes
terrorist acts, such as assaults, raids, ambushes, seizures, executions, kidnappings, sabotage, and armed propaganda. "The terrorist
act," he says," apart from the apparent facility with which it can be
carried out, is no different from other urban guerrilla acts and actions.
. . . It is an action the urban guerrilla must execute with the greatest
coldbloodedness, calmness, and decision."[19] Terrorism under urban
conditions requires good security, which is achieved in part through
tight organization. Moss explains that "members of the terrorist
group are divided into cells or 'firing groups' of from three to five
men, with a link man in each. This clearly limits the possibilities of
betrayal or of police infiltration, but it also limits the possibility of
political agitation."[20]

Of the various methods of terrorism available, political kidnapping has caught the fancy of terrorists in Latin America. Indeed, it
has been rewarding in ransom, publicity, and government reaction to
such a degree that it has become a fact of life of the 1970s. Some
governments have refused to deal with the terrorists, often with disastrous results, while others have yielded to their demands. Marighella gives three reasons for kidnapping: as an exchange for prisoners, as propaganda, and as a form of protest against U.S. imperialism. The first reason has paid rich dividends for terrorists in Brazil. In 1969 Marighella's own Brazilian National Liberation Alliance
(ALN) kidnapped the U.S. ambassador but, not taking advantage of the
worth of their hostage, demanded only 15 political prisoners for his
release. Brazil gave in easily, which whetted the appetites of the
terrorists. The next year five armed terrorists kidnapped the West
German ambassador in Rio de Janeiro, demanding the release of 40
prisoners, who were flown shortly thereafter to Algiers. Inflation
had set in. Later that same year, the Swiss ambassador was kidnapped by six ALN members who sought 70 prisoners as ransom. Although the government decided to adopt a hard line, it eventually flew
70 to Chile. Guatemala, in contrast, refused to deal with terrorists who were guilty of kidnapping. As a consequence, when the West
German ambassador was kidnapped in Guatemala City, the government refused to accept the terrorists' demand for 17 prisoners, which
was later raised to 25 prisoners and $700,000. The ambassador was
found slain a few days later. Following the Tupamaros' murder of a
U.S. police adviser in Uruguay, the terrorists responsible justified
their act by saying that they had to prove to the government that they

meant business. Of execution as a terrorist weapon Marighella states
in his Minimanual: "Execution is a secret action in which the least
possible number of urban guerrillas are involved. In many cases,
the execution can be carried out by one sniper, patiently, alone and
unknown, and operating in absolute secrecy and in cold blood."[21]

THE TUPAMAROS OF URUGUAY: A
CASE STUDY

The Tupamaros of Uruguay offer an excellent study of terrorism
that nearly caused the collapse of a government. Uruguay, traditionally
one of the most stable nations in Latin America, has been a model of
constitutional rule. Early in this century, Uruguay became a worker's paradise in Latin America, with a minimum wage, an eight-hour
day, and old-age pensions. It also boasted free university education,
divorce, and rigid control over important parts of the economy. These
remarkable feats were achieved without shedding a drop of blood.

Prosperity came to Uruguay through the export of wool, meat,
and leather. The world market for these items began to slump in 1953,
and with it went the payroll and pensions of about a third of the population. Hard times had come to this model welfare state. Borrowing
heavily to cover deficits, the country's foreign debt skyrocketed, resulting in a rate of inflation that exceeded 135 percent in 1967. The
implementation of strict wage and price controls in 1968 precipitated
violent strikes throughout the nation. The government reacted with a
show of force from the army and the utilization of emergency powers
to jail leftists. One of the aims of the Tupamaros has been the destruction of the Uruguayan economy, but in 1973 they met with virtual defeat, with about 2,500 of them in prison, 700 who had fled the country,
and only about 300 remaining in Uruguay. Ironically, their goal of
destroying the government and the economy is being achieved in their
absence. Economic chaos and severe strikes have given Uruguay one
of the few negative gross national products in the world. Daily debate
over the value of the peso has crippled ordinary business dealings.
To make matters worse, many cattlemen have taken their cattle to
Brazil in search of hard currency.

Against this background of economic turmoil, the Tupamaros
emerged as a force determined to capitalize on the situation and bring
the government down. They struggled to become known in the early
1960s by using such Robin-Hood techniques as distributing stolen food
to the poor on Christmas Eve. They surfaced from time to time,
mainly in raids on banks and business establishments, until about
1968, when they began in earnest.

The Tupamaros have never had an elaborate philosophical base, believing that the formula for revolution has already been well established in Latin America. They have had little use for organized political institutions, elections, or laws. They reiterated their belief in armed revolution as the only solution for the ills of Uruguay in a 1967 statement: "There are undoubtedly solutions for the problems of the country, but they will not be achieved without armed struggle. . . . For all these reasons, we have placed ourselves outside the law."[22] The final objective of their struggle was to set up a Socialist order under which basic industries would be owned and controlled by the people.[23] Their strategy has purposely been left vague to permit alterations as conditions change. En route, they had hoped to enlist willing workers—supporters of the Left from all walks of life, especially from the trade unions. Although the Tupamaros achieved some success, they managed to alienate many people through their militant stand. Early in 1971, they embarked on a broader program in an effort to win over the more conservative element among the workers.

In 1968, the Tupamaros began to move in a new direction against the recently elected Pacheco government, which had instituted strict control over serious economic problems. Their goal was to undermine and humiliate the government to such an extent that the government would have to resort to panic measures that would in turn alienate government support while building the terrorists' own image. They succeeded in accomplishing this to a great degree by, among other things, exposing prominent politicians and citizens to public embarrassment through stolen records and disseminating propaganda with clandestine radio transmitters. Authorities believed them to be responsible for a spectacular $1 million fire at the General Motors building just prior to Rockefeller's visit in 1969 and a lucrative $6 million robbery of a Montevideo bank the next year. The Tupamaros simultaneously mounted a wave of violence, primarily through political kidnappings and eventually murder. After kidnapping several prominent Uruguayans, to the chagrin of the government, the terrorists zeroed in on foreign diplomats in 1970. By the year's end they had kidnapped a Brazilian consul, a U.S. police adviser, and a U.S. agronomist. As before, the government regarded the Tupamaros as bank robbers, kidnappers, and common criminals and refused to bargain with them (the price was the release of all political prisoners—about 150 of them). The result was the execution of Mitrione, the U.S. police adviser, and a statement for its justification: "The logic for the technique of kidnapping to get the release of prisoners has to be followed all the way if it is to remain effective."[24] As the Tupamaros had hoped, the Uruguayan congress immediately granted Pacheco sweeping powers, including the power to suspend civil rights. Neither the government nor the Tupamaros benefited from their actions in this case. The most important diplomat to be kidnapped, though, was the British ambassador, Geoffrey Jackson, who, to the embarrassment of the government, was held in a "people's prison" somewhere in Montevideo for eight months.[25] In spite of its well-trained police, the government never succeeded in finding him. He was finally released because there was "no longer any reason to hold him."[26] Small wonder, since 106 jailed terrorists, including the powerful Tupamaros leader Sendic, had made a spectacular escape only days before from a heavily guarded government prison. These kidnappings were punctuated by numerous assassinations of Uruguayan police.

The Tupamaros' success brought continual embarrassment to the government, increased apprehension among many residents, and progressively harsher repressive measures by presidential decree. Pacheco's methods of dealing with the terrorists helped split his already shaky support and brought a wave of resignations in his government. The Tupamaros continued their pressure on the floundering economy by grightening Argentine tourists with threats of violence. Uruguay's economy had become heavily dependent on the hard foreign currency generated by the tourist industry, and the terrorists' attacks had dealt it a severe blow. By mid-1971 the Tupamaros were at their zenith when it appeared that they were on the verge of unseating the government, ruining the economy, and gaining some support for a popular revolution. The latter came about not through armed revolution as they had planned but through the traditional political process. As an alternative to the longstanding political parties, a new broadly based political force the Frente Amplio arose on the Left, which quickly developed into a party with which conservative politicians had to reckon. At first the Tupamaros were very suspicious of the movement, but in the end they offered their support. They toned down their terrorist tactics, hoping that the movement would evolve into an organization of the people to assist in bringing about their ultimate goals. The results of the November 1971 elections were disastrous for the Tupamaros and for the extreme Left because of the sound defeat of the Frente Amplio. Among the factors that caused the defeat of this movement were that it may have been associated in the minds of the voters with the Tupamaros, Chile offered a very poor example of the type of government the movement proposed, and the extreme Left has traditionally never won large numbers of votes in Uruguay.[27] Juan Maria Bordaberry, the new president of Uruguay, was not installed until March 1971 because of charges of electoral fraud by the opposition. Nevertheless, through strong-arm techniques and the use of a well-trained army, he managed to crush the Tupamaros within six months. The few remaining terrorists who had not fled the country or been jailed were forced into hiding and are capable of performing only minor terrorist acts.

The downfall of the Tupamaros and their failure to establish a
mass uprising may in part be attributed to their elitist makeup. Despite their leftist orientation they attracted few members from the
working class but were made up primarily of middle and upper-class
people. In spite of what they may have believed, their rise to power
was probably not so much a result of their goals to revolutionize Uruguayan society as of the weakness of the society itself, with its floundering economy and weak, paternalistic government. The Tupamaros'
kidnappings, bombs, and coldblooded murders also helped to alienate
their countrymen, many of whom turned to the traditional Communist
Party in their continuing struggle against the country's worsening economic situation.

ARGENTINA: ROBIN HOOD TERRORISM

Argentina has been one of the most stable countries in Latin
America, owing in measure to its position as the traditional industrial
capital of South America. Notwithstanding Argentina's political ups
and downs, its population of largely European descent has enjoyed a
generous measure of prosperity. In comparison with other Latin
American countries, a healthy portion of Argentines are middle-class,
but in contrast to neighboring Uruguay, where Montevideo is Uruguay,
Argentina has other important urban centers as well as a large rural
area, the pampa. My own research indicates that Argentines are justifiably proud of their country's progress and level of culture and education and find it difficult to believe that Argentina could ever host
acts of terrorism.

The military government of Argentina entered its third year of
rule in 1968, experiencing serious troubles with student riots, the
economy, schisms within the government, and sporadic outbreaks of
guerrilla activities in outlying parts of the country. Terrorists began
their activities in earnest in 1969, the year of Rockefeller's visit to
Latin America, by bombing supermarkets owned by a Rockefeller-
controlled company. The resultant fires caused $3 million worth of
damages. Strict government censorship and heavy-handed police
methods were followed by a government-imposed state of siege and
later on martial law, which helped to ignite wildcat strikes that crippled most heavy industry and transportation across the nation. Heavy
fighting broke out in Cordova, leaving several workers dead and many
injured. Among the arrested were several Catholic priests. At the
year's end it had become apparent that the military government was
in serious trouble. Conditions were ripe for major outbreaks of
violence.

Terrorists chose political kidnapping as the primary means to their immediate end—the termination of military rule—but they failed in their first major effort by releasing a kidnapped Paraguayan consul for "humanitarian reasons" when the government would not meet their demands—the release of two jailed comrades. Possibly to convince the government that they meant business, the terrorists later kidnapped a past provisional president of Argentina and summarily executed him without making any ransom demands. All the while, the government was undergoing a turmoil that saw a change of leader three times in two years. As part of an effort to build an acceptable image among the masses, the newly formed Peoples' Revolutionary Army (ERP) resorted to "Robin Hood" terrorism. They kidnapped a British honorary consul who was also the manager of a meat-packing factory that had laid off a number of workers the year before. His company quickly complied with the demands for distributing $62,500 worth of food to the poor. The terrorists' main victory rested in the fact that neither the army nor the meat workers' union had been able to provide the better working conditions that were established by the company as part of the terrorists' demands.

Runaway inflation at an annual rate of about 60 percent, unemployment at 8 percent, and near insolvency in the national government provided guerrilla groups with an opportunity to expand operations in 1972. In order to finance their operations, they robbed $450,000 from a state-owned bank and ransomed a wine company executive for $37,000. To enhance their image as the champions of the working class, the ERP then kidnapped a Fiat executive, stating that they would kill him unless $1 million in school supplies were distributed to the poor and all workers who had been dismissed at Fiat plants since October 1971 were reinstated. Fiat officials were willing to deal with the terrorists, but the Lanusse government refused to permit it. Not even a personal plea from the Pope was able to save the hostage, who was executed 19 days after his disappearance. Only hours before his death, the terrorists had assassinated an Argentine general. To further exploit the troubled political and economic situation, terrorists celebrated the anniversary of Eva Peron's death by burning a country club and setting off more than 20 bombs at newspaper offices and elsewhere. A joint effort of the three main guerrilla organizations in Argentina embarrassed the government by raiding a security prison in the southern part of the country and freeing a number of political prisoners, then flying them to Chile in a hijacked airliner. One week later, the government reported that 16 terrorists had been slain when they had tried to escape from another prison, but lawyers disputed the official version of the story, charging the government with "virtual execution" inasmuch as security measures at the prison precluded any mass escape attempt. This incident brought the government ill will and triggered off a wave of controversy, strikes, and bombings.

At the time of Peron's return, Argentina had three major guerrilla organizations: two pro-Peronist groups—the Montoneros and the
Armed Revolutionary Forces—and the ERP, a Trotskyite group that
refused to align itself with any organized political effort. Peron's
long-awaited return to Argentina in late 1972 failed to satisfy the
overblown hopes of many Argentines or unite opposing Peronist groups.
Just prior to the March 1973 elections that ended seven years of military rule, the ERP, which had never supported organized politics,
forced the publication of their views on the electoral process: "The
Peoples' Revolutionary Army firmly believes that the definitive road
to national and social liberation will not be realized through elections.
Power is not born from votes, power is born from gunpoint. While
these are in the hands of repressive forces and not in the hands of the
people, the generals and exploiters of the country will continue in
power."[28] What followed was a wave of kidnappings the like of which
Latin America had never seen before. The era of million-dollar
kidnappings had arrived as terrorists found that they could tap big
corporations for astronomical sums. The first kidnapping was of a
Kodak executive whose company swiftly paid $1.5 million, followed by
a First National Bank of Boston executive for another $1.5 million
and a British tobacco executive for an unspecified amount—all within
a two-week period. Argentina declared a state of emergency after
terrorists murdered the former chief of staff of their armed forces
and established special military courts empowered to decree the death
penalty for killers of military or police personnel, past or present.
The terrorists answered with a bungled kidnapping attempt of two
Ford executives. Ford yielded to their subsequent extortion demands
of $1 million worth of food, medical equipment, and school supplies
(the terrorists had threatened to kidnap more Ford executives). Officials of other foreign corporations doing business in Argentina became
worried by Ford's example, viewing it as "buying protection" from
common criminals. Indeed, Otis Elevator reacted to a $500,000 ex-
tortion attempt by flying many of its executives out of the country.
Terrorists then threatened General Motors with violence if 1,000 former employees were not rehired, but General Motors refused to cooperate. After another $1 million kidnapping, inflation set in when ter-
rorists successfully obtained $3 million in "revolutionary tax," as
they called it, in return for a Firestone executive and then asked $6
million in return for a British business executive, up from the $2
million they had asked earlier. The kidnappers finally settled for
$2 million.

Robert Santucho, a leader of the ERP, stated in an interview
that, although they were still dissatisfied with the slow action of the
new government to move toward the Left, they would not attack the
government or the police at that moment. Nevertheless, he declared

that it would be open season on "the armed forces, counter-revolu-
tionaries, foreign exploiters and Argentine capitalists."[29] Indeed,
their war continued with a $1 million extortion attempt against Coca-
Cola, which sent Coca-Cola executives packing to leave the country.
Several other lucrative kidnappings were punctuated by bombings at
ITT's Sheraton Hotel and the Bank of America and four assassinations,
all within less than two weeks after Peron took office. The icing on the
cake came, though, in 1974, when terrorists collected a $14.2 million
ransom from Exxon for the return of a kidnapped executive.

Peron's death brought to an end a short, lackluster term that
had appointed many who had expected a quick solution to Argentina's
ills. Some of his followers seemed to prefer the Peronism of days
gone by, but without Peron. He was seen by some as possibly the last
hope for democracy in Argentina. His successor, Isabel Peron, had
been in office only a short time when terrorists murdered a former
interior minister, bringing to over 40 the number of political assassinations in Argentina in the 10-month period ending in August 1974.
To avoid kidnappings like those of the past, many foreign business
executives moved their families from Argentina and altered their patterns of living in an effort to make it more difficult for would-be kidnappers.

The future of Argentina is cloudy, to say the least. The ERP
has become an uncontrollable third force, after the Peronist government and the military, and is highly unpredictable. Whether it will
successfully continue its reign of terror or go the way of the Tupamaros remains to be seen. So far the government has seemed reluctant to use the heavy-handed techniques of Uruguay.

OUTLOOK FOR THE 1970s

In Latin America guerrilla groups have largely shunned the traditional political process for change, preferring armed revolution.
At the moment few of them seem interested in obtaining power, were
they ever to arrive at that point. Lacking a comprehensive political
program, they desire more to pressure existing systems into far-
reaching socialism than to be placed in the position of responsibility
themselves. Indeed, one wonders if the spirit of adventure connected
with the means is not more appealing than the responsibility associated
with the end. After all, the guerrilla groups in Latin America today
attract mostly young people whose machismo has been overblown by
years of cultural tradition. Nevertheless, terrorists have cultivated
a situation that inspires a definite hardness when governments seek a
solution to social ills and a tough reaction, often overreaction, from
the opposition. Without a doubt, terrorism has established itself in

the means that obtains near instant results, whether they be positive or negative, and inasmuch as patience is running short in Latin America and social and economic conditions do not improve substantially, we can expect that terrorists will not only continue, but will expand, their operations.

The effectiveness of terrorist actions in Latin America is closely aligned with their degree of association with the legitimate political process. While the Tupamaros in Uruguay acted without the benefit of a complex philosophical foundation, they came dangerously close to their goals of bringing down the government and causing economic chaos. However, once they gave support to the Frente Amplio their effectiveness as terrorists diminished and it became a millstone leading to their downfall. Again, in Argentina, the most effective of the terrorist groups was the ERP, which refused to support any political ideology, including the popular doctrine of Peronism. Indeed, groups described as "Peronist" have not flourished like the ERP. The immediate acts of random terrorism and not the detailed philosophical justifications have created the greatest atmosphere of terror. However, as Ronfelbt Einaud notes, "Despite the volume of violent terrorist tactics, the revolutionary insurgents do not appear to be gaining a strategic advantage for themselves, whether measured by organized popular support, elite fragmentations, or institutional collapse."[30]

NOTES

1. See Robert Moss, Urban Guerrillas (London: Temple Smith, 1972), pp. 130-31.

2. See the New York Times, July 2, 1968, p. 1.

3. See Robert Moss, "Revolution in Latin America," Economist Brief no. 24 (April 1971), pp. 3-4.

4. Quoted in Moss, Urban Guerrillas, op. cit., p. 7.

5. See Richard Gott, Guerrilla Movements in Latin America (London: Thomas Nelson and Sons, 1970), pp. 11-12.

6. In its timing Venezuela is a notable exception. There, urban guerrillas nearly succeeded in causing the overthrow of the government in the early 1960s.

7. Gott, op. cit., p. 66.

8. Moss, "Revolution in Latin America," op. cit., p. 16.

9. See Alphonse Max, Guerrillas in Latin America (The Hague: International Documentation and Information Center, 1971), pp. 54-55.

10. See the New York Times, July 14, 1967, p. 11.

11. See the Canadian Association of Latin American Studies Newsletter no. 15 (December 1973), p. 4.

12. Robert Moss, Urban Guerrilla Warfare, Adelphi Paper no. 79 (London: International Institute for Strategic Studies, 1971), p. 3.

13. Donald C. Hodges, Philosophy of the Urban Guerrilla (New York: William Morrow and Co., 1973), p. 30.

14. See Charles A. Russell et al., "The Urban Guerrilla in Latin America," Latin American Research Review 9, no. 1 (1974).

15. Hodges, op. cit., p. 30.

16. Moss, Urban Guerrillas, op. cit., p. 13.

17. Moss, Urban Guerrilla Warfare, op. cit., p. 20.

18. Moss, Urban Guerrillas, op. cit., p. 36.

19. Quoted in Moss, Urban Guerrilla Warfare, op. cit., p. 36. See also p. 30.

20. Ibid., p. 3.

21. Ibid., p. 34.

22. Moss, Urban Guerrillas, op. cit., pp. 216-17.

23. Maria Esther Gilio, The Tupamaros (London: Secker and Warburg, 1972), pp. 128-37.

24. Quoted in Moss, Urban Guerrillas, op. cit., p. 228.

25. This "people's prison" is believed to be located in hot, humid underground tunnels where prisoners are kept blindfolded and/or drugged to avoid trouble (see the New York Times, April 4, 1971, p. 25).

26. See the New York Times, September 10, 1971, p. 11.

27. See Moss, Urban Guerrillas, op. cit., p. 238.

28. Quoted in the New York Times, March 9, 1973, p. 12.

29. New York Times, June 9, 1973, p. 8.

30. David F. Ronfeldt and Luigi R. Einaudi, "Prospects for Violence," in Beyond Cuba: Latin America Takes Charge of Its Future, ed. Luigi R. Einaudi (New York: Crane, Russak and Co., 1974), p. 37.

4

STRATEGY, TACTICS, AND TERROR: AN IRISH PERSPECTIVE
J. Bowyer Bell

Since 1969 Ireland has been gripped by murder in the streets of Belfast, bombs in supermarkets, ritual riots, and random murder.[1] Neither elegant position papers nor historical rationalizations nor moral justification can hide this slaughter of the innocents. Yet despite the record of terrible deeds and ruthless brutality, Ireland admits to no "terrorists." The gunmen, whether or not they wear uniforms, act within a tradition. They are legitimated by legend, habit, and an act of Parliament. The Paras, the Prods, and the Irish Republican Army (IRA) may call each other terrorists, but they are not terrorists in their own eyes. From their point of view their strategy, tactics, intentions, and perceptions are perfectly justifiable. In a sense, these rather ordinary men and women have become locked in a historical process that defies easy academic definition or comfortable categorization by those who have never been subject to institutional injustice, the threat of alien occupation, or the danger of murder from a ditch.

Northern Ireland is a small, intensive country. Even the weapons are small—a .50 caliber machine gun is rarely used. The bombs may be cleverly put together, but they are usually fashioned by amateurs and are years behind the times. Killing in Ireland is done by hand, one or two at a time, and almost as many deaths result from incompetence as from malice.

THE IRISH HISTORICAL EXPERIENCE

On August 12, 1969, in Derry, the Protestant Apprentice Boys, a masonic lodge dedicated to ritual displays of past victories over the Catholics and a continuing interest in maintaining their own ascenden-

65

cy, once more marched along the city walls. Below them lay the
Catholic Bogside ghetto that stretched to the new housing estates on
the Creggan. This time, however, the Bogside Catholics—"Nationalists" in Irish terms—were seized with a new militancy as a result of
nearly two years of civil rights agitation seeking to dismantle the
discriminatory system that had created a Protestant state for a Protestant people, centered at the provisional assembly at Stormont, outside of Belfast. The young people, particularly those who for the first
time had been able to go on to the university, wanted an end to sectarian hiring, ghetto housing, weighted voting, and all the paraphernalia
of discrimination cloaked in democracy. In effect, institutionalized
injustice had been fashioned in a part of the United Kingdom—one that
had seldom attracted London's attention until the Royal Ulster Con-
stabulary (RUC) was televised clubbing civil rights demonstrators,
including members of the Westminster parliament. What London
thought or how deep the resentment of the Bogside Catholics was
meant little to the Apprentice Boys, who were determined on one
more demonstration of their superiority. They would recall the hal-
lowed motto "No Surrender" that had kept Londonderry for the Protestants during the long siege centuries before—a battle as new and
significant to them as the recent scuffles of the civil rights demonstrators.

   This time the rite did not go off as planned but collapsed into a
riot as the Catholics responded to provocation with stones. Sealing
off the Bogside from the enraged Orange and Protestant mobs as well
as the RUC and the police militia (the B-Specials), the nationalists
organized an ad hoc defense of Free Derry. To lessen the pressure
on the Bogside by the police, on August 14 nationalist demonstrators
came out into the streets of Belfast, regularly the site of past Protestant pogroms. Thus the rioting and violence spread through the
Belfast Falls Road district and soon that city, like Derry, was out of
control with gas, Molotov cocktails, occasional shots, surging mobs,
and the constant crash of broken glass. On the night of August 14,
six people were shot to death in Belfast as the city slipped into anarchy. The RUC, despised by the Catholics, could not or would not
keep order. The Northern Ireland prime minister discovered that he
directed a police state with insufficient policemen. It was apparent
that, exhausted after two days of constant rioting, the RUC could no
longer maintain order, hold back the Protestant mobs (assuming they
wanted to do so), or break through the Catholic barricades and clear
the streets. On August 15, the British cabinet sent the army into Belfast and Derry.

   There was no immediate peace. Gunfights continued along the
Falls Road. The barricades remained up in the Bogside and Creggan
creating no-go zones. Houses continued to burn and the British pub-

lic could watch the chaos each evening on television. Gradually, the
British army assumed control. The British cabinet ignored the call
from Dublin for UN intervention and instead turned security in the
province over to Lieutenant General Sir Ian Freeland and prepared to
contemplate various political options that would ease the Stormont system without engendering another Protestant backlash. In the meantime, the army remained in place. All through the uneasy and often
violent autumn of 1969, British officials and fascinated observers
sought a rational explanation of this sudden plunge into sectarian violence in the mid-twentieth century.

The explanation of the real meaning of the new Irish "Troubles"
soon produced various and often contradictory theories. The violence
could be viewed as a religious war in a province in which the issues of
the Reformation remained alive or as a tribal confrontation by peoples
who looked alike but went to different churches, had different myths,
and sang different songs, and who, from the cradle, were taught to
suspect each other. There were those who saw Northern Ireland as a
postimperial colony or as the prize sought by capitalists manipulating
the working class with religious symbols. The Irish Republican movement saw the unfailing source of Ireland's woes in the British occupation of the six counties of Ulster. The Protestant Orangemen saw
"civil rights" as a disguised attempt by the IRA to create a united
Catholic Ireland. Outside the province, sympathy went to those who
sought civil rights. The young, dynamic university students, especially Bernadette Devlin, elected to Parliament at Westminster at the
age of 20, could in the welter of strange historical references, ancient
feuds, and unfamiliar myths, be recognized as decent. The closer the
observer came, however, the more difficult it became to distinguish
between the forces of justice and those of bigotry, the past and the future, and the advocates of nonviolence and the gunmen. For most,
over the next five years, Ireland would continue to remain a distress-
ful country where armies without banners bombed and murdered in
back lanes. The legendary IRA reemerged and divided into two quar-
reling segments, the Officials and the Provisionals. Novel political
institutions rose and fell, and parties and programs disappeared over
night. Neither British political magic nor recourse to the less savory
strategems of Perfidious Albion could effect any significant change.
In five years, at one time or another, the province had become a
proving ground for every sort of violence short of conventional war—
torture, assassination, car bombs, mutilation, random murder, and
eventually the export of bombs to London and Manchester and Dublin,
where explosions killed those often innocent even of knowledge of the
Northern Ireland issue. The crisis moved through unseen stages—
the Catholics at first cheered by the arrival of the British army, soon
became alienated and turned to the new Provisional IRA—the "Provos"—

for protection. In turn, the Provos provoked the British army into
repressive measures that guaranteed their own base and permitted
an IRA offensive campaign of liberation. This escalating wave of
sniping and bombing in turn provoked the British security forces at
the insistence of Stormont to introduce internment without trial in
August 1971. Internment engendered serious urban guerrilla warfare,
first in Belfast, then in Derry, and soon an intense IRA campaign
existed throughout Northern Ireland. In March 1972, the British government closed down Stormont, and by July the Provos had bombed
their way to the conference table—a conference that produced only a
short-lived truce and a return to guerrilla war. After July 1972, the
British sought to fashion new and moderate political institutions in Ireland and crush the Provos. The Official IRA had gone over to "the defensive." The Protestants, horrified by the end of Stormont and un-
satisfied with the level of repression, created their own paramilitary
forces and began an almost spontaneous campaign of vengeance against
the disloyal Catholics. This Protestant militancy, which spawned a
welter of groups—the Ulster Volunteer Force (UVF), the Vanguard
movement, the Workers' Councils, the Red Hand Commandos—in a
way horrified observers less than the revelations that the supposedly
civilized British army had been accused of torture, murder, and provocation. There could be no evading the fact that, in January 1972, during a rally in Derry, British paratroopers had shot and killed 13
Irishmen, none of whom had weapons or belonged to the IRA. In point
of fact, no one who went about Northern Ireland with a gun under any
auspices had kept a clean copybook.

During the five violent years of the Irish crisis, none of the participants advocated the use of "terror" or admitted that their strategies, much less their tactics, could be so categorized. The various
political parties, of course, had no registered gunmen, but the politicians, if they did not urge violence, often seemed to tolerate it.
The security forces, of course, simply performed their legal duties.
British army interrogation could not be called torture, according to the
official investigation, because the soldiers did not enjoy giving pain.
The Provisional IRA bombs that killed innocent civilians were regrettable, for warning had been given. The assassination of politicians
or soldiers or informers by the Official IRA was simply one facet of
revolutionary politics by the people's army of defense. A bomb in the
Tower of London, detonated without warning amid a crowd of tourists,
became an act of war. The rising toll of civilians gunned down in the
streets by British soldiers—suspects who turned out to be priests,
children, a deaf-mute—was discounted by official spokesmen—deplora-
ble but unavoidable, and certainly not a matter of policy or even faulty
training. And, as for the Protestants, the random murder of "them"
—the Mickies, Fenians, papists—by the Ulster Volunteer Force or

the Red Hand Commandos was a justifiable act of revenge against traitors, an act that would discipline the unruly minority, prevent IRA operations, and protect the Protestant way of life from papal interference. Each group, however, agreed that their enemies had been guilty of recourse to terror. For those involved, it was one of the few areas of agreement.

Today there is a general consensus by the uninvolved on several matters. First, the present troubles have roots deep in the Irish past—some have in fact traced their roots to the Anglo-Norman invasions of the 11th century. Second, in a maze of complex issues and conflicting priorities, few of those involved have emerged spotless. The Protestant militants are unsavory at best. British officialdom has been hypocritical and the security forces biased and crude. The Irish Republicans have proved as ruthless as they are narrowminded. The Dublin government has been inept and the Nationalist politicians self-serving. Few have retained their innocence or kept their reputation. Third, while violence has changed much, it has solved nothing. To seek a fourth point—that all, or none, of the participants could be labeled terrorists—would be a sticky point for many. It would be wiser to examine the question of strategy and tactics, and perception and reality, without applying the terrorist tag.

THE BRITISH ARMY

On August 15, 1969, the British cabinet committed the army to maintain order in the streets, prevent further riots, and keep the peace. Intended to supplement the police, the army largely replaced them, accepting the burden of maintaining order with the aid of the RUC. Welcomed particularly in the Catholic districts, where the minority feared that their own feeble defenses would collapse under the pressure of the Orange mobs, no one believed that the Protestant RUC, or B-Specials, would intervene effectively. The Catholics, for their purposes, had ample evidence that the only difference between the police B-Specials and the Orange mobs was that the former were better armed—and the RUC was little better. In effect, the Catholics believed that the police had inspired, or at least tolerated, disorder. They assumed that the British army would pursue an evenhanded policy. Consequently, the soldiers were welcomed with relief and enthusiasm in the Bogside and on the Falls.

Several factors began to erode the Anglo-Irish honeymoon. First, the British army, ignorant of Irish matters, discovered two "tribes." One professed loyalty to Britain, flew the Union Jack, wanted no change in the status quo, and was led by articulate and intelligent men who often held official positions. The other proved poorer, a bit scruffy, often lived in housing estates or marginal slums, was Irish not British, often flew the Tricolor, wanted instant change, and was often led by self-appointed spokesmen warped by deep grievances. Obviously, it was easier to identify with the Loyalists, who had familiar symbols if odd habits. Also, while neither side trusted any outsider, including the British army, the Loyalists could depend on existing and legal institutions—their police, their prisons, their courts—to defend them, while the Nationalists, long victims of those institutions, increasingly turned for protection to the IRA as a neighborhood militia—just in case. Neither IRA at this time had the slightest interest in any military program except self-defense and did not even have the capacity for that, but the British army could hardly look with favor upon the creation of secret, underground armies officially dedicated to their expulsion. Finally, no army, even when properly trained in peacekeeping, is a police force. The military response to disorder and provocation is almost always far harsher and far more extensive than that which the police would consider appropriate.

In Northern Ireland, after the autumn of 1969, when the British army intervened between the two "tribes" to restrict or end ritual violence and mute spontaneous confrontations, there was a tendency to follow accepted military procedures and go in heavily. Since, after interposition, the British army found the provocation to be coming on the average from the Nationalists, a tendency arose to apply the techniques of repression more readily against them. More than anything else, the massing of troops, the arrival of armor and the paraphernalia of war, and the indiscriminate use of CS gas in response to teenage rock throwing, gradually transformed the image of the army in Nationalist eyes. The British army was seen as alien, an institution not unlike the RUC, dedicated to maintaining an odious system. Such a shift in perception proved to be an incalculable asset to the two IRAs busily recruiting local defenders but with an eye on a future campaign.[2]

The army thus faced a decaying situation, particularly dangerous because within one tribe was the germ of a revolutionary movement—disciplined, trained, experienced, dedicated, and eager to exploit further disorder. The IRA leaders were not simply local defenders thrown up after the riots. The British army's position worsened because London did not dismantle the Stormont system and pushed reforms that had little impact in the Nationalist ghettos. Without a political initiative to undermine these grievances, the British army had to stay in place, alienating the minority through recourse to tactics that encouraged the further growth of the IRA, whose leaders began to provoke further British repression. Given all, from August 1969 until the beginning of 1971, the British army had a long run, kept the peace, acquired some knowledge of the local scene, and maintained discipline

under provocation. There had been no outrageous incident and no scandal—only the slow erosion of Nationalist trust and the ominous growth
of the IRA. The British army had tactics but no "strategy," for the
civilian government in London had to fashion a political initiative that
would satisfy the minority without unleashing majority violence. In
the meantime, the British army intended to maintain order by the
techniques and tactics of the manual, a manual that was more fitted
for use in an urban guerrilla campaign than in peace keeping. The
Nationalist distaste for these orthodox tactics would in 1971 produce
conditions that would narrowly limit London's strategic choices. By
then the British army's tactics would create conditions that would encourage a real Provo insurgency—bullets instead of bottles.

THE PROVISIONAL IRISH
REPUBLICAN ARMY

The Provo Army Council, while not unmindful of the experience
of others, felt little call to fashion its revolutionary strategy from
alien cloth. Irish experience extended over several hundred years
and could be grounded in the largely successful Tan War (1918-21).
The first and most important step for Northern Ireland was to provoke
the British security forces into a repression that would alienate the
Nationalist population. This task was greatly facilitated by the tendency of the British army to view its task in similar terms of antiin-
surgency and to make use of historical analogies, such as Cyprus,
South Arabia, and Palestine. Then, when the Provo's offensive campaign began sniping and bombing the IRA strategy was to make Northern Ireland ungovernable while simultaneously eroding the desire of
the British public to support continued repression. During the halcyon
days of 1971 and 1972, when IRA volunteers were bombing the centers
of Belfast and Derry, the Provo Army Council was inclined to think
that the British government would concede as a result of the level of
pressure alone. The Provos did not quite plan to win in the field but
did anticipate a British military withdrawal, because the cost to stay
would be too great—the Provo Army Council knew exactly how many
British soldiers had been killed in South Arabia before the British
army evacuated in 1967. When there was no British evacuation from
Northern Ireland, even when the toll rose above that of South Arabia,
but rather a decline in Provo capacity, the campaign was continued
with the expectation that in a war of attrition the British public would
tire first. One of the means to encourage such exhaustion was to
open a second bombing front in Britain. Hundred of bombs have been
planted—small and large, symbolic, specific, and random, in the
Tower of London, soldiers' clubs, Harrods' department store, shops,

and tube stations. The bombing in Britain has not been particularly intense, but it has been persistent. The Provos thus felt that the military campaign, largely directed against the security forces in Northern Ireland, coupled with the British bombs, would in time convince the British public that the advantages of holding on to the six counties were minimal. In the process of a campaign of attrition, the Provos realized that if the British public were horrified, disgusted, and appalled at the "mindless Provo violence," then the prospects of evacuation would be greater.

While individuals, recognizing the pragmatic aspects of bombs, were willing to kill the innocent without warning, the Provo Army Council had always opposed operations against the innocent, advocated military operations, and insisted on bomb warnings. This warning policy had not been uniformly extended to Great Britain, and in mid-November 1974, Dave O'Connell, spokesman for the Provo Army Council, indicated that, in the case of economic and military targets, no warning would be given. There was, in fact, a warning just before the Birmingham bomb that killed 17 people in two pubs exploded. Mistakes have clearly been made: an army bus was bombed, but soldiers' dependents were killed; car bomb warnings were given too late; and civilians were killed in cross-fire. Objectively, each of these accidents increased British disgust with the entire Irish involvement. So too did the assassination by the Provo Belfast Brigade on Army Council orders of two justices, both highly respected, both relatively moderate, one Catholic and one Protestant. Whether any but the Provos would consider the judiciary to be a legitimate target, there was no doubt that the killings produced widespread, outraged indignation and disgust. Whether this disgust could be translated into a net Provo gain remained uncertain, as the British public seemed equally disgusted with the lack of Protestant gratitude.

At the end of 1974, the Provos still intended to continue their war of attrition, for to call a halt would all but ensure that the capacity to act on events would disappear and any future return to guerrilla war would be very difficult. This war of attrition could not really erode the capacity of the security forces to respond, nor, probably, could new and violent Provo tactics provoke the British army into counterterror. Thus, the victim of Provo violence, whether an innocent civilian or a "legitimate" paratrooper, was not the target. The target was British public opinion. In time, the British public, disgusted with the violence and exhausted by the pointless sacrifices for the ungrateful Irish, would demand a British evacuation that at the very least would save the lives of British soldiers, not to mention a good deal of money. The Provos felt that their strategy, adjusted to reality, was sound and their tactics, limited only by logistical problems and the erosion of the trained volunteer was effective. As

for the legitimacy of the campaign that killed the innocent and, so
said many, risked civil war in the North, the IRA has always claimed
the moral right to seek the Republic, denied the pretentions of the Dublin government, and presented tenuous legal arguments for its own
continued existence. And if it is regularly denied in public and at the
polls, there is evidence that many Irish Nationalists, both in the North
and in the South, tolerate its presence, understand its motives, doubt
its means, yet recognize its self-declared mandate.

THE OFFICIAL IRISH REPUBLICAN ARMY

Of all the groups involved in the Irish Troubles, perhaps none
has given as long and as thoughtful consideration to the fashioning of
an appropriate and evolving strategy, the selection of relevant tactics,
and the relation of political and military priorities as the Official IRA.
The Officials scorn the simpleminded "pure" military strategy of the
Provos and the parochial ward politics of the Nationalist politicians.
They are appalled by the ill-articulated, highly emotional response of
the militant Loyalist working class, which the Officials feel should
be a natural ally but which has been manipulated for capitalist gain.
They recognize the British army as a faulty tool doomed to refining
"military" tactics without strategic political relevance. Nor is the
Official IRA without talent—it could probably supply a front bench
equal to any in Ireland. The end result of this Official exercise,
however, can in retrospect be seen to be an appalling mix of revolutionary models inappropriate for Ireland—rhetoric without substance,
rationalization passing as analysis, dreadful blunders in the field,
and spontaneous decisions that often reveal an emotive response little
different from that of the Loyalist militants in a direction indistinguish-
able from that of the Provos.

The early, tortuous Official attempts to apply theoretical Marxist models of revolutionary stages (a "democratic" Stormont as a
necessary stage) simply collapsed under their own weight when Northern events outran theory. Holding fast to old Republican conventions
and assured by revolutionary colleagues elsewhere, the Officials believed in the ultimate collapse of working-class prejudice in Northern
Ireland. The Officials insist that the Protestant working class has
been deluded by British capitalism and will eventually recognize the
necessity for class solidarity. The deluded Protestants, despite occasional whimpers of interest, have failed to act as programmed by
the Officials over a period of five years. The hope remains, however,
occasionally fed by contacts and overtures. In any case, coupled
with this class analysis came the contradictory impulse to defend
"our" people—obviously Catholic, albeit often working-class. It was

thus a tremendous relief to many Officials when, under Provo provocation, the British army—the traditional foe, the tool of the bosses in London, and the protector of the Stormont puppets—became the prime enemy during 1971. During the Officials' campaign against the army, before the self-imposed truce in May 1972, both ideology and sentiment were served. Other Official ventures, no matter how closely reasoned, hardly seemed to be cunningly crafted "political" operations but were rather raw vengeance coupled with incompetence. The assassination attempt on John Taylor, a member of Stormont, failed, while amateur panic resulted in the "assassination" of Senator Barnhill. In response to Bloody Sunday in Derry, when the British killed 13 demonstrators, the Officials threatened vengeance in like numbers —hardly a Marxist-Leninist tactic—but their bomb at the Aldershot regimental headquarters of the paratroops killed cleaning women and a Catholic priest to boot. Stripped of revolutionary verbiage, this was at worst vengeance and at best intimidation. Thus, even when Official analysis appears to be in phase with Northern Irish reality, Official operations occasionally raise doubts about the depth of any ideological commitment.

By May 1972, for a variety of reasons and at the end of several dubious operations, the Officials decided that further offensive attacks would be self-defeating. IRA attacks simply alienated the Protestant working class. The Provos' bombs were sectarian. The Officials would only defend the people, but even defensive actions not tied to the conversion of the masses to Official principles could only save lives and not prepare for revolution and a new Ireland. The Officials' military truce, occasionally ignored for local reasons or as a result of official exceptions, continued, as did political agitation. There were in 1973 and 1974 sufficient hints that the increasingly militant Protestant working class might just consider an alliance to maintain hope in a workers' revolution. There was only limited evidence at the polls, particularly in the south, that there was a swing to the Officials and the strains caused by the continued Provo campaign while the Officials practiced restraint resulted in internal dissent and the expulsion of the advocates of greater militancy. In sum, over five years, the Officials' strategy proved to be a mixture of Republican and orthodox revolutionary ideas that often failed as a guide to action, a tactical incompetence and indiscipline that frustrated strategic intentions, and a faith in the call of class that has yet to be answered.

PROTESTANT MILITANTS

Almost from the moment that it became clear that the civil rights movement was more than a wee ripple in 1968, the Loyalist response was swift, harsh, and traditional. Inspired by inflammatory oratory and without the need for excessive organization, the self-appointed defenders of the system came down hard with the boot. When this proved ineffectual, the agencies of the state often made abundantly clear their marginal interest in protecting the protesters from physical violence. In fact, it became difficult to distinguish—and properly so—the formal and the informal defenders of the system inasmuch as the order imposed by the agencies of the Stormont state equaled oppression in the eyes of the demonstrators. Derry in August 1969 became a battlefield for the aggressive police and the unintimidated Nationalist minority.

With the arrival of the British army—"their" British army in Loyalist eyes—there was no longer an immediate need for an aggressive, if informal, defense of the Stormont system. Only when the British army truly attempted to act as a peace-keeping force rather than as a surrogate of the Stormont system did the Loyalists react—and with violence—coming out into the streets for nightlong clashes with the soldiers. From late 1969 to the beginning of the shooting war between the Provos and the British army in February 1971 and to internment in August 1971, the traditional, ritual humiliation of "them," the Protestants assumed that order would be imposed by the British army. The Stormont systems, with the odd concession to placate London, would be retained, and the comfortable past would return. It did not. The Provo-Official IRA campaign did not wane but escalated. By December 1971, the Conservative minister of home affairs, after a whirlwind visit to Northern Ireland, could hope only for a tolerable level of violence. Bloody Sunday in Derry made it very difficult for the Dublin government to close down the IRA in the south and attracted swarms of foreign journalists. There was a growing Loyalist unease that not only were the Provos not about to be humiliated but they were actually on the crest of a wave. The British, unable to impose order, might actually concede to the bombers. And this, indeed, proved to be the case.

In March 1972, Stormont was promulgated. The Loyalists felt betrayed. The papist Provos had bombed away their birthright. In July it was discovered that the Provos had even bombed their way to the bargaining table, meeting with a British minister outside of London. Violence had paid. The Loyalists took note and began organizing. Hurriedly, a variety of "leaders," arising out of the disarray of the Stormont system or up from the mean streets of East Belfast, began to compete in the Loyalist marketplace. The most militant fashioned paramilitary groups and prepared informally and secretly to wreak vengeance on "them." Overnight the Belfast Tartan street gangs became Loyalist defenders, while older and cruder men fashioned instant commando units or local battalions from the lads down the lane. The politicians sought to capture the center or sweep up the Right, harness working-class energy in the new Vanguard movement or devise a new formula like direct rule, that would appeal to all. The old monolithic Unionist Party collapsed into those who supported the new power-sharing assembly and those who looked to the past or to a different future. Seemingly at every opportunity, the Protestant population drifted to the Right, away from concession. All the while the Loyalist gunmen went right on killing in a campaign so disorganized that the murder went unrecognized. There was no Loyalist desire to rationalize the random murders with an elegant ideology or a foundation of moral justification.[3]

The British attempt to build a middle ground on which to plant the new assembly, thus eroding IRA strength and lessening Loyalist anguish, faltered as the center dissolved. The assembly collapsed when the Protestant workingmen organized a general strike—a strike that the cabinet in London, apparently on the advice of the British army, reluctantly refused to break with force. The tactics of the general strike, enforced by militant gunmen, in no way interrupted the random murders—killings that, when recognized, resulted in a cycle of vengeance by Catholic gunmen uninterested in the restraints of Republican ideology. On their part, the Loyalist gunmen, unable to depend on the government in London, the British army, the old Unionist leadership, or the new political prophets out of the middle class, relied on the gun, held fast to the old slogans, recognized the enemy as "them," and maintained with minimal thought and negligible organization a murder campaign. Tactics were for the Loyalist gunman strategy.

THE COUNTERINSURGENT—THE BRITISH ARMY

In the study of political violence, the inclusion of authorized force employed by the security agencies of the state has often been neglected. This has particularly been true with advanced, highly legitimate, democratic regimes, for the assumption by the comfortable has been that state recourse to counterterror—torture in the basement or the murder of prisoners—has largely been limited to either authoritarian states or insecure regimes in the underdeveloped world. Police brutality, for example, is, for those who have not been brutalized, a political slogan. When this assumption proves false, public opinion is scandalized at the "exception"—My Lai or torture in Algeria. War—and irregular war in particular—is always a brutal business, and that the rebels have adopted means often defined as illicit by those in authority should not really come as a surprise. Again the assumption has been that the truly frustrated are the rebels

—the terrorist guerrillas—not the security forces. Yet it is the very irregular nature of the war that is apt to frustrate the security forces into mimicking what they perceive as rebel willingness to use any means, however illicit. When the security forces are found out by those with qualms, by journalists, or by their own excesses, the public in Britain or France or the United States is assured that such lapses are exceptions that are in no way related to the accepted tactics of war. And somehow it is the special, individual nature of such aberrations that horrifies. Strategic carpet bombing, even Hiroshima, can be explained to the public's satisfaction more easily than one dead child in an Asian ditch. And insurrections produce murder from a ditch as a matter of course.

In the case of Northern Ireland, the British public has assumed that any lapse from appropriate legal behavior by the security forces is rare and is then only the result of outrageous provocation and is always vastly exaggerated by "the terrorists." Everyone knows that the British soldier is under severe restraint in the north, must account for his actions and for any shots fired, and has a special card listing the rules. The British army, furthermore, has shown more restraint than any other force would have in a similar situation, as the record has indicated in Palestine, Aden, and Malaya. This is, however, faint comfort for the "exceptional" victim. In the recent Irish experience, what cannot be avoided, even by Anglophiles, is the systematic use of military force beyond that conventionally employed by any police force to maintain order and in ways not congenial to disinterested public opinion. This excludes the various "legal" problems surrounding the use of extraordinary powers to arrest, detain, ban, fine, question, and imprison without trial—to in fact pass laws that permit the normal canons of law to be set aside because of the needs of the moment. To be snatched from bed without explanation, questioned for days, verbally threatened, interned again without explanation for years while one's family is harassed by repeated searches, however unpleasant, falls only on the margin of the authorized use of state violence. When a suspect is tortured, a wanted man murdered in the street, an "illegal" crowd machine-gunned, or a captive killed, either as a matter of policy or without penalty, then the agencies of the state have gone beyond the conventions of democratically controlled security forces. In Northern Ireland, British security forces have overstepped that bound, whether it be systemically, erratically, or inevitably.

The British army has seen and been allowed to see as a primary mission the defeat of the Provos—Irish terrorists engaged in an urban guerrilla war with British soldiers as their prime target. In following the evolving British military doctrine fashioned to respond to Provo tactics and Provo assets, British units have transformed the

original peace-keeping mission into a low-intensity war more congenial to army doctrine. The result, perhaps inevitably, has been a
high level of military violence despite avowed efforts to restrict individual initiative, limit wild firing, and control spontaneous brutality.
For the vulnerable, the efforts have not been particularly impressive.
Over 50 civilians, for example, have been killed by error. Many of
these "accidents" were reported first as deaths of suspects until
eyewitness accounts indicated the contrary. The single most distressing such incident, Bloody Sunday in Derry, revealed that efforts had
been made to plant weapons on the dead, and the ultimate British in-
vestigatory report by the chief justice of England, Lord Widgery, despite his vast credulity, could not quite clear the British army. The
security forces had somehow killed 13 innocent people by mistake.
The weight of the evidence since 1971 is that, despite real efforts to
restrict the men in the field, a remarkable number of innocent civilians have been killed in error. The Nationalist population, justifiably
alarmed, has been fearful that this might be a consciously crafted
British campaign to intimidate them.

Such an assumption seems more logical to the threatened not
only because of the discovery of British soldiers in civilian clothes
hiding in ambush positions waiting for "suspects," but also because
of the evidence of brutality surrounding the initiation of internment in
August 1971. The British deep-interrogation process differed from
torture only in that the soldiers involved did not enjoy inflicting pain,
according to the official published British investigation. That sophisticated psychological techniques were coupled with pain has been
demonstrated, and this, unlike "accidental" shootings, was demonstrably official army policy. The distinction between the interroga-
tor's liking or not liking his work was lost on those involved, Nationalist opinion, and disinterested observers. That deep interrogation
has been suspended so that those questioned as suspected "terrorists"
are now far less likely to be brutalized and that torture in any case is
not to the British advantage may be true, but again the threatened
feel that the new restraint of the British army could be only momen-
tary, retained through the fear of future exposure. And in any case,
spontaneous, ruthless brutality continues when suspects are arrested
or stopped, during searches and sweeps. Rubber bullets hit too
many women and old men. The toll of civilians who have been shot
by mistake grows. The rumors of British assassination squads find
many takers.

What is clear is that the low intensity campaign waged under
British military doctrine has stretched the bounds of the permissible,
at least for operations within the United Kingdom that are readily
visible on the evening news. Way off in Aden or Kenya, the army
may have justified its reputation for restraint, but under the televi-

sion cameras in Northern Ireland, the security forces have demonstrated that their actions are difficult to reconcile with the pronounced
ideals of British society. For much of the British public, which is
convinced that other armies would be more dreadful and that the IRA
provocation has been unbearable, the lapses, even if systematic, have
been easy to excuse. In the heel of the hunt, counterinsurgency is a
brutal business, and while the security forces may not be waging a
campaign of terror against the Provos, they have still terrified the
innocent without intimidating the guilty.

THE URBAN GUERRILLA—THE PROVISIONAL IRA

That the Provos are guilty of terrible deeds has become axio-
matic and, even within Republican circles, produces only painful
rationalizations that it cannot be denied that the innocent must pay a
price for Irish freedom, willingly or not. The tactics and techniques
of the traditional rural guerrilla have, over the years, been gradually
legitimized. In theory, uniforms are worn, prisoners taken, torture eschewed, and civilians respected. In practice, irregular rural
wars tend to lead to irregular practices by both the guerrillas and
their opponents. In the countryside, as often as not uniforms are
discarded or ignored, and torture is defended by elegant rationalizations or resorted to at the first opportunity. Civilians are assassinated, carpet-bombed, and shot as suspects or informers. Prisoners
are not taken. Still, relatively speaking, the distinction between
civilians and combatants, military operations and open murder—the
limits of violence—are recognized, if occasionally with reluctance.
Rural guerrilla war is more or less a conventional form of violent
confrontation. Such insurrections may be unconventional in form, but
they are clearly military in intent. The same partial legitimacy is
not as clear with urban guerrilla war, and despite the scenic and apparently rural setting of Northern Ireland, there is little jungle to
hide guerrilla operations. IRA operations in the countryside are not
very different from those in Belfast or Derry. Whatever the traditional limits of rural guerrilla warfare, they barely apply in Northern
Ireland.
The Provos only rarely wear their "uniforms" consisting of
combat jackets and black berets, and then only in the no-go zones of
Derry and Belfast or at commemorations in the south. Bombing operations are regularly and overwhelmingly directed at economic targets
—shops, garages, and hotels—rather than at military targets, with
the not unexpected loss of civilian life. Improved British security
has even forced the introduction of the proxy car bomb, with which the

driver is forced to protect his hostage family by taking the vehicle to
its target. Informers, off-duty policemen, soldiers on leave, strike-
breakers, and suspected Protestant vigilantes become "legitimate"
targets for Provo volunteers. Women who collaborate with the British
are tarred and feathered. Men who are judged criminal are shot in
the kneecap when they refuse to reform. All this is official IRA policy. For some less discriminating volunteers or simple lads down the
lane, any Protestant or any "suspect" becomes a victim in an atmosphere of moral decay and wanton murder. In the spiral of what theoretically passes as low-intensity war, with Provo ambushes in crowded
streets, bombs detonating without warning, the assassination of
judges, bank robberies for the cause, and hooded bodies shot in the
neck, only the most determined can detect the limits on Provo violence or the bounds of urban guerrilla war. The Provos do, of course,
have bounds. It is policy to give bomb warnings—at least in Northern
Ireland—so that not too many innocent civilians will involuntarily have
to pay a price for Irish freedom. Others, in the north or in Britain,
as unofficial participants in the bombing campaign have felt no com-
punction about denying a warning to the enemy, but Provo policy remains the same. If the Birmingham bomb that killed 17 people were a
Provo bomb, then it is also clear that the IRA technical capacity to
deliver an effective warning has remained the same—doubtful. Certain targets are avoided as well—not only hospitals and the like but
crucial "Protestant" targets such as the shipyards of Belfast, for
these would be sectarian operations and certainly ensure Protestant
retaliation. More symbolic sectarian targets have been bombed, in
particular the towering statue of the Hero of the Londonderry Siege,
which has been destroyed. The Provos have also largely avoided certain currently fashionable tactics, such as kidnapping, hijacking, assassinations in Britain, and certain strategic options—there are no
operations in Southern Ireland. It is also Army Council policy to opt
for the military target if possible, but this has hardly been obvious
except in the repeated urban snipes and rural ambushes. Even when
the target is a soldier, too often he is off duty and lured into a trap or
killed by a mine or shot in the back, so that the means seems as illicit
as the act.

The fact that the Provos attempt, as a matter of policy, to limit
their military activities to those that are easily recognized as unconventional but within the guerrilla tradition can hardly convince the
skeptic examining the evidence of the past four years. It may be that
urban guerrillas, including Provos, are by nature violent, brutal,
immune to humane considerations, willing if not eager to risk civilian
lives, cunning, and callous, but in Northern Ireland the Army Council
restraints and limitations imposed on the volunteers as a matter of
policy have often been counterproductive and have permitted the war

of attrition to drag on when an intensive dose of the horrors might have disgusted the British into withdrawal or counterterror. Certainly the long, drawn-out dose has currently disgusted much of the British public and created an atmosphere in which evacuation has become a real possibility. In any case, the Provos do not see their actions as a campaign of terror. They intend not to intimidate either the Protestant population or the British army, but to create disorder and chaos, to force the British taxpayer to underwrite the destruction, and to affect British public opinion. That a great many people in Northern Ireland are terrified can hardly be denied, but the Provos, recognizing the results of the IRA bombing campaign in Britain of 1938-41 and the Blitz, accept that the British public cannot be coerced or terrorized.

At present, the Army Council is disappointed that the level of 1971-72 cannot at least be maintained with present equipment but feel sure that the campaign of attrition can be continued and perhaps widened in Britain with more bombs. That innocent people are killed and blunders made are part of wars of liberation, and as far as the Provos can see neither the British army nor the Protestant vigilantes have shown much restraint. Still and all, despite the logical Provo strategy and predictable rationalizations, despite the recognized desire of the Provo Army Council to pursue a military campaign, many observers are convinced that the Provos are no more than bloodthirsty murderers who are incapable of thinking beyond the next bomb and so incompetent that more volunteers kill themselves than are killed by the British. Their "military" campaign has left a ruined province and a toll of innocent victims, destroyed the political center, and contains only the promise that sectarian and intercommunal violence will escalate, perhaps into a general civil war beyond even the capacity of the British army to monitor. The critics of the Provos feel that not only are the means horrid but also the aim—a united Ireland.

THE ARMED AGITATOR—THE OFFICIAL IRA

The most articulate and knowledgeable critics of the Provos' pretensions can be found within the ranks of the Official IRA. After all the shifts and turns of Official analysis, and after deeds as bloodthirsty, horrid, and incompetent as those of the Provos, the present position of the movement stresses the political aspects of the crisis far more than the military possibilities. Putting aside the Provos' political aspiration—a four-province, federated Ireland of workers and small farmers as window dressing for more bombs—the Officials fear that continued violence, even directed against the British army, will further alienate the Protestant working class. By mid-1974, this

was particularly galling because there were signs that the Protestants
were turning from the old symbols toward a new class solidarity. The
spontaneous general strike with a leadership emerging from those involved was impressive not simply for the Protestants' capacity to
prevent an imposed British "solution," but for their demonstration of
class solidarity without the need for elite leadership. There were
even talks with the Ulster Workers' Council and Official Sinn Fein representatives. All this might be a long way from the Officials' ultimate goal, which includes a united Irish Republic, but did give hope
that the Belfast working class could at least begin a dialogue about its
own future. Thus the Provo bombs only weakened class ties and led
to demands for vengeance that, when effected, produced, even in official volunteers, a demand to continue the cycle. More distressing,
when the Officials got in the way of the Provo-British army war, the
volunteers were even less interested in showing restraint in regard to
the occupying power. The Army Council's insistence that the Official
IRA volunteer was an armed agitator, a member of a people's army,
and a defender of life on the one hand and an advocate of revolution
on the other might sound splendid at Gardner Place in Dublin, but
many of the lads off the Falls wanted action. In the past, under provocation or as a result of policy, the Dublin center had initiated operations that had satisfied this urge to act even when the act had proved
difficult to explain ideologically. Also, in the past, Official volunteers
had not waited for the good word from Dublin.

By 1974, then, putting aside the Officials' pretensions of being
the army of the people with a right to act for all the Irish people, the
position of the Official Republican movement had evolved into a revolutionary, political posture with a detailed if idealistic program, with
a searching if optimistic Socialist analysis of the Northern Ireland
situation, and with the gun as only a last resort. Over the course of
the preceding five years, however, the Officials had been involved in
a variety of operations—some of which had been authorized only by a
bare majority and were soon the subject of serious recrimination—
that had placed the gun in the forefront of policy. What tended to differ about Official operations—and the distinction is by no means clear
—is that while the Provos waged a "campaign," Official operations,
however brutal, had been tied to specific events or existing political
conditions. Officials tended to see movement, change, new options,
and a dynamic political process, while Provos viewed events through
traditional Republican glasses and hence produced traditional Republican answers: physical force will break the connection with England
and there will be a new Ireland. The Officials scrambled to find the
endless stages of political development in order to exploit the moment.
That many of these "exploits" proved disastrous—the botched assassination attempt on Taylor, the unintended death of Senator Barnhill,

the murder of a local Derry soldier home on leave from the British army, the Aldershot explosion—and that many were initiated locally in competition with the Provos has been obvious if not always admitted at Gardner Place. If Official analysis is now more rigorous and related more closely to Irish reality than to distant dialectics, if Official operations are now more politically fashioned and rigorously controlled, there are many who can easily recall the past blunders. And, more than anything else, the Officials' gun, when it is to be used, will be used in the name of working-class unity and with the belief that Protestants will in time opt for class interests. Scientific analysis aside, this is a proposition that many cannot support, and hence the elaborate Official rationalization for the revolutionary use of violence seems to some to be as simpleminded as the Provo exercise. In any case, the Officials' course record differs from that of the Provos more in degree than in kind.

THE SECTARIAN VIGILANTE—THE PROTESTANT LOYALIST

The Loyalist gunman in the Red Hand Commandos or the Ulster Volunteer Force certainly can see little difference between the Provos and the Officials. Both organizations, except for the odd showpiece Protestant, are wholly Catholic and dedicated to the establishment of a united Ireland that would be dominated by Catholics, who have always been manipulated by the hierarchy. The 26-county Irish Republic has a "Roman Catholic" constitution, and there has been ample evidence that the Church has intervened in politics, which has not even been denied in Dublin. Any 32-county Ireland, then, would be ruled by Rome. Objectively, no matter what they say or think, IRA gunmen are papal outriders. The entire rhetoric of the Loyalist-Protestant-Orange establishment, whether found in the speeches at Stormont or on the walls of the Shankhill in Belfast, has stressed defense of their way of life—"Not an Inch," "No Surrender." Since the entire Stormont system was fashioned to maintain Protestant domination within the six counties, there was little need for an unofficial defense. Why bother with a posse when the B-Special police militia could do as well? Why intimidate Catholic voters when the voting system was rigged? Why organize to oppose an IRA campaign when the province of Northern Ireland had paramilitary police and the British army on call? Thus the monolithic Protestant community, united in the Orange lodges, controlling the Stormont state, and tied to Britain, could defend their own without recourse to covert violence. In fact, during the IRA campaign between 1956 and 1962, Stormont seldom had to call on the British army—the RUC and B-Specials did the job.

The Protestant monolith began to show signs of stress after
1962 when the premiers at Stormont and Dublin exchanged visits and
proper people began talking of bridge building. Whatever the economic
and social advantages of a rapprochement, the stern Loyalists saw
none. A sign of the times was the creation of a new UVF under Gusty
Spence, a little band of bigots whose "armed struggle" consisted of a
miserable shooting in a Belfast side street of men innocent of anything
but their faith. There was general indignation and no further unofficial violence until the beginning of the civil rights campaign. Then
counterdemonstrations, led by various self-appointed leaders like the
Reverend Ian Paisley, and the partisanship of the police did not have
the traditional effect—even worse members of the Unionist leadership
in Stormont began making reform noises with a weather eye toward
Westminster. The riots of August 1969 and the arrival of the British
army reassured some of the militants so that Protestant violence was
sporadic, spontaneous (at times even directed against the British
army), and traditional in form—riots, arson, and screaming mobs.
When the Unionist premier Terence O'Neill appeared to be too moderate, a few bombs and some political infighting produced a change, but
it soon became apparent that it was not one for the better. The politicians seemed too interested in British opinion, and the British army
seemed too restrained in dealing with the Mickies. The last conventional response of the old system came with the introduction of internment in August 1971, and that produced war, not repression. As the
months passed and the IRA campaign escalated, the militants lost
faith in the British army. There followed one blow after another, until Stormont disappeared in March 1972.

Over the next two years, the various Loyalist schisms, splinters,
alliances, and alignments became far too complex for distant observers. Conventional politicians attempted to form parties, fronts, or
umbrella organizations that would direct fear and anguish into the appropriate channels. Britain tried to devise formulas or institutions
that would again permit conventional politics and incorporate reforms
from the discarded system. All the right people in London, Dublin,
and the North urged moderation and restraint and pointed to the dangers of polarization. All this movement passed over the heads of the
hard men in the back lanes of East Belfast or along the Shankhill. If
Britain, the British army, the Unionist politicians, and the RUC
would not or could not defend the system, then they would.

A variety of uncertain and often ephemeral groups clustered
around one man or one area appeared. The most famous and the only
one with even a fragment of continuity was the UVF. The original
anti-Home Rule militants had organized the UVF in 1914, and Gusty
Spence appropriated the title for his little group. Spence, while out
on parole, was "kidnapped" and briefly rejoined the new UVF,

oddly enough bringing with him some of the discipline, organization, and ideals of the IRA volunteers he had met in prison. Essentially, the UVF and most of the other defenders were small, ill-formed bands of vigilantes, sometimes with elegant titles and formal meetings, other times with nothing but three men, a lifted car, a couple of guns, and the desire to knock off a Fenian. Over two years, various groups arose, merged, melted, and disappeared. In some areas the "defenders" went into rackets, in others serious efforts were made to link up all the vigilante groups. The politicians saw the potential danger of armed bands of men of no property roaming the streets and established their own paramilitary organizations. The main impact of the new militancy was the campaign of random assassination of Fenians, largely limited to Catholic males who stumbled into the wrong streets, worked in the wrong areas, or simply presented a target of opportunity to a cruising carload of armed defenders.

The purpose, if the killers could have articulated it, was simple and crude and might even in time have become effective—the Catholics would be punished for past errors, intimidated from future ambition, and, if need be, driven from the province. Since all Catholics were guilty of disloyalty, all were legitimate targets. Efforts to concentrate on the specifically guilty—Provos or Officials—were crude, ineffectual, or abortive. Almost no IRA man was a victim, even though the total number of victims in two years was well over 200. The campaign waged by crude men, often cruel and unsavory, attracted few idealists or politicians. Occasionally there would be anonymous explanatory leaflets, but few of those involved had the time or the interest to read reasoned statements. The militants could and did supply volunteers for a few more elegant exercises in violence. Thus, the cunningly timed car bombs in Dublin in 1972 assured that harder Irish security laws would be passed. Another bombing operation in the spring of 1974 that had been timed to kill pedestrians in Dublin and Monaghan was also intended to affect Dublin policy. In both cases, there were those who thought that the bombers had been used, perhaps even by the British army. While there had been "operations" in the Irish Republic by the UVF and others, the two major bombing operations appeared atypical. A typical UVF operation consisted of a burst of machine-gun fire through the window of a Catholic pub—hardly elegant, but effective.

The dubious battle against the Fenians spread from the mean streets of Belfast to other towns and finally to the countryside. There can be no firm numbers, but the death total had risen to about 250 and during the autumn of 1974 showed no signs of easing off.[4] The Protestant militants, however, did not see themselves as murderers and terrorists: "The world is condemning us as murderers—we call ourselves patriots. We are fighting for Ulster's freedom." There

are no motiveless murders, according to militant spokesmen, because
if the background of the victim is examined, "Republican connections"
can be found. With the odd exception, such rationalizations (and many
Protestant gunmen don't bother) are hardly convincing. What is clear
is that the murders are not motiveless and that vengeance and intimidation are unpleasant, particularly when the victim is randomly chosen.
The victims are chosen, if indiscriminately, from the pool of the disloyal—male Catholics—all, even if unwittingly, traitors and potential
"Republicans."

The assassination campaign of the militants has deep roots,
building on a tradition of pogroms, riots, authorized arson, and tolerated violence against the Fenians. For over a century Belfast has
had repeated riots and for over a century the respectable Protestant
community has "understood" the anxiety of "their" working class when
threatened by Catholic domination. With the presence of the British
army limiting the traditional riotous pogrom, the militants had simply
shifted tactics and extended the time scale. The killings may indeed
have the desired effect of intimidating the Catholic population, coerc-
ing a mass emigration to the south, eroding the IRA base and thus
saving the Loyalist way of life.

CONCLUSION

The burden of the present argument is that the definitional question of what is terror very much concerns the legitimacy of political
violence. In the Irish case, none of those who have had recourse to
force perceive their actions as illicit—illegal yes, but illicit no—and
none advocate the use of terror. They are not murderers, but soldiers or volunteers, patriots or revolutionaries. Many would accept
that they have made mistakes, that there have been excesses, but it
is the others who have used systematic terror. Their own strategy
and tactics, while open to misinterpretation, are sound, viable, and
given the situation, within permissible limits. The Protestant gunmen may choose random victims, but they do not set bombs that maim
women and children. The British soldiers may use excessive force
in interrogation or shoot civilians by mistake, but they do not murder
from a ditch or booby-trap bodies. The IRA volunteers may execute
an informer, but they do not drop screaming prisoners from a helicopter or shoot their next-door neighbor simply because he goes to a
different church. What becomes clear is that all the violent actors
in the Irish crisis respond to events within a clearly defined historical tradition that to them—and often to them alone—legitimize their
tactics and determine their strategy.

The organization most readily visible as legitimate is the British army, which is licensed to kill within certain bounds by a recognized state. To a large degree, even the IRA accepts the validity of that license and so defines "army terror" as those acts performed beyond the conventional limits. And for the Irish, like many other rebels before them, it is the British hypocrisy in denying any transgressions—torture without pleasure, murder by mistake—that so enrages them. If it were another army, not based on the admired British ideals, there would be less distaste, but the Irish, at least, have experienced hundreds of years of vengeance disguised as crown justice. In any case, hypocrisy aside, the British army has crossed its own limits, not so much as a matter of policy but rather because there has been a systematic reluctance to punish the "guilty," thus encouraging subsequent transgressions.

Of all those involved, surely the assassination campaign of the Loyalist gunmen falls completely outside of conventional bounds. Yet the vigilante is hardly novel, even if the choice of random victims has had fewer takers. Given their record, it is small wonder that the Protestants fear "them," assume that all will be disloyal, and, if not disciplined, will strike back at the system. Thus, the Protestant community has regularly permitted or encouraged violent onslaughts on "them" in defense of the established system. In Northern Ireland, particularly in Belfast, the pogrom had almost been institutionalized as a means of control, and even with the establishment of the Stormont system in 1921, extralegal violence was not entirely eschewed. Thus, the Red Hand Commando is a patriot to his neighbors even when arrested by the RUC for a "motiveless" murder for his neighbors and the RUC know the motive even if they do not know the victim's name.

While the British army is not unduly troubled by problems of legitimacy and the question seldom concerns the UVF, the Republican movement has a highly complex historical and legal justification for the use of the gun, institutional restrictions on tactics, and a continuing concern with the issue. Ireland is a moral country and there must be a sound justification for political murder, no matter what the goal, if the volunteer is not to have a troubled mind and the public withdraw toleration. There are legal reasons why the present IRA, Provo, or Official, depending on one's interpretation, can claim to be the real army of the Republic, authorized by the Second Dail (parliament), while the "Free State Army" was a child of an illegal Dail. This is too arcane for most volunteers and the public at large. For a great many years, every Irish politician has publicly proclaimed the end of partition a goal and a united Ireland the grail of hundreds of years of struggle. Privately their views vary and, patently, beyond oratory the Dublin governments have done little. For 50 years, history as taught in a great many schools in Ireland has been a serious

factor in persuading many young men to continue the struggle. And
less visible but more real has been the collective memory of repression and struggle, a doubt about the moral authority of the state, and
an admiration of those who resist. Even the establishment of an Irish
state has not eroded the love of a rebel. Although few will vote for
trouble or want his own involved, a general toleration exists. Recent
events often encouraged this tendency because so many in Ireland see
the IRA as the only viable defender of the Northern Catholics. Consequently, the IRA volunteer can be assured of the toleration of many,
the support of some, but, most important, the comfort of a very long
tradition that insists that his actions are legitimate, his goals those
of the nation, and his ideals those of the people. His army may not
have banners, but it is an army, not a vigilante mob; his army may
not have uniforms, but it fights for the Irish people, not to maintain
a British colony.

In sum, all the actors feel legitimate and all act within a tradition that authorizes their strategies and limits their tactics. Each is
a patriot, none a murderer. All are rational, some even reasonable,
their course, if singleminded, set from a partially understood past
toward a specific if improbable goal. As with most other lethal political questions, the ground has been strewn with myths, special plead-
ing, fine slogans, and elegant rationalizations. The distant observer
may select from the lot; but the burden here is relatively simple.
Even if the perceptions of those involved differ from those of the
alien eye, the gunmen are not mindless and their strategies and tactics are shaped by tradition and policy.

NOTES

1. There has been as yet no definitive study of the present
Troubles (the crisis constantly outruns the final chapter) although
there has developed a massive literature. See J. Bowyer Bell, "The
Chroniclers of Violence in Northern Ireland: The First Wave Interpreted," Reivew of Politics 34, no. 2 (April 1972): 147-57; and "The
Chroniclers of Violence in Northern Ireland Revisited: The Analysis
of Tragedy," Review of Politics 36, no. 4 (October 1974): 521-43.

2. The stress on Provo cunning and British army ineptitude
(J. Bowyer Bell, "The Escalation of Insurgency: The Provisional
Irish Republican Army's Experience, 1969-1971," Review of Politics
35, no. 2 [July 1973]: 398-411) is disputed by knowledgeable Republican critics who doubt Provo foresight and British army spokesmen
who point out the complexity of the problem.

3. To date the most thorough investigation of Protestant political murder can be found in Martin Dillon and Denis Lehane, Political
Murder in Northern Ireland (Baltimore: Penguin, 1974).

4. Although the security forces announce a running count on the number of deaths arising from the Troubles, there is no agreement on the exact numbers (and less on who is responsible for each), where crime ends and politics begins, or who should be included.

POLITICAL TERRORISM:
THE BRITISH EXPERIENCE
Thomas E. Hachey

THE HISTORICAL EXPERIENCE
IN ENGLAND

With the notable exception of Ireland, political terrorism has
not been a prominent feature in the national experience of modern
Britain. Radical revolutionaries of the Irish Republican Army (IRA)
have in recent years extended their activities to England and, in the
summer of 1974, these terrorists even detonated a bomb in the Parliament building at Westminster. But contemporary IRA violence, despite its expanding scope and intensity, is an aberrant phenomenon in
Britain's otherwise relatively tranquil history. Indeed, terrorist tactics of a political character have had a lower incidence of occurrence
in Great Britain than in any other great nation since 1815.[1]

One of the most evident factors contributing to this happy cir-
cumstance has been Great Britain's geographic insularity. In the
absence of vulnerable frontiers, this nation has traditionally felt no
compulsion to maintain a large army. Military emphasis shifted to
the navy, a largely volunteer force, which did not depend upon conscription. Since the navy did not maintain a land presence, it kept a
relatively low visibility and was not as apt as the army to become a
popular irritant. Moreover, in centuries past it was often possible
in England, but not on the Continent, for the people to oppose the king
without endangering their country from without, and it was possible
on the Continent, but not in England, for the king to use against his
own people the instrument that the necessity of national protection
had placed in his hands.

Hence, while the absolute monarchism common to the Continent
was alien to English life, that country's tradition of liberty might be
said to have been seaborne. The militarism that so often suppressed

such liberties elsewhere simply had no counterpart in English life. Even present-day IRA terrorists, who often make the British army in Northern Ireland their target, view the military as an apolitical tool of the governmental system, which they deem to be the real enemy.

Perhaps, however, Britain's manifest capacity for political, socioeconomic, and religious accommodation accounts most fundamentally for the comparative paucity of terrorist activity during the past century and a half. Class antagonisms were never as bitter as on the Continent. Concessions, while often tardy, were made in sufficient time to immunize society in England against the violent upheavals so often spawned by social unrest elsewhere. The British aristocracy was also more restricted in size and privilege than its Continental counterparts and, accordingly, occasioned less resentment. British industrial and commercial barons forced the landed gentry into sharing political control, thus altering the monolithic pattern of the traditional power structure. England's leadership also blended more readily with the middle class and helped to soften class lines. It further exhibited a keener sensitivity to the problems of the masses. France, for example, still has no equivalent of the phrase "Tory socialism," which in Britain symbolizes the awareness and readiness of conservative forces to deal with social issues. If not always in economics, at least in politics the Tories have demonstrated a healthy sense of fair play and a concern for individual conscience that would be difficult to detect among French rightists.[2]

Even religion plays a politically more constructive role in England than it does in countries like France. Anglicanism was forged by the Elizabethan compromise, and from its inception this denomination has become almost synonymous with moderation and accommodation. The nonconformist Protestant sects have helped make dissent both a respectable and an integral part of British politics, and pacifism has long been rooted in this religious tradition. For instance, Britain has provided legal status for conscientious objectors since conscription first became an issue in 1916. As with its religious divisions, Britain has amicably resolved its ideological differences. There was nothing comparable to the French revolutionary zeal that automatically polarized opinion. At least since 1848, the English have preferred petitions to barricades. Except for the Irish problem, internal unrest has posed no substantial threat in Britain for generations. Religious differences were to a significant extent successfully reconciled. Class divisions have become more a social than an economic issue and are endured with a mixed sense of forbearance and resignation. A revolutionary spirit can seldom flourish in a country that respects and safeguards the rights of the opposition, and the long absence of a real or imagined internal threat has enhanced an inclination toward a nonviolent, patient, and judicious resolution of differ-

ences. Even resurgent Scotch and Welsh nationalism, despite the periodic outbursts of vocal separatists, shows signs of being contained
by this attitude.[3]

PUBLIC AND OFFICIAL PERSPECTIVES OF
POLITICAL ACTS OF VIOLENCE

In 1815, the Congress of Vienna formally ratified the triumph of
the conservative order over the Napoleonic revolutionary forces.
European moderates and reactionaries had agreed that the evils of
egalitarian democracy imperiled the social and political order and
should be suppressed. Britain was no exception. Before the French
revolution there had been active agitation in Britain for the reform of
Parliament to better reflect population changes, particularly in the
burgeoning industrial centers, and to widen suffrage in order to embrace the middle class. But the excesses of the French revolution and
the protracted war against that people resulted in a sharp decline in
political agitation, as reformers in Britain were indiscriminately
labeled as either Jacobins or unpatriotic. In addition to the suppression of dissent, the frustrations of discontented Englishmen were
exacerbated by the economic depression that gripped Britain in 1815,
when wages were cut, factories were closed, and unemployment
soared, after the Continental countries, impoverished by war, were
no longer able to purchase English manufactures. The grievances of
the disenfranchised middle class were now coupled with the anger of
the destitute masses, who suffered greatly through unemployment.
Whether they were Tyneside coal miners, Preston cotton weavers,
or Wiltshire cloth workers, the working class demands were much the
same—employment, higher wages, and cheaper food.[4]

Despite these desperate conditions, which inspired wanton acts
of destruction and terrorism, and despite the ostensibly political
tenor of the workers' fury against the government, the dynamics of
the confrontation were demonstrably more economic than ideological.
Angry mobs destroyed the machines they thought were robbing them
of employment and sacked bakers' and butchers' shops in search of
food. Rioting and arson occurred in Norfolk and Suffolk. A militant
crowd met at Spa Field in London in 1816 for the purpose of sending
a petition to the regent but instead turned to looting nearby stores.
Popular radicalism increased as demagogues like "Orator" Hunt and
William Cobbett catered to the passions of the mob and succeeded
only in frightening off middle-class support for democratic suffrage.
It is noteworthy, however, that Cobbett, feared and hated by much of
the propertied class, sought the reform of Parliament and an extension of the franchise rather than the destruction or overthrow of the
government.

Tory ministers, rattled and angry, offered nothing but repression. In 1817 the cabinet suspended habeas corpus, passed harsher measures against seditious meetings, and urged local magistrates to enroll special constables and to make prompt arrests. The number of government spies and informers was increased, and public meetings were forbidden. Bitterness and discontent among the poor reached such alarming proportions that a mass meeting at St. Peter's Field in Manchester ended in tragedy. A throng of 50,000-60,000 people, many marching in ranks carrying banners with slogans such as "Annual Parliaments" and "Universal Suffrage," met in orderly fashion to hear a speech by "Orator" Hunt. The local magistrates permitted the crowd to assemble; then, losing their nerve, the magistrates attempted to arrest Hunt as soon as he appeared. A body of mounted yeomanry was dispatched to make the arrest. Jostled and pushed about by the indignant crowd, the yeomanry drew their sabers and had to be rescued by a troop of Hussars. In the pandemonium, many people were trampled, some were sabered, 11 were killed, and 400 were injured. Hunt and the other speakers were promptly arrested and imprisoned. The government congratulated the magistrates on their conduct, but the events in St. Peter's Field—renamed "Peterloo" in mocking comparison with the Battle of Waterloo—angered the poor and inspired public demonstrations throughout the country. Meetings in many towns demanded that the prince regent dismiss the ministry. In Italy, upon hearing the news, Shelley expressed his revulsion toward such legalized terror in the bitter lines of his "Mask of Anarchy":

> I met Murder on the way—
> He had a mask like Castlereagh
> Very smooth he looked, yet grim;
> Seven bloodhounds followed him:
> All were fat; and well they might
> Be in admirable plight.
> For one by one, and two by two,
> He tossed them human hearts to chew
> Which from his wide cloak he drew.

As one might expect, the Times of London responded to the "Peterloo" violence with a sense of outrage that was doubtlessly shared by most of the nation's conservatives. And almost as predictably, the object of that newspaper's wrath was the mob that had been the victim rather than the perpetrators of the terror and violence. Editorial comment in the Times subsequently deemed it a "catastrophe" when the government determined that the circumstances surrounding the Manchester riot would not win convictions in the courts on the charge of high treason. Demanding harsh penalties for the defendants, the Times declared, "We are indignant, ashamed, nay terrified to see the law made ludicrous, and the magistracy odious; because we are shocked to see the authorities of the State descend from their vantage ground and transfer it to mischievous demagogues." The editorial concluded that official laxity in the face of such "licentious outrage" would sweep away every trace of civil liberty in Great Britain.[5]

The cabinet next engineered the passage of six acts to suppress disorder. Three of them, which expedited trials for offenders, prohibited drilling, and authorized searches for hidden arms, were generally reasonable precautions considering the temper of the times. But the other three acts were reactionary: they restricted public assemblies, authorized the seizure of seditious literature, and increased duties on pamphlets and newspapers. The hostility between rich and poor grew more acute, and for a time the English working-man's instinctive deference to the process of law appeared to desert him just as the government's tradition for compromise was notably absent. Two events in 1820 provided the lower classes with an opportunity to express their feelings. One, an incredible scheme known as the "Cato Street Conspiracy," had as its aim no less than the assassination of the entire cabinet. It was discovered and crushed, but the working classes were plainly disappointed that the plot had not succeeded.

In that same year, a scandal in the royal family permitted the people to display their dislike of, and contempt for, their rulers. When George IV succeeded to the throne, he asked the cabinet to obtain parliamentary approval for a divorce from his estranged wife, Caroline of Brunswick-Wolfenbuttel, who was living, somewhat notoriously, in Italy on a royal allowance. When Caroline returned to England and demanded her rights as queen, the lower classes embraced her cause with enthusiasm and demonstrated wildly in her favor wherever she appeared in public. But the bill for divorce was withdrawn from the agenda in Commons when the prospect of its passage seemed dubious. Caroline surprised and disappointed the hungry poor when she accepted the bribe of an increased allowance in return for withdrawing her demand to reign as queen. There was no emotional outpouring on the part of working-class militants when their jaded heroine died one month after George IV's coronation. Yet this episode, sordid as it was, seemed to provide a safety valve for the frustrations of the poor and eased the tension between the classes. Dissent was further neutralized for a time by the improving economic conditions after 1820.[6]

Prosperity produced a period of comparative tranquility in Britain during the early 1820s, but this did not prevent the government from maintaining a vigilant guard against any semblance of insurrection or from crushing it without moderation or hesitation. In the

spring of 1820, a small body of Scotch coal miners and weavers at
Bonnymuir took up arms in a blind and desperate attempt to force an
improvement in their economic plight. Soldiers easily routed this
less-than-lethal band of confused and angry protesters, and, as in
the instance of the Cato Street conspirators, exemplary executions
followed. Among the victims was Andrew Hardie, ancestor of James
Keir Hardie, who was to become the first leader of the Labour Party.[7]
Once more the government demonstrated its readiness to respond to
the remotest hint of political terrorism with a vengeful policy of
legalized counterterrorism.

In 1830, Nor were urban areas the only settings for such fateful developments. Rural misery intensified in many regions of England following the prodigious speculative boom of 1825, due largely to the agricultural recession that it produced. The rural uprisings of 1830 were
on a far larger scale than any that had occurred before. They extended over all the southern counties from Kent to Wiltshire and Dor-
set and throughout the eastern counties and a considerable part of the
Midlands. Most of these outbreaks followed a common pattern, by
which farm laborers destroyed threshing machines and other new implements that had reduced the demand for labor and burned the hay-
stacks of exceptionally harsh landowners and farmers. Throughout
it all, the rural protesters neither killed nor wounded a single person,
while they repeatedly demanded that the Poor Law authorities grant
them living rates of relief. Their moderation did not spare them
from officialdom's counterterror, however, as commissions of judges
tried hundreds of cases as soon as order was restored by the authorities. Nine men were hanged, 457 were deported to Australia or elsewhere, and nearly as many were sent to prison for varying terms.[8]

In 1830, Lord Grey became prime minister of the first Whig
ministry in Britain since 1783. The Whigs were under considerable
pressure from an improbable coalition of forces to reform the electoral system. Upper-middle-class citizens insisted upon being given
the franchise, and they were supported in their demands by radicals
and Benthamites, who sought this concession as a first step in their
fight for universal male suffrage. When the House of Lords rejected
outright a reform bill proposed by the Whig government, large parts
of the country were rocked by turmoil. Nottingham Castle was burned,
Derby jail was sacked, militant mobs marched in the streets of London, and even the king's carriage was molested. Perhaps the most
serious uprising was in Bristol, where rioters held undisputed control
of the city for three days. Looting, pillaging, and burning were
brought to a violent end after sufficient troops were mustered to
crush the insurgents and restore order. Recognizing that nothing
less than the Reform Bill would now prevent revolution, the Tory-
dominated House of Lords gave way and the bill became law in 1832.[9]

But Whigs, no less than Tories, were appalled by the terrorism
and violence that had marred the parliamentary effort for reform. In
reporting on the Bristol riots, the Times doubtlessly expressed the
sentiment of the aristocratic majority in both parties:

> We grieve to state that in the performance of this
> indispensable and painful duty the arms of our gal-
> lant soldiers occasioned a great loss of lives, that
> between 400 and 500 of the rioters are calculated
> . . . to have been cut down by the military, or to
> have otherwise perished. Many of the misguided
> populace owe their melancholy fate to the state of
> intoxication into which they had thrown themselves.
> . . . A considerable number of them suffered the
> just retribution of their crimes, by being burnt in
> the fires which they themselves had kindled, or
> burned in the ruins of the buildings which they had
> pulled down.[10]

Distress, famine, and disillusionment over the failure of the
Reform Bill inspired a new wave of popular demonstrations in the
1830s. Chartism, a passionate and resentful protest of the poor
against the harsh conditions under which they lived, took the form of
a working-class demand for the franchise and for a radical reform of
Parliament. A six-point charter containing the principal demands of
the movement was given only cursory consideration in the House of
Commons, which promptly rejected it in July 1839. Moderates like
William Lovett and Francis Place, who had helped found the movement,
were eclipsed by demagogues like Feargus O'Connor, an Irish radical who talked wildly about violence and terrorism without understanding the implications of what he was saying.[11] Fearing that the rejection by the House of Commons would doom their movement to the same
oblivion that Robert Owen's scheme for a gigantic trade union had suffered a few years before, the Chartists led militant demonstrations
in many parts of the north and west of England during early November
1839. Troops were dispatched to troubled areas, but there was very
little conflict and still less violence or terrorism on either side.
Predictably, the Times' perception of these events bordered on the
hysterical. It insisted that the Chartist objective was a revolution
against property and lamented that the fatalities among such radicals
had not been greater:

> The accounts of Tuesday from the west of England
> will already have informed the public that an orga-
> nised and armed insurrection has broken out in the

> counties of Monmouth and Glamorgan. It is an insur-
> rection of these same fanatical rebels . . . under the
> name of "Chartists" . . . affiliations of this criminal
> confederacy extend all over the kingdom, its declared
> objects being the violent overthrow of the laws, and
> an entire revolution of property by force of arms. [12]

Two days later, the Times editorialized:

> The deaths of some dozen or so of insurgents can
> serve but little towards eradicating the fierce and
> lawless disposition from which the outbreak sprung,
> or towards insuring us against future violence of
> the same nature. . . . We say once more, that the
> Chartist rebellion, in the same way as the fatal
> riots at Bristol, and as every other atrocity which
> has desolated England during the last eight years,
> may be traced to Whig maladministration. [13]

In viewing the British experience within the context of international patterns of violence and terrorism, it is worth noting that
Chartism died in 1848, the year in which much of Continental Europe
was convulsed by revolution. In England, an enormous crowd led by
Feargus O'Connor proposed to march on Parliament to present an
enormous petition containing 5 million names. The government mustered up troops and informed O'Connor that his followers would not
be permitted to cross the Thames into Whitehall. At this moment of
crisis, O'Connor meekly directed the crowd to disperse and consented
to having the petition transported to Parliament in three hansom cabs.
The ignominy of this fiasco was compounded when the petition was
found to contain many fraudulent signatures, including those of the
Duke of Wellington and Queen Victoria. But the Chartists should not
be dismissed as mere folly. Theirs was a sincere and significant
effort of the lower classes to improve their plight by calling national
attention to the woes of the poor and further promoting the self-re-
spect of workingmen. It was, in the words of John Stuart Mill, the
victory of the vanquished. [14]

BRITISH STRATEGY AND TACTICS
ACROSS THE EMPIRE

If nineteenth-century British attitudes of the press or Parliament toward political terrorism at home were invariably hostile, terrorism or violence in any part of the empire was viewed with even

less tolerance. A notable example is eloquently illustrated in the reaction of the _Times_ to the Sepoy Mutiny, which began at Meerut, India, on May 10, 1857. The Sepoys harbored a number of grievances
against the British presence on the subcontinent, many of which were
the inevitable consequences of the arrogance and ambitions of English
merchants, particularly those of the East India Company. When the
Sepoys spearheaded a mutiny that ultimately led to the massacre of
the European residents of Delhi and Crawnpore and even to major
assaults against crack British regiments in Oudh and other districts
bordering the Ganges Valley, the London government promptly dispatched powerful forces to crush the insurgency. A parliamentary
act of 1858 subsequently dissolved the East India Company and placed
the rule of India entirely in the hands of the government on the assumption that these and other reforms might redress the major grievances
of the native population. Over the years, however, the gulf between
the English and the Indians only widened. [15]

Owing to the great distance between India and Britain, news of
the latest developments in the mutiny was often more than two weeks
old when the government or the press learned of it in England. There
was no delay thereafter, however, in either ministerial or editorial
response as both press and Parliament condemned the terrorism and
called for severe penalties for its perpetrators. On June 8, 1857, the
Times declared: "The excesses of Burrackpore and Meerut demand
prompt repression and vigilant precautions, lest they should again occur. . . . Resolution and severity are required at once."[16] The following day the Earl of Ellenborough asserted in a speech before the
House of Lords: "Open mutiny is open war, and it is to be met only
as open war carried on by an enemy in the field."[17] As more details
of the lurid atrocities and systematic butchering of Europeans were
subsequently transmitted to London, the _Times_ inveighed against the
barbaric terrorism in a tone that betrayed unmistakable racist sentiments:

> In the first place the mutiny must be suppressed,
> and in a manner as shall impress the minds of the
> natives with the nature of the power they have de-
> fied when its real strength is put forth. . . . Any-
> one who has had experience of the tiger-like feroc-
> ity of the Indian in a moment of what appears to
> him success will prepare for the result. An indis-
> criminate massacre of the Europeans was the first
> act upon which the mutineers decided, and this they
> are said to have carried out in a manner most re-
> morseless and most complete. No tenderness was
> shown to sex, no reverence to age. [18]

In much the same spirit, the Times continued the diatribe two days later:

> Justice, humanity, and the safety of our country-
> men, and the honour of the country demand that
> the slaughter of Delhi shall be punished with un-
> sparing severity. Asiatics are not people to whom
> rulers can safely grant immunity from crime. A
> native army must be made to feel that treason,
> mutiny, and murder must bring a memorable retri-
> bution . . . it is too late to talk of mildness and ne-
> gotiation.[19]

Another incident involving political violence abroad that inspired similar epithets of indignation, while also affording a further gauge of British attitudes toward terrorism, was the Orsini plot of 1858. On the evening of January 14 of that year, French Emperor Napoleon III and Empress Eugenie were the objects of an assassination attempt as their carriage arrived at the opera house in Paris for a performance of William Tell. Three bombs exploded, killing eight members of the imperial escort, wounding some 150 onlookers, and shattering windows and gas lamps throughout the area. Although the carriage was totally destroyed, Napoleon and his wife miraculously escaped serious injury and, before the night was over, police had the perpe-trators of the attempted assassination in custody. They were four Italian patriots who had been living in exile in London and had planned the attack to call attention to the plight of their country. Their lead-er, Felice Orsini, was condemned to death after a dramatic trial in which the defendant made an eloquent plea on behalf of Italian indepen-dence.[20] The Times of London promptly concluded that in the long annals of crime there was no blacker deed than the one committed by Orsini and his compatriots, for not only did they make an attempt on the life of a chief of state, but they also displayed a general disregard for the lives of innocent bystanders. Hoping that these despicable terrorists would be brought to speedy justice, the Times further added: "The only wish of all who deserve the name of men is that the cord and the axe may be their lot whenever they are taken."[21] Ten days later, the same newspaper took note of the fact that the conspiracy had been apparently planned in London and that such ac-tions should be punishable under English law.[22]

Parliamentary reaction translated that sentiment into legisla-tion when Commons next reconvened in February 1858. Viscount Pal-merston introduced a Conspiracy to Murder Bill that he hoped would deter future conspiracies of murderous elements on English soil and would reassure all foreign powers that there was no "indifference in

this country to the commission of crimes of an atrocious nature."[23]
Although the bill was defeated after a second reading on February 19,
1858, by a margin of 234 to 215, even the opposition vehemently condemned such political terrorism as Orsini's attempt at assassination.
One such opposition spokesman declared:

> As a moral and religious people we absolutely abhor
> the crime of assassination. As a people used to brac-
> ing exercise and manly strife of many descriptions
> we regard assassination as a cowardly and dastardly
> evasion of those rules of fair conflict to which we
> are accustomed.[24]

British disapproval of politically motivated violence, at least
in such reactions as are found in the influential editorial comments of
the Times, was frequently coupled with a righteous tone of condescen-
sion. This is particularly evident in the journalistic response to the
Hyde Park riots of July 19, 1866, which occurred in the wake of an
unsuccessful attempt by reformers and Whigs to introduce a new Reform Bill. There was a massive protest demonstration in the Marble
Arch vicinity of Hyde Park. Some railings surrounding the park collapsed when the crowds surged against them as they turned, peacefully, to leave the area, having made through their leaders a symbolic request to be admitted to the park. The Times reported on the
scene in a spirit of outraged indignation:

> The lowest rabble of the metropolis assembled in
> the park near Marble Arch and . . . evinced their
> zeal for Reform by doing as much injury to the
> park as they possibly could, and by insulting every-
> body who appeared to be more respectable than
> themselves. They wreaked their vengeance on the
> flowers and shrubs by wantonly plucking them up
> by the roots.[25]

The Times further noted that about 100 "roughs" later dashed
through the Pall Mall area, smashing the windows of the Athenaeum
and United Service Clubs as well as those of several private resi-
dences. The Hyde Park gathering was described as having had very
few respectable, middle-class participants, the majority being the
coarsest mob "who constitute the ordinary mass of the London multitude." Nor did freedom of speech or assembly, reasoned the Times,
justify the use of Hyde Park for political rallies by such rabble,
since it was the recreation place for the residents of the west of London. The poorer classes had parks in their own districts where they

could congregate as they pleased.[26] The aristocratic Emily Eden expressed an even more extreme sentiment in what surely was not an isolated reaction. She was convinced that the Hyde Park demonstrations heralded a coming era of class war. In a letter to a friend, Lady Eden wrote: "I attempted to drive around the Park and am so indignant at the sight [she was outraged to see where the grass had been trampled and flowers destroyed] that I felt boiling and bloodthirsty."[27]

Much of the British experience with political terrorism since 1867 has been directly related to Irish Nationalist or radical elements. The Fenians—an organization committed to the establishment of Irish independence by physical force—met with the same failure in 1867 as did the Young Ireland Rising in 1848. The majority of the Irish population refused again in 1867 to respond to the appeal for a Nationalist uprising, and British authorities had the conspiracy well in hand and nearly all the Fenian leaders in prison before the movement could achieve even a temporary victory.[28] In September 1867, Colonel Thomas Kelly, a Fenian organizer of the abortive uprising in Ireland of the previous March, was captured with a comrade in Manchester. A few of their followers succeeded dramatically in rescuing them by attacking the van in which they were being transported to prison. One of the police guards was accidentally killed while the lock was being blown off, and five men were arrested. After an unsatisfactory trial, and on rather inconclusive evidence, three men were executed. These were the "Manchester Martyrs," who at once became symbols of resurgent Irish nationalism. In England, on the other hand, the events in Manchester strengthened the impression that Fenianism was a powerful and sinister force at work in the very heart of English society, an impression that was further reinforced by the gunpowder explosion at Clerkenwell prison in London at the end of 1867 that occurred when an attempt to blow up part of the prison wall killed a number of innocent people.

If the Times's reaction is any barometer of the popular feeling toward these two events, it was hostile and uncompromising. Observing how startling it was to find an armed enemy in one of the most important cities of the kingdom, the Times was pleased to report on September 19, 1867, that the leader of the Fenian rescue party at Manchester, who was also thought to be responsible for the firing of the fatal shot, was in police custody.

> It will, we may hope, be possible to make an example of him. It is of great importance that such an outrage should be met with the utmost vigour and decision. We have displayed sufficient forbearance in our treatment of that semblance of an armed force which challenged our authority in Ireland . . . the

> law must be maintained at any cost. We can have no
> parleying with open violence.[29]

That editorial sentiment became further intensified following the bombing of the Clerkenwell jail in London. Calling it "a crime of unexam-
pled atrocity," the Times insisted that any prospect of clemency for
any previous Fenian terrorist activity was forever lost. Indeed, the
newspaper exhibited a rare concern for the violence that the Clerkenwell deaths might produce among the general populace of London, as
it concluded that "the Fenians have filled to the full the cup of wrath,
and that in dealing with them public opinion will need rather to be restrained than instigated."[30] To be sure, the mingled horror and anger that these events produced did work in two very different ways.
It reaffirmed the belief of those who felt that a repressive government
was what Ireland deserved or needed, but it also prompted thoughtful
men to look beyond the violence to what had created the violence and
to wonder if the time had not come to provide Ireland with constructive alternatives to the desperate path of political terrorism. That
one of those who began to think in this way was William Gladstone was
one of the more positive legacies left by the Fenians to posterity.[31]
Gladstone, who became prime minister in 1868, later became a champion of Irish Home Rule.

There can be little doubt, however, that the militancy that
characterized social and political movements in Britain during the
decades immediately prior to 1867 was a source of keen concern even
to moderate Whig reformers. In advocating the Second Reform Bill
in 1867, the Gladstonian Liberals advanced the view that those who
had shown themselves morally worthy should come within "the pale of
the Constitution" and be given the franchise. But the vote was a privilege to be earned, not a right. Whigs no less than Tories would
have opposed any greater extension of the franchise than was authorized under that reform bill, by which 47 percent of the adult males in
Britain received the vote. Three Victorian intellectuals who shared
the misgivings of the ruling class over the political implications of
the egalitarian trend were Thomas Carlyle, the essayist and historian; George Eliot, the novelist; and Matthew Arnold, the poet and
critic. Carlyle's reaction to the reform bill is evident from the title
of his pamphlet published in 1867, Shooting Niagara: And After?—a
reference to shooting Niagara over the falls and into "American"
democracy. George Eliot feared an era of violence and political terrorism unless the newly enfranchised workers had the wisdom not to
scorn the counsel of what she called the "endowed" classes. Matthew
Arnold felt that the unique social equilibrium in Britain, which was
so capably examined in W. L. Burn's The Age of Equipoise, was
gravely imperiled by the advent of democracy. In a book published in

1869 entitled <u>Culture and Anarchy</u>, Arnold made an impassioned plea
for authority and culture. He was fearful that chaos and violence was
a real and imminent threat to the nation.[32] Paradoxically, the next
few decades were distinguished by domestic tranquility.

LABOR, THE SUFFRAGETTES, AND
IRISH HOME RULE

        Any study of Britain's direct experience with indigenous forms
of political terrorism in the twentieth century is, as it was in the previous century, an inevitably limited inquiry because of the paucity of
that nation's exposure to nearly all varieties of physical violence.
This is not to say that the potential for extreme forms of political
terrorism did not exist in Britain. Indeed, during the first decade of
this century the intensity of revolutionary fervor among three groups
in particular was such as to imperil the very existence of England's
constitutional institutions. Indifference, insensitivity, and political
opportunism were all factors in the governmental policies that continued to exacerbate the Irish and labor issues. Social unrest in
Britain assumed a third expression in the suffragette movement, which
reached its peak between 1910 and 1914. In those years, the latent
frustrations and longstanding grievances of militant labor, women,
and Irish groups coalesced to form the most menacing threat to English democracy in modern history.
        Labor, which had formed its own political party in 1916, was
not a monolithic movement nor were all of its leaders committed to
constitutional methods in seeking reform. The outcome of the Os-
borne case, which declared that unions could not impose compulsory
levies on their members in order to raise funds for political purposes,
strengthened the influence of the more radical working-class leaders.
Many of them were drifting toward syndicalism—the notion that the
union and not the state was the center of democratic action. They
held to the belief that labor leaders should influence Parliament not
by becoming members but by direct action outside politics—by the
sympathy strike, the general strike, and even sabotage. Britain
was convulsed by strikes from 1910 through 1912 as railwaymen,
miners, and transport workers struck to dramatize their demands
for higher wages and better working conditions. Mindful that a
strike by the 2 million workers in these trades could cripple industry
and disrupt the distribution of food, Prime Minister Herbert Asquith's
Liberal government attempted to conciliate rather than coerce whenever possible. Only once—in Liverpool in 1911, in the course of the
local transport strike that was the prelude to the national railway
stoppage—was there any considerable conflict, though there were a

number of small scrimmages with the police in the mining areas of
South Wales. On August 14, 1911, the Times angrily decried the
"violence and rioting" in Liverpool, which left one policeman critically
injured and scores of other officers and civilians wounded. [33] Two days
later, the newspaper expressed its abhorrence of the means by which
the railway workers were seeking company recognition for their
union—by preventing the conveyance of all food and fuel by rail until
the demand was won. The Times wrote:

> That is not an attack on the railway companies, but
> on the public at large and the nation. These trade
> unionists in their crazy fanaticism or diseased van-
> ity are prepared to starve the whole population, in-
> cluding, of course, their own families and all the
> ranks of "Labour," to ruin the country and leave it
> defenceless to the world. [34]

Under the headline "Labour Agitations Gone Mad," the Times went on
to report that two strikers had been killed when they sought to free
some of their comrades who were being taken to prison under military
escort. Mobs were also reported to be menacing authorities in Car-
diff, but the disposition of Parliament was to avoid any unnecessary
confrontations or reactions that might inflame working-class opinion
or catalyze anarchist proclivities. [35]

Far more violent than labor was the suffragette movement,
spearheaded by Emmeline Pankhurst's Women's Social and Political
Union (WSPU). [36] The suffragettes were more radical than the labor
unions, and they did not hesitate to employ terrorist tactics when
peaceful demonstrations failed to produce their goal of political equality. In November 1910, WSPU militants broke windows at the Home
Office, the War Office, the Foreign Office, and the homes of selected
political leaders. Some 223 women were arrested, and 150 of them
were sent to prison for periods varying from five days to one month.
Released from prison in February 1912, a group of suffragettes under
the leadership of Pankhurst engaged in an assault upon the most ex-
pensive windowpanes in London's West End, including the portals of
the prime minister's residence at 10 Downing Street. Once arrested,
the women undertook hunger strikes in jail and compelled the authorities to resort to force-feeding. When public opinion recoiled from
such a spectacle and thus compelled the government to parole the suffragettes, the women responded with a still more intense campaign of
violence. Postboxes were burned, telegraph lines were cut, bogus
telegraph messages summoned army reserves hither and yon, the
glass of the crown jewel case in the Tower of London was smashed,
and houses were fire-bombed—including the uncompleted residence of

Chancellor of the Exchequer David Lloyd George. [37] The government was in a dilemma, for it truly feared that Pankhurst, once incarcerated, would kill herself with continual hunger strikes, and it did not wish to indulge her obvious desire for martyrdom; yet no sooner would she be released from jail when the emaciated and half-crippled woman would appear at proscribed meetings, where she would urge women followers on to further acts of militancy. [38]

Suffragettes were not without their defenders in Parliament, and, while clearly expressing a minority sentiment, some of these apologists even sought to exculpate the women radicals from the consequences of their actions. In a debate on the floor of the House of Commons on June 28, 1912, George Lansbury made an impassioned plea for clemency and understanding in the government's handling of the suffragette problem. Lansbury declared that the women were not hysterical agitators indulging in aimless destruction or violence but courageous people willing to sacrifice their lives for their beliefs and ideals. He found it incredible that the government had charged the suffragettes with the destruction of private property rather than accusing them of politically inspired violence. Lansbury thought that the treatment accorded the suffragettes, including the hideous force-feedings in prison, was shocking and grossly inconsistent with the government's response to what he deemed to be far more grievous acts committed by other groups in the past. Lansbury declared:

> The Home Secretary told us one night that these women were not imprisoned because of political agitation, but because they broke windows. What of the man who helped manufacture the Orsini bombs and escaped over here? The British Government, under Lord Palmerston, refused to give him up. What was the charge against him? The charge against him was not merely that he was a rebel against Louis Napoleon, but that he wanted to help the flight of Louis Napoleon to heaven—or to the other place. These women have broken windows on account of political agitation, and no amount of twisting can get rid of that fact. [39]

Lansbury concluded by reminding the House of Commons that suppression of dissent was the practice of tyrannical Russia but was a scandal to any self-respecting British Liberal government. If, he continued, the suffragettes had turned to terrorism, it was simply because they had been denied any legal channel that would enable them to pursue the fulfillment of their goals. Women lived under laws enacted by an all-male legislature. Moreover, women were expected to abide by these laws even though women as a class were excluded from the very body that formulated the laws that governed all of society. "When our fathers were in that condition they broke the laws; they rioted in Birmingham and in Bristol; they pulled down railings at Hyde Park." Why, asked Lansbury, should the government take stronger action against the weaker sex, who admittedly were resorting to unlawful, albeit not unprecedented, methods in seeking the attainment of their ends?[40]

Lord Robert Cecil, whose political philosophy and party affiliation were different from those of Lansbury, agreed with him to a degree. Cecil thought that the suffragettes truly believed, however mistakenly, that their conduct would help initiate the political changes they desired. "And therefore," he asserted, "I think to treat them as ordinary criminals is perfectly absurd and shows a complete lack of imagination and a complete failure to understand the very elements of the problem." Lord Cecil considered a reasonable solution to the suffragette problem to be the deportation of the militant lawbreakers from Britain for a considerable period of time.[41]

Another member of Commons, Harold Smith, represented an alternate point of view as he forcefully condemned the suffragettes, who were "perpetrating some of the worst offences known to our criminal law. They are preaching war upon society and inciting the public to mob law." Smith insisted that the home secretary take immediate action to punish the political terrorists, observing that the callous attitude of the suffragettes toward the life and safety of all citizens precluded any consideration for clemency that might normally be accorded lawbreakers of the female gender.[42]

For its part, the Times continued to call for imprisonment and harsh punishment for "the women who have been breaking windows in order to prove their fitness for the franchise."[43] The only consistent supporters of the suffragettes were the Labour left wing, the International Labour Party, and the London Daily Herald. Their common bond was the conviction that granting the franchise to adult females was but another step down the road toward social justice for both men and women.[44] Britain was spared further revolutionary disorders by suffragette militants with the outbreak of the First World War in August 1914. Suffragettes, no less than Socialists, responded to the call to the colors on behalf of king and country, and the movement was all but forgotten during the seemingly interminable conflict of World War I. Following the hostilities, however, the Sex Disqualification Removal Act of 1919 established a significant degree of equality for women in a typically British, that is to say constitutional, procedure. Women had the vote, though not on equal terms with men until 1928, and were given access to the universities, the professions, and Parliament itself. In the grandest English tradition, the act marked the triumph of another bloodless revolution.

If much of the suffragette support, and all of the trade unions' support, came from the Left during the years immediately preceding World War I, the British constitution was seriously imperiled at this same time by a threat generated by the Right. Irish Home Rule was the issue that provoked right-wing Tories to support unconstitutional, even revolutionary, tactics in defense of the Protestant ascendancy in Ulster. As George Dangerfield has so capably demonstrated in his excellent study The Strange Death of Liberal England, the Conservative Party in Britain gave its support to the extralegal paramilitary Ulster Volunteer militia more from a desire to destroy the Liberal Party than out of any commitment to the Protestant community of Northern Ireland. The Liberals were committed to the Irish Nationalist demand for a Dublin parliament to govern all of Ireland under a Home Rule formula. So, too, the Conservatives were committed to the support of the Ulster unionists, who rejected the Liberal proposal since it would place the Protestant community at a numerical disadvantage with Catholics in any scheme for a united Ireland. The irony of the Ulster position, which insisted on continued union with Britain, was that it fomented rebellion while claiming to be ultrapatriotic. Hence, Ulster Volunteers pledged to fight for king and country against the government as though the two were separate entities. Britain's director of military operations, Sir Henry Wilson, openly sympathized with the Ulster unionists and even encouraged English military officers to resign their commissions rather than follow any government directive that might be aimed against the armed and defiant Ulster Volunteer militias. [45] An army mutiny was conceivable and civil war probable had not World War I intervened to spare Britain from an unprecedented crisis that threatened wholesale slaughter and violence. Unlike the suffragettes' or the trade unions' general strike movements, however, the Irish question was not tempered by the war. Rather, it festered beneath the surface of British life until it erupted with appalling fury a short time later. [46]

By April 1916, Britain had been at war with the Central Powers for nearly two years, and there was no sign that the steady attrition that was depleting the kingdom's manpower and other resources would soon cease. It was at this critical moment in Britain's desperate fight for survival against the German menace that an uprising against the government occurred in Dublin. The rebellion was suppressed rapidly and bloodily, but it suggested the potential danger of rebellion and revolution within the United Kingdom. On April 30, 1916, Augustine Birrell, the chief secretary for Ireland, wrote these impressions of the Dublin insurrection to Prime Minister Asquith:

> I have seen many of the prisoners, a miserable lot
> they looked, unfit for street fighting, but under shel-

> ter of the houses dangerous and hard to dislodge.
> . . . The leaders, both fighting leaders and stump-
> orators, are criminals to whom short shrift should
> be given. [47]

It was the sort of counsel that the prime minister should have tempered with a degree of restraint. The vast majority of Irishmen had neither participated in, nor sympathized with, the abortive Easter Rising. But their attitude changed dramatically as the British condemned 90 rebels for their part in the insurrection and, despite a mounting volume of protest, summarily executed 15 of the leaders, who were promptly transformed from traitors into martyrs in the eyes of Nationalist Ireland. Panic seized the British administration in Dublin as events went from bad to worse. The pacifist Francis Sheehy Skeffington was arrested and shot without trial, although he had taken no part in the uprising. Martial law was imposed, and more people were arrested than had actually taken part in the uprising. [48]

Irish revolutionary zeal was successfully contained by British authorities, at least in terms of overt activities against the crown, until after the armistice that terminated World War I on November 11, 1918. It was to be only a brief respite for England, however, for in January 1919, the Irish Republican Army (IRA) (the name adopted by militant Nationalists seeking the establishment of an independent Republic) launched a guerrilla war against British authorities in Ireland. For two and a half years the Irish nation was convulsed by a succession of horrors that would later be euphemistically characterized as the period of "the Troubles." Repeated IRA atrocities provoked the inevitable British reprisals in a seemingly interminable era of terrorism that plagued Ireland from January 1919 until May 1921. Mounting casualties, both civilian and military, atrocity stories, and the worsening of unsolved social problems and unemployment throughout England combined to produce considerable antiwar sentiment in Britain. People in Britain soon tired of the violence and waste, especially since the Irish conflict seemed to many a senseless and immoral war. Prominent Anglican clergymen, including the Archbishop of Canterbury, the Asquith wing of the Liberal Party, and the Labour Party, joined in condemning the government's prosecution of the war in Ireland. A growing chorus of denunciations came from the pulpit, the Opposition benches in the House of Commons, and the editorial pages of the left-wing press. All argued that the terrorist tactics of the IRA did not justify reprisals that seemed little different from genocide. They demanded an end to the war and a settlement that would accord a negotiated form of Home Rule and allow the Irish people to govern themselves. [49]

Even the Times, whose uncompromising condemnation of all forms of political terrorism had been consistent for more than a century, openly conceded that the Irish terrorists were by no means solely culpable for the tragic events in Ireland. That fact is perhaps best illustrated by the newspaper's reaction to "Bloody Sunday," when, on November 20, 1920, IRA gunmen, in a meticulously synchronized attack, assassinated 14 British officers and civilians at their homes throughout Dublin. While reactionaries and moderates alike called for vengeance in speeches delivered from the floor of the House of Commons, the Times reflected a more balanced perspective:

> In so far as the power of the Government can procure the arrest and punishment of the murderers, it must be exercised to the full. . . . But an army already perilously indisciplined, and a police force avowedly beyond control, have defiled, by heinous acts, the reputation of England; while the Government, who are the trustees of that reputation, are not free from suspicion of dishonourable connivance. We and all who have protested against indiscriminate reprisals have been accused most foolishly of weakening the hand of the Irish Executive [the Government]. Yet, in the light of yesterday's event, who can doubt that the strength of the Irish Executive would in this grave emergency be ten times greater had its record entitled it to appeal for the moral support of all those Irishmen to whom murder is an abomination?[50]

The signing of an Anglo-Irish treaty in December 1921 brought dominion status to Ireland and ended that country's centuries-old struggle for separation from Britain. It did not resolve all Irish grievances, however, as the six northeastern counties of Ulster remained within the United Kingdom, and irreconcilable Nationalists continued to agitate for a united and independent Irish Republic. Occasional outbreaks of violence characterized an erratic and wholly ineffectual IRA effort to achieve that end in the years that followed. But IRA outrages did not become a serious issue in Anglo-Irish relations until the recent terrorism in Northern Ireland, which began with the 1967 civil rights movement in Ulster. Old sectarian hatreds quickly surfaced, the community became polarized, and the inhabitants of that troubled region have lived ever since under a virtual state of siege. Each day brings new horrors, and there appears to be no end in sight to the violence and political terrorism that mark this latest chapter of Ireland's long and troubled history.[51]

Irish Nationalists won only a qualified victory with the treaty of 1921, but the IRA's terrorist activities and the guerrilla tactics employed during that nation's war for independence were to provide a model for other peoples living under British rule. Political violence and official reprisals composed an unhappy legacy for the British during the twilight years of the empire. The majority of Englishmen, especially in the period immediately following World War II, seemed convinced that the demand for national independence by subject peoples should be accommodated as expeditiously as possible. Nevertheless, the British were characteristically shocked by the indiscriminate terrorism of insurgent elements that attempted to either impose their own timetable for the severing of imperial ties or enforce their own assumption of political power amid the transition from imperial governance. In Palestine, for instance, in 1948, Jews and Arabs engaged in deadly conflict while British soldiers were made the targets of both sides. In angry and indignant editorials, the Times chastised both the Irgun Zvai Leumi, a Jewish nationalist group, and similarly oriented Arab elements for the outrageous and wanton killings of soldiers and civilians throughout Palestine. [52] Britain's experience was no different in Cyprus in 1958, when the Times inveighed against the barbaric assassinations of British soldiers, the perpetrators in this instance being Greeks and Turks. [53] Unlike in the case of Ireland, however, the Times and other influential segments of English opinion did not suggest that the reprehensible violence was an inevitable by-product of British maladministration in either Palestine or Cyprus. Perhaps this apparent inconsistency in British attitudes can be explained in terms of the respectable Whig-Liberal Irish partisan tradition in England. This constituency, which composed a pro-Irish lobby within the pluralistic London establishment, included high Anglican clergymen, Fleet Street press lords, and members of both houses of Parliament. Certainly there was no such indigenous equivalent for the support of Jewish, Arab, Greek, or Turkish objectives. And, of course, it is equally conceivable that the native Briton, whether consciously or otherwise, judged political terrorism within the United Kingdom by a different standard than he did similar acts committed abroad. But that supposition is more properly the subject of a separate study. [54]

Contemporary Britain, the Northern Ireland problem aside, remains one of the least fertile societies for political terrorism among the industrial nations. Despite evidence that indicates that the number of anarchist groups in England has increased notably over the past 10 to 15 years, the probability of any imminent wave of political violence seems remote. Indeed, the kind of action in which English anarchists are currently engaged is perhaps best exemplified in their contribution to the squatting campaigns that reached their peak in London and elsewhere throughout the country in 1969. [55]

Finally, the reason for Britain's remarkable degree of immunity from revolutionary terrorism is, to a large extent, explained by the working class's sense of commitment to the political system. Since 1945, about one-fifth of the membership of the House of Commons has been working-class in origin, a better representation than exists in West Germany, Italy, or any legislature in the English-speaking world. The notion of the freeborn Englishman has long been entrenched, and assumed rights of resistance and the refusal to be objects of any arbitrary state will have, as Walter Bagehot and Elie Halevy observed in the last century, been tantamount to rights of rebellion. Moreover, the responsiveness of the political elite encourages a sense of political competence among voters. [56] A recent survey, for example, indicated that more than half of the population believed that the civil service will give serious attention to their problems and 75 percent feel the same way about the police. [57] The rising unemployment and soaring economic inflation of the mid-1970s may yet alter political patterns in Britain, particularly if Conservatives and Labourites alike appear impotent to effect the necessary changes. But the prevailing public temper toward revolutionary terrorism today, as manifested in the response to the Ulster outrages, remains as inhospitable as ever.

NOTES

1. For an examination of the intervals between different types of outbreak of violence, see Lewis F. Richardson, Statistics of Deadly Quarrels (London: Stevens, 1960), p. 128 ff.

2. Edward R. Cain, "Conscientious Objection in France, Britain and the United States," Comparative Politics 2, no. 2 (1970): 285.

3. Ibid., pp. 285-87.

4. J. A. R. Marriott, England Since Waterloo (London: Methuen, 1916), p. 26.

5. Times (London), August 30, 1819, p. 2.

6. In observing the relationship between the relief of political tensions and rising economic conditions, William Cobbett said, "I defy you to agitate a fellow with a full stomach" (see the Birmingham Journal, November 12, 1836, p. 1).

7. G. D. H. Cole and Raymond Postgate, The British People, 1746-1946 (London: Methuen, 1961), p. 230.

8. Asa Briggs, The Making of Modern England (New York: Harper & Row, 1959), pp. 249-50.

9. For a useful analysis by a contemporary, see W. N. Molesworth, The History of the Reform Bill of 1832 (London: Chapman and Hall, 1865).

10. Times (London), November 2, 1831, p. 2. In the House of Commons, Lord Cavendish, in reference to what he called the "violence and indiscriminate plunder" at Bristol, said he agreed with the king's view that the best means by which to prevent any recurrence of such excesses was to strengthen the municipal police (Great Britain, 3 Hansard's Parliamentary Debates, 9 [1831] 38. Commons, December 6, 1831).

11. For a classic study of the Chartist philosophy and leadership, see J. L. Hammond and B. Hammond, The Age of the Chartists (London: Longmans, Green, 1930).

12. Times (London), November 5, 1839, p. 4.

13. Ibid., November 7, 1839, p. 4.

14. For an analysis of the degree of influence and effectiveness achieved by Chartist groups throughout England, see Asa Briggs, ed., Chartist Studies (New York: St. Martin's Press, 1967).

15. For a detailed study of the Sepoy uprising, see Richard Collier, The Great Indian Mutiny (New York: Dutton, 1964).

16. Times (London), June 8, 1857, p. 8.

17. Great Britain, 3 Hansard's Parliamentary Debates, 145 (1857) 1394. Lords, June 9, 1857.

18. Times (London), June 27, 1857, p. 9.

19. Ibid, June 29, 1857, p. 8.

20. Gordon A. Craig, Europe, 1815-1914 (New York: Holt, Rinehart & Winston, 1966), p. 199.

21. Times (London), January 16, 1858, p. 8.

22. Ibid., January 18, 1858, p. 6.

23. Great Britain, 3 Hansard's Parliamentary Debates, 148 (1858) 933. Commons, 8 February 1858.

24. Ibid., p. 939.

25. Times (London), July 25, 1866, p. 9.

26. Ibid., July 24, 1866, p. 9.

27. Peter Stansky, England Since 1867: Continuity and Change (New York: Harcourt Brace Jovanovich, 1973), p. 12.

28. See T. W. Moody, ed., The Fenian Movement (Cork: Mercier Press, 1968), for a series of revelatory and comprehensive essays on the Fenians.

29. Times (London), September 19, 1867, p. 6.

30. Ibid., December 14, 1867, p. 6.

31. F. S. L. Lyons, Ireland Since the Famine (London: Weidenfeld and Nicolson, 1971), p. 127.

32. Stansky, op. cit., pp. 12-15.

33. Times (London), August 14, 1911, p. 7.

34. Ibid., August 16, 1911, p. 7.

35. British Home Secretary Winston Churchill told the House of Commons that, while the Liverpool disorders were a grave and seri-

ous matter, they were probably due more to sectarian hatreds than to political grievances (many of the strikers were Irish Catholic residents of Liverpool). Great Britain 5, Parliamentary Debates, 29 (1911) 1757. Commons, August 15, 1911.

36. For an autobiographical statement on the goals and objectives of the WSPU movement, see Emmeline Pankhurst, My Own Story (New York: Hearst's International Library, 1914), pp. 57-62, 279-84; 292-99.

37. According to Home Secretary R. McKenna, the damage incurred in the window smashing alone was approximately £6,000. Great Britain, 5 Parliamentary Debates, 36 (1912) 865. Commons, March 4, 1912.

38. George Dangerfield, The Strange Death of Liberal England (New York: Capricorn, 1961), pp. 194-97.

39. Great Britain, 5 Parliamentary Debates, 40 (1912) 671-72. Commons, June 28, 1912.

40. Ibid.

41. Great Britain, 5 Parliamentary Debates 50 (1913) 891-92. Commons, March 18, 1913.

42. Ibid., pp. 874-78.

43. Times (London), March 6, 1912, p. 9.

44. Cole and Postgate, op. cit., pp. 492-93.

45. For an authoritative account of the mutinous conduct of Sir Henry Wilson as well as the British military officers stationed in Ireland, see A. T. Q. Stewart, The Ulster Crisis (London: Faber, 1967), pp. 161-75.

46. For one of the most recent and best analyses of the implications respecting the unresolved Irish question, see Patrick O'Farrell, Ireland's English Question (New York: Schocken, 1971), pp. 293-307.

47. Leon O'Broin, Dublin Castle and the 1916 Rising (Dublin: Helicon, 1966), p. 120.

48. For further background and analysis, see Donal McCartney, "From Parnell to Pearse," in T. W. Moody and F. X. Martin, eds., The Course of Irish History (Cork: Mercier Press, 1967), pp. 294-312.

49. Thomas E. Hachey, The Problem of Partition: Peril to World Peace (Chicago: Rand McNally, 1972), pp. 18-24.

50. Times (London), November 22, 1920, p. 13. Passions were less restrained, however, in the House of Commons, where members shouted down Irish Nationalist M. P. Joseph Devlin when he attempted to respond to Chief Secretary for Ireland Sir Hamar Greenwood's commentary on the atrocities in Dublin. See Great Britain, 5 Parliamentary Debates 135 (1920) 35-39. Commons, November 22, 1920.

51. See J. C. Beckett, "Northern Ireland," Journal of Contemporary History 6, no. 1 (1971): 121-34. For an insightful epilogue on contemporary IRA terrorism, see Tim Pat Coogan, The I.R.A. (London: Fontana, 1970), pp. 345-55. J. Bowyer Bell examines the IRA from its inception to the present in the new edition of his definitive study on that organization entitled The Secret Army: The I.R.A., 1916-1974 (Cambridge: Cambridge University Press, 1974).

52. Times (London), February 24, 1948, p. 5.

53. Ibid., August 4, 1958, p. 7.

54. Peter Calvert has advanced the hypothesis that British governments for the past 300 years have achieved a high degree of domestic tranquility quite possibly because of a deliberate effort to preoccupy the military in resolving problems abroad rather than at home. See Peter Calvert, "Revolution: The Politics of Violence," Political Studies 15, no. 1 (1967): 9.

55. David Stafford, "Anarchists in Britain Today," Government and Opposition 5, no. 4 (1970): 496.

56. Dennis Kavanagh, "The Deferential English: A Comparative Critique," Government and Opposition 6, no. 3 (1971): 346-53.

57. For a comprehensive analysis of these and kindred political opinion samplings in Britain, see Gabriel Almond and Sydney Verba, The Civic Culture (Princeton, N.J.: Princeton University Press, 1963).

SOVIET POLICY TOWARD
INTERNATIONAL TERRORISM
Robert O. Freedman

Any analysis of Soviet policy toward international terrorism, and particularly Middle Eastern terrorism, must deal with two basic issues. On the one hand, the Soviet Union is a global power with economic, political, military, and diplomatic interests all over the world. Consequently, it is vulnerable to various forms of terrorism, such as the hijacking of Soviet aircraft, the kidnapping and assassination of Soviet officials, and the bombing of Soviet embassies and trade missions, which are precisely the types of activity carried out by elements of the Palestine Liberation Organization (PLO), a loose confederation of Palestinian guerrilla organizations united only in their determination to ultimately destroy the State of Israel.[1] On the other hand the Soviet leadership has long had the goal of weakening and, if possible, eliminating Western influence from the Middle East, and it has not hesitated to exploit the actions of the PLO, one of the most anti-Western forces in the region, to further the Soviet Union's Middle Eastern goals. Consequently, this study of Soviet policy toward the PLO will show how the Soviet Union has attempted to balance the disparate goals of opposition to terrorist activities to which the Soviet Union is itself vulnerable and support of a leading anti-Western force in the Middle East.

The Soviet leadership's attempt to exploit an organization that attempts to achieve its objectives through terrorist action will, of course, come as no surprise to those familiar with the structure of the Soviet political system and the role played by the Soviet secret police in maintaining it. The Soviet secret police is the largest governmental terrorist organization in the world, responsible for at least 5 million murders during the purges of the 1930s and countless acts of persecution against Soviet citizens since that time.[2] Lenin advocated the use of terror as a legitimate, and indeed integral, wea-

pon in the workers' "political struggle," although he warned against
the use of terror for its own sake—a warning that has been echoed by
the current Soviet leadership in its advice to the more radical factions
of the PLO.[3]

Established as a political organization by the Arab summit conference of January 1964, the PLO was the latest of a series of Arab
terror organizations attempting to prevent the settlement of Jews in
Israel. In the days of the British mandate over Palestine (1922-48),
Haj Amin El-Husseini, the grand mufti, carried on terrorist attacks
against the Jewish community that reached a level close to full-scale
war between 1936 and 1938, and his actions spawned two Jewish terrorist organizations, Irgun and Zuai Leumi Lehi, whose goal was to
match Arab terror with Jewish terror.[4] Following the establishment
of the State of Israel in 1948, when the Israelis successfully defeated
five invading Arab armies, and hundreds of thousands of Palestinian
Arabs fled the country to avoid the fighting, attacks were begun on
Jewish settlements by Arabs who crossed the border from the Jordan-
ian-occupied West Bank or the Egyptian-occupied Gaza Strip.[5]

These two areas were to have been part of the Palestinian Arab
state under the UN partition plan, which divided the Palestine mandate
into separate Jewish and Arab states.[6] Instead, they were seized by
Jordan and Egypt, which encouraged terrorist attacks upon Israeli
settlements by Palestinian Arabs called "fedayeen" who were recruited from the refugee camps which had been set up to house the
Palestinians who had fled the fighting in 1948. The refugees were unable to return home because the Arab states refused to make a peace
settlement with Israel lest it legitimize Israel's presence in the Middle
East and because of Israel's fear that the refugees would be a fifth
column within its borders. The fedayeen attacks escalated in 1955 and
1956 to the point where they became a prime cause of the Israeli attack
on Egypt in the 1956 Suez war. Following the Egyptian defeat in the
war, fedayeen activity slackened considerably—a development that
had also been helped by the establishment of a UN force between Egypt
and Israel—until the radical wing of the Ba'ath Party seized power in
Syria in 1966.

The new Syrian regime espoused not only the need for the Socialist transformation in Syria and close cooperation with the Soviet Union
but also military and financial assistance for the Fatah guerrillas led
by Yasir Arafat, who had begun a series of terrorist attacks against
Israel. These attacks placed the narrowly based Ba'ath regime in
danger of retaliatory attacks by Israel, which might have caused its
fall, and in order to avoid such a possibility the Soviet leadership
urged the other Arab states, especially Egypt, to join together with
Syria against the "imperialists" and Israel. This was the theme of
the visit of Soviet Premier Kosygin to Cairo in May 1966, during

which he called for a united front of progressive Arab states "such as
the United Arab Republic, Algeria, Iraq and Syria to confront imperialism and reaction."[7] In November 1966, the Arab united front sought
by the Soviet Union began to take shape as Egypt and Syria signed a defensive alliance, and the Soviet leaders may have hoped that this would
deter any major Israeli attack on Syria.[8] Nonetheless, the Syrian
government seized on the alliance to step up its support for Palestin-
iian guerrilla attacks on Israel, and by April 1967 the Syrian-Israeli
and Jordanian-Israeli borders had become tinderboxes.

The Israelis had initially restricted themselves to retaliatory
raids against the Jordanians, through whose territory the guerrillas
had come from Syria, but in early April they decided to retaliate directly against the Syrians, and, following the Syrian shelling of Israeli
farmers from the Golan Heights, the Israeli air force took to the skies
to silence the Syrian artillery and in the process shot down seven Syrian jets that had come to intercept them. This defeat was a major
blow to the prestige of the Syrian government, and, when coupled with
anti-Ba'ath rioting led by Moslem religious leaders in early May, it
appeared that the shaky Syrian Ba'athist government was about to fall.
These developments led the Soviets, who were concerned about the
collapse of their main Arab ally in the Middle East and the center of
anti-Western activity, to give false information to the Egyptians that
Israel was planning a major attack on Syria. Egyptian President Nasser, then at the low point of his prestige in the Arab world, apparently
seized upon this opportunity to regain some of his lost prestige and
again appear as the champion of the Arabs by ordering the UN forces
to leave their positions between Israel and Egypt and by moving Egyptian troops to the borders of Israel. In addition, he blockaded the
Straits of Tiran to Israeli shipping and, at the end of May, signed a
military alliance with his erstwhile enemy, King Hussein of Jordan.
Following the military encirclement of Israel, it appeared that war
was only a few days away, and on the morning of June 5, 1967, the
Israelis decided to strike before they were attacked. In the course
of six days, the Israelis succeeded in defeating the armies of Egypt,
Syria, and Jordan and capturing the Sinai Peninsula, the Jordanian
section of the West Bank of the Jordan river, and the Golan Heights
in Syria.[9]

SOVIET ATTITUDES TOWARD THE
PALESTINIAN GUERRILLAS

The massive Arab defeat in the Six-Day War led to the rapid
growth of Palestinian terrorist organizations which, by launching attacks (most of them unsuccessful) against Israel from Lebanon and

Jordan soon captured the imagination of an Arab public still shocked
by the defeat of the regular Arab armies by Israel. As the Palestinian guerrilla organizations increased in power, they began actively
competing with each other for recruits, funds, and prestige, while at
the same time increasingly becoming a challenge to the established
governments in the Arab world, particularly those of Jordan and
Lebanon, where large numbers of Palestinian refugees were located.[10]
While the Soviet leadership initially played down the significance of
the guerrilla organizations because it preferred to work through the
established Arab states, the Soviets could not long overlook either the
growing power of the Palestinian guerrilla movement as a factor in
Middle Eastern politics or the growing involvement of the Communist
Chinese in the movement. By providing military equipment and ideological training to a number of the guerrilla organizations, the Chinese
were seeking to increase their influence in the Middle East through
the guerrilla movement,[11] and, by early 1969, the Soviet leadership
evidently decided that it had better get involved with the guerrillas itself. It did so in a cautious manner, however, and it was not until
after the death of Nasser and the severe beating taken by the Palestinians in the Jordanian civil war that the Soviet Union began to court
the guerrillas in a serious manner.

The first evidence of a changed Soviet position toward the Palestinian guerrilla organizations came on February 18, 1969, when a
TASS press release, issued at the Soviet mission to the United Nations,
termed the Palestinian Arab terrorist activity assisted by the Arab
states a "liberation struggle" against Israel and described this "struggle of peoples against invaders and occupiers" as a "just struggle"
from the viewpoint of international law.[12] This TASS statement was
of particular importance since it appeared to contradict the Soviet
position enunciated less than two months earlier by the Soviet representative to the United Nations, Yaakov Malik. In a speech to the
Security Council on December 31, 1968, dealing with the definition of
the term "aggression," Malik had stated:

> If a state helps armed bands which are being orga-
> nized on its territory and which then proceed to the
> territory of another state to attack it, that kind of
> action must be regarded, from the point of view of
> international law, as aggressive action, and this,
> in fact, is the qualification given in the Soviet defi-
> nition of aggression proposed in 1956.[13]

In an effort to correct the apparent disparity in their position,
the Soviet Union submitted another definition of aggression to the
United Nations one week after the TASS statement. In the new defini-

tion, the Soviet leaders revised Malik's earlier statement by terming attacks by guerrilla bands operating from the territory of one nation against another only "indirect aggression":

> The use by a state of armed force by sending armed
> bands, mercenaries, terrorists or saboteurs to the
> territory of another state and engagement in other
> forms of subversive activity involving the use of
> armed force with the aim of promoting an internal
> upheaval in another state or a reversal of policy in
> favor of the aggressor shall be considered an act
> of indirect aggression.[14]

Qualifying even this weakened definition still further, Article 6 of the Soviet definition stated:

> Nothing in the foregoing shall prevent the use of
> armed force in accordance with the Charter of the
> United Nations, including its use by dependent peo-
> ples, in order to exercise their inherent right of
> self-determination.[15]

As if to underscore the altered Soviet stand on Palestinian terrorist activity, Pravda, on February 27 (one day after the submission of the new Soviet definition of aggression to the United Nations) supported a Palestinian terrorist attack against an Israeli airliner at the Zurich airport that killed the copilot and wounded the pilot as an "act carried out by patriots defending their legitimate right to return to their homeland."[16] The same article denounced the Israeli policy of reprisal against Arab states harboring the terrorists and offered a rather novel interpretation of international law to term the Israeli reprisals illegal:

> Reprisals as such are recognized in international law
> as a means of self-defense by a state against illegal
> activities of another state only within a limited frame-
> work, without the use of armed force. Therefore,
> the statement by Israeli officials about reprisals for
> the actions of partisans cannot be regarded as valid,
> since, according to international law, no state can be
> held responsible for the actions of citizens of another
> country on the territory of a third state.[17]

The Soviet Union, in less than two months, had thereby almost totally changed its position on the legality of Palestinian terrorist attacks against Israel.

The constituent members of the PLO stepped up the pace of their terrorist attacks against Israelis both in Israel and in Western Europe throughout 1969, and Israel adopted a policy of retaliation against the terrorist bases in Jordan and Lebanon. The Soviet Union, meanwhile, stepped up its support of the Palestinian guerrilla organizations, although the Soviet leadership made an attempt to fit the guerrillas into its overall strategy of weakening the Western position in the Middle East. Thus, at the seventh World Trade Union Congress in Budapest in October 1969, Soviet trade union boss and Politburo member Alexander Shelepin came out strongly in support of the guerrillas:

> We consider the struggle of the Palestine patriots
> for the liquidation of the consequences of Israeli ag-
> gression a just anti-imperialist struggle of national
> liberation and we support it.[18]

By stressing the term "liquidation of the consequences of Israeli aggression," however, Shelepin was manipulating the meaning of the guerrilla organizations' fight to coincide with the Soviet-backed UN Resolution 242, which called for the withdrawal of Israeli troops from "occupied territories," a solution to the Palestinian refugee problem, and the right of all states in the region (including Israel) to exist within secure and recognized borders. By contrast, the guerrilla organizations were unanimous in proclaiming their intention to liquidate Israel itself rather than aid the Arab states in recovering the land lost to Israel in 1967. By the end of 1969, however, after observing how clashes with the guerrillas had shaken both the Lebanese and Jordanian governments, the Soviet leadership may have begun to envision the Palestinian movement as a useful tool for weakening or even overthrowing the two pro-Western regimes, and replacing them with governments more friendly to the Soviet Union.[19]

In February 1970, Arafat, who had replaced Ahmed Shukeiry as head of the PLO after the 1967 war, was invited to Moscow, but the visit was kept low-key, as the invitation came from the Soviet Afro-Asian Solidarity Organization rather than from a higher-ranking organ of the Soviet government. The next month, however, Arafat was given a high-level reception in Peking, and the Palestinian guerrilla leader warmly praised the Chinese for their assistance. As Sino-Soviet competition for the allegiance of the guerrillas grew, the Soviet leadership decided that its position would be improved if the Communist parties of the Middle East were to form their own guerrilla organization that would be able to participate in and they hoped, influence, the PLO from the inside. Consequently, the Communist parties of Lebanon, Syria, Jordan, and Iraq formed the Ansar guerrilla organization in March 1970, but, as a Jordanian Communist party member was to complain two years later, Ansar had very little influence in the guerrilla movement. [20]

One of the greatest problems plaguing the PLO was the sharp competition among its constitutent organizations for power. Some guerrilla groups, such as the Popular Front for the Liberation of Palestine (PFLP) and the Popular Democratic Front for the Liberation of Palestine (PDFLP), were avowedly Marxist. Others, such as Asiqa (Syria) and the Arab Liberation Front (Iraq), were the instruments of Arab governments. Still others, such as al-Fatah, the largest, proclaimed themselves ideologically neutral and were willing to accept aid from all sides. By June 1970, the intra-Palestinian struggle for power had reached a peak with the PFLP openly challenging al-Fatah's leadership and seeking to bring down the regime of King Hussein in Jordan as well. By this time the guerrillas had established a virtual state within a state in Jordan, and the compromise agreement worked out in June between Hussein and the guerrillas testified to their growing power. The acceptance by Hussein of the U.S.-sponsored cease-fire agreement (Egypt and Israel had also agreed) in August set the stage for the final showdown. Fearing that the Palestinian cause would be overlooked in a direct settlement between Israel and Jordan and Egypt and feeling that the time had come to topple the Hussein regime, the PFLP embarked on a hijacking spree that resulted in the flying of three hijacked passenger planes to a guerrilla-controlled airstrip in northern Jordan and their demolition, while the troops of Hussein, which had surrounded the guerrilla airstrip, looked helplessly on. [21]

Hussein seized on this opportunity to end the guerrilla threat to his regime and began military attacks on the guerrillas. While his army was in the midst of attacking the guerrilla positions, the Syrian government, then headed by Salah Jedid, dispatched an armored brigade to help the guerrillas. At this juncture the United States moved the Sixth Fleet toward the battle area and, acting jointly with Israel, threatened to intervene if the Syrian forces were not withdrawn, as both Kissinger and Nixon clearly indicated that they would not permit the pro-Western regime of Hussein to be ousted by the invasion of a client state of the Soviet Union. [22] The Soviet leadership during this period was conspicuous by its inaction, and either for this reason, or because of the strong U.S.-Israeli stand, or, most probably, because he saw a chance to embarrass Jedid, General Assad, who controlled the Syrian air force, refused to dispatch Syrian jets to fly covering missions for the Syrian tanks. The result of Assad's decision was that the Jordanian air force and tank units badly mauled the invading Syrian army, which was forced to retreat in disarray to Syria. The emboldened Hussein then turned to finish off the guerrillas and had almost completed the job when an Arab League cease-fire arranged by Nasser went into effect. It was to be the Egyptian president's last act as an Arab leader, however, because the next day he died of a heart attack, an event that was to lead to a transformation of the Soviet position in the Middle East. As a result of the fighting, the Palestinian guerrillas suffered a major erosion of their political and military power in Jordan, and this process was to continue throughout 1971, as Hussein appeared intent on ending the PLO threat to his regime once and for all.

The spate of hijackings had other consequences, however, besides the decimation of the Palestinian guerrillas in Jordan. International opinion turned against the PLO, a development not overlooked by the Soviet Union, which nonetheless sought to blame Israel more than the PLO terrorists for the Middle East situation. Thus, in the midst of the hijackings, on September 17, Pravda termed them "regrettable" and went on to quote the British Communist daily Morning Star:

> The Palestinian guerrillas were incorrect in using the hijacking of civilian aircraft as a method of struggle, the British newspaper Morning Star wrote: "To condemn only one side and say nothing about the repressive acts of Israel, however, would be hypocritical. The Israeli occupationists' piracy and banditry on Arab territory they have seized exceeds the terrorist acts of the Palestinian extremist groups many times over."[23]

The Soviet position on hijacking was to change radically in mid-October, however, as Soviet vulnerability to hijacking was starkly underlined when two Lithuanian citizens, perhaps inspired by the deeds of the Palestinian hijackers, hijacked a Soviet domestic airliner, killing a stewardess and wounding the pilot and copilot. The Lithuanians flew the aircraft to Turkey and asked for and received political asylum.[24] While the Soviet Union had termed the terrorist attack on the Israeli airliner in Zurich in February 1969 a "patriotic act" and the Palestinian hijackings of September 1970 "regrettable," it was quick to call the two Lithuanians "criminal murderers."[25] Indeed, perhaps worried about Soviet vulnerability to hijackings, the Soviet Union supported the UN General Assembly Resolution of November 25 that called for the criminal punishment of hijackers and did so in the face of opposition from a number of Arab states, which claimed that the Resolution (which does not have the force of law) was aimed against them. O. Khlestov, director of the Soviet Ministry of Foreign Affairs Treaty and Legal Department, wrote an article in Pravda on

November 28, 1970, hailing the UN decision. Although his comments were directed specifically against the Lithuanian hijackers, they could also be seen as opposition against the Palestinian hijackers:

> Under the provisions of the resolution, any person who has hijacked a plane is liable to punishment under criminal law in the state to which the plane was hijacked, or must be extradicted for punishment to the country from which the plane was hijacked. The resolution stipulates that the hijackers of aircraft making international flights—i.e. a flight from one country to another—and the hijacker of aircraft making flights over domestic air routes within the borders of a single country are equally liable to punishment or extradition. States whose laws specify no punishments for aircraft hijacking will enact appropriate legislation.
>
> Considering that aircraft hijackers have often defended their actions on the grounds that they were perpetrated for obtaining political asylum in another country, the resolution condemns without exception all acts whereby an aircraft is seized and thus makes all such persons liable to punishment regardless of the motives or pretexts on which the hijacking may have been based.
>
> The UN's adoption of a decision on the punishment and extradition of civil aircraft hijackers is a solemn warning to those who would perpetrate such criminal acts in disregard of passengers' lives and the interests of developing interstate relations. . . . The UN decision will undoubtedly help to stop aircraft hijackings and will promote the normal functioning of civil aviation. [26]

While on the one hand denouncing the hijacking of civil aircraft—perhaps because of its own unpleasant experiences with hijackers—the Soviet leadership nonetheless continued to strive to maintain links to the PLO, and articles sympathetic to the PLO were printed in the Soviet foreign affairs weekly New Times following battles between the PLO and Hussein's army in January and April 1971. [27] It was not until the major setbacks to Soviet influence in the Middle East in the late spring and early summer of 1971, however, that the Soviet leadership made a major move to obtain PLO support. In May 1971 the new Egyptian President Anwar Sadat purged the more pro-Soviet members of his government, such as Aly Sabry and Shaari Gomaa, who had tried to overthrow him. These events occurred at the time when Sec-

retary of State William Rogers was on a visit to a number of Middle
Eastern nations, including Egypt, and it appeared to many observers
at the time that the elimination of Sabry and Gomaa was a gesture to
the United States in the interests of improved relations.[28] Two months
later an even more serious blow to the Soviet position in the Middle
East occurred when a Communist supported coup d'etat against Sudanese President Jaafar Numeiri failed and precipitated a wave of anti-
Sovietism and anti-Communism throughout the Middle East.[29]

Meanwhile, as the Soviet position in the Middle East deteriorated
so too did that of the PLO, which was again mauled in battles with Hussein's forces in July 1971. Indeed, the PLO troops were so badly
beaten that many chose to cross the Jordan River and surrender to
the Israelis rather than be cut down by Hussein's troops. Thus, by
the fall of 1971, Arafat's forces were gravely weakened and the Palestinian guerrilla organizations were no longer the independent forces
in Arab politics that they once had been. At this point the Soviet government, through its Afro-Asian Solidarity Organization, again invited Arafat to visit Moscow. The following was Pravda's description
of the talks:

> The Palestinian and Soviet sides noted the importance
> of the unity of all progressive forces of the Arab world
> and the necessity for the further strengthening of their
> alliance with the true friends of the Arab people—the
> countries of the Socialist commonwealth. In this con-
> nection, emphasis was laid on the danger of attempts
> to undermine Arab-Soviet friendship, to split the
> ranks of the Arab anti-imperialist movement, and to
> tear it from the common anti-imperialist front. These
> attempts inflict damage on the Arab People's libera-
> tion aspirations and national interests and serve only
> the interests of international imperialist and Zionist
> circles.[30]

While the Soviets were now trying to enlist Arafat and his organization in their renewed drive for influence in the Arab world, the
Palestinian guerrillas also stood to gain from his visit. Following
his return from Moscow, Arafat stated that the talks with the Soviet
leaders had been "very successful" and that he had found the Moscow
climate "warmer" than it had been on his visit in 1970.[31] The situation had changed markedly for both sides since that time. Because
the guerrillas were now in far greater need of Soviet support, the
Soviets may have assumed that the PLO would be more open to Soviet
influence. Consequently, although the Communist Chinese continued
to back the PLO (a delegation from al-Fatah went to Peking two weeks

prior to Arafat's visit to Moscow and got a pledge of continued Chinese assistance from Chou En-lai), [32] the Soviets, by reportedly pledging training, medical care, and equipment to the Palestinians, seemed for the first time to be attempting to bring them under the Soviet wing, as well as using them to help stem the tide of anti-Sovietism and anti-Communism that had swept through the Middle East following the abortive coup d'etat in the Sudan.

CONTINUING SOVIET SUPPORT OF THE PLO

The Soviet Union continued its support of the PLO throughout 1971 and during the first half of 1972, even as the Black September organization, an offshoot of al-Fatah, carried out a number of terrorist actions, including the assassination of Jordanian Prime Minister Wasfi Al-Tall, and Japanese terrorists, allied to the PFLP, slaughtered 26 Puerto Rican pilgrims at Israel's Lod airport. The Soviet goal was to forge the PLO, which still had wide appeal among the Arab masses, into a leading force in the "anti-imperialist front" the Soviet leadership was trying to create in the Middle East. This process was sharply accelerated following the expulsion of the Soviet Union from its military bases in Egypt in July 1972, as it appeared that Sadat had begun to switch his allegiance to the United States in an effort to obtain an Israeli withdrawal from the Sinai desert—something the Soviet Union had proved unable to do by diplomacy and seemed unwilling to do by force. Arafat was visiting Moscow at the time of the enforced Soviet exodus from Egypt and Pravda, on July 28, cited the PLO's statement of their appreciation of Soviet support for the Palestinian cause and their declaration that

> all attempts by the imperialist and reactionary circles to disrupt the friendship between the national liberation forces in the Arab world and the Soviet Union and other socialist states are incompatible with the interests of the Arab peoples. [33]

In return for their ringing endorsement of Soviet policy toward the Arab world, Arafat's group for the first time reportedly got direct shipments of Soviet arms (hitherto they had gone to the Arab governments on whose soil PLO units were stationed)[34] as well as much greater Soviet press coverage in their struggle against Israel and the antiguerrilla elements in Lebanon. In an extensive feature article in Pravda on August 29, Pavel Demchenko described the history of the growth of the guerrilla movement and bitterly attacked Israel for its mistreatment of the Palestinians. Perhaps hoping to maintain the So-

viet tie to the Hussein regime in Jordan, however, Demchenko made
no direct mention of Hussein's bloody destruction of the guerrilla
movement in his country in September 1970 and July 1971. The Soviet
journalist was, however, critical of "acts of desperation" such as the
hijacking of passenger planes and the blowing up of nonmilitary targets,
which did "serious damage to the entire Palestinian Resistance Movement and made its support by progressive and democratic forces more
difficult."[35]

Demchenko was also critical of the right-wing and anarchistic
groups in the Palestinian movement, which he considered tools of the
Israelis and Arab reactionaries who were "using them to set a barrier
on the path to organizational and political unity." Demchenko's solution to the dilemma of the Palestinians and their relative ineffectiveness, which he candidly admitted, was the unification of the Palestinian resistance in the framework of a national front similar to the policy the Soviet leaders were promoting in Syria and Iraq:

> The facts indicate that the forces of imperialism and
> reaction have clearly stepped up their activity in the
> Arab East recently, setting themselves the goal of
> weakening the national liberation struggle of the Arab
> peoples and liquidating the Palestinian Resistance
> movement. Naturally, this creates new difficulties
> for the movement and insistently confronts it with a
> number of cardinal problems, problems that are now
> being widely discussed by the progressive Arab pub-
> lic.
>
> Among these problems is the determination, on
> the basis of the actual correlation of forces, of the
> place and role of the Palestinian movement in the
> common front of the Arab peoples. What is involved
> here, among other things, is cooperation with the
> progressive Arab governments in the struggle for
> the elimination of the consequences of the Israeli ag-
> gression, the settlement of the Near East crisis,
> and the liberation of the occupied territories. This
> calls for advancing slogans and setting tasks corres-
> ponding to each stage of the struggle, i.e., for the
> delineation of strategic and tactical tasks. Faik War-
> rad, a member of the Palestine National Council, has
> written as follows on this score:
>
>> The experience of the Arab people of Palestine
>> and of other peoples indicates that the policy of
>> "all or nothing" does not serve the people's in-

terests. Every true revolutionary must take
into account the alignment of forces and their
correlation at every separate stage and, consequently, must distinguish what is possible and
realistic from what is impracticable.

This task can be fulfilled only after the unification
of the ranks of the Palestinian movement within the
framework, for instance, of a national front with a
political program that will take into account the diver-
sity of the situation and of the forms of struggle and
will help to begin work among the Palestinians in occupied territory and among the refugees, especially
in Jordan, since without a mass base the movement
cannot develop.

The first shifts in this direction have already become evident. At a session held in Cairo several
months ago, the Palestinian National Council came
out for the unification of the resistance movement.
Since that time, the movement's press has been unified, and a single information agency has been set
up. In July the Soviet Union was visited by a PLO
delegation headed by Yasir Arafat, the chairman of
its executive committee. During the talks that took
place, the PLO representatives reported that at
present the consolidation of the ranks of the Palestinian resistance is continuing and its unity growing
stronger on a progressive anti-imperialist basis.
. . . Recent facts make it possible to draw the conclusion that attempts to isolate the Palestinian movement, to assign it a special mission in the Arab
East, are receding into the past. What is gaining
the upper hand is the realization that a just solution
to the Palestine problem can be achieved only within
the framework of a common liberation struggle of
the Arab peoples and that the natural allies of the
Palestinian resistance movement are the Arab and
international progressive forces, the Soviet Union
and other socialist countries.[36]

Despite this extensive advice, however, it appeared that neither
the Soviet Union's national-front approach nor its attempts to forge an
anti-imperialist movement in the Middle East with the PLO as one of
its important elements would succeed in arresting the steady deterioration of the Soviet position in the region. Indeed, there is no telling

how much further this process would have gone had not a group of Palestinian terrorists killed 11 Israeli athletes at the Olympic games in Munich and set off a chain of events that greatly upset the pattern of Egyptian diplomacy and gave the Soviets an excellent opportunity to strengthen their position in the Middle East.

The immediate effect of the terrorist acts in Munich struck a major blow at Sadat's hopes of persuading the Western European and U.S. leaders to bring pressure on Israel to withdraw its troops from occupied Egyptian territory. Hardest hit were Egypt's relations with West Germany. Willy Brandt, whose government had painstakingly negotiated the resumption of diplomatic relations with Egypt less than three months earlier (after a seven-year break following West Germany's establishment of diplomatic relations with Israel in 1965), criticized the lack of Egyptian assistance in his efforts to negotiate a settlement with the terrorists. The United States, whose close alignment with Israel Sadat had hoped to sever by his expulsion of the Soviets, stood even more strongly behind the Israeli government following the Munich massacre. Indeed, the U.S. ambassador to the United Nations, George Bush, exercised a rare U.S. veto when a Security Council resolution condemning Israel for its reprisal raids against Palestinian guerrilla bases in Syria and Lebanon following the Munich killings did not also condemn the terrorist acts that had provoked them.

The Israeli government was under great domestic pressure to avenge the murders and did not hesitate long. Having suffered a similar terrorist attack at Lod airport only three months earlier, the Israelis apparently decided to attempt to strike a telling blow against the guerrillas by launching a series of air strikes deep into Lebanon and Syria against suspected terrorist bases. The air assault was followed a week later by an armored strike into Lebanon aimed at destroying as many guerrillas and guerrilla bases as possible. Lebanese and Syrian resistance was relatively ineffectual as the Israeli forces roamed at will in the two countries. Three Syrian bombers, counterattacking Israeli positions in the Golan Heights, were shot down. Nonetheless, the Israeli assaults, coming on the heels of similar although far more restricted ground strikes into Lebanon following the Lod massacre in June, served once again to underline Syria's vulnerability in relation to Israel, as did numerous statements by Israeli leaders, such as Deputy Premier Yigal Allon, that Israel would henceforth take "active measures" to "deny the Arab terror organizations the necessary bases, facilities and other assistance in their inhuman war."[37]

The Soviet Union seized the opportunity presented by the Israeli attacks to launch a special airlift of weapons to Damascus to reinforce the Syrian defenses. This airlift, which generated front-page headlines in both the Arab and the Western press, underscored the Soviet argument that the Arabs would only turn to the Soviet Union in time of need.

Following the Israeli attacks on Lebanon and Syria, the Soviets warned the Arabs that they could expect further Israeli attacks and that they could not hope for support from the West. An editorial in New Times pointedly stated:

> By bombing Palestinian refugee camps in Lebanon and Syria and villages in these countries and Jordan, killing and maiming hundreds of civilians, Tel Aviv has again shown the world the brigand nature of its policy. And its spokesmen let it be known that they do not mean to rest content with this. They openly threaten further aggressive action against Arab countries. None other than Israel's Chief of General Staff, General Elazar, has declared that air strikes "are not the only means" his army has used and continues to use. Another member of the Israeli command, asked by a newsman whether Egypt might come under attack, replied "I will answer with an Arab proverb—everyone in his turn."
>
> Public opinion in the Arab countries is drawing the inference from Israel's provocative actions which the imperialists are encouraging. What if not encouragement is the US veto in the Security Council on a resolution condemning Tel Aviv's barbarous acts? All of it is helping the Arabs to realize how illusory are hopes that the imperialists are prepared to help curb the Israeli expansionists and eliminate the consequences of their aggression. And the danger of such illusion is greater than ever now. For Tel Aviv is using them not only to hold on to the occupied territories but to make new aggressive moves against the Arab states.[38]

The Russians also utilized the Israeli attacks on the Palestinian guerrilla camps to dramatize their position as supporters of the Palestinians and thus to win more influence in the Palestinian resistance movement. While the Western press unanimously condemned the Munich murders, the Soviet press was far more moderate in tone, referring to them only as a "tragic incident."[39] The Soviets, however, denounced the Israeli attacks on Palestinian refugee camps (which often housed guerrilla bases), while most of the Western press accepted the Israeli raids as legitimate reprisals for the Munich mas-

sacre. The Soviets underlined their concern for the Palestinian cause
at this crucial time by airlifting medical supplies to Lebanon to help
treat the victims of the Israeli attacks, and the guerrillas again claimed
that the Soviet Union was shipping them arms directly. [40] Although
they had been receiving an increasingly sympathetic treatment in the
Soviet press, the Palestinian movement also again came in for some
Soviet advice. V. Kornilow, in a feature article in New Times, continued the Soviet criticism of such extremist groups as Black September and once again emphasized the need for unity among the Palestinians, although his discussion of the possibilities for unity was less optimistic than the pre-Munich Soviet commentaries on the Palestinian
movement had been:

> What the extremist groups have done and are still do-
> ing has not brought about any change for the better in
> the tragic lot of the Palestinians. Nor could it. On
> the contrary, what they have done, paradoxical as it
> might seem, has been grist to the mill of the Zionist
> ringleaders. Tel Aviv exploits the acts of terror per-
> petrated by the Palestinian extremists to pass off its
> pre-planned acts of aggression against Lebanon and
> Syria as "retaliation," and to step up its propaganda
> campaign against the Palestinians and Arabs general-
> ly, a campaign the Western bourgeois press has
> joined. All this damages the prestige of the Palestin-
> ian movement, and seriously. . . .
>
> In short, despite Israeli terror, despite the ma-
> chinations of imperialism and Arab reaction, a trend
> is emerging, albeit with difficulty, towards the grad-
> ual consolidation of the Palestinian resistance move-
> ment. There is an increasing awareness within the
> PLO that for the Palestinian movement to achieve any
> measure of success it needs a clear cut political pro-
> gram which, proceeding from reality, would set ex-
> plicit, feasible tasks. Most leaders of the various
> Palestinian organizations are coming to see more
> and more distinctly that both the extremism of cer-
> tain groups like the Black September organization
> and the attempts of reactionaries in the Arab world
> to harness the Palestinian movement to their own
> interests are equally prejudicial to the cause for
> which many Palestinian Arabs are ready to give
> their lives—the liberation of Israeli-occupied terri-
> tory. [41]

All in all, thanks to the Munich massacre and the sharp upsurge in fighting between Israel and the Arabs that followed it, the Soviet position in the Middle East had improved from its low point in early September, as the Arabs felt more dependent on Soviet military supplies for their sharpening conflict with Israel. Indeed, even Sadat had felt the need to seek an improvement of relations with the Soviet Union, and he fired General Mohammed Sadek, his defense minister and an outspoken critic of the Soviet Union, as a gesture to the Soviets. The Soviet leadership may have concluded from this that a limited degree of warfare in the region was a net bonus for the Soviet Union, as long as it did not escalate into a war between the two superpowers, since, during the period of relative Middle Eastern calm (September 1970 to September 1972), the Soviet position had deteriorated steadily. Indeed, the Soviet position had improved so much as a result of the post-Munich developments that on October 26, 1972, Numeiri, who had clashed so bitterly with the Soviets the year before over the abortive Communist supported coup d'etat against his regime, announced that the Sudan would restore full diplomatic relations with the Soviet Union by the end of the year. [42] In addition, the Soviet leadership must have welcomed the deterioration in relations between the Arabs and the West, particularly the United States and West Germany, which occurred after Munich. Interestingly enough, one of the comments made by the terrorists about the goals of their operation coincided with a similar objective of Soviet policy:

> The operation was aimed at exposing the close relations between the treacherous German authorities and United States imperialism on the one hand and the Zionist enemy's authorities on the other. [43]

UN DEBATE ON TERRORISM

While the Munich massacre led to an improvement in the Soviet Union's position in the Middle East, it also precipitated a heated debate in the United Nations on combatting terrorism, much as the Palestinian hijackings of civilian aircraft two years before had led to a discussion of the need to curb hijacking. In this case, however, with the Soviet Union in a relatively weaker position in the Middle East than it had been in 1970, it adopted a far less clear stand, probably in an effort to avoid antagonizing the more radical Arabs, on whom it had come to depend in the Middle East. Thus, the Soviet Union vetoed a compromise resolution worked out by France, Britain, Italy, and Belgium that would have both called for a cessation of military action in the Middle East (clearly meaning Israeli reprisal raids

against guerrilla bases in Lebanon and Syria) and condemned all acts
of terrorism.[44] In an appearance before the United Nations on September 22, Soviet representative Malik stated that the Soviet Union
was opposed to terrorism, particularly violent acts committed against
heads of state and diplomats in foreign countries. Interestingly enough,
however, instead of citing acts by Palestinian terrorists, he mentioned a number of what he called "terrorist acts" carried on by "Zionist activists" in New York against the Soviet mission to the United
Nations.[45] Malik also challenged the title of the draft Western European resolution, which called for "measures to prevent terrorism and
other forms of violence which endanger or take innocent human lives
or jeopardize fundamental freedoms." Malik claimed that such a resolution, if approved, could be used by "neo-colonialists to suppress
the liberation movements and to justify various barbarous forms of
violence in areas where armed conflicts are taking place."[46]

Soviet Foreign Minister Andrei Gromyko told the United Nations
that the Soviet Union opposed acts of terrorism and "acts of violence
that serve no positive ends and cause loss of human life."[47] Gromyko
went on to condemn both the "criminal actions" on the part of the
Munich terrorists and Israel's reprisal attacks, which he also termed
"criminal":

> It is certainly impossible to condone the acts of ter-
> rorism committed by certain elements from among
> the participants in the Palestinian movement that
> have led, notably, to the recent tragic events in Mu-
> nich. Their criminal actions deal a blow also at the
> national interests and aspirations of the Palestinians;
> these acts are used by the Israeli criminals in order
> to cover up their policy of banditry against the Arab
> peoples.[48]

Gromyko then summarized the Soviet position on terrorism, outlin-
ing in his statement the areas in which the Soviet Union was the most
vulnerable:

> The Soviet Union, from positions of principle, op-
> poses acts of terrorism that disrupt the diplomatic
> activity of states and their representatives, trans-
> port ties between them, and the normal course of
> international contacts and meetings.[49]

The Soviet leadership's fears regarding their country's vulnerability to international terrorism were most clearly expressed in an
exchange between Dmitry N. Kolesnik, a Soviet foreign ministry legal

expert, and Jamil M. Baroody, the outspoken representative of the
Saudi Arabian mission to the United Nations, who compared the Pales-
tinian terrorists to Robin Hood. In replying to Baroody's comments,
Kolesnik told the United Nations:

> I think the comparison is not accurate, especially
> with regard to the scale of danger which can be
> created by the modern terrorists. . . . Modern
> terrorists prefer to have rifles and bombs, and to-
> morrow it is quite probable they will have death-
> carrying germs or maybe stolen atomic bombs . . .
> and with the help of these bombs, they can blackmail
> any government. . . . The struggle against interna-
> tional terrorism is a common cause of all peace-
> loving nations. [50]

The Soviet representative went as far as to urge an international
treaty "to thwart criminal terrorism," although he rejected as "pre-
mature" a U.S. proposal that the United Nations convene a meeting
early in 1973 to consider the adoption of a convention to prevent and
punish terrorism. [51]

As the debate on terrorism continued, the majority of Afro-
Asian nations supported the demands of the Arabs that the United Nations explore the causes of terrorism rather than attempt to deal with
the terrorist acts themselves. The Soviet Union, in an obvious effort
to gain Arab support, sided with Arab demands, and the final vote was
76 to 35 with 17 abstentions to study the causes of terrorist acts rather than to draw up international legislation aimed at stemming the
acts of terrorism on the model of the antihijacking resolution of November 1970. The United States opposed the resolution, and Bush
warned that it had been drafted "in such a way as to be susceptible of
being interpreted as aimed at raising, rather than lowering, the level
of violence in our troubled world." [52]

Three months later, one Belgian and two U.S. diplomats were
murdered by Black September terrorists in the Saudi Arabian embassy
in Khartoum, the Sudan. Pravda, perhaps mindful of the vulnerability
of Soviet diplomats stationed abroad, condemned the killings but cited
Arab sources to demonstrate that its condemnation was not anti-Arab
or even anti-Palestinian:

> Such actions, in the opinion of numerous representa-
> tives of the Arab public, are doing great harm both to
> the Palestinian Liberation Movement and to the Arab
> countries' common struggle against the consequences
> of Israeli aggression. [53]

However, following Hussein's decision to execute the imprisoned
Black September terrorists whose release had been demanded by the
Black September organization in Khartoum, the Soviet Union appealed
to Hussein on "humanitarian grounds" to spare the lives of the terror-
ists. On March 9, 1973, Pravda printed the following appeal by the
Praesidium of the Supreme Soviet of the Soviet Union to Hussein:

> Guided by humanitarian considerations, the Praesi-
> dium of the USSR appeals to King Hussein to spare
> Abu Daoud, a prominent leader in the Palestinian re-
> sistance movement and other Palestinians arrested.
> . . . This humane act would be in keeping with the
> interests of uniting the patriotic forces of the Arab
> people in the struggle against Israeli aggression and
> would meet the approval of all friends of the Arab
> peoples. [54]

This sign of concern for the Palestinian terrorist leader was
yet another example of the Soviet Union's attempt to utilize the Palestinian guerrillas as a component part of an anti-Western front in the
Arab world. Indeed, at the end of November 1972, less than two
months after the Munich massacre, and while the UN debate on terrorism was still in progress, an all-Arab Popular Congress of the
Palestine Revolution was held in Beirut under the sponsorship of the
Arab Communist parties. This congress set up the Arab Front for
Participation in the Palestinian Resistance, and a declaration approved by the meeting pledged to "liquidate the imperialist presence
and its strategic and economic interests in the Arab homeland." [55]
Attending the conference were the Communist parties of the Arab
world, along with delegations from the Iraqi, Syrian, South Yemeni,
Algerian, and Egyptian governments and representatives of the Soviet Union and Soviet Bloc states in Eastern Europe. An editorial in
the February 1973 issue of the World Marxist Review hailed the formation of the Arab front:

> The formation, at a conference in Beirut last Novem-
> ber, of the Arab Front in support of the Palestinian
> Revolution, in which communists, revolutionary-dem-
> ocrats, and other patriotic parties and organizations
> of 14 Arab countries are represented, is evidence of
> the increasing cohesion of the anti-imperialist forces. [56]

While seeking to forge the Palestinian guerrillas into a component part of its anti-Western Middle East front, the Soviet leadership
also continued to exploit the effects of Palestinian terrorist activity,

much as it had done following the Munich massacre. Thus, when the
Israeli government, in the face of the rest of the world's unwillingness to take action against Palestinian terrorism, decided to take
preemptive action against the terrorists, the Soviet Union was quick
to exploit the Israeli action. On April 9, following a Palestinian terrorist attack on the home of an Israeli diplomat on Cyprus, Israeli
commandos raided Beirut and killed the three Palestinian guerrilla
leaders thought to be the masterminds of the terrorist campaign
against Israeli citizens in Europe and responsible for the murder of
the Israeli athletes in Munich. As might be expected, the Soviet Union
seized upon this incident to discredit the United States by linking it to
the Israeli action and to again urge the Arabs on to "anti-imperialist
Arab unity." Writing in New Times, Dmitry Volsky asserted:

> An examination of the Beirut provocation leads many
> observers to the conclusion that it was carried out
> with direct assistance from Western Secret Services.
> In its statement the Palestine Liberation Organiza-
> tion, for example, accused the CIA of complicity in
> the murders. . . .
> The need to unite on an anti-imperialist basis is
> one of the main conclusions of the Beirut events made
> by all progressive Arab opinion. The importance of
> unity is being stressed by papers in Cairo, Damascus
> and Baghdad. Unity is the motto of numerous pro-
> test manifestations now sweeping the Arab world.
> Concerted actions by the Arab peoples, with the sup-
> port of their friends, can create an insurmountable
> barrier in the path of Tel-Aviv's encroachments.[57]

Arab-Israeli tension continued to escalate following the Beirut
raid, and the Soviet Union underscored its support of both the Arab
states and the Palestinian guerrillas with shipments of arms as well
as by diplomatic support in the United Nations. The Soviet Union's
close ties to the Palestinian guerrillas was indicated in August 1973
when Arafat was an honored guest at the World University games in
Moscow[58] and the PLO was allowed to open an information office in
East Berlin.[59] In October, another major war between the Arabs
and the Israelis erupted—the fourth since the State of Israel was proclaimed in 1948. While initially appearing to profit enormously from
the war, given the Arab oil embargo against the United States and the
establishment of the "anti-imperialist Arab unity" they had so long
wanted, the Soviet leadership saw its improved position in the Middle
East begin to deteriorate following the war when Secretary of State
Kissinger worked out an Israeli-Egyptian disengagement agreement

without the help of the Soviet Union. In the process, Kissinger secured
the resumption of U.S.-Egyptian diplomatic relations, which had been
broken after the 1967 Six-Day War, and the steady stream of U.S. bus-
inessmen traveling to Cairo seemed to underscore the fact that Sadat
was once again moving toward the United States.

As U.S. influence in Egypt began to rise, despite Soviet warnings, the Soviet leaders sought to counter this by deepening their relationship with the PLO—one of the most anti-American forces in the
Middle East—by floating a trial balloon for the establishment of a Palestinian state. Thus, a joint communique issued with visiting Yugoslav leader Josef Tito that was published on the front page of _Pravda_
on November 16 stated that "the lawful national rights of the Palestinian Refugees must be implemented as part of a peace settlement."[60]
Five days later, Canadian Foreign Minister Mitchell Sharp commented
in a press conference after conferring with Soviet leaders that the Soviet Union would give the Palestinians strong support.[61] Then, on
October 22, Arab diplomats in Moscow stated that a PLO delegation
had met with Politburo members "at a very high level."[62] This burst
of Soviet activity on behalf of the Palestinians came just before the
Arab summit conference in Algiers called by Sadat to coordinate Arab
strategy and helped enhance the stature of the PLO at the conference,
which recognized the PLO as the "sole legitimate representative" of
the Palestinian people. In thus giving stronger backing to the Palestinians than ever before, it appeared as if the Soviet goal, in addition
to countering the U.S.-Egyptian rapprochement, was to establish a
Palestinian state on the West Bank of the Jordan River and in the Gaza
Strip. These areas, occupied by Israel since the 1967 war, had earlier been administered by Jordan (the West Bank) and Egypt (the Gaza
Strip) after the two Arab states had occupied the territories during
the 1948-49 Arab-Israeli war (instead of allowing them to be the basis
of a Palestinian Arab state as the UN Resolution of November 1947
had decreed).

It appears that the Soviets worked for the establishment of a
Palestinian state of limited size (they had to convince many Palestinians as well as the Western powers) not only to defuse the Arab-Israeli conflict (if this was their aim at all) but to secure another area
in the Middle East where they could exercise influence, along with
South Yemen, Iraq, Syria, and, to a lesser degree, Egypt, where
their influence was declining. It may have also been Soviet reasoning
that the location of a pro-Soviet regime in the midst of such pro-Western states as Israel, Jordan, and Lebanon would serve to further
weaken the position of the United States in the region while strengthening that of the Soviet Union.

Meanwhile, following the signing of the Israeli-Egyptian disengagement agreement, Kissinger embarked on the difficult task of

achieving a similar agreement between Israel and Syria. Despite two Palestinian terrorist attacks on Israeli settlements aimed at sabotaging the peace talks—one of them, at Maalot, killed 24 schoolchildren—Kissinger was ultimately successful and an agreement was signed at the end of May. Following the Syrian-Israeli agreement, President Nixon made a triumphant tour of the Middle East, much to the chagrin of the Soviets, and then traveled to Moscow for his third summit conference with Soviet leader Brezhnev. In their final conference communique, Brezhnev and Nixon issued the following statement:

> Both sides believe that the removal of the danger of war and tension in the Middle East is a task of paramount importance and urgency, and therefore, the only alternative is the achievement, on the basis of Security Council Resolution 338 (which ended the October war) of a just and lasting peace settlement, in which should be taken into account the legitimate interests of all peoples in the Middle East, including the Palestinian people, and the right to existence of all states in the area.
>
> As co-chairmen of the Geneva Peace Conference on the Middle East, the USSR and USA consider it important that the conference resume its work as soon as possible, with the question of other participants from the Middle East Area to be discussed at the conference. Both sides see the main purpose of the Geneva Peace Conference, the achievement of which they will promote in every way, as the establishment of a just and stable peace in the Middle East.
>
> They agreed that the USSR and the USA will continue to remain in close touch with a view to coordinating the efforts of both countries toward a peaceful settlement in the Middle East. [63]

Soviet propaganda highlighted the final communique's emphasis on the role of the Palestinians in a peace settlement in an effort to reinforce the Soviet Union's relations with the PLO as a counter to Sadat's Westward move and the possibility of a similar move by Syria. Gromyko had met with Arafat on a regular basis during the negotiations for the Syrian-Israeli disengagement agreement, and these meetings had been given prominence in the Soviet press. Despite their military weakness, the Palestinian guerrilla organizations still enjoyed a great deal of popularity among the more radical Arab states and among large sectors of the Arab public as well. Thus the Soviet leaders, just as after the October war, hoped that by

increasing their ties to the Palestinians they would strengthen a major
anti-Western force in the Middle East and reap the benefits of guerrilla popularity in the Arab world. For their part, the Palestinian
Arabs were now in greater need of Soviet aid than ever before because
the Israeli disengagement with Syria—which Palestinian terrorist
groups had tried to prevent with attacks on the Israeli settlements of
Qiryat Shemona and Maalot—had left the Palestinian Arabs alone, at
least for the time being, in their confrontation with Israel, despite
pledges of support from Arab leaders.

Following the Syrian-Israeli disengagement agreement, the Palestinian National Council convened in Cairo to determine the direction
of the Palestinian movement. The council was a quasi-parliamentary
organization composed of representatives from almost all of the various Palestinian organizations. After a great deal of debate, the Palestine National Council worked out a 10-point program, not all of
which was to the liking of the Soviet leadership.[64] In its first point,
the program rejected participation in the Geneva conference under
Resolution 242 as long as it dealt with the Palestinian Arabs only as
a "refugee problem."[65] The second point stated that the PLO would
struggle "by all means, fore-most of which is armed struggle, to
liberate Palestinian Land," while opposing any agreement with Israel.[66] Although disagreeing with the Palestinians' refusal to come to
Geneva or deal with Israel, the Soviet leadership warmly welcomed
the ninth point of the program, which stated that the PLO "will struggle to strengthen its solidarity with the socialist countries and the
world forces of liberation and progress to foil all Zionist, reactionary
and imperialist schemes."[67]

In commenting on the meeting of the Palestinian National Council, New Times correspondent Viktor Bukharov, citing Arab newspapers, indirectly rebuked the Palestinian guerrillas for rejecting participation in the Geneva conference and for other "extremist" positions.[68] In addition, Bukharov returned to an earlier Soviet theme,
arguing that unity was a vital necessity for the Palestinian guerrilla
organizations. While describing the Palestinian movement in generally favorable terms, Bukharov reserved his warmest praise for
the decision of the PLO executive to admit representatives of the Palestinian National Front.[69] This was a guerrilla organization made
up primarily of West Bank Arab Communists who, once dormant, were
now carrying out acts of sabotage against the Israelis. The admission
of the Palestinian National Front into the PLO executive drew warm
Soviet praise because it served as an example of both the success of
the national front strategy the Soviet leaders had been urging on the
Arab world and the way in which they could influence the PLO from
the inside.[70]

While the Soviet Union was exhorting the Palestinian guerrilla organizations to unify and warning them against "extremist positions," it was simultaneously exploiting the Israeli raids induced by guerrilla attacks to underline the "aggressive nature" of Israel and its ties to the United States. The Soviet goal in this maneuver was to prove to the Arabs that the Soviet Union was their only true friend. Pravda, on June 23, denounced Israeli attacks on the "peaceful inhabitants of Lebanon," comparing them to Nazi attacks during World War II, while branding as "absurd" Israel's justification for the attacks as responses to actions by the Palestinian guerrillas operating from Lebanon. Then, following an attack by Palestinian terrorists operating from the Lebanese port of Tyre against the Israeli coastal town of Nahariya in late June (the attack was timed to coincide with Nixon's arrival in Moscow), the Israelis retaliated with attacks against three Lebanese ports in an effort to deter the Lebanese government from granting naval staging areas to the terrorists. The Soviet leadership seized upon these Israeli attacks to offer aid to Lebanon and to pose again as the champion of the Arabs.[71]

As Arab-Israeli tensions heightened once again following the Palestinian terrorist raids against Israel and Israeli reprisals and preemptive attacks against the Palestinian guerrilla bases in Lebanon, the Soviet leadership may have hoped for a repetition of the situation of September 1972. At that time an anti-Soviet and pro-American trend was reversed by the massacre of Israeli athletes at Munich and the subsequent Israeli attacks on Lebanon and Syria, which made Soviet military aid a vital necessity for the Arab states. In any case, in early July 1974, an Arab League Defense Council meeting was called to deal with Israeli attacks on Lebanon, and Soviet comment on the conference hailed Arab "solidarity" in support of Lebanon while once again stressing support for the Arab cause.[72]

The Soviet leaders were not content, however, with merely encouraging Arab support of the Palestinians and the Lebanese in the face of Israeli reprisal attacks. With the reconvening of the Geneva peace conference under active discussion, the Soviet leaders continued their efforts to persuade the Palestinians to participate in the Geneva conference with the ultimate goal of creating a Palestinian Arab state on the West Bank and in Gaza. Izvestia correspondent Igor Belyaev wrote the following in a key article on the Middle East on July 9:

> Back in November 1947, the 1947 UN General Assembly adopted a resolution on the division of Palestine into two independent states—Jewish and Arab. Israel was created in 1948. The Arab Palestinian state never became a reality. . . .

> The Palestinian Arabs must now have the opportu-
> nity to decide their own fate. The Geneva Peace Con-
> ference on the Near East can and must be the most
> suitable place for a discussion of their legitimate
> rights. [73]

While the Soviet leadership thus came out more strongly than
ever before in favor of a Palestinian state and tried to win the Palestinian Arabs over to their point of view, the Soviet Union's relations
with Egypt again deteriorated, and the Soviet leaders utilized the Palestinian issue in an effort to isolate and embarrass Sadat because of
his increasingly close political and economic ties with the United
States. New Times correspondent Y. Potomov attacked Sadat for his
agreement with Hussein in mid-July that the Jordanian monarch and
not the PLO represented the Palestinians living in his kingdom—including the West Bank. While Sadat was later to change his position
on this matter, Potomov seized the opportunity to use the PLO and
Libyan leader Mu'ammar Quaddafi to demonstrate that Sadat was isolated from the mainstream of Arab thinking on the Palestinian question:

> The leaders of the PLO and several other Arab coun-
> tries disagree with the proviso contained in the com-
> munique on the recent talks between President Anwar
> Sadat of Egypt and King Hussein of Jordan that "the
> Palestinian Liberation Organization is the legitimate
> representative of the Palestinians with the exception
> of those dwelling in the Hashemite Kingdom of Jordan."
> The communique has been trenchantly criticized by
> the press in a number of Arab countries.
>   On July 23 PLO Executive Chairman Yasir Arafat
> met Libyan leader Muammar Kaddafi. According to
> Libyan newspapers, they were of one mind in noting
> that the Jordanian communique cut across the deci-
> sions of last year's Arab summit conference in Al-
> giers which recognized the PLO as the sole legiti-
> mate representative of the entire Palestinian people. [74]

The Soviet embrace of the Palestinian cause, which was part
of the overall Soviet strategy of encouraging anti-Western trends in
the Middle East, reached a new high at the end of July, when the Soviet leadership invited Arafat to come to Moscow. At the time of
Arafat's visit, the Soviet press gave unprecedented coverage to the Palestinian question, including a six-page report in New Times and a
3,700-word article in Izvestia. [75] During the talks with Arafat and

his delegation, the Soviet leaders again emphasized their recognition of the Palestinians as the "sole legitimate representative of the people of Palestine,"[76] thus indirectly attacking Sadat. According to the description of the talks in <u>Pravda</u>, the Soviet Union also expressed its support for the participation of the PLO at the Geneva conference "on an equal basis with the other participants" and agreed to the opening of a PLO mission in Moscow.[77] In return, the PLO delegation, which included a Jordanian Communist (probably as a sop to the Soviets) gave its usual lip-service praise of the Soviet Union for its "unvarying support and assistance" and for its "principled policy."[78]

As the Soviet Union stepped up its support for the Palestinians, it appeared to be Soviet strategy that the PLO could be the instrument to both isolate Sadat from the other Arab leaders and lead the anti-Western coalition in the Middle East. It seemed that the Soviet hope was to establish a radical, anti-Western Palestinian state on the West Bank and in Gaza, situated between pro-Western Lebanon, Israel, and Jordan, which would be dependent on Soviet military aid and diplomatic support. At the very minimum, the PLO, in pursuing its policies under Arafat's leadership, would be an effective anti-Western force in the Arab world even if it pursued its extremist aim of dismantling the State of Israel, because the United States continued to support Israel's right to exist. The Soviet strategy seemed to achieve a major success at the summit conference of Arab leaders at Rabat, Morocco, in October 1974, where the PLO was unanimously acclaimed as the "sole legitimate representative" of the Palestinian people. Interestingly enough, however, Soviet reporting of the Rabat conference stressed the importance of a speedy return to the Geneva peace conference,[79] while a number of the more radical groups within the PLO, such as George Habash's PFLP, angrily withdrew from the executive committee of the PLO because they claimed that Arafat was planning a deal with Israel.

CONCLUSION

In analyzing Soviet policy toward Palestinian terrorism in the period 1967-74, it is clear that there has been a steady progression in the Soviet Union's support of the PLO—the loose confederation of Palestinian terrorist groups dedicated to the destruction of the State of Israel and willing to use terrorist means to achieve their desired goal. At first the Soviet Union was hesitant about supporting the PLO, preferring to achieve its goal of eliminating Western influence from the Middle East by working through the established Arab governments. As the Palestinian terrorists increased in power, however, and as Communist China began to actively support them, the Soviet Union changed its position. Another major stimulus to the Soviet Union's decision to support the Palestinian guerrillas was the deterioration of the Soviet position in the Middle East following setbacks in Egypt and the Sudan in 1971 and 1972. This coincided with a weakening of the PLO position following Hussein's crackdown on the guerrillas in Jordan. Consequently, the Soviet Union and the PLO, because of their weakened positions, drew closer to each other. The PLO gained weapons and diplomatic support from the relationship while the Soviet Union gained an ally for its anti-Western and increasingly anti-Egyptian front of Arab states in the Arab world.

As the Soviet Union stepped up its support for the PLO, it was forced to modify its position toward international terrorism. Vulnerable because of its economic, political, and diplomatic interests all over the world, the Soviet Union had a clear interest in preventing the spread of terrorism lest Soviet interests be engulfed by it as well. Nonetheless, as the Soviet Union became more dependent on PLO support in the Arab world, its position on the various PLO acts of terrorism changed. Thus, when the Soviet Union enjoyed a strong position in the Arab world in 1970, it did not hesitate, despite Arab opposition, to openly condemn hijacking and work for a UN resolution opposing it— a development clearly inspired by the Soviet leadership's experience of having one of its own aircraft hijacked by two Lithuanians. Two years later, however, when the Soviet position in the Middle East had been weakened following the enforced exodus of Soviet troops from Egypt, the Soviet position changed. During the UN debate on terrorism prompted by the Munich massacre, the Soviet Union voted to support an Arab-sponsored resolution to study the causes of terrorism while opposing the draft resolution calling for action against the perpetrators of terrorist deeds.

One should also not overlook the fact that the Soviet Union profited, albeit indirectly, from the terrorist acts of the PLO at Munich. Given the world's reluctance to deal with terrorism, the Israeli government decided, in an effort to protect its citizens both at home and abroad, to attack the guerrilla bases in Lebanon and Syria. This, in turn, further inflamed the Arab-Israeli conflict and made the Arab states more dependent on Soviet military and diplomatic support. This enabled the Soviet Union to improve its weakened Middle East position as it capitalized on the major Israeli reprisal raids following the Munich massacre, much as it did following the Israeli assassination of Palestinian terrorist leaders in April 1973 in Beirut and Israeli reprisals following terrorist attacks at Maalot and Nahariyah in May and June 1974.

Throughout its relationship with the PLO, the Soviet leadership has sought to integrate the movement into its larger anti-Western front in the Arab world. In addition, it advised the PLO to give up its extremist positions, which alienated Western opinion, as well as certain of its terrorist actions, which were similarly counterproductive. Following the October 1973 war, the Soviet leadership began to advocate that the PLO establish its own state on the West Bank and the Gaza Strip. The Soviet leadership had two goals in mind. First, the proposed state would lie between Lebanon, Israel, and Jordan, all of whom were pro-Western in outlook and could be expected to oppose the new state, which was likely to engage in subversive acts against them. For this reason, the Palestinian state would be in need of Soviet support, and this would give the Soviet Union another foothold in the Arab world, and one that would partly make up for its losses in Egypt. Second, since the United States continued to support the existence of the State of Israel, the Soviet leadership probably considered it counterproductive to support the maximalist PLO goal of dismantling Israel, lest the Soviet Union jeopardize the benefits flowing to it from its detente with the United States—benefits that included U.S. technological assistance to the lagging Soviet economy and possible U.S. assistance, or at least neutrality, in the event of a major Sino-Soviet war.

The Soviet relationship with the PLO has thus been basically an exploitative one. The Soviet leadership has been attempting to exploit the activities of the PLO to improve the Soviet Union's position in the Middle East and weaken that of the United States. For its part, the PLO has proved only too willing to accept Soviet military aid and diplomatic support as it pursued its own goals. Nonetheless, the policy of supporting terrorism holds dangers for the Soviet Union, and, despite lip service to the contrary, the Soviet leadership is helping to foster and encourage international terrorism in general. Therefore, it cannot be ruled out that, in a climate of rising international terrorism, the Soviet Union, with its widespread economic, military, diplomatic, and political interests, may soon find itself the victim of the kinds of terrorist activity it has itself fostered.

NOTES

1. The terms "terrorist" and "guerrilla" are used interchangeably throughout this chapter. While one man's "terrorist" is another man's "freedom fighter," depending on the perspective taken, in this analysis the actions of the constituent elements of the PLO will be the central focus. Since these actions have included assassinations, bomb attacks against civilians, hijackings, and the taking of civilian hostages, the Palestinian guerrillas will be termed "terrorists" throughout this study.

For an excellent study of the origin and development of the PLO, see William B. Quandt, Faud Jabber, and Ann Mosely Lesch, The Politics of Palestinian Nationalism (Los Angeles: University of California Press, 1973). Other studies of the PLO and its constituent members include: Ehud Yaari, Strike Terror (New York: Sabra Books, 1970); Zeev Schuff and Raphael Rothstein, Fedayeen (New York: David McKay, 1972); and John Laffin, Fedayeen (New York: Macmillan, 1973). See also Gerard Chailand, The Palestinian Resistance (Baltimore: Penguin, 1972).

For a current study of international terrorism, see Terrorism, a Staff Study prepared by the Committee on Internal Security of the U.S. House of Representatives (Washington, D.C.: Government Printing Office, 1974).

2. Given a limitation of both space and access to classified research materials, this chapter can deal only with the public record of Soviet policy toward Palestinian terrorism. The Soviet secret police maintains a huge foreign espionage network, and there have been recurrent rumors that it has helped one or another of the constituent elements of the PLO. For a recent popular study of the Soviet secret police's foreign operations, see John Barron, KGB: The Secret Work of Soviet Secret Agents (New York: Reader's Digest Press, 1974). For scholarly studies of the domestic activities of the Soviet secret police, see Simon Wolin and Robert M. Slusser, eds., The Soviet Secret Police (New York: Praeger, 1957); and Robert Conquest, The Soviet Police System (New York: Praeger, 1968). For an excellent account of the Soviet secret police from one of its victims, see Alexander Solzhenitsyn, Gulag Archipelago (New York: Harper & Row, 1973).

3. For a survey of Lenin's comments on the utility of terror, see Stefan T. Possony, ed., The Lenin Reader (Chicago: Regenery, 1966), pp. 468-75.

4. For a discussion of the events of this period, see Robert Owen Freedman, "The Partition of Palestine: Conflicting Nationalism and Great Power Rivalry" in The Problem of Partition: Peril to World Peace, ed. Thomas Hachey (New York: Rand McNally, 1972), pp. 174-212.

5. "Fedayeen" in Arabic means "self-sacrifice."

6. For a discussion of these events, see Freedman, op. cit.

7. See the report by Hedrick Smith in the May 18, 1966 issue of the New York Times.

8. Pravda, on November 22, 1966, had the following comment about the treaty: "The defense treaty signed by the UAR and Syria is called upon to play an especially important role in rebuffing the intrigues of Imperialism and Arab reaction."

9. For a useful account of the developments leading to the 1967 war, see Walter Laqueur, The Road to Jerusalem (New York: Macmillan, 1968).

10. On this point, see Quandt et al., op. cit.

11. For analyses of the relations between China and the Palestinian guerrillas, see R. Medzini, "China and the Palestinians," New Middle East, no. 32 (May 1971), pp. 34-40; and Peking and the Palestinian Guerrilla Movement, Radio Free Europe Research Report, September 1, 1970.

12. Cited in Leon Romaniecki, The Arab Terrorists in the Middle East and the Soviet Union (Jerusalem: Soviet and East European Research Center of the Hebrew University of Jerusalem, 1973), p. 3. Romaniecki's study deals with the Soviet position in UN debates on the definition of "aggression," long a knotty problem in international law.

13. Cited in ibid., p. 3.

14. Cited in ibid., p. 10.

15. Cited in ibid., p. 25.

16. Pravda, February 27, 1969.

17. Translated in Current Digest of the Soviet Press 21, no. 9: 21. For a far more traditional view of reprisals under international law, see William W. Bishop, International Law (Boston: Little Brown, 1962), pp. 745-46.

18. Cited in Paul Wohl, New Soviet Revolutionary Stance in the Middle East, Radio Liberty Dispatch, May 25, 1970, p. 2.

19. For analyses of Soviet policies toward the guerrillas during this period, see Y. A. Yodfat, "Moscow Reconsiders Fatah," New Middle East, no. 13 (October 1969), pp. 15-18; and John K. Cooley, "Moscow Faces a Palestinian Dilemma," Mid East 11, no. 3 (1970): 32-35.

20. Naim Ashab, "To Overcome the Crisis of the Palestinian Resistance," World Marxist Review 15, no. 5 (1972): 75.

21. For a description of these events, see Malcolm Kerr, The Arab Cold War (New York: Oxford University Press, 1971), pp. 144-48.

22. For an analysis of U.S. policy during Hussein's clash with the guerrillas, see Robert J. Pranger, American Policy for Peace in the Middle East, 1969-1971 (Washington, D.C.: American Enterprise Institute, 1971), pp. 39-48.

23. Translated in Current Digest of the Soviet Press 22, no. 37: 12.

24. See the report in the October 16, 1970 issue of the New York Times.

25. Cited in ibid.

26. Translated in Current Digest of the Soviet Press 22, no. 48: 23-24. The Soviet leaders were later to cite this resolution to justify

the harsh penalties against Soviet Jews who allegedly plotted to hijack a Soviet airliner. See Pravda, January 1, 1971.

27. Compare R. Petrov, "The Events in Jordan," New Times, no. 4 (1971), pp. 6-7; and V. Kudryavtsev, "On the Way to Unity," New Times, no. 17 (1971), pp. 8-9.

28. For a description of these events, see Robert Owen Freedman, "Soviet Foreign Policy Toward the Middle East Since Nasser" in The Soviets in Asia, ed. Norton T. Dodge (Mechanicsville, Md.: Cremona Foundation, 1972), pp. 77-91; and Soviet Policy Toward the Middle East since 1970 (New York: Praeger Publishers, 1975).

29. Ibid.

30. Pravda, October 30, 1971. Translated in Current Digest of the Soviet Press 23, no. 44: 18.

31. Cited in a report in the New York Times, January 1, 1972, dealing with the Palestinian guerrillas.

32. Ibid.

33. Translated in Current Digest of the Soviet Press 24, no. 30: 17.

34. See the reports by Eric Pace in the New York Times, September 18 and 21, 1972.

35. Pravda, August 29, 1972. Translated in Current Digest of the Soviet Press 24, no. 35: 2.

36. Ibid., pp. 3-4.

37. Cited in a report by Francis Offner in the Christian Science Monitor, September 23, 1972.

38. New Times, no. 38 (1972), p. 1.

39. Pravda, September 7, 1972.

40. See the report by Eric Pace in the New York Times, September 22, 1972.

41. Y. Kornilov, "Meetings with the Fedayeen," New Times, no. 42 (1972), pp. 24-25.

42. New York Times, October 27, 1972.

43. For the "Declaration" on the Munich massacre by the Black September terrorist movement, see the Middle East Monitor 2, no. 18 (1972): 4-6.

44. New York Times, September 11, 1972.

45. Ibid., September 23, 1972.

46. Ibid.

47. Ibid., September 27, 1972.

48. Ibid.

49. Ibid.

50. Ibid., November 18, 1972.

51. Ibid.

52. Ibid., December 19, 1972.

53. Translated in Current Digest of the Soviet Press 9, no. 9: 23.

54. Translated in ibid. 25, no. 10:25.

55. See the report by Anan Safadi in the Jerusalem Post, December 1, 1972.

56. "Marching Together: The Role of the Communists in Building a Broad Alliance of Democratic Forces," World Marxist Review 16, no. 2 (1973): 112.

57. Dmitry Volsky, "The Beirut Crime," New Times, no. 16 (1973), pp. 12-13.

58. For a report on Arafat's visit to Moscow, see New Times, no. 35 (1973), p. 2.

59. New York Times, August 19, 1973.

60. Pravda, November 16, 1973.

61. Washington Post, November 21, 1973.

62. Ibid., November 23, 1973.

63. New Times, no. 28 (1974), p. 23.

64. A description of this meeting together with the 10-point program is found in the Middle East Monitor 4, no. 13 (1974): 3-4.

65. Ibid., p. 4.

66. Ibid.

67. Ibid.

68. Victor Bukharov, "Palestinian National Council Session," New Times, no. 25 (1974), p. 12.

69. Ibid., p. 13.

70. For a detailed description of the activities of the Palestinian National Front on the Israeli-occupied West Bank, see the report by Terrence Smith in the New York Times, August 23, 1974.

71. See the report by Juan de Onis in the New York Times, July 12, 1974.

72. Georgi Shmelyov, "Solidarity the Keynote," New Times, no. 28 (1974), p. 10.

73. Izvestia, July 9, 1974. Translated in Current Digest of the Soviet Press 26, no. 31: 2.

74. Y. Potomov, "Middle East Settlement: Urgent Task," New Times, no. 31 (1974), p. 22.

75. New Times, no. 32 (1974), pp. 26-31; Izvestia, July 30, 1974. New Times also printed a front-page editorial supporting the PLO and a two-page interview with Arafat, who hailed the Palestine National Front and warmly praised the Soviet Union for its aid.

76. Pravda, August 4, 1974.

77. Ibid.

78. Ibid.

79. Pravda, October 29, 1974.

PART

III

ASIA AND AFRICA

7

POLITICAL VIOLENCE IN THE SOUTH ASIAN SUBCONTINENT
Saleem Qureshi

WHAT IS TERRORISM?

Terrorism is the use of violence in order to induce a state of fear and submission in the victim. The object of terrorism is to secure a change or modification in the behavior of the intended victim himself or to use him as an example for others. The violence of terrorism is the ultimate of coercion, whether actually applied or merely used as a threat. The use of terrorist violence is based on the assumption that the intended victim is unreasonable and incapable of seeing the viewpoint of the terrorist,[1] that the victim cannot be persuaded, but only compelled, in a manner by which he has absolutely no choice except to surrender. It is not necessary for violence to actually be used in order for it to be called "terrorism." The threat of the use of such violence, whether explicit or implicit, if it is perceived by the intended victim as likely to be actually carried out, also constitutes terrorism.

The questions of what specific acts constitute terrorism, which acts of terrorism are political, and which are simply crimes in terms of ordinary law have been difficult to define and to secure international consensus about, because of the differing perspectives and interests of different states. International consensus has been sought in order to prevent terrorists from seeking immunity in other states. The main obstacle to this has been the view of those states that have considered wars of national liberation and the violence of the suppressed or deprived as legitimate expressions of the right of self-determination and, therefore, violence and terrorism that accompany such wars as legitimate.

One of the earliest attempts at defining and categorizing acts of terrorism was made under the auspices of the League of Nations by

the 1937 Convention for the Prevention and Punishment of Terrorism.
The purpose of this convention was to make acts of terrorism crimes
against humanity that no state should condone on the grounds that the
acts are political in nature and directed only against a particular tyranny. Many states, sympathetic to decolonization movements, were
unwilling to support such a document, and though 24 states signed it,
only one ratified it, and it never came into force. The need for consensus has increased as acts of terrorism on behalf of political causes
have become more frequent. The antagonists of terrorism have
sought legal remedies while the supporters of the terrorists' causes
have emphasized political and social solutions. Thus, there is no
consensus even now, as none has been possible in the past, and none
seems likely in the near future.

The 1937 convention, however, is still helpful, for it attempts
to define terrorism and to categorize the acts that can be included in
the category of "terrorism." This is useful as it provides a meaningful frame of reference for this study. The convention defines as acts
of terrorism all "criminal acts directed against a state and intended
or calculated to create a state of terror in the minds of particular
persons, or a group of persons or the general public."[2] In the category of terrorism are included all acts as well as attempts that cause
death or bodily harm to heads of state or government, their spouses,
and other public figures; that cause damage to public property; that
endanger the lives of the public; and that deal with arms and ammunition for the commission of any of these offenses in any state.

This chapter, utilizing the 1937 convention's definition of terrorism and its categories, will deal with all acts of violence with a political, as against a personal, objective, whether individual or collective,
random or selective. Whether the objective was achieved, or was
achievable, or not in that particular manner or by that specific method
will not make the terrorist act more or less relevant within the frame
of reference of this chapter.

THE ASIAN DIMENSION

This chapter will deal with the subcontinent of South Asia,
whose major states are India, Pakistan, and Bangladesh, although
Sri Lanka (Ceylon), Nepal, even Burma, and sometimes Afghanistan
are also included. The subcontinent covers approximately 1.5 million square miles and is populated by roughly 750 million people.
Prior to 1947, the general designation for the area was "British India."

The subcontinent has been more a geographical than a political
entity. It has been home to a multiplicity of races, colors, religions,

and languages. It has been conquered by numerous outsiders, all of
whom, except for the most recent two, eventually merged themselves
into the native population, producing a more or less common social
and religious code. Among the two exceptions—the Moslems and the
British—the Moslems became Indians but not Hindus and the British
became neither and kept themselves apart. Thus, the history of modern India has been characterized by two essential cleavages—religious,
which separated Moslems from non-Moslems, and colonial, which
separated the natives from the Europeans. The resolution of the latter was achieved through political independence and that of the former
by a political division of the subcontinent, though on this point views
vary broadly depending upon the viewer. However, these two cleavages can account for almost all terrorist violence in the subcontinent
up to the time of independence. The religious antagonism has been
considerably reduced since independence, but it still exists and occasional religious violence does take place. The political cleavage has
also not been completely overcome, though the parties have changed—
national liberation agitators have replaced the departed colonial rulers
—and consequently the range and objective of political violence has
also changed. Prior to independence, the nationalists demanded the
removal of the political authority of the alien colonialist. Since then,
it has been the leaders of subnationalism who have been demanding the
separation of their territory and to that end have carried on intermittent violent and terrorist activities.

The political-ideological cleavage between the Communists and
the non-Communists has arisen since independence and has been the
major cause of large-scale terrorism and counterterrorism, especially in certain parts of the subcontinent.

Religion has always been an important factor in determining
moral values toward violence as well as attitudes toward people of
other religions. In the South Asian subcontinent two major religions,
Hinduism and Islam, have dominated the lives of the overwhelming
majority of people, and consequently their views on the use of violence
are important.

Among Moslems the use of force as an instrument of group policy has always been considered legitimate, and when used for religious
purposes it has been considered religiously meritorious. Mohammed,
the founder of Islam, though not fond of violence and coercion did not
hesitate from fighting wars or using force against rebels. The Islamic
dogma permits jihad (holy war) and even makes it a duty to use force
if Islam is in danger and encourages Moslems to convert the non-Moslem world into the Moslem world. Moslems have historically considered it meritorious to spread the word of God and their hegemony
far and wide, peacefully if possible, forceably if necessary. Thus,
the use of violence as well as opposition to violence by counterviolence

has been part of Moslem consciousness in terms of interactions with non-Moslems but also even among Moslems themselves.

The general view, particularly outside India, has been that Hindus are peaceful and consider nonviolence a terminal virtue. This view has been given even greater authenticity by Mahatma Gandhi and his personal identification on the one side with Hinduism and on the other with political campaigns, first in South Africa and later in South Asia, conducted without arms. There is also the absence of Hindu military activity for expansion beyond the frontiers of the subcontinent. Further, in the fourfold caste scheme of the Hindus, the apex of the pyramid is occupied by the caste identified with the absence of the use of physical force and violence. However, both in terms of sources of attitudes, such as religion and mythology, as well as in terms of recorded history, violence occupies a respectable position in the Hindu religion. Hindu behavior and mythology glorify virtuous men, gods, and demons who do not abhor violence; who resort to terrorism, such as kidnapping, deception, and extortion; and who take to war readily. The Hindu scriptures make it a pious duty to use violence, to even kill one's own kin, in the name of duty. One of the two greatest Hindu epics, the Mahabharata, tells the story of a great war, and the Bhagavad-Gita (The Song of God) is replete with divine arguments to kill the enemies of righteousness even if they are one's own kin.

The philosopher and statesman Kautalya and the sage Manu advocated the use of violence and terror. Kautalya, himself a Brahmin, engineered the downfall of the low-caste dynasty of Nandas in the fourth century B.C., put Chandragupta Maurya on the throne, and served him as prime minister. In his political classic Arthashastra, Kautalya advised the king about the systematic use of deception, violence, and internal espionage.[3] Manu described violence as an instrument of punishment "which in turn is declared to be the most important technique of power," for to Manu it was the fear of punishment that held the social order. Manu considered it a primary function of the king "to correctly measure and administer penalties in the form of violence and deprivations."[4] Sardar K. M. Panikkar, an Indian historian of considerable scholarly repute, has also asserted that there is no historical basis to the notion of Hindu nonviolence and that Hindus have used violence in the same way as any other group.[5]

Thus, both Hindus and Moslems have not only been prone to violence psychologically, religiously, and historically, but have also actually participated in the political violence that has taken place in South Asia. The motivations and objectives of the two groups seldom coincided and it may be argued that more political violence took place between the members of the two communities than between the colonialists and their opponents.

POLITICAL VIOLENCE AS AN INDICATOR
OF POLITICAL CLIMATE

Political violence, collective or individual, is closely related
to political life and "there has been a close connection between the
basic political process and the predominant forms of conflict."[6] The
nature and extent of violence emanates from political conditions, for
it is political conditions that determine what form and extent of violence
is necessary and possible. As one observer has remarked, "the character of collective violence at a given time is one of the best signs we
have of what is going on in a country's political life. The nature of
violence and the nature of society are intimately related."[7] Furthermore, "the extent of violence depends on politics in the short run as
well. Violence is not a solo performance, but an interaction. It is
an interaction that political authorities everywhere seek to monopolize,
control, or at least contain."[8]

The first modern terrorism took the form of colonialism:

> The most terroristic wars were, however, undoubtedly
> the colonial wars fought by the industrially and mili-
> tarily dominant European powers against less well pre-
> pared and less technically advanced native peoples as,
> for example, in India, China, the Sudan.[9]

In these colonial battles, countless natives were massacred and the
rest reduced to submission. The response of the native, whether immediate or delayed, was also terrorist because of his experience or
knowledge that colonialism was itself imposed through terrorism as
well as because of the nature of colonial rule, which came to be seen
as terrorist and unchanging. The reaction of the colonial regimes
has been the terrorism of repression, which has been particularly intensive because it generally involves the regime's response to a national revolutionary movement that itself resorts to terrorism. Thus,
a terrible competition in violence and cruelty is set in motion.[10]

As a result of colonialism, it can be argued, the modern political process in the subject countries started with violence and terrorism. Violence and terrorism remained constant and, in some ways,
formed the basis of the relationship between natives and colonialists
almost up to the end of colonialism. This relationship, based on coercion and terror, has become so deeply entrenched that it seems to
constitute even now the most effective political input and output in the
majority of the former colonies.

Colonialism in South Asia, though considered even benevolent
by some, was always seen as alien, and few natives identified with
it.[11] Terrorist violence is inherent in colonialism, for its authority,

whether for its imposition or for its sustenance, rests on brutal force
and has neither customary, traditional, religious, or kinship sanction
behind it. If the colonialist mingles with the conquered population and
both accept a common code, the colonialist ceases to be a colonialist
and becomes a native; but where the colonialist is physically different
from the native and keeps the distinction alive in order to distinguish
between the slave and the master, no identification takes place and the
main bond between the two groups remains coercive violence. On the
continents of Asia and Africa this has been the pattern of colonialism,
and most terrorist violence has been the result of the contest between
the two groups. The native used terror to weaken the resolve of the
colonialist to maintain his political structure and power by making the
price of this maintenance too high in terms of human lives. He also
used it to isolate the colonialist from his native supporters by making
their support costly due to their greater exposure to the terrorist.
The colonialists, in turn, used terror to silence and deactivate the
terrorist himself as well as to deter the would-be terrorist.

Colonial regimes are generally based on violence but do not necessarily and continuously use terror, because violence can occur
without terror though terror cannot occur without violence. The colonial regimes seek control of population and territory, not destruction,[12]
and use terror selectively against only those whose destruction is
considered necessary for control and as an example. This domination
has been "a form of interaction in which the superior generally acts
so as to make the subordinate react to him, but in a manner chosen
by the superior."[13] It is therefore intimidation that is the normal
method of such rule rather than a widespread use of violence. Intimidation is the general manner of ruler behavior in societies in which
power is based essentially on force. As a technique, intimidation is
designed to evoke a response of fear among the natives without actually
resorting to violence.[14]

The response of the natives—as the victim of colonialism has
generally been designated—has varied from acquiescence by the majority to determined and active resistance by the politically conscious
and concerned minority. Resistance is "an organized response to a
force that provokes it,"[15] whether it occurs immediately or is delayed.
Such resistance has taken the form of protest demonstrations, strikes,
and violent or nonviolent civil disobedience, but its purpose has always been the achievement of change in the structure of power, generally against the will of the powerholders. Whether this resistance
is ideologically clothed in nonviolence and tends to shun violent actions, emphasizing only moral persuasion, or is openly violent, it is
generally interpreted by the power holders as organized deliberate actions opposing the official will, which is normally clothed in the respectability of law. To the resisters, their actions are prompted by

the initial actions of force that established the colonial authority in the first place.[16]

The resisters have been invariably weaker than the colonialists, who control almost all the means of violence. The regime's reaction to resisters has generally been more violent, though it is projected as punishment for the contravention of the law, which is the norm established by the colonial power. Thus, the violence of the resister is termed "terrorist" whereas that of the regime is the enforcement of the law, and what distinguishes one from the other is the condition of legality. As long as the regime observes these conditions its reprisals against the resisters, no matter how harsh, are excluded from the category of terrorism, that is, the colonial governments never acknowledged their violence as terrorism. The conditions of legality are offered as temptations to the natives, who could buy peace and avoidance of punishment by abiding by the officially established norm, for colonial regimes, like despotic regimes, have been "held together by institutionalized caprice and absolute power and [have] regularly used violence to inhibit potential resistance."[17]

CATEGORIES OF TERRORISM

This chapter will deal with the period of dominant colonial rule in India, which covers approximately two centuries—from 1754 to 1947. However, the period of concentrated, explicit political terrorism, including government reprisals, spans roughly half a century—from 1895 to 1947—and while acts of terrorism that took place prior to 1895 will be mentioned, the main focus of this chapter will be on the last quarter of the colonial rule in South Asia.

The following categories will be used for the description and analysis of terrorism:[18]

1. explicit, organized, deliberate
   a. direct—rebellions
   b. indirect—tactical, selective assassinations
2. random, mass, unorganized.

Terrorism, whether in the form of independent action or reaction and reprisal, has long been part of the human condition in South Asia. Countless foreign invaders brought terror in their wakes, and one of them, the Iranian Nadir Shah, surpassed them all by ordering a general massacre of the citizens of Delhi in 1739 in reprisal for the murder of some of his soldiers. So deep was the impact of this terror that to this day the name of Nadir for "capricious autocracy" and the term "general massacre" for "total brutality" have entered

the everyday language of North India. In addition, a regular feature
of politics has been the wars of succession in which almost every succession followed a civil war and the elimination of royal rivals.
Finally, the terms "thug," "dacoit," and "loot" are India's contribution to English usage, although bandits and highwaymen have carried
on their activities in almost every society.[19] Thus, terrorism and
violence are not new to South Asia.

REBELLIONS

The first explicit, organized, anticolonial violence took the form
of religious rebellions. They were called "religious" not because
their objective was religious but because the group was organized
along religious lines and membership was restricted to the adherents
of a particular religion or sect. The second category of such rebellions was called "political" because not only was the objective political but the membership of the group was open to all, that is, to all
those who were in the category of "subject" as opposed to "ruler."

The first religious uprising was the Sanyasi rebellion. Religious
ascetics, called "Fakirs,"[20] or "Sanyasis,"[21] rebelled aginst the
East India Company in the late 1760s and early 1770s, under the leadership of Sheikh Majnu. They were powerful in Bengal and Bihar, and
between 1770 and 1772, North Bengal was virtually at their mercy.
They fought the troops of the East India Company and took over company factories. In the beginning, Hindu and Moslem mendicants
fought together, but later the Hindus separated under the leadership
of Mohan Giri.

The second religious uprising, the Wahabi rebellion, under the
leadership of Amir Khan, took place in the 1860s and 1870s. The
Wahabis were a puritanical Moslem sect,[22] and although their motivation was religious, their uprising was directed toward the expulsion
of the British. Like the Sanyasis, their stronghold was Bengal.

A third uprising took place at the same time as the Wahabi rebellion. The Kukas, a sect of the Sikhs, under the leadership of
Guru Ram Singh, revolted against the British and set up a parallel
government in the Punjab.

All three rebellions were short-lived; the British crushed them
brutally with great losses of lives on the side of the rebels.[23]

In the category of political rebellions fall three major uprisings
that directly challenged colonialism. The Sepoy Mutiny of 1857 was
the first, followed by the Ghadar[24] revolt of 1915, and finally the rebellion of the Indian National Army (INA) during World War II. The
Sepoy Mutiny was entirely confined to the South Asian subcontinent,
while the latter two were planned and organized mainly outside India
and involved Europe, Asia, and even North America.

The Sepoy Mutiny of 1857 started in January when Indian troops, both Hindu and Moslem, refused to use the cartridges for the new Enfield rifles on the grounds that they were greased with cow and pig fat.[25] On May 10, 1857, Indian troops killed their British officers at Meerut and marched on to Delhi. The mutiny became "a holocaust of blood and fire, laying a thousand homes in ashes, costing tens of thousands of lives,"[26] for the mutineers, "elated by their early successes and with none to counsel moderation . . . committed unpardonable excesses in places like Meerut, Delhi, Kanpur, Jhansi."[27] The response of the British was "primeval savagery," the governor general commenting that "no amount of severity can be too great" and writing to the commander in chief: "I should rejoice to hear that there had been no holding our men, and that the vengeance had been terrible."[28] A colonel in the British army suggested that the mutineers should be flayed alive, impaled, or burned, and the London Times added that they should be "mowed down by artillery."[29] And they were: "Rebel Sepoys were tied to the cannon mouth and blown to pieces."[30]

The emperor of India and his sons fared no better. The emperor, after being captured, was told by a Captain Hodson "that if any attempt were made at rescue he would shoot the king down like a dog."[31] The princes were accused of having tortured and slain English prisoners. After capturing them, Hodson decided to shoot them and "proceeded to do that daring, cruel, much abused, much praised deed":

> He halted his troop . . . ordered the princes to strip;
> then, taking a carbine from one of his troopers, he
> shot them with his own hand. The shuddering crowd
> gazed at this [white man] shooting one by one their
> princes. [32]

The mutiny destroyed large areas on both sides of the Ganges, "cost 40 million pounds and the lives of 2,034 soldiers in action and another 8,987 from disease . . . to say nothing of the murdered civilians and the thousands on thousands of native casualties."[33] The intensity of the violence was not the product of a sudden outburst of hatred on the part of the Indians against the British. On the contrary, anger and frustration had been building up for years and the forbidden grease in the cartridge became the spark to ignite almost the whole of North India.[34]

The causes of this anger were both economic and political; the economic cause affecting both the rich and the poor, while the political mainly affected the ruling classes and the nobility. The cotton industry in India, one of the main supports of the working classes, had been systematically destroyed in order to support the textile mills

in England. The land tenure arrangement and the control of trade by
the British were used to make the Indian peasant grow industrial raw
materials and food grains that were exported to England; later, the
processed product was sold to the Indians at a much higher price. As
a result, several famines took place in South Asia with considerable
loss of life.[35] It has been estimated that between 1754 and 1815 £1
billion was transferred from India to England and the annual average
of such transfers in the nineteenth century was about £20 million, out
of which neither India nor the Indians gained anything at all.[36] Further,
racist feeling among the British in India was so strong that they never
spared Indians any racial humiliation. Lord Cornwallis said that
"every native of Hindustan is corrupt,"[37] and Lord Wellesly described
Indians as "vulgar, ignorant, rude, familiar and stupid."[38] As late
as 1934, Indians were considered genetically inferior ("the average
amount of native qualifications can be presumed only to rise to a certain limit")[39] and therefore not qualified to hold jobs on a par with the
British. The missionaries, in their enthusiasm to save the soul of
the heathens, also added to Indian anger. Even the British soldiers
worked to convert Indian soldiers to Christianity, in reaction to
which "the Sepoys burnt with anger at the superciliousness of their
officers who added insult to injury by calling them 'niggers' and
'suars' [pigs]."[40]

While the policies and actions that followed may not be called
terrorist and violent in themselves, there is an element of psychological terrorism and violence directed against the dignity and self-re-
spect of the dominated Indians. And, if to this is added the economic,
political, military, and psychological exploitation of the Indians, it
can be argued that the Indians were so deprived that, in order to
throw off the British yoke, their response had to be violent and terrorist. Since, as we have seen, the British claim to superiority
rested on their power to destroy, the British were, in essence, running the government by violence and terrorism.

The second political rebellion, which Khushwant Singh, a highly
respected Indian author, describes as "the most powerful terrorist
movement in the history of India's freedom movement,"[41] was the
"Ghadar" that occurred during World War I. The Ghadar was a conspiracy, hatched abroad, mainly in North America, for throwing the
British out of India by terrorist means. Its main actors were the
Sikh immigrants from India who had settled in British Columbia and
on the West Coast of the United States. They were mostly uneducated
laborers, while most of their leaders were educated Hindus and Moslems. Since the Ghadarites lived outside India, the Ghadar plans and
conspiracies were spread over North America, Europe, the Middle
East, the Far East, and Southeast Asia. According to their plan, Indians abroad were to be told to return to their homeland and wait for

the signal for the general uprising; money, arms, and ammunition
were to be supplied by Germany; and Indian troops outside as well as
inside India were to be incited to revolt against the British. It was
hoped that these plans, when executed in conjunction with the war in
which Germany was expected to be dominant, would paralyze the British administration and free India.

The propaganda organ of the Ghadarites was the Ghadar, a
weekly started on November 1, 1913 by the Indians of the West Coast
of the United States and Canada, with Hardayal, a philosophy lecturer
at Stanford University, as its chief editor. The first issue of the
Ghadar, written in Urdu, highlighted its objectives:

> Today, there begins in foreign lands, but in our coun-
> try's language, a war against the British Raj. . . .
> What is our name? Ghadar. What is our work?
> Ghadar. Where will Ghadar break out? In India.
> The time will soon come when rifles and blood will
> take the place of pen and ink. [42]

The Ghadar propaganda exhorted Indian immigrants to return
to India and wait there for the signal for the revolt. They were assured that they would be supplied with arms and money from abroad,
and, since Britian was bound to lose the war, their success was assured.

The call was successful because it attracted members from all
three major religious communities: Sikhs, Hindus, and Moslems.
The Sikhs had become anti-British because of the racially discriminatory immigration policies of Canada—considered by the Sikhs to be
an extension of the government of the United Kingdom—which were
spotlighted by the case of the Komagata Maru. [43] The Hindus, as the
majority community, had been in the forefront of the independence
movement since the turn of the century, and their resentment against
the British had been intensified by the partition of Bengal. [44] The
Moslems turned against the British government because of its defeat
of the Ottoman Empire, which was then the only independent Moslem
state of any significance and whose head was considered by Moslems
to be the caliph of the world of Islam. Since Britain did not help the
Turks in the Balkan wars, and in World War I Britain itself became
the main enemy of the Turks, [45] Indian Moslems came to see Britain
as the enemy of Islam.

Thousands of Indian immigrants returned from Canada; the
United States; Hong Kong, Shanghai, and other parts of China; Malaya;
Borneo; Japan; and the Philippines in response to the Ghadar appeals.
On their way to India they contacted Indian soldiers in the British
army, exhorting them to rebel against the British and take part in the

revolution. They organized branches of the Ghadar party in Shanghai, Bangkok, and Rangoon to keep up the propaganda inciting Indian troops and Burmese Moslems against the British.[46] The response of Indian soldiers was by and large sympathetic because of their resentment toward the British for using Indian soldiers as cannon fodder while saving British soldiers.[47]

In India the returned immigrants and their supporters murdered Indians whom they considered loyal to the British and broke open jails and destroyed railways and telegraphs. As they ran short of money and arms—which were supposed to arrive from abroad but never did due to government vigilance—the Ghadarites looted government treasuries and police stations and robbed rich Indians.[48]

The main theater of Ghadar activity, beyond these murders and robberies remained abroad. After the outbreak of the war, Germany became the center of the anti-British activity of the Ghadarites. The German government offered money and arms to the Indians. Hardayal and another Indian, Chatopadhyaya, fromed the Indian Revolutionary Society in Germany with the aim of establishing a republican government in India. They were allowed to attend the meetings of the German foreign office that dealt with India. Many Indians, among them Hindus who had taken on Moslem names, worked on Indian soldiers in Egypt and Persia; others in Constantinople and Kabul established liaison with the Turkish and Afghan governments for the overthrow of the British in India. In Constantinople a fetwa (the equivalent of a papal bull) was read exhorting Indian Moslem soldiers in the Middle East to jihad against the British.

The first revolt took place on February 15, 1915 in the Light Infantry, a Moslem unit posted in Singapore. The rebels overpowered the reservists but were opposed by the Sikhs of the Malay State Guides and Sikh Sentries. In the fighting, eight senior British officers and 36 others were killed. Of the mutineers no exact number of dead is available, but 126 were court-martialed—37 were sentenced to death, 41 to imprisonment for life, and the rest received varying prison terms.[49]

In the cases of the Indian troops in Persia, Iraq, and Egypt and the 130th Baluch Regiment in Rangoon, which was to revolt on January 21, 1915, the British learned of the conspiracies in time and nipped them in the bud; no actual revolt took place. The revolutionaries were apprehended and severely punished.[50] No actual uprising in India ever took place because of the effective espionage of the government. Most of the leaders of the revolt were arrested and executed.[51]

With the entry of the United States in the war on April 6, 1917, 17 Indian revolutionaries and their German contacts and supporters were arrested, tried, and sentenced in the United States.[52] This was the last chapter in the history of the Ghadar party and its revolutionary

violence, since in India itself no revolt had taken place. The Ghadarites, being short of money and arms, could not carry on even their
stray terrorist activities for long. They also failed to arouse any
meaningful support for their cause among the ordinary people on any
significant scale and most were easily rounded up by the government,
tried, and hanged or sentenced to long prison terms.[53]

A number of factors contributed to the failure of the Ghadar conspiracy—poor planning and organizational work on the part of the revolutionaries, lack of secrecy enabling easy infiltration of government
spies into their inner councils, failure to receive arms and money in
India, embezzlement of funds by the leaders, and acrimony among
them on religious and parochial grounds. The most important reason,
however, was that the populace in India had not been prepared. The
overwhelming majority did not identify with the revolutionaries and
was completely turned against them when they started committing
dacoities and murders. The government of India, in its assessment
of the conspiracy, reached the same conclusion, adding the factors of
"the Indian habit of regarding the ideal as the fact accomplished and
bad leadership."[54]

The next organized armed attempt to overthrow the British dominance through violence did not come until World War II presented another opportunity. The hero of this attempt was Subhas Chandra Bose,
president of the Indian National Congress in 1938 and 1939, and the
vehicle was the INA. Even before 1939, Bose had believed that a serious international crisis leading to war was likely to break out and
that India should be prepared for a violent national struggle using
every possible means in order to wrest its freedom from Britain.
Failing to win support within the congress, Bose resigned as president and resolved to act on his own with the help of like-minded militants. He organized his own group, called the "Forward Block," though
within the congress, and projected a militant, Leftist, radical stance
that intensified when Britain declared India a belligerent, contrary to
the wishes of the elected provincial ministries. As an opponent of the
war, Bose was arrested in June 1940.[55]

Long before his arrest, Bose had reached the conclusion that
neither the congress, the Moslem League, or the Hindu Mahasabha[56]
saw the war as he did and were therefore opposed to obstructing the
war effort of the government of India. Bose was convinced that Britain
would lose the war, that Britain would not willingly transfer power to
the Indians, and that India would have to fight for its independence.
In order to realize his dream, Bose had to get out of prison, but the
government was unwilling to oblige. Using the famous Gandhian technique of "fast unto death," Bose compelled the government to release
him lest he die and his death spark large-scale violence. Toward the
end of January 1941, Bose succeeded in eluding the police and escaped
from Calcutta to Kabul, Afghanistan.

In Kabul, Bose made contacts with the Italian and German governments, then at war with Britain. Alberto Quaroni, the Italian minister in Kabul, after an interview with Bose on March 2, 1941, sent a report to Rome.[57] Bose had asked Quaroni, as a first step, for the establishment of a "Government of Free India," which would direct Indian military activity abroad as well as in India, for India was morally ripe for revolution, and "if 50,000 men, Italian, German or Japanese could reach the frontiers of India, the Indian army would desert, the masses would uprise and the end of English domination could be achieved in a short time."[58] Bose assured Quaroni of the desertion of Indian troops but played down the role of the terrorist organizations and the effectiveness of terrorism. However, only one month later, when Bose was in Berlin and submitted a secret memorandum to the German government, he suggested not only intensive propaganda against giving money or soldiers to the British government, against paying taxes and obeying orders, and for inducing troops to revolt, but also the organization of strikes in factories, sabotage of strategic bridges and factories, and the organization of uprisings leading to a mass revolt.[59] It seems that in talking about terrorism with Quaroni, Bose was referring to selective assassinations, of which he disapproved, while in communicating with the Germans, Bose was suggesting collective, organized terrorism, which he considered necessary and effective for bringing down the colonial government.

From the beginning, Bose concentrated on organizing Indian soldiers outside India, but the only soldiers he could reach were the prisoners of war of the Axis powers. It was out of such soldiers that he succeeded in forming units to work with the German Fifth Column Organization and established Free India centers in Rome and Paris. On hearing of the spectacular successes of the Japanese in the Far East, he transferred his base of operations to Japan.[60]

Indian revolutionaries, who had already been working in Japan, persuaded Captain Mohan Singh of the First Batallion of the 15th Punjab Regiment, which had been captured by the Japanese in North Malaya in December 1941, to work within the developing INA. Singh succeeded in persuading 40,000 Indian prisoners of war to join the INA. This conversion was attributed to terrorism commited by the leaders of the INA. At the termination of the war, several leaders were tried by the government on charges of torture and murder of soldiers who had refused to join the INA.[61]

Political authority over the INA was exercised by the Indian Independence Movement, which had been established by Rash Behari Bose, an Indian terrorist who was wanted in India for several bombings and who had absconded to Japan in 1939. After Japan conquered Southeast Asia, the headquarters of the movement were moved to Bangkok. On Subhas Bose's arrival in Bangkok for the organization of the INA

on July 4, 1943, Rash Behari Bose turned the leadership of the movement over to Subhas Bose, who was hailed as <u>Netaji</u> (Supreme Leader).
Subhas Bose established the Provisional Government of Free India on
October 21, 1943, with headquarters in Singapore and political authority over the INA. The Indian Independence Movement was merged in
this provisional government.[62] INA troops took part, along with Japanese forces, in launching an invasion of India from Burma, but neither
the Japanese nor the Indians succeeded in conquering or "liberating"
any part of India. The Japanese, who had the resources and equipment,
seemed to lack the motivation for fighting in the difficult terrain of
northeast Burma, while the Indians, who were highly motivated, lacked
the resources and freedom to operate on their own. With the U.S.
entry into the war, Japanese attention and resources were directed
toward the Pacific theater. In the end, the INA, like its patron the
Japanese army, surrendered to the British forces, and its leaders
were put on trial.

This attempt at securing India's freedom through force failed
because the Japanese were not the liberators and used Indians for
their own purposes, the INA did not succeed in "liberating" any siza-
ble Indian territory, and no significant revolts took place within India
in spite of the violence and terrorism sparked by the "Quit India"
movement of 1942.[63]

Tactical terrorism forms the second category of explicit, deliberate, organized terrorism. Unlike rebellions, tactical terrorism
is indirect. By this method a victim is used to pressure his princi-
pals or a third party into conceding to the demands of the terrorist.
In the case of India, tactical terrorism was used against the functionaries of the colonial government in order to paralyze the government
by preventing officials from discharging their duties. In this category
of terrorism are included selective assassinations, bombings, and
dacoities, both committed and attempted. Of these three, assassinations and bombings are the main terrorist acts, while dacoities are
supportive or secondary, that is, the target of terrorism is the func-
tionary or supporter of colonialism whereas the target of dacoity is
determined by the needs of the terrorist—money, arms, explosives—
and by the ease with which they may be obtained.

Assassinations and bombings both require not only the physical
courage to commit the act but also the moral or psychological courage
necessary to justify the act before it is committed and to rationalize
it afterward. There is a greater need for courage in the case of assassination than in bombing in that there is direct contact and a face-
to-face confrontation between the victim and the terrorist, which nec-
essitates a considerable amount of psychological preparation, of society as well as of the terrorist.

The indispensable role of theory and the primacy of the theoretician is obvious in the preparation of terrorists for the liquidation of

their victims. It is the theoretician who provides the moral justification and rationalization and the historical, cultural, and religious respectability and legitimacy to the act of terrorism. It is the theory
that acts as the magnet in the recruitment of terrorists. The theoretician reaches out to the recruits through the propagation of his theory,
mainly through public meetings and the circulation of literature. In
most cases, except those of government terrorism, the communication
and propagation of terrorist theory is accomplished by word of mouth
and printed material surreptitiously circulated because of the government ban that comes sooner or later. Once printed, the literature
survives and outlasts the theoretician. This literature is thus as important for the actual operation of terrorism as for its proper understanding.

The earliest and perhaps most important theoreticians of Indian
terrorism were Bal Gangadhar Tilak, a Maratha, and Aurobindo
Ghose, a Cambridge-educated Bengali, around the turn of the last century.

Tilak can be called the father of the Indian revolutionary movement and of Indian terrorism. He started public Ganpati (Hindu religious festivals) in western India as "an anti-Muhammadan movement"[6]
in September 1894 and Sivaji[65] coronation festivals in 1895.[66] Tilak's
newspaper, Kesari, started in the early 1890s, was the torchbearer
of the spirit of revolt. It urged the Marathas to rebel as Sivaji had
done two centuries earlier. Independence would be obtained not by
merely reciting the story of Sivaji but by taking "up swords and
shields [and by cutting] off countless heads of enemies [by shedding]
upon the earth the life blood of the enemies who destroy our religion
. . . kill calves and kine."[67] Hindus were exhorted to "free her
[the cow] from her trouble; die, but kill the English [and] not cir-
cumscribe your vision like a frog in a well; get out of the Penal Code
and enter the extremely high atmosphere of Srimad Bhagabad Gita
[which advises] to kill even our teachers and our kinsmen"; it would
thus be no sin for Hindus to kill the British.[68] Tilak was tried on
charges of sedition and convicted, and though the position taken by
him was one of apology for the political assassinations that had taken
place in 1897,[69] the Kesari continued to preach violence and terrorism
and considered political murders to be different from ordinary murders

> owing to the supposition on the part of the perpetrators
> that they were doing a sort of beneficent act [because]
> the very system of administration is bad, and . . . un-
> less the authorities are singled out and individually
> terrorized, they would not consent to change the sys-
> tem.[70]

Ghose, who lived in Maharashtra, came under the influence of Tilak, and it was through Ghose that the new impulse of violent nationalism was brought to Bengal. Ghose considered Tilak to be "the one possible leader of a revolutionary party."[71] Ghose had already turned away from the congress, considering its method of petitioning the British government to be useless. He believed that it was not by prayer and petition but through "purification by blood and fire" that a nation's liberty could be achieved, and he asked Indians to adopt not England as their model, but France, which had "blotted out in five terrible years the accumulated oppression of thirteen centuries."[72] Like Tilak, Ghose concluded that "the surest and the safest ground to proceed on would be religion."[73]

In the field of terrorist literature the most important journals were Kesari Kal, Jugantar, Bande Matram, Ghadar, to some extent Jahan-I-Islam, and leaflets and irregular publications like Liberty, Swadhin Bharat, Ghadar-I-Gung, and Ilan-I-Jung. Among the earliest books promoting terrorism were Bhawani Mandir (The Temple of Bhawani), Bartman Renaniti (The Modern Art of War), and Mukti Kon Pathe (What Is the Path of Salvation), all published in the early 1900s.

Jugantar, founded in 1906 as a revolutionary Bengali weekly, was even more violent and revolutionary than its Marathi counterpart, Kesari. Its message was the following:

> If it be lawful for an individual to use physical force
> for self-preservation, why should it be unlawful for
> a nation to do the same. If it not be a sin to commit
> manslaughter in order to defend one's self against
> thieves and dacoits, why should it be a sin to kill a
> few men in order that a nation might become free.[74]

In June 1908, the government passed the Press Law, and under its authority banned the Jugantar.

Swadhin Bharat propagated secret murder and eulogized it as a holy act on the part of an enslaved people.[75]

Liberty, started by Rash Behari Bose[76] in 1913, advocated:

> Revolution has never been the work of men. It is al-
> ways God's own will worked through instruments. . . .
> A grim Revolution is the greatest need of the times.
> Rise, brothers, in spirit. Individual incidents like
> the one at Delhi [the attempted murder of a viceroy]
> may strike terror into the hearts of the tyrants but
> they cannot bring you the desired goal.[77]

Bande Matram was the journal of the Indian revolutionary group in Europe. It was published in Paris under the leadership of Madame Cama, a Parsi from Bombay. Since its publication was beyond the reach of the British authorities, it was more violent and open in its advocacy of terrorism. One of its issues carried the following message:

> Terrorize the officials, English and Indian, and the
> collapse of the whole machinery of oppression is not
> very far. The persistent execution of the policy that
> has been so gloriously inaugurated by . . . martyrs
> will soon cripple the British Government in India.
> This campaign of separate assassinations is the best
> conceivable method of paralysing the bureaucracy and
> of arousing the people. The initial stage of revolution
> is marked by the policy of separate assassinations. [78]

The Ghadar, published abroad like the Bande Matram, was also very direct and violent in its advocacy of terrorism. It exhorted Indian immigrants to go back to India "with the express object of committing murders, causing revolution and expelling the British Government by any and every means."[79] It asked Indians to use their "guns and arrows . . . to fight guerrilla wars"[80] and "to rise and put Europeans to death"[81] because "the work can never be accomplished without the sword."[82] A pamphlet, Ghadar-I-Gunj,[83] issued by the Ghadar press, enjoined the revolutionaries to "commit dacoity on the Government and awake the whole nation [to] rob Europeans of their money and bring it to your own use."[84]

Jahan-I-Islam was a Turkish newspaper begun in Constantinople in 1914. It had an Urdu section edited by Abu Saiyad, a Punjabi. The Urdu section was aimed at Moslems under British authority in South Asia, Burma, and even Malaya, instigating them to jihad in solidarity with Turkish Moslems in order to weaken the British position in the Middle East, where their interests were clashing and their armies fighting. Since in this context the Turkish interests were similar to those of the Ghadar party, Jahan-I-Islam came out in support of the Ghadar call:

> This is the time that the Ghadar should be declared
> in India, the magazines of the English should be
> plundered, their weapons looted and they should be
> killed therewith. . . . Hindus and Muhammadans,
> you are both soldiers of the army and you are
> brothers, and this low graded English is your enemy

> . . . and by combining with your brothers murder
> the English and liberate India. [85]

Kal, a Marathi journal, added an idealistic and international
perspective to terrorism by endeavoring to give legitimacy to terrorist acts in the name of a higher national goal, comparing the work of
Indian revolutionaries with that of the Russians. In its issue of July
8, 1908, the Kal said that Indians were no longer singing the songs of
British glory and would do anything for Swarajya (independence). If
the terrorism of Russian bomb throwers could lead to the convening
of the Duma in spite of the lack of wide support for Russian terrorists,
then Indians were bound to get their independence, and, therefore,

> it is quite unjustifiable to call the bomb-throwers in
> India anarchists. Setting aside the question whether
> bomb-throwing is unjustifiable or not, Indians are
> not trying to promote disorder but to obtain Swarajya. [86]

In addition to regular publications, the message of terrorism
was propagated by sporadic publications printed at secret presses.
One of them was the Feringhi[87] Destroyer Press in Tinnevelly, Ma-
dras, and one of its pamphlets told Indians to

> take an oath that as long as the Feringhi exercises au-
> thority in our land of Bharata you will regard life as
> worthless. Beat the white English Feringhi you get
> hold of, even as you beat a dog, and kill him with a
> knife, a stick, a stone or even by the hand given by
> God. [88]

A similar pamplet issued by the Indian Revolutionary Committee
exhorted the revolutionaries to

> first and last spread terror. Make this unholy Gov-
> ernment impossible. Hide like invisible shadows of
> doom and rain death upon the alien bureaucracy. Re-
> member your brothers who are perishing in jails and
> rotting in swamps. [89]

The three books Bhawani Mandir,[90] Bartaman Rananiti, and Mukti
Kon Pathe, were used along with such other works as the Bhagavad-
Gita, the writings of Vivekananda, and the lives of Mazini and Garibaldi
for the revolutionary education of the terrorist initiates, presenting
terrorism as legitimate and meritorious in religious and political
terms. Bhawani Mandir exhorts Hindus to acquire mental, physical,

moral, and spiritual strength, to copy the methods of Japan and fight against the British. <u>Bartaman Rananiti</u> preaches the inevitability of war when oppression cannot be ended by other means and tells the youth to acquire heroic qualities by facing dangers. <u>Mukti Kon Pathe</u> is a reprint of articles published in the <u>Jugantar</u>. In essence it says that no special physical strength is needed to kill Europeans, that arms can be acquired by dacoities and weapons can be prepared secretly, and that Indians could go to foreign countries to learn the art of making weapons.[91]

Terrorist organizations were the instruments for giving effect to what the theoreticians and publications were preaching. Because of their need for secrecy, their illegal character, and the repulsive nature of their work, very little was known about them at the time of their existence. The legal ban on them, after their work was discovered, drove them underground, and the only information that was made public came through police sources, and only when the police found any documents. Documents, however, cannot be considered reliable sources of accurate information, for in many cases what actually existed by way of an organization was no more than a name.

This much, however, can be stated with certainty: the earliest organizations were formed in Maharashtra, then in Bengal, and later in other parts of South Asia. Even in Bengal the ideas and impetus came from Maharashtra, but once Bengal turned terrorist it was Bengali organizations and terrorists that spread throughout the country. Hardly a single terrorist conspiracy, bombing, or murder took place anywhere in South Asia in which Bengali terrorists were not involved.

The earliest terrorist organization seems to have been the Chapekar Association of Maharashtra, founded by the Chapekar brothers sometime prior to 1897. Its existence came to light as a result of the murder of the plague commissioner of Bombay. Mitra Mela was started around 1899 by the Savarkar brothers and in 1900 developed into the Abhinav Bharat of Young India Society. This society aimed at an organization modeled on the revolutionary societies of Russia. It had members in various parts of western India and a secret branch in Satara. The investigations in connection with the Nasik conspiracy exposed this society. The Gwalior conspiracy led to the discovery of the Nav Bharat Society of Gwalior.[92]

In Bengal the secret societies were organized under the innocuous names of <u>Akharas</u> and <u>Samitis</u> in many important centers like Calcutta, Dacca, Bakarganj, Faridpur, Mymensingh, Dinajpur, Chittagong, and Cooch Bihar. Among the most important and terroristically effective ones were the Dacca Anusilan <u>Samiti</u>, founded in 1905; the Calcutta <u>Samiti</u>; and the Manicktola Garden House Secret Society, founded in 1907. At the beginning of 1912, Anusilan <u>Samitis</u>[93] were established throughout Bengal as well as in Behar, Uttar Pradesh, and the central provinces. In Uttar Pradesh, the center of terrorist activity was Benaras, but there as well as all over northern India the terrorists were mainly Bengalis and Marhattas.

The umbrella organization of northern India, and also the most influential, was the Hindustan Republican Association, formed with the combination of the Anusilan Party in north India and Sanyal. The objective of this organization was to establish a federal India through an armed revolution. This seems to be one of the earliest leftist parties; its ideal was the Soviet Union and it wanted to end the exploitation of man by man. Another important revolutionary terrorist organization in northern India was the Hindustan Socialist Republican Association. It was to this organization that the famous Indian revolutionaries Chandra Shekhar Azad and Bhagat Singh belonged. [94]

Among the less well-known organizations, the Independent Kingdom of United India revealed its existence through a letter by the finance secretary of its Bengal branch to a victim of dacoity in 1916, thanking him for Restitution 9,891-1-5, which was to be repaid with 5 percent interest after the Independent Kingdom had materialized. [95]

A leaflet published in December 1917 reveals the existence of the Indian Revolutionary Committee, which seems to have been based in Calcutta. The discovery of this leaflet on the person of a terrorist and his connection with a gang based in Chandernagor provides circumstantial evidence about this group. [96]

As secret societies, the Samitis were very restrictive in their membership, especially that of their inner circle. Mainly college graduates were recruited, and before they could be admitted to the inner circle their antecedents were verified and they went through a probationary period. In the initiation ceremony they took an oath

> lying flat on a human skeleton with a revolver in one hand and a [Bhagavad-] Gita in the other. [The chief of the Samiti] held a sword with the point resting on the forehead of the postulant as he knelt and solemnly swore that if it were demanded of him, he was prepared to sacrifice even his life for the independence of the country. [97]

In addition to the initiation ritual, the Samitis had elaborate rules for the conduct of their members. Among them were that members must consider the Samiti a military organization and the violation of any rule involved punishment in proportion; that members were working for a revolution for the establishment of righteousness and not for personal enjoyment; and that traitors among members were to be executed. [98]

The documents pertaining to the organization of the Samitis
were discovered by the police in the course of arrests and searches.
The document on general principles obtained on September 2, 1909,
from a house in Calcutta, shows that the work of the party was divided
into two parts, general and special. The former included organization, propaganda, and agitation; in the latter category, the military
work included chemistry (preparation of explosives) and finance,
meaning the imposition of taxes on the rich.

Information on the district organization scheme and the rules
for members was obtained in documents found on the person of a member of the Dacca Anusilan Samiti who was arrested on February 27,
1913. It seems that there was one headquarters with several subordinate centers, further divided along the lines of divisions of the government.

A pamphlet found in another search in September 1916 gave information about the duties and responsibilities of the leader.[99]

While Samitis sometimes worked together, there was no single
headquarters and no single command. The Sedition Committee, in its
investigations, did not find the existence of one conspiracy, and therefore members of one group could not be held responsible for the actions of another group, though the objectives of all of them were the
same. "We may go further and say that there is evidence that particular outrages were not always approved of as a matter of policy by
groups other than that which committed them."[100]

The Samitis achieved such success within such a short time of
their creation that the government sought to curb their terrorist activity by imposing a ban through the Criminal Law Amendment Act
XIV of 1908.[101] The extent to which the government was frightened
can be judged by the provisions of the act—an abridged form of preliminary investigation and trial by a Special Bench of the High Court
without assessors or jurors. Under this statute the following Samitis
were banned in 1909: Dacca Anusilan Samiti, Dacca; Swadesh, Band-
hab Samiti, Bakarganj; Brati Samiti, Faridpur; Suhrid and Sadhua
Samitis of Mymensingh.[102] However, their terrorist activities did
not cease, and the Samitis continued to operate (for example, the
Dacca Samiti was involved in dacoities and murders in 1911 and
1912).[103]

The principal weapons used by the terrorists were revolvers
and bombs and occasionally knives and wooden sticks. The last two,
although easily available and not illegal to possess and carry, were
not very effective. Revolvers were stolen, bought, or smuggled from
abroad, while all bombs were manufactured within India, most of
them at one or two centers; however, the formulas for bombs were
imported from Europe. The explosives for bombs—dynamite, various
acids, and chemicals—were all obtained locally. In addition, the

chief of the Dacca <u>Samiti</u> discovered a formula for a deadly poison to be applied to arrowheads.[104]

Bomb making by terrorists was started in 1907. The first bomb makers were Ullaskar Dutta and Hem Chandra Das, members of the Manicktola Garden House Secret Society in Calcutta. Their bombs were used to blow up trains and for assassinations.[105] After the banning of the Manicktola society, bomb-making activity was shifted to Chandernagore, then a French enclave in Bengal. Most of the bombs used throughout India were manufactured in Bengal.

Three types of bombs were generally used. The first was a round bomb that used picric acid. It was one of these that killed two women in 1908. The second were the comparatively harmless "coconut bombs." One of these was used against Lord Minto. The third was a cylindrical bomb filled with high explosives, jute needles, and pieces of iron. This kind of bomb was used in Calcutta, Lahore, Delhi, Sylhet, Mymensingh, and Midnapore.[106]

In addition, a special bomb, called the "book bomb," was invented in 1908 in order to kill a notoriously harsh magistrate of Calcutta. The book bomb was sent in the mail as a book. The magistrate received the parcel but got suspicious and turned it over to the police for examination. The police found that

> the parcel did contain a book; but the middle portion
> of the leaves had been cut away and the volume was
> thus in effect a box and in the hollow was contained
> a bomb with a spring to cause its explosion if the
> book was opened.[107]

This device was described by Muspratt Williams, chief inspector of explosives of India, as "a most destructive bomb."[108]

The first political murders were committed by members of the Chapekar Association. The victims were Rand, the plague commissioner, and a Lieutenant Ayerst, killed by the Chapekar brothers on June 22, 1897, in Poona as they left the celebrations for the 60th anniversary of Queen Victoria's coronation. Rand was the marked victim and Ayerst was killed accidentally. Tilak, in an article in the <u>Kesari</u> of May 4, 1897, described Rand as "tyrannical" and stated that "the Government was practising oppression" through compulsory visitations by medical authorities in order to control the epidemic,[109] and "it has been ascertained later that both the Chapekar brothers and their club were inspired by Tilak's ideas and methods."[110]

The Chapekar brothers were tried, and one of them, Damodar, was hanged for the murder. Two years later, the Chapekar Association attempted to assassinate a policeman in Poona and later killed two brothers who had given information leading to the arrest and conviction

of Damodar Chapekar. As a result of these murders, four members
of the Chapekar Association were hanged and one was sentenced to 10
years' rigorous imprisonment.[111]

Many more assassinations and unsuccessful attempts followed.
Narendra Nath Gosain, an approver, was killed in the Alipore Jail in
August 1908 by revolvers that had been smuggled in, for which the two
assassins were hanged. Jackson, the district magistrate of Nasik,
who had sentenced Ganesh Savarkar, a terrorist, was killed by Anant
Lakshman Kanher of the Abhinav Bharat Society in December 1909 with
a pistol that had been sent from England by Ganesh's brother in the
false bottom of a suitcase. For this murder, three terrorists were
executed. O'Brien, an engineer with a jute mill, kicked an Indian
employee to death, for which he was fined only 50 rupees. This fine
was considered an insult to Indians, and in retaliation, members of
the Attonanti Samiti and the Mukti Sangha attempted to murder O'Brien
but failed. In 1910, Shamsul Alam, a deputy superintendent of police,
was killed inside the Calcutta High Court, and in 1911, Ash, collector
of Vinnevelly, was murdered. In 1913, a head constable was killed
in Calcutta and an inspector of police in Mymensingh; in 1915, a deputy superintendent and an inspector of police as well as a constable
were killed in Calcutta; in 1916, a subinspector of police was killed
in Barisal. A school headmaster was shot in March 1915 on the assumption that he was reporting to the government on the activities of
students involved in anti-British activity, and in December 1915, terrorists killed a member of their own Bajitpur revolutionary gang because he was believed to be acting as a police informer.[112]

The arrival of the Simon Commission[113] in India in 1928 aroused
considerable opposition among Indians, mostly due to the fact that
there was not a single Indian among the commission's members.[114]
A number of demonstrations in protest against the commission took
place, which the government tried to break up by violence. In one of
them Gala Lajpat Rai, a famous congressional leader, was beaten by
the police with a steel-mounted stave and died. Azad and Bhagat
Singh decided to take revenge. They ambushed Saunders, the English
police official responsible for the fatal assault on Rai, and killed him
along with his Indian orderly within a month after Rai's death.[115]
Azad was finally surrounded by police in 1931, but they only got his
corpse after riddling him with bullets.

Terrorist activity, which had slackened in the 1920s, intensified
in the early 1930s. Lowman, the inspector general of police in Bengal, and Hodson, the superintendent of police in Dacca, were shot in
1930, Lowman fatally. This was the time when the Round Table Conference to deal with Indian political developments was taking place in
London. Sir Tej Bahadur Sapru,[116] a member of the conference, remarked that "Benoy Bose [the assassin] accomplished half the task of

the Round Table Conference."[117] Bose went on to shoot another Englishman—Simpson, the inspector general of prisons—and, in order to
avert arrest, shot himself dead. Ahsanullah, a Chittagong police inspector who was notorious for his brutality, was shot dead by a 15-
year-old boy who, because of his age, was not hanged but sentenced to
life imprisonment. In that same year, terrorists threw a bomb at the
car of Sir Charles Tegart, the police commissioner of Calcutta. Tegart escaped, but a nonofficial Englishman and one of the assailants
were killed. The other assailant was hanged. Between 1930 and 1933,
three magistrates of Midnapore—Peddie, his successor Douglas, and
his successor Barge—were shot dead one after the other. The terrorists themselves were either shot dead on the spot by the police or
hanged, but they succeeded in making it almost impossible for British
officers to rule, and finally the government had to appoint a Bengali
magistrate.[118]

Not all of the terrorists were men. Two girls, Suniti Choud-
huri and Santi Ghosh, shot Stevens, the district magistrate of Comil-
la, dead, and Bina Das unsuccessfully tried to shoot the governor of
Bengal in 1930.[119]

The police and administrative officials were not the only targets
of terrorism. Several provincial governors as well as governors
general were the victims of terrorism.[120] In protest against the partition of Bengal, which created a Moslem majority in the eastern part,
approximating the area that in 1947 became Eastern Pakistan, Hindu
Bengalis made several vehement protests. In 1907, two attempts
were made on the life of Sir Bamfylde Fuller, lieutenant governor of
Eastern Bengal, and in that same year a bomb was thrown at the special train of Sir Andrew Fraser, another lieutenant governor of Bengal. Both escaped unhurt.[121] Sir Stanley Jackson, governor of Bengal, was shot at on the occasion of the Calcutta University Convocation
in 1930, but escaped. Later, Sir John Anderson, another governor of
Bengal, was shot at in Darjeeling and barely escaped.[122]

It was an attempt on the life of a viceroy that constituted the very
first act of selective assassination in India. Lord Mayo was visiting
the Andaman Jail[123] when on February 8, 1872, Sher Ali, a Wahabi,
stabbed him. The Wahabi rebellion had resulted in the exile of the
Wahabi leader Amir Khan in 1871. In retaliation for this exile, Abdullah, a Wahabi, stabbed to death Norman, the presiding magistrate
in whose court Amir Khan had been tried. Abdullah was hanged, and
it was in retaliation for this hanging that Mayo was stabbed.[124] An
attempt on another viceroy was made on November 13, 1909, when
two bombs were thrown into the carriage in which the Viceroy Lord
Minto and his wife were driving in Ahmedabad. They escaped unhurt,
but the head of the man who found one of the bombs was blown off.[125]

On the transfer of the capital from Calcutta to New Delhi in
1911, the Viceroy Lord Hardinge made a ceremonial entry into the
new capital on December 23, 1912, riding a decorated elephant. A
bomb was thrown at him, which only wounded him but killed the Maha-
wat (elephant driver).[126] Seventeen years later on exactly the same
day, an attempt was made on the life of yet another viceroy when terrorists tried to blow up the special train of Lord Irwin. The viceroy
barely escaped.[127]

Sir John Simon, head of the Simon Commission, was also marked
as a target, but before he could be attacked, the bombs the terrorists
were taking from Benaras to Bombay to blow up his train went off and
killed the terrorists as well as several other passengers.[128]

The terrorists also brought their political violence to England
itself. One of their terrorist acts was the assassination on July 1,
1909 of Colonel Sir William Curzon Wyllie, the political aide-de-camp
at the India Office, at a gathering at the Imperial Institute in London
by Madan Lal Dhingra. This murder was in retaliation for the life imprisonment of Ganesh Savarkar,[129] as shown by a statement found on
Dhingra's person after his arrest, which read: "I attempted to shed
English blood intentionally and of purpose as an humble protest against
the inhuman transportation and hangings of Indian Youths."[130]

The work of the terrorists could not be carried on without money
and arms. In the beginning, the financial needs could be met by dues,
but as the work expanded expenses increased and this proved insufficient. Consequently, if their work was to be carried out on a large
scale, money had to be obtained by force. The fact that their revolutionary work was meant for the good of society and not for individual
benefit was used to justify the collecting of money from society.
Therefore, the theoreticians argued that, while ordinary dacoity vio-
lates the principles of good society, political dacoity does not:

> No sin but rather virtue attaches to the destruction
> of this small good for the sake of some higher good.
> Therefore if revolutionaries extort money from the
> miserly or luxurious members of society by the ap-
> plication of force, their conduct is perfectly just.[131]

Between 1907 and 1917 alone, 130 political dacoities were committed. In at least 25 of them, the amount of money extorted ranged
from 10,200 rupees on April 22, 1911 to 80,000 rupees on October
17, 1916. The number of dead in these 25 dacoities averaged one per
dacoity, while the number of wounded was considerably larger. The
most audacious and frightening to the authorities, however, were the
dacoities for arms, two of which particularly merit description:
Rodda's arms robbery of August 26, 1914 and the Chittagong armory
raid of March 12, 1930.

Up to the time of the August 1914 robbery, terrorists used to obtain revolvers and pistols by forcible seizure or theft from the Anglo-Indians or from foreign sailors or through purchases, such as from Nur Khan of Chetta, an arms dealer, and from Kishore Mohan Sapui, who imported revolvers from France and regularly allocated a portion to the revolutionaries.[132] The theft of pistols from Rodda and Company, a firm of gun manufacturers in Calcutta, is described as "an event of the greatest importance in the development of revolutionary crime in Bengal,"[133] for this theft placed 50 Mauser pistols and 46,000 rounds of ammunition at the disposal of the terrorists. A Mauser pistol has a .300 bore, "is sighted up to 500 yards and if held straight, is a very formidable weapon."[134] The theft itself was more a matter of conspiracy than daring. Of the 202 cases of arms and ammunition that arrived from Europe and were cleared through customs regulations, only 192 reached the firm's warehouse. The clerk of the firm, responsible for this clearance, returned to get the remaining ones. He was never seen again, nor were the remaining 10 cases. The authorities soon found out that, of the 50 pistols, 44 had almost at once been distributed to nine different revolutionary groups in Bengal, and in almost every "revolutionary outrage" that took place in Bengal since August 1914, Mauser pistols stolen from Rodda had been used.[135]

The Chittagong armory raid took place on the heels of Gandhi's Dundee (Salt) march, which began on March 12, 1930. On April 18, 1930, terrorists raided the armory and with the help of the loot formed a provisional government with Surjya Sen at its head. The British residents of the port fled and took shelter in the steamers, and for three days the British government ceased to exist. With the arrival of reinforcements the provisionals had to retreat, though battles took place at the Jalalabad Hills and Dhalghat. Surjya Sen and his associate Tarakeswar Dastidar were arrested, tried, and hanged.[136]

RANDOM MASS TERRORISM AND
GOVERNMENT REPRISALS

Mass terrorism, also called communal riots, were random, unorganized, and specifically Indian in origin. They seem to be unique to South Asia and will be treated here as a distinct category, for seldom was the colonial regime the object of this terrorism, especially in the period between the two world wars. Though the first recorded communal riot took place in 1893,[137] constant communal tension and almost regular communal bloodshed did not become common until the end of World War I. It is the period between the wars when communal riots, the nonviolent noncooperation of Gandhi, and government reprisals converged to create a situation of almost constant violence. In this triangular situation the central position was occupied by Gandhi and his nonviolent, noncooperation movements because, to a considerable degree, communal riots on the one side and government reprisals on the other emanated out of Gandhi's movement.

Between 1917 and 1942, nine civil disobedience movements were launched by the Indian National Congress under Gandhi's personal leadership: Champaran satyagraha (1917), Kheda, or Kaira, satyagraha (1918), Rowlatt Act satyagraha (1918), nonviolent noncooperation (1920-22), Bardoli satyagraha (1928), Civil Disobedience (salt law breach) (1930-31), Civil Disobedience for Swaraj (1931-32), Individual satyagraha (1940-41), and "Quit India" (1942-44).[138]

Gandhi developed and applied the technique of nonviolent noncooperation—Satyagraha (soul force), also called civil disobedience—in South Africa against the government's harsh and racist policies. Because of the successes he achieved there, he seems to have been convinced that similar results could be obtained in South Asia. An important point about Satyagraha was Gandhi's conviction that, since, at least theoretically, this disobedience did not use physical force, no violence or terrorism took place if the campaigns were confined to Gandhi's instructions. This view, however, may be disputed on the grounds that force, whether moral or physical, is force, and to the extent it succeeds in breaking the will and the resistance of the adversary it is terrorism, even if it is only moral terrorism. It seeks intimidation of the adversary and intimidation is a powerful weapon. Another significant point about these movements is that the level of communal violence seems to have increased with new campaigns and the frequency of this violence so institutionalized the relations between Hindus and Moslems that even personal altercations between Hindus and Moslems could turn into riots, and on numerous occasions actually did so.[139]

The movement of 1919, called the Rowlatt Satyagraha, was launched as a protest against the Rowlatt Act, which allowed arrest without warrant of a suspected person and imprisonment without trial. The act resulted from the Rowlatt Report on sedition and revolutionary crime in India during 1893-1918.

The Satyagraha demonstrated in protest in Delhi. The police, in trying to break them up, shot at the demonstrators, causing several deaths and many injuries. The casualties added reasons for more demonstrations, which now took place in many parts of India. In mob retaliations in Amaritsar, five Europeans were killed and a missionary woman, Sherwood, was beaten.[140] The government retaliated by imposing martial law, summary trials, and public floggings and by making Indians crawl on all fours when passing through the site of Sherwood's beating. General Dyer, the military commander of the area,

ordered a ban on all public meetings on April 12, 1919, but failed to
inquire as to whether his order had been fully publicized or not. The
next day, 20,000 men, women, and children assembled in Jallianwallah
Bagh—a rectangular enclosure with only one exit—in Amaritsar. Dyer,
accompanied by 150 soldiers, marched into the meeting place "to do
all men to death till they were going to discontinue the meeting." The
total ammunition that Dyer's soldiers had—1,650 rounds—were fired
and 1,000 persons killed.[141] To the committee, appointed by the government to investigate what were called the "Punjab disturbances,"
Dyer declared: "For me the battle field of France or Amaritsar is
the same," and General Drake-Brockman declared that "force is the
only thing that any Asiatic has any respect for."[142] For his part in
governmental terrorism, Dyer was presented with a sword of honor
and a purse of £26,000.[143] Because of this large-scale violence,
Gandhi suspended the Satyagraha after 12 days.

The nonviolent noncooperation movement of 1920-22 was started
both as a protest against the Hunter Committee Report, which white-
washed the brutalities related to the Jallianwallah Bagh tragedy and
the restrictions imposed by the Rowlatt Act, and in support of the
Khilafat demands of the Moslems—the restoration of the throne, dig-
nities, and lands of the Ottoman emperor, who was the sultan/caliph
of the Moslems of the world. Gandhi, sensing the possibility of Hindu-
Moslem unity against the British (the reasons for their respective opposition to the British were different), took up the directorship of the
joint campaign. Under his leadership, the Moslem leaders incited
Moslems against the anti-Islamic policies of the British while the
Hindu leaders aroused Hindus against the satanic and immoral nature
of the British rule.[144]

The Khilafat agitation was interpreted by Moslems as a call to
their own independence, and in south India, particularly in the Malabar
area, it sparked the Mopalah Rebellion in August 1921.[145] It was

> the revolt of an ignorant and fanatical people undoubt-
> edly engineered by the preachings of Hindu and Mus-
> lim agitators, a revolt which soon turned against the
> Hindu community and resulted in the sacking of Hindu
> temples, the forcible conversion of Hindus to Islam
> and the death of many innocent persons.[146]

When the government took action and imposed martial law, the terrorists took to the hills and waged a guerrilla war. Of the government
troops, 43 were killed and 126 wounded, and 3,000 of the Mopalahs
were killed, which gives an indication of the extent of the terrorism
that made Sir Sankaran Nair, congress president in 1895 and later a
member of the viceroy's executive council, lament that

thousands of Mahomedans killed and wounded by troops,
thousands of Hindus butchered, women subjected to
shameful indignities, thousands forcibly converted,
persons flayed alive, entire families burnt alive, women in hundred [sic] throwing themselves in wells to
avoid dishonour, violence and terrorism, threatening
death standing in the way of reversion of their own religion. This is what Malabar in particular owes to the
Khilafat agitation, to Gandhi and his Hindu friends.
The President of the Indian Muslim League . . . justified the Mohamedan atrocities as an act of war against
the Hindus and the Government.[147]

A second case of mass terrorism arising out of this very movement occurred in Chauri Chaura in north India in the United Provinces.
On February 4, 1922, some congress volunteers and peasants, whom
the volunteers had incited against the government, raided the police
station of Chauri Chaura. The 21 policemen and a rural watchman,
finding themselves outnumbered by the Satyagrahis, took shelter in
the police station, at which the agitators set the building on fire and
burned the inmates alive. On February 7, 1922, Gandhi called off the
Satyagraha because of mob violence.[148]

The Mopalah terrorism showed how deep religious fanaticism
was and how easily it could be turned into mass violence. The Chauri
Chaura terrorism indicated the ease with which mobs, once excited,
could turn against anybody and could commit the most brutal violence
in the name of nonviolence. However, it seems that the lessons of this
mass terrorism were not learned by the congress leadership and Gandhi. Perhaps the successes of the Bardoli Satyagraha of 1928, which
was against the raising of rents, and of the 1930-31 Civil Disobedience
(the Dundee march and the Salt Law breach)[149] gave the impression
that Indian agitators had learned the art of nonviolent noncooperation,
though even in the latter case some mob violence did take place.

The Civil Disobedience movements of 1932-34 and 1940-41 and
the "Quit India" movement of 1942 could hardly be called nonviolent
since they led, on the one side, to the intensification of Hindu-Moslem
killings and mass terror and on the other to government reprisals.
As one latter-day commentator remarked:

Whatever the Congress apologists might argue, the
national movement of August 1942 was far from being a peaceful and constitutional agitation confined
to the limits of the law. The Quit India Movement,
as it was termed, virtually developed in no time into
a mighty revolutionary movement producing violence,
bloodshed and terror.[150]

No sooner had the "Quit India" movement been launched than almost the entire top leadership of the congress was incarcerated. Without leadership, frenzied masses, driven to desperation, turned to violence. Radio broadcasts by the Axis powers and the news of the events in Southeast Asia added fuel to the fire:

> The fury of the masses burst forth and almost in no time the whole of India was in the throes of a devastating revolution. Miles and miles of railway lines were uprooted, post offices were pulled down, police stations were burnt and crores[151] worth of Government property looted or destroyed.[152]

The British government, desperate in its own worst predicament, retaliated with fury and violence.

> Then followed rule by ordinances, firings, lathi charges . . . even bombings from airplanes were reported from some places. . . . It is estimated that more than 2,000 unarmed and innocent people were shot down and about 6,000 were injured by the police and the military. Tens of thousands were wounded by lathis, about 150,000 were jailed, and about a million and a half were imposed as collective fines. There is record of tortures, burning of houses, looting, and other atrocities by the police and military.[153]

Communal riots have taken place sporadically since 1893, but after 1917 some of the worst random terrorism occurred as a result of the mass political participation that Gandhi's nonviolent noncooperation entailed. Gandhi was severely chastised for it, but there is no evidence to show that he learned the lesson, and it seems that neither did the other political leaders. It should have been obvious that mobs brought out in the streets for political agitation could not be controlled except by the show or the use of massive force. In 1946, the Moslem League, which had studiously remained aloof from Gandhi's civil disobedience movements and criticized him for riots and bloodshed, decided that it must also call out its supporters in the streets if its demand for Pakistan was to be realized. It was the league's decision to call for "direct action,"[154] to show the political clout of the league and the vehemence of the Moslems' disgust with both the British and the Congress, which engulfed the whole of northern India in the worst mass terrorism ever recorded in history.

The "direct action," theoretically intended for peaceful mass demonstrations by Moslems against the "Congress-British collusion,"

was launched in Calcutta in August 1946 and immediately turned into
an orgy of murder, mayhem, and destruction of property. Like wild-
fire it spread throughout Bengal, then Bihar and Uttar Pradesh, and
on to the Punjab and the North West Frontier Province (N.W.F.P.),
involving Hindus, Moslems, and Sikhs with terrible brutalities committed on all sides.[155] The inability of the leaders of the Hindus and
the Moslems to control their followers, the lack of power of the government to suppress it by force, and the unwillingness of Westminster
to prolong its responsibility for the administration of India combined
to secure the abatement of the riots through partition. The partition
plan led to the mass exodus of the minority communities, which in
turn exposed them to even worse brutalities and terrorism. As a result, 16 million people left their homes and at least 1 million perished.
If there ever was a case of mass terrorism for gross political objectives, it was this one, and while the subcontinent became independent
and the Moslems got their Pakistan, the bitter legacy has survived to
this day. Governments in all the states in South Asia claim to have
eradicated this terrorism, and to a considerable extent they have succeeded, yet the corpse of communal riots has not been buried or not
been buried deep enough, for it rises periodically and claims its innocent victims.

OVERVIEW

The long history of political terrorism involving the people of
the Indian subcontinent and the large areas over which it has been
spread gives the impression that most people must have participated
in it. Closer scrutiny, however, reveals something quite different.
The area most affected by political violence lies north of the line con-
necting Bombay to Calcutta. Hardly any communal riots and very few
selective assassinations took place south of this line. All religious
communities were involved in communal riots, but in selective assassinations, bombings, and political dacoities, no Moslems were involved, though there were Moslem victims of tactical terrorism just
as there were Hindu and English victims. Mass Moslem participation
in politics seems to have been confined to the Khilafat and the Pakistan agitations. The Khilafat agitation coincided with the Ghadar agitation in time; thus whatever seems to be Moslem participation in the
Ghadar actually pertained to the Khilafat question. The terrorists
involved in the Maharashtra assassinations and related conspiracies
belonged to Chitpavan Brahmins, the same caste to which such moderates as Gopal Krishna Gokhle and Mahadev Govind Ranade belonged.
These terrorists were all ultraorthodox, strongly anti-British, and
also anti-Moslem. Most of the Bengali terrorists belonged to Bhad-

ralok (gentlefolk); they were Hindu, mostly upper caste, educated, high school and college graduates, and spoke English.[156] Both Bengali and Marhatta terrorists belonged to the well-off middle classes. Up to the time of Ghadar in 1915 particularly, but even later, practically all terrorists involved in selective assassinations and bombings anywhere in India were Marhattas and Bengalis, more Bengalis than Marhattas. In the smuggling of arms both Marhattas and Bengalis were involved, but bomb manufacturing seems to have been a Bengali specialty, though in police searches the same formula for making bombs that was found in Bengal was also found in Nasik and Satara in the Bombay Presidency as well as in Hyderabad Deccan.[157]

The main period of selective assassinations and bombings stretches from 1897 to 1915, with its latter half being most intensive in tactical terrorism. This coincides with the period in which the Congress party was controlled by the moderates, the extremists having been expelled at the Surat Congress in 1907. In 1916, Gandhi assumed the leadership of the Congress and turned it into a mass organization by bringing the extremists back within the Congress fold as well as by launching the nonviolent noncooperation movements. During this period of mass agitational politics, tactical terrorism of selective assassinations and bombings seems to have been suspended, but in the late 1920s, when mass agitational politics appeared to be diminishing, tactical terrorism picked up again with the bombing of Lord Irwin's train in 1929 and several assassination attempts in the early 1930s. With the grant of provincial autonomy and the elective, responsible government under the Government of India Act (1935), tactical terrorism seems to have come to an end. The next phase of sustained violence started with the launching of the "Quit India" movement in 1942, which in 1946 led to the most intensive communal terrorism. It seems that the periods of dominance of tactical terrorism coincided with those of moderate organized political agitation, but when organized political agitation became transformed into violence, tactical terrorism ceased to occur or became very low-key.

In selective assassinations of harsh civil and police officials, the victims, in addition to Englishmen, were Hindus as well as Moslems, while the terrorists were almost always Hindus. But there does not seem to be a single case of such an assassination leading to a Hindu-Moslem riot. In contrast, however, some of the worst terrorism followed the launching by the Congress of the civil disobedience movements against the British. The most obvious example of such terrorism was the Mopalah riots, which followed on the heels of the Khilafat movement, a movement considered to be the high-water mark of Hindu-Moslem unity and of joint Hindu-Moslem demands and pressures on the British. With very few exceptions, and in almost all civil disobedience movements, some communal violence always took place, and it was this violence that became the background and therefore the basis for the uncontrollable terrorism that raged between 1946 and 1948.

British colonialism came to an end in South Asia with the granting of independence to India and Pakistan in 1947. Terrorism emanating from colonialism should also have come to an end at the same time. That this has not been so is evident from the violence for independence or autonomy that has since taken place in the Naga and Mizo lands in India and in Baluchistan and the Pakhtoon areas in Pakistan. Guerrilla warfare and government reprisals, armed attacks, hunt-and-destroy methods, and bombing have taken place in all these areas. The governments of India have used the carrot-and-stick technique, while the governments of Pakistan have tended to rely on the stick. The establishment of Nagaland and Mizoram as constituent units within the Indian Union seems to have pacified the majority, while the armed forces have crushed the guerrilla rebellions. However, the Baluchistan and Pakhtoonistan movements seem to have become endemic with periodic violence and government reprisals in attempts to crush the agitators. Violence and terrorism may be said to have become a way of life in those areas.

Similar problems, but on a much larger scale, have presented themselves in Kashmir for India and in East Pakistan. In Kashmir, as in the case of the Nagas and Mizos, the government of India used a two-handed approach and although political violence did take place, it never reached the level that would have required massive government reprisals. In East Pakistan, almost from the beginning, demands for autonomy were met by central government-imposed repression, which in turn led to more violence and harsher governmental reprisals. In 1971, the central government decided to use massive terrorism to subdue the rebellious elements. Governmental terrorism led to the exodus of millions of refugees into India, which India used as a pretext to invade East Pakistan and destroy the state of Pakistan. The defeat of the Pakistani armies brought about a reign of terror by the guerrillas against the sections of population that had remained loyal to the central government.

Riots up to 1947 were almost all of a communal character and were blamed on the British for the imperial policy of divide and rule, but since then, while the British have left, riots have not only not ended but their variety and frequency has increased. Thus, since independence, in addition to communal riots, four different kinds of riot have taken place—language, industrial, ideological, and sectarian.

The major language riots took place in East Pakistan in support of the Bengali language in 1952 and in Sind in 1972 against the Urdu language. In South India the peak of language riots against the imposition of the Hindi language was reached in 1965.

Industrial riots have taken place in many parts of India but particularly in West Bengal. The rioters, in addition to intimidation through violence, invented the technique called "gherao," which means the encirclement of the management within the business premises and detention until the management gives in or the government breaks up the encirclement through the use of force.

Ideological terrorism by the Communists has, in a way, grown out of industrial riots and spread into the rural areas. The victims of ideological terrorism have been the landlords and capitalists, mercilessly butchered by the terrorists called Naxalite, after Naxalbari, an area in West Bengal where the movement started.

Sectarian riots may be described as the terrorism of the majority sect against the minority sect within the same religion. The most outstanding examples of sectarian terrorism were the anti-Qadiani riots of 1952 and 1974 in Pakistan.

In terms of selective assassinations, the murder of Gandhi by an Indian and a Hindu showed that one does not have to be a tyrant to be the victim of an assassin's bullet.[158] Between Gandhi's assassination in 1948 and that of L. N. Mishra, the Indian railway minister, in 1975,[159] countless assassinations of famous and not-so-famous political personalities have taken place. In a similar way, the line of selective political assassinations in Pakistan stretches from that of the first prime minister, Liaquat Ali Khan, in 1951 to that of Hayat Mohammad Khan Sherpao, home minister N.W.F.P. in February 1975, with numerous assassinations and attempted assassinations taking place in between.

The phenomenon of continuing political violence despite the termination of colonialism seems explicable on two grounds. First, what has ended is only the racial feature of colonialism, not its structure. There are groups of people whose perception of politics is different from what seems to be the case on the surface. These groups, though not very different racially or in color from the dominant group —as was the case with European colonialism—nonetheless do not identify with the dominant group and, finding no means for their own independence, feel compelled to resort to terrorism. The cases of Nagas, Mizos, Kashmiris, Bengalis, Baluchis, and Pakhtoons could be explained in terms of such "structural colonialism." Second, it is the insitutionalization of violence that may explain the terrorism of riots and selective assassinations. Historically, in this part of the world there have been no regularized channels for political input. European colonialism simply supplanted the traditional arbitrary, autocratic government, and while European education instilled the ideas of popular participation and political independence, the institutions of colonialism did not provide any means for the realization of these aspirations. In the absence of normal peaceful, regularized channels, vio-

lent terrorist means came to be seen as one possible way of political
input. In South Asia, as it would seem in many areas of the world
where even limited self-government did not evolve, government has
come to be identified with arbitrariness and caprice. Consequently,
social morality accepts as justifiable any means of cheating and opposing the government if one finds government policies unacceptable, provided one can get away with it. And in cases in which government policies or government functionaries are seen as obviously inimical and
not amenable to modification by persuasion, violent opposition through
demonstrations, riots, and even assassinations is considered not only
justifiable but necessary. There is a long history in South Asia of
people achieving by violence in the streets what cannot be obtained by
peaceful petition. Political terrorism, therefore, needs to be dealt
with at the political level and through policies that will eliminate the
political causes of violence. If, however, it is only terrorism that
is dealt with at the legal level and through government reprisals,
then the reprisals are likely to arouse terrorist retaliation and the
vicious circle may perhaps never be broken or broken only by the
destruction of one or the other party.

NOTES

1. The perpetrator of terror would not see himself as a terrorist and would use such terms as "commando," "guerrilla," "revolutionary," or "freedom fighter." In the context of this chapter, the
term "terrorist" will be used to cover all these terms.

2. For the text of the convention, see Proceedings of the International Conference on the Repression of Terrorism, 1937, C.94
M.47. 1938 V.; and for a discussion of the problems of the definition
of terrorism, see John Dugard, "International Terrorism," International Affairs 50, no. 1 (1974): 67-81.

3. Max Weber said that Machiavelli's Prince was harmless in
contrast to the Arthashastra.

4. G. Buhler, trans., The Laws of Manu, The Sacred Books of
the East, vol. 25 (London, 1886), p. 219.

5. Sardar K. M. Panikkar, Asia and Western Dominance (London: George Allen and Unwin, 1959).

6. H. D. Graham and T. R. Gurr, eds., The History of Violence in America (New York: Praeger Publishers, 1969), p. 2.

7. Charles Tilly, "Collective Violence in Eastern Europe," in
ibid., pp. 4-5.

8. Ibid., p. 41.

9. Paul Wilkinson, "Three Questions on Terrorism," Government and Opposition 8, no. 3 (1973): 294.

10. Ibid., pp. 297-98.

11. An Indian author has written that "men may dread, but can never love and regard those who are continually humiliating them by the parade of superiority." See V. B. Kulkarni, British Dominion in India and After (Bombay: Bharatiya Vidya Bharvan, 1964), p. 92. Also, see Sir John Malcolm, A Memoir of Central India (London: Kingsbury, Parbury & Allen, 1823), vol. 2, p. 438.

12. In this context colonial regimes, as established in Asia and Africa, were different from regimes colonizing what they thought were almost empty spaces, such as the European colonization of the Americas. Here the colonizers were not interested in controlling the natives but instead sought the destruction of the natives in order to control the land.

13. Kurt H. Wolf, trans. and ed., The Sociology of Georg Simmel (Glencoe, Ill.: Free Press, 1950), pp. 188 ff.

14. J. B. S. Hardman, "Intimidation," Encyclopedia of Social Sciences, vol. 8, p. 239, in E. V. Walter, Terror and Resistance (New York: Oxford University Press, 1969).

15. Walter, op. cit., p. 20.

16. See C. M. Case, Non-Violent Coercion (New York, 1923), reproduced in Walter, op. cit.

17. Walter, op. cit., p. 61.

18. In modern literature a distinction is made between the terms "terrorist" and "revolutionary," "guerrilla" and "commando." Some Indian historians have also made this distinction, such as J. C. Chaterji: "The Indian revolutionaries were not terrorists, they were not anarchists, they were inspired and conscious revolutionaries." See Indian Revolutionaries in Conference (Calcutta: Firma K. L. Makhopadhyay), p. 1. But the British government did not seem bothered by this semantic difference and used the term "revolutionary." See Sedition Committee, 1918, Report (Calcutta: Superintendent Government Printing, 1918) (hereafter referred to as Report).

19. The highway bandits, who established a reign of terror through torture, murder, mayhem, and extortion in Central India in the early nineteenth century, were called "thugs," their armed robberies with violence were called "dacoities," and what they stole or extorted was called "loot."

20. "Fakir" is a Persian term meaning "the contented one," one who is indifferent to the material world. Here the term means "a mendicant" and is usually applied to a Moslem.

21. Sanyasi is a Sanskrit word meaning "one who has abandoned the material world," "an ascetic," or "an abstinent." This term is usually applied to a Hindu.

22. It is the same sect to which the ruling dynasty of Saudi Arabia belongs.

23. Details of these rebellions are given in J. C. Chaterji, op. cit.

24. The word "Ghadar" means "a violent and bloody upheaval." In addition to being used for the revolt, it refers to the Ghadar party, which organized the revolt, and to the Ghadar journal, which was its propaganda organ.

25. For Hindus the slaughter of cows, which are considered holy, is religiously reprehensible, and to chew cow fat is a sin. For Moslems the pig is a dirty animal and its eating is sinful, as it is for Jews.

26. R. Collier, The Great Indian Mutiny (New York: Ballantine Books, 1965), p. 12.

27. V. B. Kulkarni, op. cit., p. 95.

28. Ibid., p. 99.

29. Ibid., p. 98.

30. Michael Edwardes, Red Year: The Indian Rebellion of 1857 (London: Hamish Hamilton, 1973), p. 144.

31. W. H. Fitchett, The Tale of the Great Mutiny (London: John Murray, 1939), p. 335.

32. Ibid., pp. 340-41.

33. John Harris, The Indian Mutiny (London: Hart-Davis Mac-Gibbon, 1973), p. 202.

34. North India alone would exceed the whole of Western Europe both in territory and population. The confinement of violence to this region and the support that the British received from other Indian quarters should not be interpreted to mean that feelings against the British were shared by only a handful of people and that the whole affair had only a local context, in the same way as a revolt in Portugal, Denmark, or Holland against a foreign overlord (Holland was a colony of the Habsburgs) would not be interpreted as only a local affair. Besides, it was north India that had the seat of the independent sovereign kings of India and where the domination by the British came to be seen as real, and hence the greater development of frustration among Indians of the north over the loss of positions of power and privilege. Since the Moslems had constituted the majority of the ruling aristocracy prior to the British, it was the Moslems who were in the forefront of the mutiny and who also had to pay a very high price for their part in it.

35. For details, see Tara Chand, History of the Freedom Movement in India (New York: International Publications Service, 1973), vol. 1; and A. K. Cranell and P. Kegan, The Economic Revolution of India (London: Trench, 1883).

36. D. Kincaid, British Social Life in India (London: George Rutledge, 1938); and R. Dutt and P. Kegan, India in the Victorian Age: An Economic History of the People (London: Trench, 1904).

37. Kulkarni, op. cit., p. 92.

38. T. G. Spear, The Nabobs (London: Oxford University Press, 1932), p. 145.

39. Dispatch to the Government of India, December 1934, in Kulkarni, op. cit.

40. Ibid., p. 94.

41. Khushwant Singh and Satindra Singh, Ghadar 1915, India's First Armed Revolution (New Delhi: R. K. Publishing House, 1966).

42. Ibid., p. 19.

43. The Komagata Maru was a Japanese ship chartered by the Sikhs in Hong Kong to carry Indian immigrants to British Columbia. The ship brought about 400 people, who were prevented from landing, and the ship was turned back at gunpoint, leading to numerous deaths among the passengers. For details see Singh and Singh, op. cit., pp. 30-34; and L. P. Mathur, Indian Revolutionary Movement in the United States of America (New Delhi: S. Chand & Co., 1970), pp. 66-69.

44. Report.

45. See Choudhry Khaliquzzaman, Pathway to Pakistan (Lahore, W. Pakistan: Longmans, 1961).

46. Mathur, op. cit., pp. 78-81.

47. Singh and Singh, op. cit., pp. 35-45.

48. Mathur, op. cit., pp. 41-51, 71, 114-15.

49. Singh and Singh, op. cit., pp. 46-47.

50. Singh and Singh, op. cit., pp. 46-47.

51. Mathur, op. cit., pp. 80-81.

52. Ibid., p. 52.

53. Report, pp. 149-57.

54. Isemonger Report, An Account of the Ghadar Conspiracy (Lahore: Government Press, 1922).

55. For a detailed account, see Netaji Research Bureau, Subhas Chandra Bose, The Indian Struggle: 1920-1942 (London: Asia Publishing House, 1964).

56. The Moslem League was an exclusive Moslem political party, while the Hindu Mahasabha was exclusively Hindu.

57. An abridged version of the report of Alberto Quaroni is given in ibid., pp. 415-18.

58. Ibid., p. 416.

59. Ibid., pp. 421-22.

60. For details of this phase, see Chand, History of the Freedom Movement in India (New York: International Publications Service, 1973), vol. 3.

61. For details, see Bhulabhai Desai, I.N.A. Defence (Delhi: Delhi Printing Works, 1945). The charges are given on pp. xv-xvii.

62. For details, see Uma Mukherjee, Two Great Indian Revolutionaries (Calcutta: Firma K. L. Mukhopadhyay, 1966), pp. 145-55.

63. This will be discussed in detail later on in this chapter.

64. See Report, p. 1.

65. Sivaji was a Maratha chieftain who waged guerrilla warfare against the Mughal Emperor Aurangzeb. While Moslems consider Sivaji an anti-Moslem rebel, Hindus look upon him as a nationalist fighting against the alien Moslem overlordship in India.

66. For details, see Mukherjee, op. cit.

67. Ibid., pp. 5-6.

68. Report, p. 3. Also, see Kesari, June 15, 1897.

69. Mukherjee, op. cit., p. 6.

70. Kesari, June 22, 1908.

71. Mukherjee, op. cit., pp. 10-11.

72. Ibid., p. 10.

73. Intelligence Branch, "Note on the Growth of the Revolutionary Movement in Bengal," in Mukherji, op. cit., p. 14.

74. Jugantar, June 9, 1907.

75. Mukerjee, op. cit., p. 32.

76. Bose was one of the two great Indian revolutionaries in Mukherjee. See Two Great Indian Revolutionaries, op. cit.

77. Mukherjee, op. cit., p. 116.

78. Reproduced in Report, op. cit., p. 11. This particular article was written on the assassination of a British official by an Indian in London on July 1, 1909.

79. Report, pp. 145-46.

80. Singh and Singh, op. cit., p. 19.

81. Mathur, op. cit., pp. 50-51.

82. Singh and Singh, op. cit.

83. Report, p. 151.

84. Ibid., p. 151.

85. Jahan-I-Islam, November 20, 1914, reproduced in Report, op. cit., p. 169.

86. Quoted in Report, pp. 7-8.

87. The word literally means "French" but has been used to mean Europeans in general.

88. Report, pp. 164-65.

89. Ibid., p. 108.

90. Bhawani is a manifestation of Kali, the goddess of death.

91. Details given in Report, pp. 23-35.

92. For more details, see Report, pp. 4-11.

93. An Akhara is a place of physical exercise while a Samiti is a social organization, and an Anusilan Samiti is a cultural organization.

94. J. C. Chaterji, op. cit., pp. 24-27.

95. Report, pp. 78-110.

96. Ibid.

97. J. E. Armstrong, superintendent of police, in a secret report (Introductory Note to the History of the Dacca Anusilan Samiti, dated April 25, 1917) to the chief secretary, government of Bengal, quoted in Mukherjee, op. cit., pp. 16-17, 23-24.

98. Report, p. 98.

99. Ibid., pp. 93-99.

100. Ibid., p. 102.

101. Already in 1908, 11 political assassinations of officials and their supporters had taken place.

102. Report, p. 40.

103. Ibid., pp. 52-63.

104. Intelligence Branch Records, Government of West Bengal, File No. 1270/1913.

105. Mukherjee, op. cit., pp. 12, 104-05.

106. Report, pp. 12, 104-05.

107. Ibid., p. 32.

108. Intelligence Branch Records, government of West Bengal, File No. IV/1085/1909.

109. Report, pp. 2-3.

110. Mukherjee, op. cit., p. 11.

111. Report, p. 4.

112. Report gives an estimate of 54 murders, mainly of officials, excluding assassination attempts and dacoities—in which more were wounded than killed—between 1907 and 1917 alone.

113. Sir John Simon was the leader of the British Parliamentary Commission, which visited India to study the political situation and make recommendations for the decennial installment of political concessions to India.

114. The commission was a joint parliamentary body consisting of members of the Houses of Commons and Lords, and since no Indian was a member of either house, no Indian was included in the commission.

115. Chaterji, op. cit., p. 27.

116. Sapru was a prominent Indian politician. He was a lawyer, a constitutionalist, and a moderate and had been the Law Member of the Viceroy's Executive Council.

117. Quoted in Chaterji, op. cit., p. 30.

118. Ibid., pp. 30-31.

119. Ibid.

120. The offices of viceroy and governor general were combined in the same person.

121. Chaterji, op. cit., p. 12.

122. Ibid., pp. 30-31.

123. The Andaman Islands are situated in the southeastern part of the Bay of Bengal. The British used them as a penal colony for

Indian criminals serving life sentences, much as they had used Australia for their own hardened criminals.

124. Chaterji, op. cit., pp. 3-4.

125. Ibid., p. 14.

126. Ibid., p. 16.

127. Ibid., p. 29.

128. Chaterji, op. cit., p. 27.

129. Ganesh was the brother of Vinayak Savarkar, who had established a revolutionary group in London whose members used to practice revolver shooting. Ganesh was convicted of waging war against the king through the publication of inflammatory poems and propaganda.

130. Mukerjee, op. cit., p. 73.

131. Quote from Mukti Kon Pathe (What Is the Path of Salvation?) cited in the section dealing with ideas and literature dealing with terroism.

132. Intelligence Branch Records, Government of West Bengal, File No. 757/13, given in Mukerjee, op. cit., p. 46.

133. Report, p. 66.

134. Hughes Butter, inspector general of police, Calcutta, File No. 229/15, in Mukherjee, op. cit., pp. 53-54.

135. Ibid., pp. 53-54.

136. Chaterji, op. cit., p. 30.

137. Report, p. 1.

138. For details, see J. S. Sharma, India's Struggle for Freedom (Delhi: S. Chaud & Co., 1962), vol. 1, pp. 82-121.

139. For a discussion of the institutionalization of violence in a pattern of politics, see F. Gross, Violence in Politics (The Hague: Mouton, 1972), p. 7.

140. Kulkarni, op. cit., p. 127.

141. Report of the Commissioners Appointed by the Punjab Subcommittee of the Indian National Congress, 1920, p. 57. Sharma, in India's Struggle for Freedom, op. cit., gives the figure of 400 shot and 2,000 wounded (see pp. 84-91).

142. See Report of the Committee Appointed by the Government of India to Investigate the Disturbances in the Punjab, 1920, p. 116. This committee is also called the Hunter Committee.

143. See Kulkarni, op. cit., pp. 126-27.

144. Sharma, op. cit., pp. 84-91.

145. The word "Mopalah" in the language of Malabar means "son-in-law." Mopalahs are the descendents of Arabs who went to Malabar as traders, married local girls, and settled down there. In many ways they should be considered the most integrated of all Moslems in India; however, as this rebellion showed, their view of themselves was very different—they were Moslems first and last.

146. Kanji Dwarkadas, India's Fight for Freedom, 1913-1937 (Bombay: Popular Prakasham, 1966), p. 179.

147. Sir Sankaran Nair, "Gandhi and Anarchy," quoted in Dwarkadas, op. cit., p. 180.

148. Dwarkadas, op. cit., p. 194.

149. For details, see Sharma, op. cit., pp. 93-95.

150. Mukherjee, op. cit., p. 7.

151. One crore is equal to 10 million rupees.

152. S. C. Bhartarya, The Indian Nationalist Movement (Allahabad: Indian Press [Publications] Private Ltd., 1958), pp. 230-38.

153. R. R. Diwakar, Satyagraha: The Power of Truth (Hinsdale, Ill.: Henry Regency Co., 1948), pp. 84-85.

154. For details of the events leading to this action, see the author's Jinnah and the Making of a Nation (Karachi: C.P.S., 1959); and "The Consolidation of Leadership in the Last Phase of the Politics of the All India Muslim League," Asian Profile, October 1973; also, see Khaliquzzaman, op. cit.; and Maulana Abul Kalam Azad, India Wins Freedom (Calcutta: Orient Longmans, 1959).

155. For a non-Indian and neutral perspective, see Lieutenant General Sir Francis Tuker, While Memory Serves (London: Cassells & Co., 1950).

156. Report, pp. 13, 27.

157. Ibid., p. 104.

158. For details on Gandhi's assassination, see Pyarelal, Mahatma Gandhi, The Last Phase, vol. 2 (Ahmedabad: Navajivan Publishing House, 1958), chap. 24.

159. News India (New Delhi), February 1975.

8

CHARACTERISTICS OF TERRORIST
MOVEMENTS IN AFRICA

The basic trait of South African terrorist movements is that they are territory based, nonideological (in the primary sense), and noninternationalist.[1] Their common denominator is their aim to evict governments consisting primarily of whites of European origin and substitute themselves, that is, black Africans. Their claims to legitimacy are based on historical assertions, usually unsubstantiated, that black governments were ousted by white invaders and on the pronouncements of liberal European political theory, such as that government should be based on the consent of the governed and the paramountcy of majority rule. The fact that these theories are rarely if ever practiced elsewhere in Africa seems of little relevance to them.

The consideration that the status of these movements is variable —it ranges from extinction through merger or other total loss of identity to the attainment of complete international legitimacy through accession to governmental function, the realization of their purpose— is only marginally relevant to this chapter. The fact is that terrorist movements are in the process of forming the governments of Angola and Mozambique, did so recently in Guinea-Bissao, and may form all or part of the governments of Rhodesia and/or Southwest Africa (Zimbabwe or Namibia) in the near future.

The organizational headquarters of the terrorist movements has been centered since its establishment in 1963 around the Liberation Committee of the Organization of African Unity (OAU) in Addis Ababa. Originally the committee consisted of nine members: Algeria, Congo-Kinshasa (later Zaire), Ethiopia, Guinea-Conakry, Nigeria,

194

Sengal, Tanganyika, Uganda, and the United Arab Republic. The first chairman was Oscar Kambana, Tanganyika's foreign minister. Somalia and Zambia joined two years later. At present, all members of the OAU have observer status.

So-called field headquarters were established in Lusaka and Dar es Salaam. In the former, in a cubicle compound named "Liberation Center," are offices of the African National Congress (South Africa) (ANC), the Movimento Popular de Libertacao de Angola (MPLA), the Uniao Nacional para a Independencia Total de Angola (UNITA), the Frente de Libertacao de Mocambique (FRELIMO), the South-West Africa Peoples' Organization (SWAPO), and the Zimbabwe African National Union (Rhodesia) (ZANU). It may be assumed that the anti-Portuguese organizations are now established within Angola and Mozambique. The Pan-Africanist Congress (PAC) and FRELIMO were based mainly in Tanzania. The Governo Revolucionario de Angola no Exilio/Frente Nacional de Libertacao de Angola (GRAE/FNLA) are based in Zaire.

Extra-African support for terrorist organizations emanates primarily from the Soviet Union and the People's Republic of China. Token offers of governmental contributions, primarily for nonmilitary purposes, come also from Sweden, Norway, Finland, Holland, Canada, and Israel. However, African leaders have shown no concerted intention of subserving their national aspirations to any form of internationalism, not even Marxism, in spite of the support they are receiving from its disciples.

One African writer put it very succinctly:

> If our leaders used the small segment of the radical left among the whites in our political life, it was literally to use them. Naive minds interpreted this as a subordination of African interests to the whims of white Marxists. American political scientists saw this as the thin end of the wedge for Moscow to come in. Nothing could have been more ridiculous than to see white and black anti-communists provide America with just the kind of lies that would justify its material support of Boer fascism. To use whites politically where one finds a genuine radicalism is not to seek cultural integration or assimilation in a country where Blacks are such an overwhelming majority as in South Africa. You could count with the fingers of your hand Africans who were ideologically Marxist. Nationalism has always been the dominant motive in liberation politics in South Africa whatever the rhetoric.[2]

Since at this time terrorist activities in Southern Africa are directed only against South Africa, Rhodesia, and South-West Africa, these are the three areas that will be examined in this chapter.

SOUTH AFRICA

While the policy of apartheid—or what was designated by the late Prime Minister Hendrik Verwoerd as "separate development"—may have lately gained a measure of acceptance outside the boundaries of the Republic, the demographic imbalance within, coupled with the slow but steady awareness of status by the Bantus, must make the preservation of the status quo increasingly difficult as time passes. South Africans within the government and outside of it are fully aware that the "wind of change" predicted by the then British Prime Minister Sir Harold MacMillan, in his February 3, 1960 Cape Town speech, will increase in intensity and blow existing institutions away. They hope, however, that the storm is still far off and that something, as yet unknown, will enable them to brace the gale.

South Africa is a tense place, apprehensive of subversion by a number of terrorist organizations, various church groups, and "international Communism." In its nervous state, itchy trigger fingers could at almost any time repeat the Sharpeville incidents of 1960. There is a mistrust and animosity even among members of the white community. Afrikaners mistrust Englishmen, who are still often emotionally more attached to queen and old country than to the Republic. The Dutch Reformed Church mistrusts all other doctrines. The United and Progressive parties are trusted less by the ruling Nationalist Party than behooves the usual relationship between government and loyal opposition. And within the National Party the verkramptes (closed-minded persons) mistrust the verligtes (enlightened ones).

The following are the main antigovernment organizations active in South Africa at the present time.

The ANC was founded in 1912, shortly after the passage of the Act of Union (1910), which established South Africa as a dominion within the British Empire. The basic purpose of the ANC was to facilitate the attainment and preservation of the political rights of the nonwhite peoples in the area. It was supposed, essentially, to be nonviolent. Its "freedom charter," formulated in 1955 under the leadership of the Nobel Peace prize winner (1960) Chief Albert J. Luthuli, calls for human rights for all people in South Africa.

A splinter group of the ANC, under the leadership of Robert Sobukwe, broke away in 1959 and formed a new organization, the PAC, whose military section styled itself "Poqo" (pure). Most terrorist activities inside the Republic are attributable to Poqo. The ANC also

spawned a militant group, "Umkhonto Wesizwe" (spear of the nation),
which, however, is far less active.

Both organizations, the ANC and the PAC, are more active outside South Africa than inside. This activity is primarily political,
aimed at discrediting the government of the Republic and its policies.
Another facet of activity is fund raising. The ANC receives substantial
support from the Soviet Union, and the PAC from China. Both receive
OAU assistance. The ANC maintains offices in Dar es Salaam, Lusaka,
Algiers, Cairo, New Delhi, and London. In London its publication
Sacheba appears monthly and Spotlight on South Africa weekly. Its
headquarters is in Morogoro, Tanzania.[3]

In 1971 another organization received considerable publicity.
The Unity Movement of Southern Africa, founded in 1943, with headquarters in Lusaka, allegedly instigated active terrorism, in spite of
its original manifest aim of bringing peaceful pressure to bear upon
the government of South Africa for the purpose of securing economic,
social, and political justice. Fourteen members were charged under
the South African Terrorism Act, which will be discussed below.

South Africa, in its fear of an externally induced violent change
of government, enacted stringent anti-Communist legislation. Whites,
by and large, enjoy in South Africa the same personal rights and priv-
ileges often referred to as "the traditional rights of Englishmen."
The South African writ de homine libero exhibendo resembles the
English habeas corpus and was introduced through the Roman-Dutch
law. The major exception to this is the Suppression of Communism
Act No. 44 of 1950 (amended several times at later dates), which in
addition to giving a passable definition of "Communism" also includes
the advocacy of any doctrine or scheme "which aims at bringing about
any political, industrial, social or economic change within the Union
by the promotion of disturbance or disorder" or that aims at bringing
about these changes "under the guidance of or in co-operation with
any foreign government or international institution whose purpose or
one of whose purposes (professed or otherwise) is to promote the establishment within the Union of any political, industrial, social or
economic system identical with or similar to . . . a despotic system
of government based on the dictatorship of the proletariat under which
one political organization only is recognized and all other political
organizations are suppressed or eliminated." The act further includes
any doctrine or scheme "which aims at the encouragement of feelings
of hostility between the European and non-European races of the Union."

Obviously, this act, which permits the minister of justice, among
others, to isolate or banish any individual for suspected activities
coming under this umbrella definition of "Communism" is so broad
and so widely applied as to constitute a serious abrogation of personal
freedom in the Republic.[4] It must be added, however, that legal ave-

nues of appeal have been provided for, though in practice they usually prove futile.[5]

The South African government is confident that it possesses the manpower, equipment, and popular support to suppress internal terrorism at this time. This confidence extends to any assistance that may be tendered by other African governments. The major anxiety focuses on the possibility that the Communist countries, perhaps as a result of setbacks in the Middle East, may concentrate in the future on South African liberation movements, supporting them with materiel, manpower, financial assistance, and a diplomatic offensive. Although South Africa is becoming increasingly self-sufficient and hence less vulnerable to international pressures, the fear of external Communist support for internal subversion is acute.

South Africa's political future, especially in the African context, appears to be on the upswing. The Republic retained diplomatic contact with neighboring black states, the former High Commission territories (Lesotho, Botswana, and Swaziland), Malawi, and the Malagasy Republic (until the ouster by military coup of President Tsiranana in 1972), and surreptitiously with Zambia, Ghana, the Ivory Coast, and others. These relations were primarily economic, although a modicum of mutual goodwill toward some political accommodation is present. Contributing factors are South Africa's economic strength, its ability to facilitate economic development in underdeveloped black Africa, and an increasing acceptance of the "separate development" policy's assertion of leading toward independent Bantustans. Should a modus vivendi with the members of the OAU be reached, terrorism in South Africa would be choked off, having been deprived of most of its ideological rationale and its foreign bases. On the other hand, should South Africa's fear of increased Communist support for terrorism be realized, based on the obvious desire for increased influence, the possibility of civil war must be considered, and the South African government, largely with military equipment supplied by France and by a growing domestic armament industry, is facing this alternative realistically.

South Africa's antiterrorist (or anti-insurgency) potential is formidable. Of a gross national product of $18.4 billion, the government spends $442.4 million on defense, or 2.5 percent. The army consists of a standing force of 32,000 and a trained reserve of about 220,000, including 75,000 "kommandoes" (home guards, mainly infantry and armored corps). These forces are supported by about 1,000 armored vehicles, including 240 Centurion and Comet tanks, 550 armored cars, and 200 scout cars (all figures are for 1971). These figures do not include recent purchases from Italy and France exceeding $200 million and Centurion tanks sold by Jordan in 1974. The air force consists of 8,000 highly trained personnel, deployed in 28 squadrons.

The South African police numbers about 55,000 officers, of whom more than half are black, colored, or Asian. It includes an antiterrorist force of about 3,000 equipped with antipersonnel carriers, riot trucks, heavy infantry equipment, cavalry, and trained dogs.

At the UN-OAU Conference on Southern Africa held in Oslo on April 9-14, 1973, the ANC and the PAC admitted in effect that antigovernment activities within South Africa are, except for rare token instances, practically nonexistent.[6]

Important ameliorative changes in the attitudes of the South African government regarding the nonwhite population of the Republic were indicated in a speech to the senate by the prime minister on October 23, 1974. What these changes will portend for the extraparliamentary opposition is too early to assess. So far, however, many facets of so-called petty apartheid have been abandoned. Also, the prime minister visited Liberia early in 1975 as an indication that the black African community of nations is attaching credence to the new policy.

RHODESIA

The basic problem for Rhodesia is its staggering demographic and economic imbalance. About 94 percent of its 5,773,600 inhabitants are Bantus, mainly Matabele and Mashona (1973). About 5 percent are white, mainly of British origin. About 1 percent are Orientals. It is assumed that the latter two groups own about 80 percent of the country's economic product. The bicameral parliament is composed of an assembly of 66 members, of which 50 are white and 16 black. The senate consists of 23 members.

Rhodesia was a self-governing British colony from 1923 to November 11, 1965, when it passed the Unilateral Declaration of Independence (UDI), an act not recognized elsewhere. In 1970, Rhodesia proclaimed itself a republic. Democratic republican parliamentarism is applied only to the white community of about 280,000, which also enjoys one of the highest standards of living in the world. Nevertheless, because of isolation imposed by the outside world, with the partial exception of South Africa, the prevailing state of mind is a _laager_ mentality—a defensive tenacity imposed by the Rhodesian Front government but not shared universally even within the white "encampment."

The Rhodesian Front captured all 50 seats in the summer 1974 election because of the single-member constituency system. It received 77 percent of the vote case. Four other white political parties exist and form an extraparliamentary opposition. The main opposition party, the Rhodesian party, received 18 percent of the vote and no seats. In parliament a token African party, the United People's

Party (UPP), has legal recognition as an opposition party and in the
1965 election received less than 800 votes.[7]

The first ANC of Rhodesia was founded in 1934.[8] Similar to its
namesake in South Africa, its original aims were to peacefully achieve
political and economic rights for Africans. In 1951 the ANC and other
political bodies joined forces to form the All-Africa Convention, primarily for fighting against the proposed Federation of the Rhodesias
and Nyasaland. Six years later, under the leadership of Joshua Nkomo,
the ANC was reconstituted. The ANC is not a political party; its main
purpose is to give a voice to the African majority and as such is recognized by the Rhodesian government under its current spokesman, Bishop
Abel Muzorewa. Nkomo founded the Zimbabwe African People's Union
(ZAPU) in 1957. The party was banned in 1959; its leader, when not
negotiating with the Ian Smith government, is in detention. In 1963,
dissidents formed ZANU, since they objected to what they considered
a lack of militancy on the part of ZAPU. ZANU is, of course, also
banned, and its leader, the Reverend Ndabaningi Sithole, shares
Nkomo's fate.

Currently, apart from leading occasional joint terrorist forays
into Rhodesia, the alliance between the two banned parties is tenuous.
In 1971, a joint formation was announced called the "Front for the Liberation of Zimbabwe" (FROLIZI) and declared its intention "to wage a
resolute, long-term people's struggle against British colonialism and
its Hitlerite agents in Zimbabwe."[9]

Terrorist incursions began in 1966 and initially took the form of
small bands infiltrating from Zambia or Mozambique to mine a road
or attack an isolated farm or an African village for the purposes of
"recruitment" or punishment of "collaborators." Of late, actions re-
sembling military confrontations on a larger scale have been noted.
Actions by infiltrators against civilians are marked by exceptional
cruelty and the use of torture. There are few planned battles with the
armed forces, and when they do occur or when a band is overtaken the
results are usually disastrous for the terrorists. If captured terrorists are identified as natives of Rhodesia, they are charged as common
criminals, and, if convicted of murder, the penalty may be death.

The military forces of Rhodesia consist of approximately 5,000
regular personnel, about 10,000 officers and men in the Territorial
Force, and about 30,000 in the reserves. The air force includes about
75 pre-UDI aircraft, except for perhaps 10 French Alouette helicopters.

The police, about 7,500 officers, has reserves of about 30,000.
The organization is paramilitary and operates in conjunction with the
army.

In statements to the UN-OAU Oslo conference, ZAPU requested
that the following should be accepted and taken as a working basis for
support:

(a) That the people of Zimbabwe have suffered and continue to suffer violent oppression.

(b) That the oppression suffered by the people of Zimbabwe is being carried out by the United Kingdom using its settler racists and fascists as direct agents.

(c) That economically and in other forms of war logistics the United Kingdom in Rhodesia is reinforced, for its oppression of the people of Zimbabwe, by its NATO allies, particularly the United States, West Germany, France, South Africa and Japan.

(d) That the current armed liberation struggle launched by the people of Zimbabwe in resistance to this oppression is the only just and inevitable means of liberating themselves.

The immediate needs of ZAPU are:

(i) Sufficient, substantial, direct financial assistance to service all our liberation activities, such as fuel for transport, repairs and replacement of parts. Grant of financial assistance should take into account that the Rhodesian fascist regime apart from military hardware spends $50 million annually to service its forces of oppression.

(ii) Sufficient transport in the form of jeeps, heavy-ton carriers (lorries) and fast manoeuverable cars suitable for mobility and speed in this type of struggle, considering the sophisticated transportation and communication system of the enemy.

(iii) Relevant hardware and technical equipment with the imparting of the necessary skills.

(iv) Information dissemination equipment—typewriters (portable and large carriage), duplicators (small and large) plus relevant equipment and spares; printing machines (manageable), photostat machines (large and small) and the relevant equipment.

(v) Material needs—shelters, blankets, large quantities of all types of clothing (male and female)— to meet the needs of freedom fighters as well as for welfare purposes.

(vi) Medicines for casualty and tropical disease purposes plus hospital equipment and assistance for professional medical training.

(vii) Education and technical training for mechanical, civil, agricultural, chemical and electrical engineering, book-keeping and accountancy. [10]

ZANU's statement is more militant and relates to other liberation movements. Thus

> the reformist ameliorative politics of the ANC, NDP
> and ZAPU, it unequivocally rejected as sterile. It
> opted for action. It had analysed the situation and
> come to the obvious conclusion in view of what hap-
> pened to the ANC, NDP, ZAPU, that a racist, fascist
> minority regime which depended on force, intimida-
> tion and terrorism, could only be removed by force.
> No amount of persuasion or reasoning could make it
> change. It must be forced off the saddle of political
> power if justice was to return to Zimbabwe. [11]

The scope, method, and results of ZANU's activities are stated in the manifesto:

> Today ZANU operations cover an area of 50,000 sq.
> miles in the east-north east, north and northwestern
> parts of the country. The area has an African popu-
> lation of between 1.5 and 2 million. White farmers
> in the area are living in a state of fear. Many have
> moved their families out in fear and make their farm-
> steads available for use by so-called security forces.
> Some women and children who have remained on the
> farmsteads sharing with the soldiers have been killed
> or injured in confrontations between ZANLA [the Zim-
> babwe African National Liberation Army, the mili-
> tary wing of ZANU] and the defenders of settlerist
> colonialist oppression of our people. [12]

Practically the whole of the army, police, and air force is on permanent duty. Units of reservists and territorials have been called out.

Another segment of the ZANU manifesto states:

> Three years ago we decided on a new strategy; at the
> end of that period towards the end of 1972, in quick
> succession, Altena farm, belonging to a settler
> farmer Marc de Borchgrave, and used by the rebel
> regime's forces as an anti-freedom fighter operation
> centre, was attacked, and two whites were injured.
> Shortly afterwards Whistlefield farm, also used as
> an army command post, was also attacked by ZANU
> forces, with the loss of twenty-five white soldiers,

and two trucks carrying the forces of repression were blown up by ZANLA laid mines killing or wounding many white soldiers. On December 30 another truck carrying fifteen white soldiers was blown up by a mine; and on January 6, 1973, a police station and the local army officers' mess were attacked by ZANU forces at Mt. Darwin. Two days later two police reservists working under cover as land inspectors were killed by ZANU forces and a third was taken captive. The regime in utter desperation turned against and closed the border with neighbouring Zambia. That the decision was ill-considered and taken in panic is clear from the fact that at first the closure was total, then it excluded copper in transit to the seaports, and finally it was withdrawn altogether. [13]

It is a common assumption that in guerrilla warfare, the defense forces should outnumber the guerrillas by a ratio of ten to one. The expenses of the defenders are also much larger proportionally. While there is practically no chance that ZAPU/ZANU could defeat Rhodesia in battle, the price it pays in mobilized manpower, military procurement, and economic damage caused by a tightening blockade may induce the Smith government or its successor to come to terms with the representatives of the black population.

SOUTH-WEST AFRICA (NAMIBIA)

South-West Africa (Namibia), which had been the protectorate of German South-West Africa (Deutsch Sudwest Afrika) since 1884, was captured by the forces of the then Union of South Africa in 1915, during World War I. The Union was granted a League of Nations mandate in 1922. After World War II and the demise of the League of Nations, South Africa refused to place South-West Africa under the new UN trusteeship system. [14] The UN General Assembly declared the mandate annulled in 1966 and established an 11-nation administrative council to lead South-West Africa toward self-government in 1967. The council renamed the country "Namibia" in 1968. South Africa does not recognize these actions, arguing that the United Nations had no rights to do so under its charter. The International Court of Justice, after an initial decision favoring the status quo ruled in support of the UN resolutions in 1971. [15] The UN commissioner for Namibia, who, of course, cannot enter the territory, is Sean MacBride of Ireland, who shared the Nobel Peace Prize for 1974.

In effect, the territory is governed by an administrator appointed by South Africa and an 18-member white elected legislative assembly. It has six seats in the South African assembly and four appointed senators.

In 1973, part of northern South-West Africa was established as a homeland of the Ovambos. Ovamboland has limited self-government.

The South-West African population of 760,508 is composed of Ovambo—by far the largest nation—Damara, Herero, Nama, Okavango, East Caprivians, Coloreds, Basters, Kaokovelders, Tsaranas, and Bushmen. Whites, who include many Germans, constitute about 15 percent.

SWAPO of Namibia, formed in 1957, is the major terrorist movement in the area and alleges support from most tribal groups. Another terrorist movement, SWANU (South-West African National Union) is supported only by Hereros and is not recognized by the OAU.

The UN General Assembly and Security Council supported SWAPO and its leader Samuel Nujoma by SC Resolution 269 of August 12, 1967, which, by a vote of 11-0-4, recognized "the legitimacy of the struggle of the people of Namibia against the illegal presence of the South African authorities in the territory." The United States supported GA Resolution 2145 of 1966 terminating the mandate and declaring South Africa's continued presence illegal and has accepted the advisory opinion of the International Court of Justice affirming this position.[16]

SWAPO headquarters are in Dar es Salaam, though chances are that it will move to Angola after the Portuguese exit. It maintains offices in Algiers, Cairo, Helsinki, London, Lusaka, New York, and Stockholm. The Namibia News is published in London.

SWAPO's military achievements are few and are limited primarily to the topographically favorable Caprivi Strip. They usually involve small, foreign-trained cadres of from 6 to 25 persons who attack patrols and small settlements, lay mines, damage property, and retreat. It is estimated that the total number of active SWAPO adherents is about 2,000, of whom not more than 10 percent are in South-West Africa. Well-publicized actions have taken place. The August 26, 1966 Ongulambashe incursion, considered the "opening shot of the liberation," involved two SWAPO groups, one of 6, another of 10, who trained 30 local Bantus, who remained in their villages. The SWAPO units were intercepted by a Bantu chief and his villagers and handed over to the South African police.[17]

SWAPO attempted vengeance by attacking the homes of officials of the Department of Bantu Affairs at Oshikango on September 26, 1966. Although the terrorists burned houses and used machine guns, there was only one casualty. There were no soldiers or police present during the attack; they arrived later by helicopter and captured some of the attackers, who were subsequently tried with other captured SWAPO members. The dramatic transcript of the trial is available and has been widely publicized.[18]

The prosecution claimed that they had taken part in a terrorist conspiracy to overthrow law and order in Namibia. They had been trained in the use of firearms and explosives and in hand-to-hand fighting and karate, it was charged; they had infiltrated into Ovamboland to recruit others to help in the uprising and had engaged in acts of violence (including one murder) and robberies.

The trial evoked widespread international protest. The Council for Namibia and the Special Committee of 24, the Assembly, the Commission on Human Rights, and, finally, the Security Council denounced the illegal arrest, deportation, and trial of the Namibians as a flagrant violation of human rights and of the international status of the territory. The vague provisions and severe penalties of the law, the ill-defined charges, the retroactive prosecutions, the removal of the defendants from Namibia to South Africa, and the conduct of the trial itself were condemned. Despite demands that it be discontinued, Prime Minister Vorster declared that South Africa would not allow anything or anybody to interfere with the trial.

Early in 1968, the verdicts were announced. The judge found 34 defendants guilty; two were acquitted (one defendant had died during the trial). Nineteen of the men were sentenced to life imprisonment; the others received terms of up to 20 years.

Again, there were strong protests. The Security Council unanimously censured South Africa's flagrant defiance of its earlier call for discontinuance of the trial and of UN authority.

Another group of eight Namibians went on trial in the summer of 1969 in Windhoek. The defendants, who reportedly had been imprisoned in Pretoria for as long as three years before the trial, faced charges similar to those that had been made in the previous trial. Their court-appointed lawyers admitted the guilt of five of the men, who were sentenced to life imprisonment. A sixth received an 18-year term; two were acquitted.

It is also of interest to refer to news out of Uganda in 1974, where nine Africans were allegedly executed by firing squad on the charge of "suspected terrorism."

The Terrorism Act (No. 83 of 1967, South African Government Gazette 1971) was made retroactive to July 27, 1962, when the first men were recruited for training abroad, and provided that a person convicted under it could be sentenced to death, but that if he were sentenced to imprisonment it must be for a period of at least five years. The powers of this act were extended to South-West Africa.

Among the objections raised around the world to the Terrorism Act was one relating to the retroactive clause. Logically, however,

one should surely acknowledge that the act did not actually create a
completely new crime unexpectedly; it merely defined the new crime
clearly committed by those who left the country from 1962 onward to
receive military training designed to attempt the collapse of constituted authority. As the South African Department of Foreign Affairs
has argued in its monograph "South Africa and the Rule of Law" (April 1968): "If terrorists began an offensive in 1962 which only came
into effect in 1966, why should the counter-offensive not also be valid
from the first date?"[19]

SWAPO's major successes have been political. In spite of deep
divisions and a traditional enmity among several tribes in South-West
Africa, SWAPO succeeded in creating an image of a unified but oppressed nation deprived of its traditional homeland. Only the present
artificial climate in the United Nations—an attitude of "let's correct
injustice elsewhere but not interfere in my own internal affairs"—supported by the new majority of underdeveloped (even if, occasionally,
oil-rich) nations and the Communist states, would fail to observe that
empiric reality is far from the picture of Namibia painted by SWAPO.

CONCLUSION

In light of the recent ultimate successes of terrorist organizations in Angola, Mozambique, and Guinea-Bissao, the question arises
as to whether similar results can be obtained in the remaining white-
ruled territories in South Africa.

First, these successes were only in small measure achieved in
battle. Terrorist losses in armed encounters usually exceeded by a
wide margin those incurred by the police and the military. However,
the reserves in manpower and materiel available to the terrorists exceeded those of the Portuguese. The war in Portugal's African territories ended as an internal contest between large competing tribal
groups, utilizing only a fraction of available forces in the field, supported by supplies from friendly governments, basking in worldwide
sympathy, and based in sanctuaries, against unenthusiastic draftees
with no real direct interest in or patriotic feeling about the area, derived from a shrinking human pool, draining the limited resources of
a poor country, ostracized by allies, and vilified by the international
community. This contest brought about disenchantment in the metropole and a subsequent change in government and disengagement in Africa.

Second, a completely analogous situation does not exist in South
Africa, South-West Africa, or Rhodesia. In South Africa and Rhodesia, whites, most of whom were born in Africa, are resisting in the
knowledge that they have nowhere else to go. Settlers in Portuguese

Africa participate in a limited measure, knowing that the metropole is available as a refuge.

Third, unless large tribal units participate in an insurrection, which so far has not been the case, the manpower available to terrorist groups in the three territories is very limited. As was shown above, South Africa and Rhodesia are capable of total mobilization. South Africa also enjoys considerable fiscal resources.

Fourth, the governments in the three territories are aware that the status quo cannot be maintained and are eager to reach accommodations with their opponents. Since the political elements behind the terrorist movements are fully aware of the utility of cooperation with the whites in government and in the economy and the limitations of concessions that can be wrought out of the whites, they may offer a realistic compromise, involving a period of transition and mutual readjustment, which could establish a modus vivendi.

Fifth, in South-West Africa, where whites number only about 100,000 and are adjacent to South Africa, a surrender of the mandate for the purpose of incurring international goodwill is feasible, in spite of the military ineffectiveness of SWAPO.

Sixth, in South Africa an accelerated divestiture of black ethnic groups into homelands could change the demographic ratio sufficiently to make the truncated Republic acceptable to black Africa. An added impetus is derived from South Africa's economic and technical utility to potential friends.

Seventh, Rhodesia realizes that the present situation is not tenable indefinitely. The government is acutely aware of growing isolation and the erosion of support. It stands to reason that the December 1974 feelers extended to the ANC and the terrorist organizations, which led to preliminary discussions in Lusaka, will eventually lead to realistic negotiations and culminate in a compromise.

In summary, unless a force majeure intervenes in South Africa, the realization by all parties that a military impasse has been reached and that external pressure on the white governments may be a very slow process in a fast-moving age may lead to a triumph of reason over terror.

NOTES

1. The term "terrorist" as used here should be considered synonymous with other descriptions used in this context, such as "guerrilla," "freedom fighter," and "insurgent." There is no judgment attached, as either one may form a government within the target territory if successful. The term "terrorist" is in current use by the de facto governments in the area and is therefore used in this chapter.

2. Ezekiel Mphahlele, The African Image, rev. ed. (New York: Praeger Publishers, 1974), p. 28.

3. U.S. Congress, House, Report of Special Study Mission to Africa, 92d Cong., 2d sess., 1972.

4. For an illustration of Banning Orders, see Allen Drury, A Very Strange Society (New York: Trident Press, 1967), pp. 461-65.

5. One may also speculate that South Africa's peculiar internal situation would justify restrictive legislation under the Holmes "clear and present danger" doctrine (Schenck v. United States, 249 U.S. 47 [1919]).

6. See O. Stokke and C. Widstrand, Southern Africa: The UN-OAU Conference (Uppsala: Scandinavian Institute of African Studies, 1973), vol. 2, Papers and Documents; PAC, "Mounting Black Resistance Inside Azanda," vol. 2, p. 173; Potlako Lebello, "The Struggle Against Minority Rule and Apartheid in South Africa," vol. 1, p. 135; ANC, "The Liberation Struggle with South Africa and the International Community," vol. 2, p. 183.

7. E. S. Efrat, ed., Introduction to Sub-Saharan Africa (Lexington/Toronto: Xerox College Publishing Co., 1973), pp. 163 ff.

8. M. Morris, Terrorism (Cape Town: Howard Timmins, 1971), pp. 12 ff.

9. U.S. Congress, Report, op. cit., p. 223.

10. Stokke and Widstrand, op. cit., vol. 2, pp. 141-42.

11. Ibid., p. 147.

12. Ibid., p. 149. See also the section "The Freedom Struggle in Zimbabwe," ibid., vol. 1, pp. 125 ff.

13. Ibid., vol. 2, p. 148.

14. See United Nations, Office of Public Information, A Trust Betrayed: Namibia (New York, 1974).

15. See Anthony Lejeune, comp., The Case for South-West Africa (London: Tom Stacey Ltd., 1971).

16. U.S. Congress, Report, op. cit., p. 226.

17. Morris, op. cit., pp. 91 ff.

18. A Trust Betrayed, op. cit., pp. 30-32; and Morris, op. cit., pp. 103 ff.

19. Morris, op. cit.

9

FROM TERRORISM TO WAR: THE ANATOMY OF THE BIRTH OF ISRAEL
Yonah Alexander

In 1962, Pope John XXIII began his unprecedented encylical with the words "pacem in terris"—peace on earth. Although this far-sighted message has not eliminated war, it has inspired certain moves toward ideological reconciliation and theological fraternalism. Indeed, the phenomena of detente and ecumenicism reflect contemporary efforts to establish coexistence between opposing political systems and to promote interfaith tolerance.

Suffice it to mention the unfreezing of the Cold War between the superpowers, the improved diplomatic relations between the United States and the People's Republic of China, the mutual recognition of the two Germanys, and the Bangladesh-Pakistani peace settlement. And on a religious plane, the Vatican, determined to foster closer ties with other faiths, announced in 1974 the formation of one commission for Judaism and another for Islam.[1]

Unfortunately, this hopeful trend has evaded the Middle East for over a quarter of a century. For at the core of the Arab-Israeli conflict is the confrontation between two seemingly uncompromising ideologies—Arab nationalism and Zionism. The former is dominated by the struggle of individual Arab countries to achieve and maintain sovereignty; by the Pan-Arab dream of uniting all Arabic-speaking peoples, Moslems and Christians alike, in a united entity; and by the Pan-Islamic idea of bringing under one flag all Moslems, Arabs, and non-Arabs.[2] The latter is the religious and political ideology of the Jewish national liberation movement, out of which the modern State of Israel emerged and to which it is still committed.[3] Stemming from the territorial rift over the control of Ottoman and subsequently British Palestine, each ideology is based on the deep conviction that its cause is moral and just. The Arabs feel that they are a peace-loving people who are plagued with a belligerent enemy that threatens the very survival of the Arab nation. Constantly alert to Israel's "bound-less territorial ambitions," they are bent, in the words of Egypt's President Anwar Sadat, to "liberate our Arab land, drive out the rob-ber and restore the rights of the Palestinian people."[4]

Israel, on the other hand, having fought four bloody wars with her Arab neighbors—three for survival in 1948, 1967, and 1973 and one for security in 1956—believes that it is right and the other side is wrong. With sober awareness of what would have happened if the Arabs had won, Israel is determined to hold out without peace, if need be indefinitely. In fact, it insists that it is the Arabs who must decide between coexistence and nonexistence.

Admittedly, some rays of hope for a negotiated settlement have broken through the clouds of the October 1973 war (also known as the Yom Kippur War by the Jews and the Ramadan War by the Arabs). For the first time in the history of the conflict, a peace conference opened at Geneva the following month. In a relatively optimistic mood, Israel's Abba Eban addressed the conference with the plea, "Let us atone for twenty-five years of separation by working now towards a cooperative relationship similar to that which European states created after centuries of war."[5]

A new climate of intensive Middle East negotiations sponsored by the United States developed in subsequent months. But now that the Rabat summit conference of the Arab heads of state has recognized the Palestine Liberation Organization (PLO) as the "sole legitimate representative of the Palestinian people,"[6] the prospects for a transi-tion from a state of belligerency to total peace are more remote than ever before.

After all, it is the relentless and indiscriminate waves of ter-rorism initiated, planned, and executed by the PLO and other extrem-ist Palestinian Arab nationalists that have consistently and massively blocked any attempt at rapprochement between the antagonists, let alone a durable peace. Believing that a resort to wanton violence would escalate into a prolonged resistance or guerrilla warfare, which, in turn, would precipitate in all-out war leading ultimately to a decisive victory over Zionism, militant Palestinian Arab leaders have traditionally looked upon terrorism as a practical and unequivocal expression of their intention to deny the right of self-determination to the Jewish people. Indeed, this theory and its application in practice are not new elements in the Arab-Israeli conflict; they are as old as the confrontation between Arab nationalism and Zionism. Ever since the inception of the British rule in Palestine at the end of World War I, then, terrorism has been employed to prevent the growth of the yishuv (Jewish community in Palestine) and the establishment of Is-rael.

THE EARLY JEWISH-ARAB ENCOUNTER,
1880-1914

One of the fundamental bases of Zionism is the unbroken historical bond between the Jews—the oldest Palestinian people still surviv-
ing—and the "land of their fathers," the roots of which go back some
4,000 years. Although the vast majority of Jews were scattered to
every corner of the earth after the destruction of the Second Commonwealth, continuity of Jewish life in Palestine has been maintained.
In addition, during the centuries of exile, the millenial hope for national restoration survived and was expressed in the form of numerous
attempts to resettle the Promised Land.[7]

The unique mystical attachment and loyalty of "a people without
a country to a country without people"[8] have been reinforced in the
Zionist ideology by the fact that the Jews have neither abandoned Palestine nor renounced their title to it. In modern times an increasing
number of olim (immigrants), influenced by the rise of nationalism in
Europe during the nineteenth century,[9] spurred by the brutal pogroms
in Czarist Russia[10] and the virulent antisemitism rampant in the
West,[11] and inspired by the crystallization of a national consciousness
advocated by chovevei Zion (lovers of Zion), began to settle in Ottoman
Palestine in the 1880s. These early halutzim (pioneers) purchased
and toiled the land, drained its marshes and swamps, reclaimed the
uninhabited and barren desert, cultivated and irrigated the exhausted
soil, established agricultural settlements, and built new towns.[12]
To them and to the other settlers of the first and second aliyah (immigration),[13] confrontation with the indigenous Arab population in Palestine was not a major concern, nor did they envision the necessity
of having to resort to force in order to secure the right to rebuild a
national entity in Zion, their only source of physical and spiritual
safety and vitality.[14] Since they regarded their ideology as reasonable,
uniquely humane, and even messianic, they saw no inherent and objective reasons for conflict between Jews and Arabs.[15] Indeed, they believed that the aspirations and interests of both peoples were comple-
mentary and interconnected, and that the Arabs, in particular, would
benefit considerably from Jewish achievements.[16]

Theodore Herzl, the father of the Zionist movement, and his
associates and successors[17] who sought in Palestine a political and
territorial solution to the Jewish problem[18] concentrated therefore
on the attainment of two objectives:[19] to convince the Jewish masses
in the European Diaspora that such a redemption was both necessary
and practical,[20] and to influence the custodians of the Holy Land and
the important world powers to permit Jewish settlement there and to
secure some kind of autonomous status for those who would hearken
to their call and come. Diplomatic interventions with the sultan of

the Ottoman Empire, the kaiser of Germany, other European poten-
tates of that time, and the statesmen of the British Empire, whose influence on all areas bordering on the routes to the East was burgeoning, were the principal political preoccupations of the early Jewish
nationalist functionaries. The achievement of these stated goals, the
Zionist leaders assumed, could be done without the slightest detriment
to the Arab population in Palestine. Underlying this assumption was
Herzl's guiding pledge: "It goes without saying that we shall respect-
fully tolerate persons of other faiths and protect their property, their
honor, and their freedom with the harshest means of coercion. This
is another area in which we shall set the entire world a wonderful example."[21] Committed to this principal, the Zionist movement looked
forward to Jews and Arabs living in peace, side by side within the
envisaged Jewish state, enjoying rights and opportunities.

During this same period, contemporary Arab nationalism re-
vived dreams of independence from the Ottoman Empire. But as soon
as the Arab press published reports on the emergence of Zionism as
a national ideology, some concern for the fate of Palestine as part of
the Arab world began to be articulated.[22] In Palestine itself, opposition to the semilegalized Jewish immigration and settlement took the
form of protests by some Arab notables to the Ottoman authorities,
who at times acceded to Arab requests to impose various restrictions
on Jews. But these demands did not stem from nationalistic motivations, but were rather expressions of religious and ethnic assertive-
ness. In fact, since Palestine was regarded by Turkey as the southern
part of the Syrian province, the Palestinian Arabs sought to merge this
sector of the Middle East with "greater Syria" on the basis of common
political, judicial, social, and economic foundations. It is not surprising, therefore, that no distinct Arab political-ideological parties
developed in Palestine simultaneously with other Arab national movements elsewhere prior to World War I.

Indeed, any sporadic, small-scale attacks by Palestinian Arabs
on the early Jewish settlements in the country occurred primarily because of fear, envy, and greed. That is, sometimes Arab peasants
and Bedouins were apprehensive that their rights of ownership and
grazing would be threatened by the newcomers. Also, there were
Arab raiders who desired to enrich themselves at the settlers' expense.

Since the Turkish administration did little to check such incidents, the Zionist pioneers had initially to rely on hired local Arab
and Circassian guards[23] to defend their vulnerable villages. Only in
1907 did some of the settlers form a Jewish armed militia, the "Bar
Giora," named after a Jewish leader of the rebellion against Rome in
the first century. Two years later it was succeeded by "Hashomer"
(the watchman), which soon provided protection to Jewish settlements
in the Galilee and Judea.

BRITISH PLEDGES TO THE ARABS AND
PROMISES TO THE JEWS, 1914-23

When World War I broke out and Turkey entered the conflict on the side of the Central Powers, Arabs and Jews both appealed to the Allies for assistance in realizing their national aspirations in the Middle East.

During the period between July 1915 and March 1916, letters were exchanged between Sherif Hussein of Mecca on behalf of the Arabs and Sir Henry McMahon, the British high commissioner in Egypt, on behalf of the British government. This correspondence culminated in the British promise of Arab independence in the Middle East in return for an Arab agreement to revolt against the Turks. Consequently, Bedouin tribesmen, supported by British funds, arms, and advisers, such as the legendary Lawrence of Arabia, began to sabotage Turkish installations. Other Arab units, led by Hussein and his son Emir Faisal, helped the Allies to hasten the disintegration of the Ottoman Empire, already in its death throes.[24]

About the same time, many Palestinian Jews, jointly with their brethren from other countries, fought alongside British forces in the Middle East in the hope that this effort would lead to Allied support of Zionism.[25] This expectation materialized on November 2, 1917, when Lord Arthur James Balfour, foreign secretary of Britain, in a letter sent to Baron Edmond Rothschild, a prominent Jewish leader, declared, "His Majesty's Government views with favor the establishment in Palestine of a National Home for the Jewish people and will use their best endeavors to facilitate achievement of this object."[26]

Regarding this declaration as official British support for Zionist aims in Palestine, Jewish battalions fought within the British army in Palestine in the closing stages of the war. On December 9, 1917, some 400 years after the Ottoman rule over the Holy Land had begun, the Turks surrendered Jerusalem to General Allenby, and a British military administration was set up in Palestine.

At the San Remo conference of April 25, 1920, the victorious powers of World War I, acting as the Supreme Council of the League of Nations, decided to place Palestine in the British sphere of influence.[27] On July 1 of that year, a civil government was established in the country. The League of Nations, on July 24, 1922, approved the final draft of the Palestine mandate and incorporated the Balfour Declaration into the document. It charged the mandatory power with "placing the country under such political, administrative and economic conditions as will secure the establishment of the Jewish National Home."[28]

But the promise given to the Jews in the Balfour Declaration, which was originally understood to cover all historic Palestine—on

both sides of the Jordan River—was successively whittled down by the
British. They created in 1921-23 the emirate of Trans-Jordan, four-
fifths of the territory of Palestine assigned to the mandate, in order
to accommodate a loyal ally, Abdullah, and thereby fulfill the wartime
pledge to his father, Hussein, recognizing this area as Arab and independent.

AN ARAB-JEWISH DIALOGUE THAT FAILED, 1918-20

The conclusion of World War I signaled a brighter era for self-
determination of nations, peace, and prosperity in the Middle East.
The prospects for mutual recognition of the aspirations of both Arab
nationalism and Zionism were forecasted by the leaders of these two
liberation movements. On March 23, 1918, Hussein, the exponent of
Pan-Arabism, wrote in the daily paper of Mecca Al-Qibla, "We saw
the Jews . . . streaming to Palestine from Russia, Germany, Austria,
Spain, America. . . . The cause of causes could not escape those who
had the gift of deeper insight: They knew that the country was for its
original sons, for all their differences, a sacred and beloved homeland."
Stronger support of the Arab nationalist movement for Zionism
came on January 3, 1919, when Feisal, acting on behalf of the Arab
kingdom of Hedjaj, signed a formal agreement with Chaim Weizmann,
president of the World Zionist Organization, which called for "all necessary measures . . . to encourage and stimulate immigration of
Jews into Palestine on a large scale, and . . . to settle Jewish immigrants upon the soil." The preamble of the agreement stated, "mindful of the racial kinship and ancient bonds existing between the Arabs
and the Jewish people, and realizing that the surest means of working
out the consummation of their national aspirations is through the closest possible collaboration in the development of the Arab state and
Palestine, and being desirous further of confirming the good understanding which exists between them, [we] have agreed upon the following. . . . "29
Feisal's stand was reaffirmed in his subsequent correspondence
with Felix Frankfurter, a prominent American Zionist, with the hope
of obtaining the assistance of influential world Jewry in achieving the
goals of the Arab movement for sovereign independence. On March
3, 1919, he wrote, "We Arabs, especially the educated among us,
look with deepest sympathy on the Zionist movement. . . . We will
wish the Jews a hearty welcome home. . . . We are working together
for a reformed and revised Near East, and our two movements com-
plement one another. The movement is national and not imperialistic.

There is room in Syria for us both. Indeed, I think that neither can be a success without the other."[30]

These communications obviously asserted that the Arabs looked upon the Zionists and their envisaged state as a potential ally. Following this signal, the Palestinian Arabs were at first friendly to the idea of a Jewish national home. Their initial reaction, therefore, was not marked by violence, as most of them showed a lack of political sophistication and expressed little interest in obtaining much more in the way of home rule or exclusive tenure than they had enjoyed under the Turkish regime. The Zionist leaders consistently assured them that their interests would be safeguarded. As Weizmann put it, "cooperation and friendly work with the Arab people must be the cornerstone of all our Zionist activities in the land of Israel."[31]

But these early hopes were shattered by two events. First, the Pan-Arab kingdom, in whose name Feisal spoke, never came into being. Therefore, those Arab leaders who were willing to recognize a Jewish state in Palestine could not implement the Feisal-Weizmann agreement. Second, and perhaps more important, the Palestinian Arabs turned all their efforts against the fulfillment of the Zionist vision. This occurred when an extremist minority faction of Palestinian Arabs assumed control over their own people and introduced terrorism as a way of achieving specific political aims: first, to reduce, if not eliminate, the Jewish presence in Palestine and to frustrate Zionist designs to establish a distinct state there; second, to reject any efforts of Jewish-Arab coexistence and cooperation; third, to persuade or force the mandatory power to relinquish its policy as expressed in the Balfour Declaration; and, finally, to achieve national independence in Palestine under Arab control.

These goals were set down at the All-Arab Palestine Conference, which met in Jerusalem in January 1919.[32] Palestinian Arabs, jointly with their supporters in the General Syrian Congress, declared the following June: "We reject the claims of the Zionists for the estalishment of a Jewish commonwealth in that part of southern Syria which is known as Palestine, and we are opposed to Jewish immigration into any part of the country. We do not acknowledge that they have a title, and we regard their claims as a grave menace to our national, political and economic life."[33] Similar aims and demands were reiterated by the Third Palestine Arab Congress, meeting in Haifa in December 1920, and by subsequent gatherings during the mandatory period.[34]

Leading and inspiring these ultranationalists was Haj Amin El-Husseini, then president of the Supreme Moslem Council, which had managed Moslem affairs in Palestine.[35] The grand mufti of Jerusalem had assembled a personal countrywide religious-political machine and thereby also presided over the Arab Higher Committee (formerly the Supreme Arab Committee), charged with the coordination of the work

of Arab nationalists. He and other members of the prominent Husseini family were the only Arab personalities in British Palestine
with whom the Zionist leaders did not meet to discuss a basis for mutual understanding, for they bitterly disavowed any proposals that did
not entail the total abandonment of Zionist principles. Their constant
incitements to violence against the Jewish community in Palestine resulted in the waves of Arab terrorism of the 1920s and 1930s.

THE FIRST WAVE OF ARAB TERRORISM, 1920-21

The first wave of Arab terrorism in Palestine began spontaneously. Arab rioters attacked isolated Jewish settlements in Upper
Galilee in early 1920. Two villages, Metulla and Tel Hai, succumbed
to the overwhelming mob and had to be abandoned. The heroic deaths
of Joseph Trumpeldor, the defender of Tel Hai, and his comrades became a symbol of dedication and sacrifice for future generations of
Jews.

Palestinian Arab hostility against the Jews spread to Jerusalem,
the City of Peace. On April 20, thousands of Arab pilgrims who had
arrived for the Moslem festival of Nebi Musa were roused to join in
an anti-British political demonstration. Soon the march turned into
an outburst of anti-Jewish frenzy. Leaders and provocateurs shouted
insults against their neighbors ("el Yahood calabana"—"the Jew is our
dog") and incited the mob to attack their enemy ("itbah el Yahood"—
"kill the Jew").

Thereupon the marchers became an explosive force and went after the "children of doom" with sticks and knives. The Arab police,
which was under British control, did not make any attempt to stop the
violence and, in some cases, even joined their fellow Arabs in the
rioting and plunder.

These disorders claimed the lives of five Jews and injured 211
others. Four Arabs also died in the incident. British troops who arrived on the scene arrested several hundred Arabs for the night. The
following morning, disturbances broke out again when the detainees
were released. Order was finally restored several days later, but
not before the government had been forced to disarm the Arab police,
proclaim martial law, and ask the British troops to assume full control.[36]

The military governor of Jerusalem dismissed the Arab mayor
of the city, Mussa Kazim El-Husseini, for inciting the anti-Jewish
rioters. Soon afterward, El-Husseini was elected president of the
Arab Executive Committee, the leading Palestinian Arab umbrella
organization representing local political parties, which would not co-

operate with the British authorities and refused to negotiate with the Jews.

Another member of the prominent Husseini family, Haj Amin, at that time the president of the Arab Club in Jerusalem (the organization that supported an all-Syrian unity), was sentenced by a British military court to 15 years' imprisonment in absentia for his more direct responsibility for the 1920 disturbances. Bowing to Arab pressure, the British allowed him to return to Palestine from his Trans-Jordanian refuge.

To be sure, the authorities in Jerusalem set the tone for an "even-handed" policy. Thus, Zeev (Vladimir) Jabotinsky, a Zionist leader and one of the commanders of the Jewish Legion of World War I, was sentenced by the British to 15 years' imprisonment for his part in organizing the defense of the Jewish quarter of Jerusalem during the 1920 riots. But his sentence was commuted because of strong Jewish protests.

But these developments only tended to bolster the yishuv's determination that, in order to defend Jewish life, property, and honor, it must rely on Jewish protection. The "Haganah" (defense), the citizen-soldier militia organization, was thus established in the wake of the 1920 riots. Formed by members of the earlier defense group Hashomer and veterans of the Jewish Legion of World War I, it was soon to face its first test. [37]

On May Day of the following year, an Arab mob took advantage of a clash in the Jewish sector of Jaffa between a government-authorized Jewish labor organization's procession and a counter-parade by illegal Jewish Communists and unexpectedly attacked both groups. This was followed by the massacre of 13 Jews by a berserk crowd in the Immigration House in Jaffa. On the outskirts of the city, Joseph Chaim Brenner, a leading Hebrew writer, was murdered, along with the family with whom he was visiting at the time.

A series of reprisals by Haganah members followed in the Jaffa area. A number of people were killed, and many were wounded on both sides. Subsequently, violence spread to other regions in the country. Armed Arabs attacked and looted several settlements. The most serious onslaught befell Petach Tikvah, the oldest Jewish agricultural colony, which traditionally had enjoyed good relations with its neighbors. The settlement was able to hold its own against some 2,000 attackers until it was saved by an Indian cavalry squadron that happened to be passing by. Another Arab attack on Petach Tikvah was checked by a squadron of British planes and then dispersed by an Indian military unit. Some 50 Arabs and 4 Jews died in this incident. [38]

The Haycraft Commission, sent to Palestine to investigate the causes of the 1920-21 disturbances, reported "that racial strife was begun by Arabs who were generally the aggressors; that the outbreak was unpremeditated and unexpected; that the general body of Jews was anti-Bolshevist; that the fundamental cause of the riots was a feeling amongst the Arabs of discontent with, and hostility to, the Jews, due to political and economic causes, and connected with Jewish immigration, and with their conception of Zionist policy as derived from Jewish exponents."[39]

ARAB AGITATION AND THE SECOND OUTBURST OF VIOLENCE, 1922-29

In reaction to the 1920-21 wave of terrorism and the Haycraft report, the mandatory government in Jerusalem sought to appease the Arab nationalists. When they refused to accept the establishment of a legislative council in Palestine that would have provided a considerable measure of self-government because it would have meant cooperation with the Jewish community, the mandatory administration formed, in January 1922, the Supreme Moslem Council, to administer the affairs of the Moslem community in the country. Haj Amin El-Husseini, who had been appointed the mufti of Jerusalem (religious official who issues rulings in response to questions) by Sir Herbert Samuel, the first high commissioner of the civilian administration in Palestine, a year earlier, was elected president. Although El-Husseini had promised to exercise his great spiritual and social influence to assure peace in Jerusalem, the council soon became the mufti's powerful instrument to fight Arab political opponents, Zionism, and the mandate's policy regarding the establishment of a Jewish national home in Palestine.

Several months later, Samuel announced at a gathering of Arab leaders at Ramleh that Jewish immigration would be reduced. This declaration was formalized with the publication of the British white paper of June 3, 1922, which proposed establishing a quota on such immigration to be determined by the economic absorptive capacity of the country.[40] However, the Arab nationalists were not completely satisfied with the document because it did not put an end to the development of the Jewish national home in Palestine as envisaged in the Balfour Declaration.

In the following year, the British banned the Haganah as an illegal organization. It went underground and prepared itself to defend the yishuv in the face of continued Arab agitation reinforced by rising nationalism. But, in the absence of any representative institution in Palestine, resulting directly from Arab objections, the mandatory government permitted the establishment in 1926 of the Vaad Leumi (National Council), to serve as a sort of cabinet for the Jewish community in the country.

Fortunately, the years 1922-28 passed without any serious outburst of violence. Jewish immigration in the country almost doubled, and when an economic crisis developed in Palestine in 1926-27, Arab nationalists expected that the Zionist effort to establish a Jewish entity would collapse from within. But the economic conditions improved, and the British strengthened the Palestinian Zionists by recognizing the Jewish Agency as a world Jewish body to advise and cooperate with the mandatory government on matters concerning the national home.[41] These developments, coupled with an increase in the ferocity of the Arab extremists, suddenly changed the relative peace in the country.

It all began as a consequence of tensions connected with the Wailing Wall dispute.[42] The mufti, who fostered the Islamic character of Jerusalem, injected a religious character into his struggle with Zionism when, in 1928, he challenged the right of Jews to bring prayer appurtenances to the wall in the Old City of Jerusalem, the most sacred site of Judaism. Jews, on the other hand, disputed the right of the Moslem Waqf (the Moslem religious foundation) to build on that part of Haram al-Sharif (the Temple Mount, with the mosques of al-Aksa and the Dome of the Rock holy to Islam), immediately overlooking the wall. A British white paper was issued in November that favored the Arab position.

On August 23, 1929, Jews obtained permission for and carried out an orderly demonstration to protect this concession and to reaffirm Jewish rights at the wall. The Arab leadership in the Old City then incited mobs to participate in a countermarch. Aroused by inflammatory speeches, the protesters burned petitions placed by Jewish worshipers in Wailing Wall services.

Rumors that Jews were planning to appropriate the Haram al-Sharif and to burn down the holy mosques situated there brought to the Old City thousands of Arabs ready to protect their sacred sites. The following day, on the Jewish sabbath, the mob attacked throughout Jerusalem, including the Mea Shearim quarter inhabited mainly by orthodox Jews. The Arab police in the Old City were ineffective, and the British forces were delayed in providing assistance; as a result, the Jewish community suffered badly.

Violence spread to the outlying vicinities of the Old City, to the Jewish agricultural colonies of Artuf and Motzah, where an entire family was slaughtered. Settlements in the southern district of the country, Hulda and Beer Tuvia, were also assaulted. But in these colonies the Haganah was able to hold the Arabs at bay.

The most brutal attack that sabbath day was aimed at the religious center of Hebron, which consisted mostly of older people supported by charitable contributions from abroad and a group of young Talmudic academy students. Almost the entire community was wiped out in a terrible ordeal: more than 60 Jews were killed and over 50 wounded, including women and children; the synagogue was profaned; the Jewish clinic (which had provided treatment for both Arabs and Jews) was ransacked; and other Jewish property was destroyed.

On August 28, 1929, another devastating pogrom-type operation took place at Safed, also an old center of Jewish piety. Here too the toll was high: 45 Jews were killed or wounded, houses of worship and learning were desecrated, and homes were pillaged and burned.

In less than one week, a total of 133 Jews had died and 339 others had been injured in Jerusalem, Hebron, and Safed. In other mixed cities, such as Gaza, Jenin, Nablus, and Tulkaram, the Arabs expelled their Jewish neighbors from their midst. In different parts of the country, Jews were forced to abandon a total of 11 communities. By the time order was restored, 116 Arabs had also been killed and another 232 wounded. [43]

In the wake of this wave of terrorism, the British government established in the fall of 1929 a commission headed by Sir Walter Shaw to investigate the reasons for the disturbances. Its report blamed the Arabs for the outbreak of violence but emphasized their fear of, and opposition to, the continuing development of the Jewish national home. It recommended, therefore, that Zionist immigration to Palestine be more tightly controlled. [44]

SPORADIC ARAB TERRORISM, 1930-36

The years 1930-36 witnessed a third wave of intermittent Arab-initiated disturbances and violence. These events unfolded in the wake of increased Jewish immigration to Palestine, many Jews having left Germany under the impact of Nazi repression and Polish anti-Semitism.

El-Husseini, who had become the most important leader of the Palestinian Arabs after the 1929 riots, increased, with the backing of the extreme political faction of the Supreme Moslem Council, his pressure on the mandatory government to stop the flow of Jewish immigrants. Mobilizing support from coreligionists outside Palestine, delegates from some 22 countries met at a Moslem congress in Jerusalem in December 1931 and warned against the dangers of Zionism. Similarly, the Arab Executive Committee, representing local nationalist parties, in its manifesto of March 1933, asserted that the Zionists had designs to take possession of the country, with the active support of the British, and urged the Arabs to sacrifice themselves in the battle with the enemy.

This call struck a responsive chord, and the Arabs launched a campaign of violence against the mandatory government. The general strike of October, protesting the accelerated Jewish immigration, led to anti-British riots in Jaffa, Haifa, and Jerusalem. It resulted in the deaths of 26 Arabs and one policeman. The following year, an Arab terror group began to operate against the authorities, but the British forces killed and captured all of its members. Throughout this period, there had also been a number of assassinations of Jews, attacks on Jewish farms, acts of vandalism against orchards and crops, and deliberate maiming of cattle belonging to Jews. [45]

The dramatic events of the 1929 terror and its aftermath shocked the yishuv. In fact, it rather expected that the national aspirations of the Arabs would be satisfied by the creation of Jordan and the establishment of other new Arab states and, therefore, that they would not object to the establishment of a single Jewish state in the area. After all, the Zionists rationalized, the Arabs had neither a legal nor a moral title to Eretz Yisrael. Such a claim, they asserted, was refuted by the fact that the Arab population of Palestine was of mixed races and did not constitute a distinct people and by the failure of the Palestinian Arabs throughout history to fight for independence rather than surrender the land to successive conquerors.

The official Jewish leaders therefore attempted to reach agreements with the more moderate Arab leaders. For example, David Ben-Gurion and Moshe Sharett, representing the yishuv, met with Musa Alami, a prominent Palestinian spokesman, and agreed that there should be further discussion between the two communities regarding the establishment of a Jewish entity, on both sides of the Jordan River, connected to an Arab federation in the neighboring countries. Ben-Gurion and Alami met several times in the following year to continue their talks.

Also, unofficial Jewish leaders had attempted to improve relations with the Palestinian Arabs. The best-known group was the "Brith Shalom" (Covenant of Peace), led by Judah Magnes, the then president of the Hebrew University, and included a group of noted Jewish scholars of Jerusalem. Founded in 1925, this organization aimed at the establishment of a biracial commonwealth in Palestine, in which both Arabs and Jews would enjoy equal rights without regard to the demographic differences between majority and minority. In the meantime, it promoted active intellectual and social cooperation between Arabs and Jews in Palestine. It was also instrumental in bringing Jewish and Arab political leaders together on several occasions. One example is the July 18, 1934 meeting between Ben-Gurion and Magnes and the leader of the Istiglal (Arab nationalist party) in Palestine, Abdul Hadi, who stated that, if the Arabs became united with the aid of the Jews, then they would agree to accept even 5 to 6 million Jews in Palestine.

But these contacts consistently failed. Arab apprehension in Palestine was converted into hostility by the more extreme Palestinian leadership orchestrated by the mufti and his followers.

THE ARAB REVOLT, 1936-39

Encouraged by the failure of the mandatory authority to exercise its police power or moral persuasion effectively, particularly when Jewish interests were at stake, and by the inability of the League of Nations to check the aggression of Italian facism and German nazism, the militant Arab leadership decided to rise up in open revolt against both the British administration and the Jewish community.

To be sure, two immediate events precipitated the most intensive wave of Arab violence in the pre-1948 period. First, the Arab Higher Committee, the all-embracing body representing the Arab parties in Palestine, was formed in April 1936 under the chairmanship of El-Husseini, the mufti of Jerusalem. Despite some internal disagreements, this political machinery enabled the militant nationalists to command greater obedience from the population and to direct the revolt without challenge from any other Arab leader. Second, the mufti realized that, with the growth of Jewish population in the country and the determination of the yishuv to strongly resist Arab violence, terrorism must become a new type of warfare in the form of organized and efficient bands of fighters replacing mob outbursts. Thus, after El-Husseini set up his storm troops in Green Shirt semimilitary units, the ground for the insurrection was prepared. [46]

The terrifying bloodbath of the rebellion began on April 15, when a mufti group held up 10 cars on the Tel Aviv-Haifa highway, singled out three Jews, put them in a truck, and shot them to death. Four days later, an Arab attack in Jaffa resulted in three Jewish fatalities.

On April 25, the Arab Higher Committee organized a general strike in the country until their demands for a fundamental change in British policy in Palestine were met. This strike was accompanied by violence. Jews were assaulted and stoned in various cities. In rural areas Arab farmers attacked Jewish settlements and the British police. These activities were supplemented by guerrilla warfare carried out by organized Arab units from the hills.

Open support for Palestinian terrorism from the neighboring Arab countries came almost immediately. Their officials justified the bloodshed on the grounds that the Arabs had lost faith in the value of British "pledges and assurances for the future." They also protested the mandatory government's use of force against the Palestinian Arabs.

This political support was supplemented by the training of local bands by outside guerrillas, such as Syria's Fazi al-Qawugji, who also joined the Palestinians in fighting. In fact, the local Arabs were reinforced by volunteers from Lebanon, Syria, and Trans-Jordan. As a result of this escalation, sabotage and murder increased. Roads were mined, railways damaged, and the oil pipeline between Iraq and Haifa broken.

This stage of the Arab insurrection came to an end by October, some six months after the outbreak of the revolt, as a result of the intervention of some of the Arab countries. That is, Iraq, Saudi Arabia, Trans-Jordan, and Yemen requested (at Britain's invitation and after prearranged agreement with her) the Palestinian Arabs to stop the bloodshed, and the violence was halted, but only after it had claimed the lives of some 80 Jews and injured some 400 others.

To investigate these events, the London government established the Palestine Royal Commission headed by Lord Peel. Its report, published in July 1937, declared the mandate unworkable and the British pledges to both parties mutually irreconcilable: "To put it in one sentence, we cannot—in Palestine as it now is—both concede the Arab claim to self-government and secure the establishment of the Jewish National Home."[47] The commission therefore recommended the partition of Palestine into a Jewish state and an Arab state that would be united with Trans-Jordan as the best possible solution to the problem.

Although this proposal did not meet with full Jewish expectations, the Zionist Congress, meeting in August, decided to enter into negotiations with the British government for the creation of a distinct Jewish entity in Palestine as a decisive step in fulfilling Zionist aims.

On the Arab side, Trans-Jordan's Emir Abdullah favored the partition proposal, hoping to incorporate the Arab portion into his kingdom. Abdullah's supporters among the Palestinian Arabs, such as Ragheb Al-Nashashibi, were inclined to accept this plan, but the strong opposition of the extreme nationalists, led by the mufti of Jerusalem, and the initiation of an internal bloodbath against the Arab moderates, coupled with the resumption of the insurrection with greater vigor, finally shelved the Peel proposal. When the British district commissioner in the Galilee was murdered, the mandatory authorities retaliated by outlawing the Arab Higher Committee on October 1, 1937, for its role in the rebellion. Five of the most important members of the committee were arrested and deported to the Seychelles, a group of islands in the Indian Ocean.

The mufti of Jerusalem, who was dismissed by the mandatory authorities from his position of president of the Supreme Moslem Council, which was disbanded, fled the country to Lebanon and then took up residence in Syria. From his exile, El-Husseini continued to direct the rebellion in Palestine, and his followers resumed operations on a large scale.

Attacks against individual Jews and Jewish settlements were stepped up. One such attack was the October 4, 1938 Tiberias Massacre. Two large Arab units attacked the city for several hours before government troops drove them away. The shooting, stabbing, and burning left 19 Jews dead and 3 wounded, including women and children.

Violence was also directed at British police stations as well as at Arab towns where local residents opposed the militant Arab nationalism. But with the intensification of British military action coupled with the support provided by the indigenous Arab Peace Bands established by the authorities to fight the guerrillas, the revolt began to lose momentum by the spring of 1939.

Meanwhile, in another effort to resolve the Palestinian problem, the British government invited the representatives of the Arab and Jewish communities and, for the first time, also delegates of the Arab states, to the St. James Round Table Conference, held in London in February 1939. Since the Arabs refused to sit with the Jews at the same table, the British had to meet separately with them and the Jewish delegation. When the conference ended in a deadlock, the mandatory government reverted to ruling Palestine by decree.

Then, on May 17, Malcolm MacDonald, the colonial secretary, published a white paper enunciating a new policy whereby existing rights of Jews to immigration and land purchases were curtailed and the Balfour Declaration's goals were deferred. It also announced a plan for an independent Palestine in 10 years, which would relegate Jews to a permanent minority status.

The white paper further established that Jewish immigration would be limited to a total of 75,000 during the next five years and that additional Jewish immigration into Palestine would depend upon Arab consent. Finally, the document determined that the transfer of Arab-owned land to Jewish ownership would be regulated by an interim government.[48]

London's anti-Zionist policy, military realities, the severe economic damage suffered by the Arabs, and a joint appeal by pro-British leaders of the neighboring countries finally convinced the Arab Higher Committee to end the revolt and urge quiet. The British agreed to permit the guerrillas to escape and made no attempt to disarm the bands. The general strike was called off, and the organized violence ceased, although sniping and other individual attacks continued.

By the time World War II broke out in September 1939, the Arab revolt had virtually been suppressed. The toll was frightening: 517 Jews, 3,112 Arabs, and 135 British dead; 2,500 Jews, 1,775 Arabs, and 386 British injured.[49]

THE JEWISH RESPONSE TO THE ARAB
REVOLT, 1936-39

The Jewish losses from the Arab revolt would have been much greater had it not been for the defense efforts of the yishuv, with some support given by the British authorities, against whom the Arabs had also directed their attack. The Jewish Agency, representing the yishuv, adopted a twofold policy: havlagah (self-restraint) and haganah (self-defense). This meant a deliberate decision of the Jewish community not to meet Arab terrorism with counterterrorism, but to take appropriate defensive measures.

More specifically, the Haganah, which was closely linked to the Histadrut (General Federation of Jewish Labor in Palestine), bore the main responsibility for the implementation of this policy.[50] It fortified Jewish villages with barbed-wire fences, redoubts, and searchlights; provided settlements and towns with fighting men; established dozens of stockades and watchtower outposts in areas where no Jewish settlements had previously existed; made available armed escorts to protect vehicles and convoys; constructed new roads to enable greater safety of communications; and gradually organized operations against terrorist bands and their bases.

The mandatory government, in cooperation with the Jewish Agency, formed an auxiliary police known as "Ghafirs," or "Notrim" (Guards), often serving as a cover for the Haganah underground in communications, arms procurement, equipment transportation, and training. These units guarded railways, airfields, and government offices.

Protecting villages against incursions by Arab bands was the responsibility of the Jewish Settlement Police, set up by the authorities, and of the Haganah's "Peluggot Sadeh" (Field Companies). Finally, "Special Night Squads," consisting of regular British forces and Haganah members and commanded by Captain Orde Wingate, undertook guerrilla-type operations against the terrorists.

Throughout the period of the Arab revolt, the Haganah continued to strengthen its underground forces. It purchased weapons inside and outside the country, developed its own arms industry, and trained its increasing membership. The cost of these activities and the security expenses in general were met by Kofer ha-Yishuv, a voluntary tax that the Jewish community in Palestine imposed upon itself.

Simultaneously with such defense efforts, Jewish leaders, both official and unofficial, tried to improve relations with the Arab Palestinian community. These attempts were mostly initiated by a few social, business, and labor groups. Several clubs to cultivate closer social relations were sponsored by the League for Arab-Jewish Relations. There were also sporadic instances of Arab-Jewish cooperation by the business leadership of both communities. The Arab chairman of the Nablus Chamber of Commerce participated in a Jewish nutrition conference in Tel Aviv, and a number of joint meetings of Arab and Jewish orange growers were held. Histadrut, then an all-Jewish labor organization, launched a parallel Arab labor union, and the two groups cooperated in organizing joint strikes around the country and in initiating joint cooperatives. However, these efforts proved abortive because radical Arab nationalists discouraged and eventually, through intimidation and terror, stopped any contact with Jews. One newspaper correspondent concluded, "Extremist Arab followers of the Mufti . . . are rapidly achieving their aims by eliminating political opponents in Palestine who are inclined toward moderation."[51]

The Jewish leadership also attempted to persuade moderate Arabs from the neighboring countries to begin a dialogue among themselves regarding the possibility of a peaceful resolution of the opposing nationalistic aims. Thus, Ben-Gurion and Magnes met with George Antonius, a Christian Arab historian and theoretician of the nationalist movement. Eliahu Elath, a representative of the Jewish Agency, held meetings with Faud Bey Hamaz, the foreign minister of Saudi Arabia; Chaim Weizmann saw Shabander, an adviser to Syria's president; and Magnes met Iraq's Nuri Pasha.

As these contacts also proved fruitless and the Arab revolt in Palestine continued with greater vigor, the Haganah's policy of self-restraint and defense began to have its critics, particularly among the more militant members who owed allegiance to the Revisionists, the extreme nationalist wing of the Zionist movement.[52] Revising an earlier split, they seceded from the Haganah in 1937 and formed the Irgun Zvai Leumi (National Military Organization), or, in its abbreviated form, Etzel (IZL), led by David Raziel.[53] It not only advocated a strong defense posture but also insisted on retaliation against Arab terrorists and, at times, even against innocent Arabs. Etzel bombed Arab marketplaces, cafes, and buses throughout the country, killing scores and wounding hundreds of people. The British response to this wave of violence was severe. In the summer of 1938, the authorities hanged an Etzel member who was captured in an abortive attack on an Arab bus in Galilee.[54]

Despite the activities of Etzel and the constant Arab provocations, the yishuv's policy of havlagah prevailed. But a more militant attitude, particularly toward the British, developed within the Jewish community with the publication of the pro-Arab white paper of May 1939. The yishuv denounced this document as not in accord with the Balfour Declaration and the British obligation under the League of Nations mandate. Ben-Gurion asserted at a meeting of the clandestine Haganah, "Until now, we have acted according to the spirit of the law. From now on some of our activities will be directed against the law and with the aim of making that law powerless."[55]

When the British foreign secretary announced an immediate suspension of Jewish immigration to Palestine for six months, beginning on October 1, 1939, Ben-Gurion declared, "The British closed legal entry to Palestine, so the Jews would force their way by the back door."[56]

To facilitate the organization and coordination of illegal immigration, also known as aliah bet (class B immigration), [57] particularly in light of the worsening situation of the Jews in Europe, the Haganah set up a special underground body, the "Mosad" (the Institution). In addition, the Haganah formed a unit to carry out anti-British operations, including attacks on telephone lines, railroads, and other government property.

As might be expected, Etzel's response to the white paper was more violent, and many of its activities were directed against the British authorities. When it called off its operations on the outbreak of World War II, a more extreme splinter wing formed the "Lohamei Herut Yisrael" (Fighters for the Freedom of Israel), also known as "Lehi" and "the Stern group" (named after its first commander). [58] Interestingly, Lehi initially sought to cooperate with Britain's enemies, the Axis powers, in an effort to obtain from them firm support for the creation of a Jewish state in Palestine.

WORLD WAR II, VIOLENCE, AND
REPRESSION, 1939-45

Although Arab terrorism ended at the outbreak of World War II, the Jews of Palestine were alarmed by the growth of Trans-Jordan's Arab Legion and Frontier Forces, officered and trained by the British, who were also stationed in camps west of the Jordan River.

Despite this apprehension, the yishuv's attention was turned to the struggle against nazism. Some 136,000 volunteers, almost the entire Jewish population between the ages of 18 and 50, registered for national service. Nearly 30,000 Palestinian Jews, including members of the Haganah, acting on its orders, joined military units within the framework of the British army, among them the Jewish Brigade. They were equipped and trained by the British and fought alongside the Allies throughout the war. Some of them were recruited for special missions against the advancing Germans in the Middle East in 1941-42 and for guerrilla action in occupied Europe.

No similar war effort was contributed by the Palestinian Arabs. In fact, the mufti of Jerusalem had established a direct contact with Hitler in Germany and encouraged the faithful in Iraq to join Rashid Ali's pro-Nazi coup against the British in April 1941. In a Berlin broadcast, the mufti declared the following:

Salaam Aleikum, children of Allah, Moslems of the World; this is your leader talking to you wherever you may be. This is Amin Al-Huesseini, calling on you in the name of Allah, besides whom there is no God

and Muhammad is his messenger, to take up arms in
this Jihad [holy war] against the infidel British who
want to subdue all children of Allah and kill all his
soldiers, and against the cunning Jews who desire to
rob you of your sanctuaries and rebuild their Temple
on the ruins of our Mosque of Omar in al-Quds. Children of Allah, this is a Holy War for the glory and
honor of Allah, the merciful and beneficent. If you
die in this war, you will sit in Heaven on the right
side of the Prophet. Children of Allah, I call on you
to fight. Heil Hitler. [59]

Although the Iraqi revolt failed, the mufti continued his collaboration with Hitler in planning and executing the "final solution" of Europe's Jewry. At a rally in Berlin in November 1943, El-Husseini declared, "The Germans know how to get rid of the Jews."

The impact of these activities is illustrated by the deep emotional
sympathy of the Arabs for Hitler. In the streets of Palestinian cities,
Arab crowds saluted the Fuhrer. Moreover, many Moslems volun-
teered for Nazi units operating in occupied territories in the Soviet
Union and Yugoslavia and for the mufti's legion carrying out sabotage
activities in British Palestine. This wartime assistance was provided
by the mufti in return for Germany's assurances to liquidate the foundation of the Jewish national home after victory.

Notwithstanding the Jewish and Arab contributions to the war effort, throughout the period the mandatory government persisted with
its white paper policy. When the British were about to deport 1,700
illegal immigrants aboard the ship Patria in November 1940, the
Haganah sabotaged its departure. The boat sank and 250 Jews were
drowned in Haifa Bay. [60]

The authorities also continued the cordon-and-search tactic
against the Jewish underground movements. In October 1939, 43
Haganah members were arrested for carrying arms and participating
in a military training course. They were sentenced to five years'
imprisonment. In other instances, the British forces discovered hidden arms and ammunition in Jewish villages. [61]

These arms searches and arrests were suspended as the Italian
and German threat to the Middle East became more acute. The
Haganah cooperated with the British in the invasion of Vichy-French
Syria and Lebanon in 1941. Hundreds of the Haganah's "Palmach"
(Shock Troops)—permanently mobilized commando units—were trained
by British officers in guerrilla tactics in preparation for a resistance
movement in case Palestine were occupied by enemy forces.

But as soon as the war tide turned in favor of the Allies, relations between the yishuv and the mandatory government deteriorated.

The authorities resumed their arms searches, staged political trials against Haganah members, and blocked attempts at illegal entry into Palestine. In February 1942, the <u>Struma</u>, carrying 169 Jewish refugees on their way to Palestine, was sunk in the Black Sea.[62]

In response to these events, an extraordinary conference of Zionist leaders from Palestine, the United States, and Europe was held at the Biltmore Hotel in New York City. On May 11, 1942, the conference adopted the Biltmore Program demanding the opening of the gates of Palestine for Jewish immigrants and the establishment of the country as an independent Jewish commonwealth. This plan met with strong opposition, particularly from Etzel and Lehi. Supporting a more radical solution, they insisted on a Jewish state within the historical boundaries of the ancient kingdom of Israel.

Meanwhile, acts of terrorism by Lehi continued intermittently throughout the war. In January 1942 there were a series of armed robberies and murders of senior British officers in the Tel Aviv area. A month later, Abraham Stern himself was killed. Attempts by members of the group to assassinate the inspector general of the police and one of his assistants in reprisal on April 22 failed.[63]

Lehi did not hesitate to carry its campaign against the British even outside Palestine. On November 6, 1944, two of its members assassinated Lord Moyne, British resident minister in Egypt, who was known for his anti-Zionist attitude. The assailants were arrested, tried, and executed in Cairo on March 22, 1945.[64]

Etzel was also active during the last two years of the war in an attempt to force the British government to reverse its anti-Jewish policy. In 1944 there were attempted assassinations of British officials, murders of police and military personnel, and attacks on mandatory facilities as well as on police and military installations.[65]

This wave of Jewish violence was strongly condemned by the yishuv leadership.[66] It called upon the dissident groups to put an end to terrorism, hoping that, with the end of the war approaching, the British would take a more pro-Jewish disposition. But Etzel and Lehi rejected this request and continued with their violence against the British in the belief that, if they were to destroy British prestige in Palestine, "the removal of their rule would follow automatically."

The Haganah, not wanting to lose its respectability in relation to the mandate authorities, undertook some strong action against Jewish terrorists, including the surrender to the British police of a number of Etzel and Lehi members.

The mandatory government, for its part, resorted to repressive measures against all those suspected of belonging to Jewish terrorist groups. In October 1944, the authorities deported 251 suspects to a detention camp in Eritrea. Simultaneously with this response, London adopted a pronounced pro-Arab policy toward the end of the war

by encouraging the creation of the Arab League. It was formally established on March 22, 1945, in Cairo, by Egypt, Iraq, Lebanon,
Saudi Arabia, Syria, Trans-Jordan, and Yemen. The Arab Higher
Committee of Palestine was admitted as a permanent and voting member. The goal of the league became immediately apparent—an eventual unification of all Arab states, including independent Palestine.

POSTWAR DISAPPOINTMENT AND THE
JEWISH STRUGGLE AGAINST THE BRITISH,
1945-47

After World War II ended in Europe and the calamity of the Holocaust became known, the yishuv expected the British government in
London to reopen the gates of Palestine to the Jewish survivors ga-
thered in displaced persons camps established by the Allies. But
President Truman's appeal to London to permit 100,000 Jews to immi-
grate to Palestine was not heeded. The newly elected government,
whose leaders, Prime Minister Clement Attlee and Foreign Minister
Ernest Bevin, had promised their support for Jewish aspirations before coming into office, stood firmly by the prewar white paper, re-
stricting Jewish immigration and, in effect, opposing the establishment of a Jewish state in Palestine.

The yishuv's response was swift. The Mosad, the Haganah's
clandestine organization for illegal immigration from Europe, jointly
with the "Brihah" (Flight), another body set up for the purpose of assisting displaced Jews to settle in Palestine, intensified their activities. A few boats with illegal immigrants began to arrive, but most
were intercepted by the British navy, and their passengers were interned.

These developments resulted in a unique display of the yishuv's
unity. The three underground organizations—the Haganah (headed by
Moshe Sueh), Etzel (commanded by Menachem Begin), and Lehi (led
by Nathan Friedman-Yellin)—decided, in spite of ideological differences between them, to cooperate in a newly formed Jewish resistance movement. The Haganah contributed to the movement a static
force of 40,000, consisting of settlers and townfolk; approximately
16,000 people attached to a "field army" based on the Jewish Settlement Police; and the Palmach units with a membership of 2,000 to
6,000, including reserves. The contributions by the other paramilitary organizations were far smaller. Etzel had a force estimated at
between 3,000 and 5,000, and Lehi had between 200 and 300 members.[67]

Determined to engage in sabotage activities against the mandatory
government in order to influence London to change its policy, each of
the component units of the movement carried out, under a common au-

thority, specific operations separately.[68] The first operation of the
movement took place on October 10, 1945, when a Palmach unit
breached the walls of the fortified Athlit internment camp and freed
208 illegal immigrants who were being held there. On November 1,
the Haganah launched a major attack on the Palestine railway system
at 153 different points, completely disrupting it. Several coastal pa-
trol boats at Haifa and Jaffa were destroyed. Etzel caused heavy damage to the Lydda station, and the Haifa refineries were sabotaged by
Lehi.[69]

On the following day, Kol Israel (the Voice of Israel), the underground broadcasting station of the resistance movement, called these
activities "an expression of our strength and decision." It also declared: "We lament the British, Arab and Jewish victims who fell in
the attack on the railways and ports of Palestine. They are all victims
of the White Paper."

A second warning to the British government of the consequences
that would follow if it did not modify the Palestine policy was given by
the Jewish resistance movement in subsequent months.[70] In a series
of operations in February 1946, attacks were directed at police posts,
coast guard stations, radar installations, and airfields.[71] Describing
these events, Kol Israel, in its March 3 broadcast, said:

> This last fortnight has seen a renewed intensity in the
> struggle of the Jewish people against the forces which
> aim to throttle them and their national aspirations for
> normal nation-hood in their National Home.
> The attack on the Radar Station on Mount Carmel
> was aimed at destroying one of the principal agents
> of the Government in its hunt for Jewish refugees.
> The sabotage of the airfields was the sabotage of a
> weapon which has been degraded from its glorious
> fight against the evil forces of Nazism to the dishon-
> orable task of fighting against the victims of Nazism.
> Those three attacks are symptomatic of our strug-
> gle. In all cases the onslaught was made against the
> weapon used by the White Paper in its despicable bat-
> tle to repudiate its undertaking to the Jewish people
> and the world, and not against the men who use this
> weapon. It is not our object to cause the loss of life
> of any Briton in this country; we have nothing against
> them because we realize that they are but instruments
> of a policy, and in many cases unwilling instruments.[72]

When London rejected a recommendation for the speedy admission of 100,000 Jewish refugees into Palestine, this time offered in

the report of the Anglo-American Commission of May 1, 1946,[73] Kol
Israel made the following broadcast:

> The Jewish Resistance Movement thinks it desirable to
> publish the warning it intends to lay before His Majes-
> ty's Government. Present British policy is executing
> a dangerous maneuver and is based on an erroneous
> assumption: Britain, in evacuating Syria, Lebanon
> and Egypt intends to concentrate her military bases
> in Palestine and is therefore concerned to strengthen
> her hold over the mandate; and is using her responsi-
> bility to the Jewish people merely as a means to that
> end. But this double game won't work. Britain can-
> not hold both ends of the rope; she cannot exploit the
> tragic Jewish question for her own benefit as manda-
> tory power, while attempting to wriggle out of the
> various responsibilities which that mandate confers.
> From the Zionist point of view, the tepid conclusions
> of the Commission bear no relation to the political
> claims of the Jewish people, but, even so, in the exe-
> cution of these proposals, the British Government is
> displaying a vacillation at once disappointing and dis-
> creditable. We would therefore warn publicly His Ma-
> jesty's Government that if it does not fulfill its respon-
> sibilities under the mandate—above all with regard to
> the question of immigration—the Jewish people will
> feel obliged to lay before the nations of the world the
> request that the British leave Palestine. The Jewish
> Resistance Movement will make every effort to hinder
> the transfer of British bases to Palestine and to pre-
> vent their establishment in the country.

In an attempt to disturb British communications, the Haganah,
on the night of June 16, blew up roads and bridges linking Palestine
with its neighboring countries.[74] Two days later, five British officers were kidnapped from a military club in Tel Aviv.[75] On June 23,
Kol Israel announced that three of the officers would be kept as hostages for two Etzel members who were under sentence of death. Subsequently, the British high commissioner granted an amnesty to the
two resistance members.[76]

In light of these events, the mandatory government decided to
take firm steps against the yishuv's leadership.[77] On June 29—also
known by the Jewish population as "Black Saturday"—the authorities
arrested many Jewish leaders and conducted searches for arms caches
in dozens of settlements. In the following days, thousands of suspected

Palmach members were interned, and the British continued with their searches for weapons throughout the country.[78] Also, in a stiffening shift of its policy, London determined to intern all apprehended illegal immigrants in refugee camps in Cyrpus rather than in Palestine, as it had done previously.[79]

But the unity of the Jewish resistance movement collapsed on July 22, 1946. In one of the most dramatic actions of that year, Etzel blew up the wing of the King David Hotel in Jerusalem that contained the British military headquarters in Palestine and the offices of the government secretariat (except those of the high commissioner). The total casualties were 91 killed and 45 injured, including soldiers and civilians (British, Arab, and Jewish). On the following day, the Voice of Fighting Zion, Etzel's clandestine radio station, declared that "the tragedy was not caused by Jewish soldiers, who carried out their duty courageously and with self-sacrifice, but by the British themselves, who disregarded a warning and refused to evacuate the building."[80]

This action was strongly denounced by the Jewish Agency. It requested Etzel and Lehi to halt their terror activities against the British. But the dissident groups continued with their violence. They ambushed and killed British policemen and soldiers, attacked government installations and army camps, blew up railways, and mined roads. In a daring operation they freed their comrades from the Acre fortress prison.[81] Etzel even extended its sabotage beyond Palestine. On October 1, 1946, the British embassy in Rome was badly damaged by bomb explosions.[82]

Realizing that it could not bring about the formation of a new, more moderate Jewish leadership in Palestine, the mandatory government released many Jewish Agency and Haganah members. A new London-initiated proposal, the Morrison-Grady plan of July 1946 (named after Herbert Morrison, lord president of the council, and Henry F. Grady, an American special envoy), based on the division of Palestine into semiautonomous Jewish and Arab sectors, with a central British authority retaining supreme power for another four years, was rejected by both Jews and Arabs.

THE UN DEBATE, 1947

Unable to find a satisfactory solution to the mounting violence in Palestine, and in the absence of any willingness on the part of the two Palestinian communities to accept various proposals for the future of the mandate,[83] Britain asked on April 2, 1947, for a special session of the UN General Assembly to consider the question of "constituting and instructing a special committee to prepare for consideration of the questions of Palestine."[84]

The Arab members of the United Nations objected to the terms of the British request because they implied recognition of Jewish claims, and the Arabs therefore demanded that the forthcoming meeting alternatively consider the questions of the termination of the mandate over Palestine and the declaration of independence. [85]

But when the special session of the UN General Assembly convened on April 25, 1947, [86] the British item was placed on the agenda. The assembly agreed to hear the cases of the Jewish Agency for Palestine, the Arab Higher Committee, and other interested nongovernmental parties. [87]

The Jewish representatives complained of the British restrictions on immigration to Palestine. The Arab delegates, on the other hand, stated that the Balfour Declaration had been made without consent or knowledge of the people most directly affected—the Arabs of Palestine.

Subsequently, the special assembly set up a UN Special Committee on Palestine (UNSCOP)[88] to prepare the Palestine item for consideration by the forthcoming regular assembly. The Arab countries announced that they would boycott UNSCOP.

After intensive investigation of the various aspects of the problem, UNSCOP, on August 31, 1947, issued its report to the General Assembly. [89] It unanimously resolved that the mandate be terminated. The majority recommended that Palestine be divided into an Arab state, a Jewish state, and an international status for Jerusalem, all linked in an economic union. They further recommended that the Arab and Jewish states become independent after a transitional period of two years, to begin on September 1, 1947, during which the United Kingdom would progressively transfer the administration of Palestine to the United Nations; that Jerusalem be placed under an international trusteeship system with the United Nations as the administrating authority; and that provisions for the preservation of, and free access to, the Holy Places be contained in the constitutions of both the Arab and the Jewish states.

As a preferable alternative to the partition of Palestine, a minority recommendation proposed a single, independent, federal state, comprising independent Arab and Jewish states, with Jerusalem as its capital. [90]

The Arab states and the Arab Higher Committee immediately rejected UNSCOP's recommendations. When Great Britain informed the regular session of the General Assembly on September 29, 1947 that it had decided to evacuate Palestine, the Arab Higher Committee proposed an alternative plan to the UNSCOP report, with these recommendations: that an Arab state be established in the whole of Palestine; that this state respect the rights and fundamental freedoms of all persons before the law; that the Arab state protect the legitimate rights and interests of all minorities; and that the Arab state recognize freedom of worship and access to holy places, including Jerusalem.

But this proposal for the future constitutional organization of Palestine was not accepted by the United Nations and the Jewish party. Rather, the General Assembly, in its November 29, 1947 session, adopted Resolution 181(II) on the "Plan of Partition with Economic Union of Palestine," as recommended by UNSCOP.[91] It established the UN Palestine Commission to implement the resolution and directed the Security Council to assist in implementation as well as to take additional measures, if necessary, to maintain peace in the area.

Although this recommendation fell short of the Balfour Declaration, which, according to the Jewish Agency, referred to the whole of Palestine, the yishuv readily accepted the partition plan. The major reservation registered by the Agency stated that, since West Jerusalem was heavily populated by Jews, it should become the capital of the Jewish state and not be placed under an international administration, as proposed by the resolution.

The Arab delegates at the United Nations asserted that they would oppose the implementation of the partition plan. Several weeks later, on December 14, 1947, the Arab League, at the conclusion of its Cairo conference, released the text of letters sent to the United Nations, the United Kingdom, and the United States warning that the partitioning of Palestine would be considered a "hostile act towards 400 million Moslems."

Britain alone capitulated to this pressure, declaring that it would not cooperate in the implementation of the UN resolution.

THE ARAB ARMED INSURRECTION AND
THE JEWISH RESPONSE, 1947-48

Since the scene in Palestine from the end of World War II up to the UN vote of November 29, 1947 was dominated by British-Jewish confrontations,[92] a strange lull in relations between Arabs and Jews settled in during this period. But, as soon as news of the General Assembly's recommendation reached the country, a wave of Arab terrorism, followed by an armed insurrection and culminating in a military invasion of the newly born State of Israel some six months later, began. On the morrow of the UN resolution—November 30—a bus was fired on by Arabs and five Jews were killed. The Arabs proclaimed a general strike and, on the next day, a mob of some 200 youths broke their way into the Jewish commercial section of Jerusalem, smashed windows, looted shops, set goods on fire, and stabbed a number of people.[93] Riots also took place in Haifa and in the mixed quarter between Tel Aviv and Jaffa, and convoys were attacked in different parts of the country. Dozens of Jews lost their lives in these incidents. [94] On December 30, some 2,000 Arab employees of the oil refineries in the Haifa-Acre area attacked their Jewish colleagues and massacred 41 of them. [95]

The situation in the country approached administrative chaos and political anarchy. The British did not make any serious effort to prevent the intensification of Arab terrorism. In mid-January 1948, an Arab bomb planted in a postal delivery truck exploded in the heart of the Jewish business center of Haifa, causing nearly 50 casualties. [96] Several days later, in the Hebron hills, a group of 35 men, almost all of them Hebrew University students, were murdered, and their bodies were mutilated by their attackers. [97]

In addition to Palestinian Arab armed bands led by local leaders such as Abd Al-Qadir El-Husseini and supported financially by the neighboring states, the Arab League also began recruiting volunteers for an irregular Arab force for the purpose of participating in the Palestine struggle. Haj Amin El-Husseini, the former mufti of Jerusalem who, after World War II, had escaped arrest and settled in Egypt, was particularly active as president of the Arab Higher Committee in this effort.

Early in 1948, the Arab Liberation Army, or "Army of Deliverance" (Jeish al-Inqadh), commanded by Fawzi Al-Qawuqji, who before had headed volunteers to assist the guerrillas during the Arab revolt, sent some 5,000 men, mostly Iraqis, Syrians, and Lebanese, into Palestine. [98] Only after the force had been entrenched in the country, an increasing number of Palestinian Arabs joined in. The army used small units to attack specific targets, usually Jewish settlements or convoys moving between settlements in northern and central Palestine. Other volunteers were sent to the southern part of the country by Egypt's Moslem Brotherhood, an ultraconservative religious and political organization.

Jewish response to the wave of Arab terrorism and its escalation into an organized armed insurrection was swift. While the Haganah focused on defensive actions, Etzel and Lehi, which continued to operate independently, did not exclude strong retaliation. On December 11, 1947, six Arabs were killed and thirty wounded when bombs were thrown at Arab buses in Haifa. There were also many casualties in an attack on an Arab village near the city. Two days later, 18 Arabs died and 60 were injured in several attacks in Jerusalem, Jaffa, and the Lydda area. Houses blown up in an Arab village near Safad on December 18 left 10 people dead. [99]

In an attack on Balad-ei-Sheikh, on the slopes of Mount Carmel, on January 1, 1948, apparently in retaliation for the oil refinery massacre of the previous month, many Arab villagers were killed and wounded. [100] On the same day, 10 Arabs were killed in a Jaffa cafe explosion.[101] During that same month, there were heavy Arab casualties in Etzel and Lehi attacks on the Arab National Committee in Jaffa, an Arab-owned Semiramis Hotel in Jerusalem, and on Arab crowds in various cities.[102]

As terrorism increased daily in the country, the UN Palestine Commission sent its first special report to the Security Council on February 16, 1948. It criticized "powerful Arab interests" in and out of Palestine for "a deliberate effort to alter [the partition plan] by force" and "certain elements of the Jewish community" for "irresponsible acts of violence which worsen the security situation." The commission called on the council to establish "an adequate non-Palestinian force which will assist law-abiding elements in both Arab and Jewish communities." Without such a force, the report warned, there will be "uncontrolled, widespread strife and bloodshed" at the termination of the mandate. Finally, it also quoted official British figures on casualties in Palestine during the period from November 30, 1947 to February 1, 1948: 869 killed, including 427 Arabs, 381 Jews, 46 British, and 15 others.[103]

The Security Council, aware of the seriousness of the situation, had conducted long series of debates on the question of maintaining peace in Palestine.[104] But both sides, during the same period, continued with violence and counterviolence. Moreover, there was apparently some British involvement on the side of the Arabs. On February 1, the editorial offices of the Palestine Post, a Jewish-sponsored English newspaper in Jerusalem, was demolished by the explosion of a British armored car loaded with explosives and parked outside the building. Some 20 people were injured.[105] Similarly, on February 22, British armored cars parked near an apartment building on Ben Yehudah Street in the Jewish sector of Jerusalem exploded, destroying several houses and killing more than 50 residents.[106]

In light of these and other incidents, the general feeling prevailing within the Jewish community was that the authorities, on the whole, intervened on behalf of the Arabs. Etzel delivered a warning to the British stating that, since London was interested in kindling the fight between Arabs and Jews in order to remain in Palestine, it would direct its activities against the authorities inside and outside Palestine until "freedom is achieved." Etzel, as well as Lehi, was subsequently involved in exploding trains in the country, sending letter and parcel bombs to England, and placing explosives in a government office in London.[107]

London immediately denounced these actions and condemned the Jewish Agency for its failure to take steps to suppress "Jewish terrorism." In a statement addressed to the agency, the government concluded that the

Haganah have from time to time foiled the terrorist
groups, but there still remains no method of dealing
effectively with these people except the use of the machinery provided by the law. The Government, confronted with the deliberate policy of the Jewish Agency
to render their task as difficult as possible, desires
to bring once more to the attention of the Jewish community the fact that the continuance of indiscriminate
murder and condoned terrorism can lead only to for-
feiture by the community of all right in the eyes of the
world to be numbered among civilised people.[108]

Early in March, the Va'ad Leumi (National Council of Palestinian Jews) in accordance with the UN partition resolution, set up an interim government to serve as a provisional organ of the Jewish state
following the termination of the British mandate. The Arab response
to this unilateral political act was more violence. Jerusalem was besieged by Arab irregulars and cut off from the coast, and Jewish settlements in the Galilee were attacked by Arab volunteers. Clashes
between Arabs and Jews near Tel Aviv resulted in the deaths of 17
Haganah members and 15 Arabs. On March 11, a device was smuggled into the courtyard of the Jewish Agency headquarters in Jerusalem in a car belonging to the American consulate in the Old City,
driven by an Arab. The explosion wrecked a section of one of the
wings and caused 13 deaths and other casualties.[109] Toward the end
of the month, Arabs carried out persistent raids on highways, blocking traffic and the movement of people.

Lehi, during this period, was particularly active. In one operation it heavily damaged the Haifa headquarters of an Arab military
group under the direction of Iraqi and Syrian officers. In the same
city, Lehi destroyed vehicles with explosives in the Arab sector, killing 17 and injuring 100. Its units also mined a Haifa-Cairo train and
caused a heavy toll in dead and wounded.[110]

In April, the Arab boycott policy against the Jews of Palestine,
which was formally adopted by the Arab League Council on February
12, 1945, was further intensified. The government of Iraq stopped
delivery of oil through the pipeline from Iraq to the refineries in Haifa.

Encouraged by this display of support by neighboring countries,
the local Arabs blockaded the Jewish quarter of the Old City of Jerusalem, cutting off the supplies of food, water, and medicine to the
noncombatant residents of this sector.[111] A medical convoy, consisting of 75 Jewish doctors, nurses, and teachers, was attacked on its
way to the Hadassah Medical Hospital on Mount Scopus, and most of
them were killed. Other units were ambushed elsewhere, such as a
relief convoy of 46 people, which was destroyed near Yechiam, a kibbutz in the Galilee.[112]

In spite of these setbakcs, the Haganah was able, during the
month of April, to rapidly establish control over the entire area allot-
ted to the Jewish state in the UN partition plan. It opened the road to
Jerusalem by occupying Arab areas on both sides of the road, routed
the Qawuqji forces in the Jezrael Valley, and drove the Arab units
from Safed, Tiberias, and Haifa.

Etzel and Lehi, meanwhile, continued to operate unilaterally
and sometimes jointly against both the Arabs and the British. On April 6, a military camp at Pardes Hanna, near Haifa, was attacked, and
several British soldiers were shot, some in the back. This incident
brought a strong denunciation from the colonial secretary in London,
who declared that it was "cold-blooded murder for its own sake and
nothing else" and added, "Such senseless crimes, committed by members of a community which aspires to recognition by the world for acceptance into the community of nations, continue to blot the record of
the Jews of Palestine."[113]

A more dramatic incident took place on April 9 during a combined military operation of Etzel and Lehi against the Arab village of
Dir Yassin, near Jerusalem. Some 200 Arab civilians, most of them
women and children, died when they failed to heed the repeated loud-
speaker warnings in Arabic advising them to evacuate the village.[114]
This tragedy was unreservedly condemned by the Haganah and all responsible leaders of the yishuv.

The Arab reaction was bitter. Husein Khalidi, secretary of the
Arab Higher Committee of Palestine, stated that there were 250 dead
at Dir Yassin, including 25 pregnant women, 52 mothers "with suck-
lings up to a few months old," and about 60 other women and girls.[115]
He also asserted, "We realize that the Jews have been treated in this
manner by the Nazis. We know of their suppressed hatred of their
persecutors. But now their hatred is directed against the Arabs,
among whom the Jews lived for thirteen centuries. . . . The Arab reaction is not for me to say, but there will be no reprisals."[116] Clearly,
this and similar statements by the Arab leadership influenced passions
and, in fact, increased the panic among the Arab population, resulting
in a mass exodus in subsequent weeks.

At the United Nations, meanwhile, diplomatic activity continued.
The second special session of the General Assembly, which began on
April 16, rejected a U.S. plan for a temporary trusteeship for Palestine as a move to stop the violence there. The Arabs favored the plan
because it implied a single rather than a partitioned state; the Jews
opposed it, holding that the trusteeship proposal was untenable and
would negate the partition resolution.

The Security Council, for its part, fully aware of "the increasing violence and disorder in Palestine," adopted on April 1 a resolution that called upon the antagonistic Arab and Jewish armed groups

"to cease acts of violence immediately."[117] Having failed to achieve
this truce, the council called again on the parties, on April 17, to stop
all confrontations, to refrain from provocative political activity, and
to safeguard the Holy Places.[118] On April 23, the Security Council
created a Truce Commission, composed of representatives of the
United States, France, and Belgium, to assist in carrying out the proposed cease-fire arrangements.

As the United Nations was unable to stop the bloodshed, Golda
Meyerson (who later became Golda Meir), in an attempt to avert what
seemed to be a threatened invasion by the neighboring countries, met
secretly on behalf of the Jewish Agency with King Abdullah of Trans-
Jordan on the night of April 30. Although the Arab monarch was prepared to recognize some sort of autonomy for Palestinian Jews, he
could not resist both British and Pan-Arab pressures advising him
against concluding a separate agreement with the Jewish Agency. The
dialogue thus failed, and the parties braced themselves for the inevitable confrontation.

The final two weeks of the prestate period were costly to the
yishuv. Trans-Jordan's army, better known as the "Arab Legion,"
commanded by British officers, entered the fighting in and around
Jerusalem. In one of its military operations, the legion cordoned
off Kfar Etzion on the Hebron–Jerusalem road. After the inhabitants
surrendered, they were murdered by Arab villagers. Only 4 out of
110 men and women who were in Kfar Etzion at the time managed to
escape. The other three Jewish settlements in the region were also
overwhelmed by the superior Jordanian forces.[119]

On May 14, 1948, the mandate of Palestine ended and the British
completed the withdrawal of their forces. That day the Jewish Provisional State Council proclaimed the birth of Medinat Yisrael (the State
of Israel). The Proclamation of Independence of the State of Israel
made a special plea: "In the midst of wanton aggression . . . we extend the hand of peace and good neighbourliness to all the neighboring
States and their peoples and invite their cooperation and mutual assistance." It also called "upon the Arab inhabitants of the State of
Israel to preserve the ways of peace and play their part in the development of the State on the basis of full and equal citizenship and due
representation in all its bodies and institutions—provisional and permanent."

The Arabs responded to this appeal by sending the invading forces
of Egypt, Iraq, Jordan, Lebanon, and Syria, in order to destroy the
Jewish state on the very first day of its existence. Azaam Pasha, the
secretary general of the Arab League, outlined its purpose: "There
will be a war of extermination and a momentous massacre which will
be spoken of like the Mongolian Massacres and the Crusades."[120]

But the infant state survived the first onslaught.

EPILOGUE

The foregoing examination leads one to the inescapable conclusion that the evolution of the Middle East conflict was the direct outcome of several irrational and reactionary forces prevailing at that time in the region and beyond.

The major contributing factor to that development was the hostile attitude and the resulting rampant terrorism of the Palestinian Arab nationalists toward the yishuv. Unilaterally proclaiming self-determination for themselves, they denied without any understanding and compassion the same right to the Jews, who also had deep historical roots and a continuous presence in Palestine.

Admittedly, there were many instances of good neighborly relationships between the two communities before World War I. But Arab opposition to the Zionist experiment in the form of editorials in the local press coupled with pressure on the Turkish authorities to place restrictions on the early pioneers were also present during this period.

The situation deteriorated with the establishment of the British mandatory rule when extremist Arab leaders such as Haj Amin El-Husseini, the then mufti of Jerusalem, assumed almost total control over the Arab population, encouraging it to look upon Jews as hated foreigners, to reject purchased land transfers to them, and to protest Zionist immigration and settlement in the country.

This extremist leadership rejected not only the Balfour Declaration and all of the manifold proposals submitted during the mandatory period but even also the November 29, 1947 UN Resolution, which afforded the Palestinian Arabs an historic opportunity to assure the establishment of their own distinct state. Terrorism, in the form of sabotage and murder, was deliberately introduced by the mufti and his followers among the Palestinian Arabs as a way of achieving a determined political aim, namely, to guarantee the abrupt and conclusive demise of the envisaged Jewish sovereignty.

Thus, this illicit violence was not a product of frustration or despair of a possible political solution to the confrontation with Zionism; in fact, it was initiated even before all pacific alternatives had been exhausted. More specifically, terrorism against the yishuv in the 1920s and the early 1930s became a routine and squalid weapon of war by other means, escalating into prolonged guerrilla warfare during the Arab revolt of 1936-39 and reemerging in the unceasing and ghastly waves of outrages in the 1947-48 period, culminating in the first round of open hostilities between the Arab states and Israel.

Clearly, the Palestinian Arab campaign of violence, which began spontaneously and continued more methodically, had its roots in the unrestrained malice toward the Jewish community and in the blind passion to destroy the national home even before its inception. It had borne some fruit in the coldblooded murder and vicious attacks, for the toll of dead and wounded was heavy, and the economic cost was high.

But despite these effects, Palestinian Arab terrorism proved futile in its primary purpose. It did not at any time seriously jeopardize the growth and development of the yishuv, nor did it pose a real threat to the formation of a Jewish state at the conclusion of the mandate. In fact, as soon as it became apparent in the final days of the British rule in Palestine that the local insurrection, supported by outside volunteers, had failed in its "liberation" efforts, it was necessary for the regular armies of the neighboring countries to intervene.

A second cause of the pre-1948 Arab-Jewish estrangement and violence lies in the negative behavior of the Arab states. Admittedly, moderate leaders from Egypt, Iraq, Saudi Arabia, Syria, and Trans-Jordan met at different times with representatives of the yishuv and the World Zionist Organization inside and outside the Middle East. In view of international realities and the Jewish presence in Palestine, they were willing to consider and initially even agree to tolerate Jewish national aspirations, at least within their vision of an essentially regional map based on sovereign Arab states or an amalgamated Arabdom.

But extremist and anti-Zionist forces ultimately overwhelmed any reasonable trends within the neighboring countries, and therefore moderate voices had no influence whatever on the tragic turn of events. Providing political support, financial aid, and volunteers in the 1936-39 period, the Arab states assumed a greater role in the Palestinian problem with the establishment of the Arab League in 1945.

When the UN General Assembly adopted the partition resolution, the Arab states staunchly backed and encouraged the Palestinian Arabs to reject it. Furthermore, they decided, even against the advice of their military leaders, to take up arms to prevent the partition plan from ever being consummated.

At midnight on May 14, 1948—the first day of existence of the new state of Israel—all of the surrounding Arab states launched armed invasions and called upon the Arab residents of Israel to rise up and destroy the new nation forthwith.

And finally, the ambivalent, and, on many occasions muddled, approach of the mandatory British administration in Jerusalem and the often contradictory policies of the government in London were, no doubt, catalytic in creating an atmosphere of friction leading to outbreaks of violence between the Arab and Jewish communities. By not reinforcing the pledge of assisting in the establishment of a Jewish homeland, by not permitting unlimited Jewish immigration or, alternately, abrogating definitely its obligations in that regard, the British gave a strong stimulus to the development of Arab extremist nationalistic tendencies. By allowing leaders such as the mufti to impose their wills, often by intimidation and violence, on political opponents and by reacting halfheartedly to waves of terrorism against the yishuv, the mandatory power ironically convinced the extremists that terrorism would pay off. For instance, as a result of the Arab revolt, the British white paper of 1939 virtually accepted Arab demands, thus further strengthening the spirit of disorder and lawlessness in the country.

The local Arabs were also greatly assisted by the actions of the British administration when it began to withdraw from Palestine in a situation approaching administrative chaos and political anarchy. This attitude also acted as a tempting enticement to the surrounding Arab countries to send troops into Palestine in order to prevent the creation of the new state.

To be sure, any discussion of the origins of the pre-1948 collision in the Middle East must also consider the Jewish input. Although the Zionists, in the process of creating Israel, brought grave emotional and physical calamities on the Palestinian Arabs, they did not bring these disastrous consequences on their neighbors because of a sinister ideology bent on their obliteration. On the contrary, all of the yishuv's proposals for some sort of formula for accommodation— federal or confederal, or even binational—failed to strike a responsive chord in the influential Palestinian Arab leadership. Moreover, it was the yishuv that accepted the partition plan of 1947, albeit with misgivings, as a still further whittling down of the homeland area promised by the Balfour Declaration.

Even in the face of mounting Palestinian Arab terrorism, the overwhelming majority in the Jewish community subscribed to a policy of self-defense and self-restraint. For example, it was only after a bitter controversy that the Haganah leadership decided to resort to offensive tactics against Palestinian Arab terrorist bases during the Arab revolt. Any indiscriminate vengeance directed by Etzel and Lehi against the local Arabs was strongly repudiated by the yishuv's leadership. This was the official policy also during the insurrection of 1947-48. Whenever violent outrages occurred, such as the Dir Yassin massacre—and they were rare—the spokesmen for the mainstream of the community disassociated themselves from such crimes.

It was only out of despair and, indeed, it was only natural that the yishuv resort to force in resisting British policies barring the immigration of the death camp survivors. But in all acts of sabotage, such as the destruction of British radar stations used to intercept illegal ships, maximum care was taken to avoid the loss of innocent lives. In fact, when the dissident groups began a campaign of violence against British officials, police, and the military, the Jewish Agency and its leaders denounced these acts as "lunatic crimes" and "works of agents provocateurs." The yishuv made it very clear that "Jewish Palestine and terrorists cannot co-exist," and therefore counterterrorist measures were undertaken against Etzel and Lehi.

In light of this evidence, it can be concluded that, had it not been for the uncompromising position of the Palestinian Arabs and their consistent resorts to terrorism, the encouragement and support of the neighboring states, and the British bankrupt policy that created unfavorable conditions for a peaceful resolution of the Palestine question, the historical events in the Middle East would have been dramatically different.

Now, 27 years after the establishment of Israel, the conflict lingers on. Terrorism is implanted as deeply as ever in the politics of the region. The Palestinian Arab "freedom fighters," represented by the PLO, continue to be as nihilistic as their predecessors were during the mandatory period; their avowed and entrenched aim is still the liquidation of the existence of a sovereign Jewish state in Palestine, and they are unwilling to negotiate for anything short of that. That is, their dogma is "politicide" and their modus operandi is terrorism, both as means and as ends.

But unlike the early experience of the "liberators," at present the terrorists are better equipped in terms of personnel, finances, arms, and political support. Instead of the mufti mobs and gangs, they are organized in fedayeen and fatah movements; in lieu of charity from Arab states, they enjoy lavish monetary support from oil-rich Middle East countries; knives and guns have been replaced by the most sophisticated weaponry, including computer-guided missiles; and past skepticism and lukewarm support have been succeeded by official sanction and protection by the Arab world and by universal recognition of the PLO at the United Nations.

But ironically, as in the past, these "heroes" constitute a force of anarchy against their own brethren. Not only do they terrorize Palestinian Arabs who do not cooperate with them, but often they undermine the stability of Arab states and inflict bloody civil wars, as in Jordan and Lebanon. Moreover, they are threatening the texture of international life by injecting violence into vulnerable lands and among defenseless and innocent people with no direct connections with the Middle East conflict.

Obviously, permissiveness of and capitulation to Palestinian-Arab terrorism that has been immeasurably magnified by the mass media invite further expansion of violence. They encourage and nourish hopes about the imminent destruction of Israel, and, failing that, it is not unlikely that terrorism will elevate the already dangerous Middle East collision course into another eyeball-to-eyeball confrontation on the battlefield.

The tragedy of such an eventuality is that it will not only bring untold suffering to the parties concerned but will also contain the seed of nuclear escalation that may engulf the entire world in a global confrontation that no one wants. The Yom Kippur War, for instance, became the most serious crisis between the Soviet Union and the United States since the dramatic events of June 1967. While nuclear calamity was somehow averted in October 1974, there is unfortunately no assurance that a new war in the region will not engage the interests and prestige of the superpowers again and drag the entire world to the brink of disaster.

If these frightening developments are to be averted, it will be necessary—indeed, imperative—for the international community and, in particular, the Arab states, to face the moment of truth and to take the following concrete steps: reverse their endorsement of PLO terrorism as an approved value; register a sense of revulsion at all acts of violence; cease financial support, stop the flow of weapons, and deny any facilities and sanctuaries to terrorist groups; cooperate with national and international bodies such as Interpol in the suppression of terrorism; and finally, impress upon terrorist groups the fact that the only alternative to tolerance and coexistence is self-destruction.

NOTES

1. See the New York Times, October 23, 1974.

2. For Arab treatments of the subject, see, for example, George Antonius, The Arab Awakening (Beirut: Khayat, 1955), 3rd ed.; Hazem Zaki Nuseibeh, The Ideas of Arab Nationalism (Ithaca, N.Y.: Cornell University Press, 1956); M. A. Aziz, "The Origins of Arab Nationalism," Pakistan Horizon, March 1956, pp. 29-37; "The Foundations of Arab Nationalism," Egyptian Economic and Political Review, September-October 1958, pp. 10-15, 20-24; Albert H. Hourani, Arabic Thought in the Liberal Age, 1798-1939 (New York and London: Oxford, 1962); Khaldun S. Al-Husfi, Three Reformers: A Study in Modern Arab Political Thought (Beirut: Khayats, 1966); Hisham B. Sharabi, Nationalism and Revolution in the Arab World (Princeton, N.J.: D. Van Nostrand, 1966); and Zeine N. Zeine, The Emergency of Arab Nationalism: With a Background Study of Arab-Turkish Relations in the Near East (Beirut: Khayats, 1966). For non-Arab perspectives, see, for instance, Leonard Binder, The Ideological Revolution in the Middle East (New York: John Wiley and Sons, 1964); Herman Finer, "Reflections on the Nature of Arab Nationalism," Middle Eastern Affairs (October 1958), pp. 302-13; Nastollah S. Fatemi, "The Roots of Arab Nationalism," Orbis, Winter 1959, pp. 437-56; Hans Kohn, The Age of Nationalism: The First Era of Global History (New York: Harper & Row, 1968); and Hans E. Tutsch, Facets of New Nationalism (Detroit: Wayne University Press, 1965).

3. The best sources on Zionism in its true philosophical and historical perspectives are Joseph Heller, The Zionist Idea (New York:

Schocken, 1949); Oskar Rabinowicz, Fifty Years of Zionism (London: Robert Anscombe and Co., 1950); Israel Cohan, A Short History of Zionism (London: Frederick Muller, 1951); Harry Sacher, Israel: The Establishment of a State (London: Weidenfeld and Nicholson, 1952); Norman Bentwich, Israel Resurgent (New York: Frederick A. Praeger, 1960); Ben Halpern, The Idea of the Jewish State (Cambridge, Mass.: Harvard University Press, 1961); and Arthur Hertzberg, ed., The Zionist Idea (New York: Herzl Press, 1963). For an official statement of the Zionist position, see Memorandum Submitted to the Palestine Royal Commission (Jerusalem: Jewish National Council, 1936); Memorandum Submitted to the United Nations Conference on International Organizations, San Francisco, April, 1945 (New York: Jewish Agency for Palestine, 1945); The Jewish Case Before the Anglo-American Committee of Inquiry on Palestine (Jerusalem: Jewish Agency for Palestine, 1947); and The Palestine Issue: Preliminary Memorandum Submitted to the Special Committee of the U.N. (Jerusalem: Jewish Agency for Palestine, 1947). For the Zionist view as expressed by Israeli leaders, see, for example, Robert St. John, Ben-Gurion (London: Jarralds, 1959); Naphtali Lau-Levie, Moshe Dayan (London: Vallentine, Mitchell, 1968); Terence Prittie, Eshkol: The Man and the Nation (New York: Pitman, 1969); Marie Syrkin, Woman with a Cause (New York: Putnam's, 1963); and Zalman Shazar, Morning Stars (Philadelphia: Jewish Publication Society of America, 1967). For a brief analysis of "Jewish" or "Israeli" nationalism, see Israel Kolatt, "Theories on Israel Nationalism," in Confrontation: Viewpoints on Zionism (Jerusalem: World Zionist Organization, 1969).

4. Quoted by As-Sayad (Beirut), September 28, 1973.

5. Quoted by the Jerusalem Post, December 22, 1973.

6. See Brief (Tel Aviv), no. 92 (October 16-31, 1974).

7. See, for instance, The Historical Connection of the Jewish People with Palestine (Jerusalem: Jewish Agency for Palestine, 1936).

8. Israel Zangwill, "The Return to Palestine," New Liberal Review 2 (December 1901): 627.

9. See Ben Halpern, "Zionism and Israel," in Benjamin Rivlin and Joseph S. Szyliowicz, The Contemporary Middle East: Tradition and Innovation (New York: Random House, 1965), pp. 276-82, for a comparison between Zionism and other nationalistic movements and for an analysis of the reasons for the unique characteristics of Jewish nationalism.

10. See Simon M. Dubnow, History of the Jews in Russia and Poland, 3 vols. (Philadelphia: Jewish Publications Society, 1916-20); and L. Greenberg, The Jews in Russia (New Haven, Conn.: Yale University Press, 1951), vol. 2.

11. See James Parks, Antisemitism (London: Vallentine Mitchell, 1963); and A. Roy Eckardt, Elder and Younger Brothers (New York: Charles Scribner's Sons, 1967).

12. Among the earliest pioneers were students from Eastern Europe belonging to an organization called "BILU" (initials of the Hebrew words "beth Yaacov luhu venelha"—"house of Jacob, come ye, and let us walk" [Isa. 2:5]). See, for example, Leon Pinsker, Auto-Emancipation: A Call to His People by a Russian Jew (London: Rita Searl, 1947); David Ben-Gurion, Rebirth and Destiny of Israel (New York: Philosophical Library, 1954), pp. 270-72; and Alex Bein, The Return to the Soil (Jerusalem: Youth and Hechalutz Department, World Zionist Organization, 1952).

13. The Jewish population in Palestine in 1882 reached 24,000. During the first aliah (1882-1903), some 25,000 Jews immigrated to Palestine. In the second aliah (1904-14), nearly 40,000 immigrants arrived.

14. For background accounts on Arab-Jewish relations, see, for example, Michael Assaf, History of the Arabs in Palestine, vol. 3, The Arab Awakening and Flight—Nations and States Contend for Palestine, 1876-1948 (Hebrew), (Tel Aviv: Tarbut We-Hinukh, 1967); Shimon Shamir, A Modern History of the Arabs in the Middle East (Hebrew) (Tel Aviv: Reshofim, 1965); and Aaron Cohen, Israel and the Arab World (London: W. H. Allen, 1970).

15. See "The Spiritual and Pioneering Mission of Israel: The Eternity of Israel," Ayanot (Hebrew), 1964, p. 74. See also statement by David Ben-Gurion before the Knesset, January 2, 1956, as quoted in Israel Peace Offers (Jerusalem: Ministry of Foreign Affairs, 1958), p. 56; and Martin Buber, "Zion and Youth" (1918), in Mission and Destiny (Hebrew), vol. 2, p. 219.

16. See, for example, Cmd. 1700, p. 8; Financial Aspects of Jewish Reconstruction in Palestine: How the Arabs Have Benefited Through Jewish Immigration (London: Jewish Agency for Palestine, 1930); and Zionism and the Arab World (New York: Jewish Agency for Palestine, 1946).

17. For the basic ideology of Zionism by the founder of the Zionist movement, see Theodor Herzl, The Jewish State (New York: Scopus Publishing Co., 1943); Old New Land (Altneuland), trans. Lotta Levensohn (New York: Herzl Press, 1960); The Complete Diaries of Theodor Herzl, ed. Raphael Patai, trans. Harry Zohn (New York: Yoseloff, 1966), 5 vols.; and The Diaries, trans. and ed. Marvin Lowenthal (New York: Grosset and Dunlap, 1962). For works related to Zionism by other Zionist leaders, see Nahum Sokolow, History of Zionism (London: Longmans, Green and Co., 1919), vol. 1; Arthur Rupin, The Jewish Fate and Future (New York: Macmillan, 1940); Chaim Weizmann, Trial and Error: The Autobiography of

Chaim Weizmann (New York: Harper and Brothers, 1949); David Ben-Gurion, The Rebirth and Destiny of Israel, op. cit.; Louis Lipsky, A Gallery of Zionist Profiles (New York: Farrar, Strauss, and Giroux, 1956); and Nahum Goldman, "Zionism: Ideal and Realism," in Confrontation: Viewpoints on Zionism (Jerusalem: World Zionist Organization, 1970). For diagnoses of Zionism's founders relative to the processes dominating Jewish life in the Diaspora, see, for example, Martin Buber, "Aus einer Rede," Die Welt, March 29, 1912, reprinted in Juedische Bewegung (Berlin: Juedische Verlag, 1916), p. 195; A. D. Gordon, "The Congress" (1913), in The Nation and Labor (Hebrew) (Jerusalem: Zionist Organization, 1952), p. 198; Ber Borochov, On Zionist Theory (1915), in Writings (Hebrew) (Tel Aviv: Am-Oved, 1943), vol. 1, p. 2; Chaim Weizmann, "The Jewish People and Palestine" (Statement made before the Palestine Royal Commission in Jerusalem, November 25, 1936); and David Ben-Gurion, "From Class to People," Ayanot, 1955, p. 23.

18. Theodore Herzl stated that "the Jewish Question exists wherever Jews live in perceptible number. Where it does not exist, it is carried by Jews in the course of their migration." The Jewish State (Hebrew) (Warsaw: Tusiah, 1896), vol. 1, pp. 21-22. For a recent analysis, see Jacob Neusser, "Zionism and the Jewish Problem," in Confrontation: Viewpoints on Zionism (Jerusalem: World Zionist Organization, 1970), pp. 3-14.

19. For the Zionist objectives as formulated in the first Zionist Congress, see Protokoll des I. Zionistenkongresses in Basel vom 29 bis 31 August 1897 (Prog., 1911), p. 131. See also Constitution of the Zionist Organization (Jerusalem: World Zionist Organization, 1938); Israel Cohen, The Zionist Movement (New York: Zionist Organization of America, 1947); Gavriel Stern, "70th Anniversary of the First Zionist Congress," Israel Horizons 15, nos. 9 and 10 (November-December 1967): 20-23; K. Israel, "The Zionist Movement and the Jerusalem Programme, 1968," in Confrontation: Viewpoints on Zionism, op. cit., pp. 3-12; and Eliezer Schweid, "Israel as a Zionist State," in Confrontation: Viewpoints on Zionism, op. cit.

20. Some Jews rejected the concept of unity of the Jewish people with Palestine as a beacon of national security. For anti-Zionist works, see, for instance, Morris R. Cohen, Zionism: Tribalism or Liberalism (New York: American Council for Judaism, 1946); Alfred M. Lilienthal, What Price Israel (Chicago: Henry Regnery Company, 1953); Moshe Menuhin, The Decadence of Judaism in Our Time (New York: Exposition Press, 1965); Benjamin Matov, "Zionist and Anti-Semite: 'Of Course!,'" Issues (Spring 1966), pp. 21-26; and Jakob J. Petuchowski, Zion Reconsidered (New York: Twayne Publishers, 1967).

21. "Diary" (June 1895), in Writings, op. cit., vol. 2, p. 71.

22. Anis Sayegh, in her study Palestine and Arab Nationalism (Beirut: Palestine Liberation Organization Research Center, n.d.), reports that during this period the first articles attempting to expose the "Zionist plot" appeared in Al-Manor (Cairo) and Al-Carmel (Haifa). For a pro-Arab anthology of readings of the history of Zionism and Palestine from 1897 until the establishment of Israel, see Walid Khalidi, From Haven to Conquest (Beirut: Institute for Palestine Studies, 1971). See also Nevill Mandel, Turks, Arabs and Jewish Immigration into Palestine, St. Anthony's Papers no. 17, Middle Eastern Affairs no. 4 (Oxford: Oxford University Press), p. 80; and Nagib Azoury, Le Reveil de la Nation Arabe (Paris, 1905).

23. Circassians are members of a Moslem ethnic group from the Caucasus region who were transported to Palestine in the 1800s by the Ottoman Turks.

24. For a general discussion of the period, see Suleiman Mousa, T. E. Lawrence: An Arab View, trans. Albert Butros (New York: Oxford, 1966).

25. Some Palestinian Jews, at least initially, favored wartime cooperation with the Central Powers. See Alexander Aaronsohn, With the Turks in Palestine (New York: Houghton Mifflin, 1916), for a personal narrative of a well-known Palestinian Jew concerning the early part of World War I in Palestine. See also Yigal Allon, Shield of David (New York: Random House, 1970), pp. 32-34.

26. For text, see United Kingdom, Balfour Declaration, November 2, 1917, quoted in report of Royal Commission, Cmd. 5479 (London, 1937), p. 16. For resolutions, statements, and views by Jewish organizations relating to the Balfour Declaration, and for press comments, see Great Britain, Palestine and the Jews: Jewry's Celebration of Its National Charter (New York: George H. Doran, 1918). See also Blanche Elizabeth Dugdale, The Balfour Declaration: Origins and Background (London: Jewish Agency for Palestine, 1940); Leonard Stein, The Balfour Declaration (New York: Simon and Schuster, 1961); and Richard H. S. Crossman, "The Balfour Declaration, 1917-1967," Midstream 13, no. 10 (1967): 21-28.

27. This was done in accordance with the wartime secret Sykes-Picot Treaty of May 9, 1916, whereby Britain and France agreed to divide the eastern Middle East between them. For an examination of the British and French roles in the Middle East, see Jukka Nevakivi, Britain, France, and the Arab Middle East, 1914-1920 (London: Oxford University Press, 1969); John Morlowe, Arab Nationalism and British Imperialism (New York: Praeger Publishers, 1961); and Elizabeth Monroe, Britain's Moment in the Middle East, 1914-1956 (Baltimore: Johns Hopkins, 1963). For an interpretation of Britain's Palestine promises, see Fayez Sayegh, "Two Secret British Documents," Hiwar (Beirut), no. 8 (January-February 1964), pp. 17-32; and the Times (London), April 16, 1964.

28. See United Kingdom, Final Drafts of the Mandates for Meso-
potamia and Palestine for the approval of the Council of the League of
Nations (London, 1921), Cmd. 1500, and Cmd. 1785, pp. 1-11, for
official documents of the mandate. See also Albert M. Hyamson,
Palestine Under the Mandate, 1920-1948 (London: Methuen, 1950),
for a Zionist view by a former mandatory official. For other works,
see Norman and Helen Bentwich, Mandate Memories, 1918-1948 (New
York: Schocken, 1965); and Edwin Samuel, A Lifetime in Jerusalem:
The Memoirs of the Second Viscount Samuel (Jerusalem: Israel Universities Press, 1970).

29. Quoted in report of Royal Commission, Cmd. 5479 (London,
1937), pp. 19-20; and the Jewish Agency for Palestine, Documents
Relating to the Palestine Problems, 1945, pp. 17-18.

30. Quoted in Chaim Landau, ed., Israel and the Arabs (Jerusalem: Central Press, 1971), p. 48. See also letter by Sir Henry Mac-
Mahon in the Times (London), July 23, 1937; Chaim Weizmann's
speech to the Zionist Congress (1931), quoted in Jewish Agency for
Palestine, Memorandum to the Palestine Royal Commission, 1936, pp.
87-89; and N. Mandel, "Attempts at an Arab-Zionist Entente, 1913-
1914," Middle Eastern Studies 1, no. 3 (1965): 238-67.

31. Speeches (Tel Aviv: Gitzpe, 1937) (Hebrew), vol. 1, p. 141.

32. ESCO Foundation for Palestine, Palestine: A Study of Jewish, Arab and British Policies, vol. 1 (New Haven, Conn.: Yale University Press, 1947), p. 473 (hereafter referred to as ESCO Palestine
Study).

33. Quoted by Antonius, The Arab Awakening, op. cit., p. 441.

34. For details, see Issa Sifri, Arab Palestine Between the Mandate and Zionism (Jaffa, 1937); Robert John and Sami Hadawi, The
Palestine Diary, vol. 1, 1914-1945 (Beirut: Palestine Research Center, 1970); Don Peretz et al., A Palestine Entity (Washington, D.C.:
Middle East Institute, 1970), pp. 1-21; and A. Kayal, ed., Documents
on Palestinian Resistance to the British Mandate and Zionism, 1918-
1939 (Beirut: Institute for Palestine Studies, 1969).

35. Maurice Pearlman, Mufti of Jerusalem: The Story of Haj
Amin Al Hussein (London, 1947); Eliahu Elath, Haj Mohammed Amin
El-Husseini (Hebrew) (Tel Aviv: Reshafim, 1968); and Ha'aretz (Tel
Aviv), March 1, 2, and 6, 1970.

36. ESCO Palestine Study, op. cit., pp. 132-33.

37. For details, see, for instance, Munya Mardor, Haganah
(New York: New American Library, 1966).

38. ESCO Palestine Study, op. cit., pp. 269-70.

39. Ibid., p. 271.

40. Weizmann, Trial and Error, op. cit., p. 342.

41. See The Hope Simpson Report (Jerusalem: Government
Press, 1929), pp. 53-54, 78-79.

42. See, for example, Jewish Agency for Palestine, Memorandum on the Western Wall (Jerusalem: ˜Azriel Press, 1930); ESCO Palestine Study, op. cit., pp. 608-09; and United Kingdom, International Commission for the Wailing Wall Report, December, 1930 (London: His Majesty's Stationery Office, 1931).

43. A Survey for Palestine, prepared in December 1945 and January 1946 for the information of the Anglo-American Committee of Inquiry (Jerusalem: Government Press, 1946), vol. 1, p. 24. See also Arye Hashavia, "This Month—Forty Years Ago, the Hebron Massacre" (Jerusalem: Prime Minister Office, 1969).

44. See Cmd. 2530. For another proposal to limit Jewish immigration, see The Hope-Simpson Report, op. cit.

45. See A Survey for Palestine, op. cit., pp. 30-31.

46. See Leila S. Kadi, Basic Political Documents of the Armed Palestinian Movement (Beirut: Palestine Liberation Organization, 1969).

47. United Kingdom, Palestine Royal Commission Report, Cmd. 5479, July 1937 (London: His Majesty's Stationery Office, 1937), pp. 110-11.

48. For an excellent analysis of Arab, Jewish, and British policies from 1936 to the breakdown of the mandate, see Jacob C. Hurewitz, The Struggle for Palestine (New York: Greenwood Press, 1968).

49. See A Survey for Palestine, op. cit., and ESCO Palestine Study.

50. For details, see Mardor, op. cit.; Ephraim Dekel (Krasner), Shai: Historical Exploits of Haganah Intelligence (New York: Yoseloff, 1959); and Munya Mardor, Haganah (New York: New American Library, 1966).

51. New York Times, October 15, 1938. For Arab attitudes, see, for instance, Cmd. 3530, 5479, 5854, 6808, and 7044.

52. The Revisionists established the World Union of Zionists Revisionists in 1925 and a youth movement, Betar (Brith Trumpeldor). In 1935 it seceded from the official Zionist organization, only to rejoin it in 1946. Its leader was Zeev (Vladimir) Jabotinsky. See his presentation on The Story of the Jewish Legion (New York: Ackerman, 1945).

53. The first split occurred in 1931 when these dissidents left the Haganah. However, most of them rejoined it in 1936. For details on Etzel by commanders who succeeded Raziel, see Yaacov Meridor, Long Is the Road to Freedom (New York: United Zionists Revisionists, 1961); and Menachem Begin, The Revolt: Story of the Irgun (New York: Henry Schuman, 1951).

54. Keesing's Contemporary Archives 3 (1937-40): 3177A, 3312A, 3513, 3642B.

55. Quoted by Michael Bar-Zohar, The Armed Prophet: A Biography of Ben Gurion (London: Barker, 1967), p. 53.

56. Ibid., p. 74.

57. For details, see Bracha Habas, The Gate Breakers (New York: Yoseloff and Herzl, 1963); and Jon and David Kimche, The Secret Roads (New York: Farrar, Straus, and Cudahy, 1955).

58. For an insight into the workings of Etzel and Lehi, see Gerold Frank, The Deed (New York: Simon and Schuster, 1963). For a description by a former member of Lehi of some of the organization's activities, see Avner (pseud.), Memoirs of an Assassin (New York: Yoseloff, 1959). See The "Activities" of the Hagana, Irgun and Stern Bands (New York: Palestine Liberation Organization, n.d.); and "Zionist Terrorism," UN Doc. A/C.6/C.876, November 22, 1972, for Arab perspectives.

59. Quoted in the American Professors for Peace in the Middle East Newsletter, October 1969. See also Joseph B. Schechtman, The Mufti and the Fuehrer (London: Yoseloff, 1965); and Seth Arsenian, "Wartime Propaganda in the Middle East," Middle East Journal 2 (October 1948): 417-29.

60. See Munya Mardor, Strictly Illegal (London: Robert Hale, 1964), pp. 56 ff.

61. Survey of Palestine, op. cit., 1: 58, 61, 63.

62. See Thierry Nolin, La Haganah: L'Armee Secrete d'Israel (Paris: Ballard, 1971), pp. 159-63.

63. Keesing's Contemporary Archives 4 (1941-42): 6798A.

64. "The Assassination of Lord Moyne," Jewish Agency's Digest of Press and Events, November 11, 1944, pp. 1-3. For a basic study, see Gerold Frank, The Deed, op. cit., and "The Moyne Case: A Tragic History," Commentary 2 (December 1945): 64-71. See also Isaac Zaar, Rescue and Liberation (New York: Bloch, 1954), pp. 38-43; J. Bowyer Bell, The Long War (Englewood Cliffs, N.J.: Prentice-Hall, 1969), pp. 12-13; and "Assassination in International Politics: Lord Moyne, Count Bernadotte, and the Lehi," International Studies Quarterly 16, no. 1 (March 1972): 59-82; and Ha'aretz, March 26, 1975.

65. A Survey of Palestine, op. cit., 1:63, 72; and Keesing's Contemporary Archives 5 (1943-45): 6798.

66. For details, see Palcor News Agency Cables, March 27, April 13, November 20 and 22, 1944. Arab reactions are cited in Jewish Agency's Digest of Press and Events, April 10 and November 21, 1944.

67. See Report of the Anglo-American Committee of Inquiry on Palestine, Cmd. 6808 (1946), pp. 40-41.

68. For activities prior to the merger of these groups, see Valia Hirsch, "The Truth About the Terrorists," Today 1 (January 1945): 10-

12; and Frank Gervasi, "Terror in Palestine," Colliers, August 11, 1945, pp. 64-65.

69. See George Kirk, Survey of International Affairs: The Middle East, 1945-1950 (London: Royal Institute of International Affairs), p. 195; and Hamaas (Lehi's publication), no. 2 (November 1945).

70. See Palcor News Agency Cables, November 29, 1945; and Jewish Telegraphic Agency, December 26, 1945.

71. Herut (Etzel's publication), no. 55 (February 1946).

72. Eshav (publication of the Jewish resistance movement), no. 116 (March 4, 1946). For other activities by the movement, see Palcor News Agency Cables, April 4 and 24, 1946.

73. This commission was formed by the British government in November 1945 for the purpose of involving the United States in the responsibility for a solution to the Palestine problem (see Anglo-American Committee of Inquiry, op. cit).

74. R. D. Wilson, Cordon and Search: With 6th Airborne Division in Palestine (Aldershot: Gale and Polden, 1949), p. 262.

75. Keesing's Contemporary Archives 6 (1946-48): 7983.

76. Itzhak Gurion, Triumph on the Gallows (New York: Brit Trumpeldor of America, 1950), pp. 80-81.

77. Prior to this action, the British, for instance, had imposed all-night curfews. See Palcor News Agency Cables, April 30, 1946.

78. New Palestine News Reporter, July 12, 1946; and Palcor News Agency Cables, July 30, 1946.

79. Emanuel Celler stated that "terrorism in Palestine is a symbol of despair resulting from British action and would be a tragedy if the British used it as a pretext to deny entrance of 100,000 Jews into Palestine." Congressional Record, July 24, 1946, pp. 9944-45.

80. Keesing's Contemporary Archives 6 (1946-48): 8103. See also Begin, op. cit., pp. 212-20.

81. Palcor News Agency Cables, October 9 and 30, and November 7, 1946; and Keesing's Contemporary Archives 6 (1946-48): 8222.

82. Palcor News Agency Cables, November 12, 1946; and Begin, op. cit., p. 234.

83. See, for example, Jewish Telegraphic Agency, February 9, 1947; and Palcor News Agency Cables, February 11, 19, 20, and March 3, 12, 1947.

84. UN Doc. A/286.

85. UN Doc. A/287-291, April 22, 1947.

86. For an excellent presentation of the Palestinian question as discussed by the special session of the General Assembly, see Jacob Robinson, Palestine and the United Nations: Prelude to a Solution (Washington, D.C.: Public Affairs Press, 1948).

87. When the Charter of the United Nations came into force on October 24, 1945, the Arab states of Egypt, Iraq, Lebanon, Saudi

Arabia, and Syria were among the original members of the world organization.

88. Members of UNSCOP were Australia, Canada, Czechoslovakia, Guatemala, India, Iran, the Netherlands, Peru, Sweden, Uruguay, and Yugoslavia.

89. UN Doc. A/364.

90. The minority proposal was submitted by India, Iran, and Yugoslavia.

91. The assembly vote was 33 to 13 with 10 abstentions.

92. See, for instance, Palcor News Agency Cables, May 15 and August 4, 1947; the New York Times, August 1, 1947, and September 4, 1947.

93. Palestine Post, December 3, 1947.

94. See, for example, the New York Times, December 11, 12, 13, 1947.

95. Palestine Post, December 31, 1947.

96. Ibid., January 15, 1948.

97. Ibid., January 20, 1948.

98. See Fawzi Al-Qawuqji, "Memoirs, 1948," part I, Journal of Palestine Studies 1 (Summer 1972): 25-28, and part II, Journal of Palestine Studies 2 (Autumn 1972): 3-33.

99. Keesing's Contemporary Archives 6 (1946-48): 9237.

100. Ibid.

101. New York Times, January 2, 1948.

102. Keesing's Contemporary Archives 6 (1946-48): 9238.

103. UN Doc. S/616.

104. UN Doc. S/PV.253, February 24, 1948.

105. Palestine Post, February 2, 1948.

106. Ibid., February 23, 1948.

107. Ibid., February 29, 1948; and the New York Times, February 21, 22, 23, 24, 1948.

108. Keesing's Contemporary Archives 6 (1946-48): 9238.

109. See Netanel Lorch, The Edge of the Sword: Israel's War of Independence, 1947-1949 (New York: Putnam, 1961), p. 63.

110. Keesing's Contemporary Archives 6 (1946-48): 9239.

111. The siege of Old Jerusalem ended on May 28, 1948, when the Jewish quarter surrendered to the Arab Legion. See Harry Levine, Jerusalem Embattled (London: Gollancz, 1950); and John Bagot Glubb, A Soldier with the Arabs (London: Hodder and Stoughton, 1957), pp. 129-30.

112. See Lorch, op. cit.

113. London Times, April 7, 1948; and Keesing's Contemporary Archives 6 (1946-48): 9239.

114. See "Dir Yassin," West Asia Affairs (Summer 1969), pp. 27-30; the New York Times, April 10, 11, 12, 1948; Edgar O'Ballance,

The Arab-Israeli War, 1948 (New York: Praeger, 1957), p. 58; Arthur Koestler, "The Other Exodus," Spectator, May 18, 1961; and Christopher Sykes, Crossroads to Israel (Cleveland: World, 1965), pp. 416-17.

115. New York Herald Tribune, April 12, 1948.

116. Quoted by Guy Ottewell, "Deir Yassin: A Forgotten Tragedy with Present-Day Meaning," Perspective (April 1969), p. 6.

117. UN Doc. S/PV.277.

118. UN Doc. S/723.

119. See Lorch, op. cit., p. 129; Edgar O'Ballance, op. cit., pp. 65-66; and Dov Knohl, Siege in the Hills of Hebron: The Battle of the Etzion Bloc (New York: Yoseloff, 1958).

120. BBC News Broadcast, May 15, 1948.

**PALESTINIAN TERRORISM:
VIOLENCE, VERBAL STRATEGY,
AND LEGITIMACY**
Edward Weisband
Damir Roguly

THE FOCI AND THE MEANING OF MODERATION

This chapter will be an analysis of Palestinian terrorism. It starts by asking who the actors and the groups involved are and how they became organized. Around what factors—class, religion, geographical identity, educational experience, and so on—did the leadership of the Palestinian resistance coalesce? According to what ideological precepts did they organize their followers?

The next section will detail some of the major acts of violence that have been committed. Palestinian terrorism has gone through a number of phases involving major tactical, if not strategic, changes.

We will be primarily interested in the ways in which the different actors justify their actions. Violence in order to be terrorism must be political. Since terrorist violence tries to create the framework for political interactions, terrorists are forced to locate their actions in some political or moral context.

To do this, they use words. They adopt certain verbal strategies that announce how their actions should be interpreted. Verbal strategies help to create a terrorist's reputation for behavior; they explain the goals he is seeking. They attempt to provide a normative context for action by, in whatever way possible, endowing the brutality of terrorism with social meaning.

This chapter proceeds from the assumption that terrorism, to be politically meaningful, must be conciliatory as well as chiliastic. It must be norm-creating as well as norm-destroying, dialogical as well as diabolical. It must, in the words of Albert Camus, "aspire to the relative." Terrorism is different from criminal violence in that its purpose is symbolic, its means psychological, and its ends political. Terrorism often serves as the cutting edge of a revolutionary movement, but, precisely because it is the vehicle of organized insurgency, it must point the way to a political resolution. It must negate its nihilism. For a terrorist, to want too much is to seek too little. This is especially true of Palestinian terrorism, since the Palestinian resistance is, at its core, a movement toward national sovereignty.

Al-Fatah, an acronym devised by reversing the letters of the Arabic words for "Palestine National Liberation Movement" means "opening" or "conquest," and the two weeks between October 28 and November 13, 1974 may well be remembered as the beginning of a new era. During these two weeks, the international community, or at least that large body of countries loosely identified as the Third World, conferred quasi-governmental status upon the Palestine Liberation Organization (PLO). Yasir Arafat, its leader, was given a reception at the United Nations on November 13, 1974, reserved for chiefs of state. His address began at noon, the time at which heads of state speak before the General Assembly; moreover, the beige armchair, the United Nations' symbol of chief-of-state status, was brought into the hall of the General Assembly to be used by Arafat, who, in turn, received a minute's long standing ovation when he rose to speak.[1]

The event at the United Nations was perhaps of less immediate consequence than the decision that had been taken two weeks earlier at the meeting in Rabat of Arab heads of government—to recognize the PLO as "the sole legitimate representative of the Palestinian people." The Rabat resolution endowed the PLO with the right to assert "national authority" and committed the Arab nations to this authority's support "in all respects and at all levels."[2] Thus, the PLO and its main constituent organization, al-Fatah, achieved standard-bearer primacy in the Palestinian cause.

The significance of the Rabat resolution rests in its recognition of the PLO and, by implication, al-Fatah, as the central political force of the Palestinian people. The 20 Arab states at Rabat confirmed the right of al-Fatah alone to act on behalf of all the Palestinians, a right that had in the past been challenged by the Arab states themselves and by other organizations within the Palestinian resistance movement.

The history of the Palestinian resistance has been characterized by two tendencies—what one observer refers to as "fission and fussion"[3] and by what another calls "an endless dance of unification and separation, always changing partners and breaking off again."[4] When, on January 5, 1968, al-Fatah issued a call to all "active" "fedayeen" organizations to establish a "consultative committee," it listed 12 separate groups, including the PLO and al-Fatah itself.[5] This attempt to create a modicum of coordination among the fedayeen organizations typifies al-Fatah's role as a unifying force in the movement. The

events of October and November 1974 openly confirmed what had been
evolving since 1956, namely, the gradual emergence of al-Fatah as
the umbrella of all Palestinian terrorist organizations. Since 1970, it
has acted as the major power center within the PLO; since 1968, it
and it alone had accurately claimed to appeal to the majority of Palestinians.[6]

Yet it has not claimed open responsibility for terrorist violence
outside Israel, like the notorious European airplane hijackings, nor
has it generally appeared willing to be associated with the more virulent expeditions inside Israel, like the one at Maalot. The military or
commando arm of al-Fatah, Quwat al-Asifa (Forces of the Storm),
explicitly aims at such targets as "roads, dams, bridges, railways,
water pipes, pumping stations, police stations, tractors, fuel installations, industrial complexes, ammunition dumps, military vehicles."[7]
The PLO has attempted to coordinate the campaigns of all the fedayeen
units, but it has also apparently preferred for the most part to be
identified as a force that tends to attack targets, primarily military
ones, in Israel—no more and no less.

The notion that certain of the fedayeen organizations are "moderate" is often treated simplistically. All commando organizations are
equally tenacious in their aim to eliminate the State of Israel and to
vindicate Palestinian claims to what is regarded as their traditional
homeland. All perceive violence as the instrument with which to liberate the Palestinian people.

This applies to al-Fatah. One Egyptian weekly summed up the
political thinking of al-Fatah as follows: "The political ideology of
al-Fath's organization is based on revolutionary violence. . . . As
the rifle is the outer image of al-Fath, the bullet is the ideology."[8]
All fedayeen organizations, including al-Fatah, are led by professional
terrorists whose trade is political violence. But precisely because of
the political role that terrorism plays, certain groups and sets of
leaders appear to be more aware than others of the need for effective
discipline in the use and justification of violence. Al-Fatah may be
said to be moderate in the strict sense that, given its clear-cut military program and salient political objectives, this organization seemingly possesses the ideological capability of engaging in terrorist violence selectively and of entering into negotiations with other Arab
states and possibly with Israel designed to construct a normatively
viable resolution to the conflict, that is, of entering into a peace based
on political compromise.

How and in what ways any of the fedayeen groups can appro-
priately be deemed "moderate" can only be interpreted against the
background of these elements.

TERRORISTS—WHO THEY ARE, WHAT THEY
BELIEVE, WHERE THEY BELONG

The early manifestations of Palestinian terrorism against the Jewish community in Palestine date back to 1929-32 with the formation of the so-called Green Hand gang and the secret cells organized under the inspiration of At-Din Al-Qassam. Despite the complex pattern of twists and turns in the interrelationships among the terrorist groups since that time, four axes can be discerned within the resistance movement. Two of them have already been mentioned—the PLO and al-Fatah; the other two are the Popular Front for the Liberation of Palestine (PFLP) and the Vanguards of the Palestine Popular Liberation War, from which come the al-Sa'iqah forces, which are wholly dominated by the Syrian government.

Throughout its history, al-Fatah has experienced its most important advances when the fate of the Palestinians was at its lowest ebb—in 1948, 1956, and 1967. A central figure from the very beginning has been Arafat, who in 1948 fought in the irregular cadres organized by Abd Al-Qadir El-Husseini.[9] After the war, Arafat and other displaced Palestinians went to Gaza, where they attempted to form the "All-Palestine Government."[10] These attempts faltered,[11] and in 1951, Arafat began his studies in civil engineering at what is now the University of Cairo.[12] During this period, Arafat organized the General Union of Palestine and received military training at an Egyptian military college. In 1956, he fought against the British and the French, specializing in sabotage and demolition.[13] Certain common experiences, such as fighting in the wars of 1948 and 1956 and becoming politically active in Gaza during the turbulent years of the early 1950s, brought several young Palestinians, including Arafat, together. They formed the nucleus of what would become the leadership of al-Fatah. This group, molded by Gaza, Cairo, and Suez, included Abu Iyad (Salah Khalaf) and Abu Jihad (Khalil Ibrahim Wazir),[14] alleged to be one of Arafat's closest companions.

Al-Fatah, although conceived in Gaza and Cairo, actually had its birth within the well-to-do Palestinian community in Kuwait, for Arafat lived there between 1957 and 1964. Although the term "al-Fatah" is alleged to have been devised in Gaza during the aftermath of the 1956 Suez crisis, it took seven years—until 1963—to form a commando-type organizational structure.[15] Nearly two full years would elapse after this before al-Fatah could engage in its first military operation. This occurred on December 31, 1964, and its first military communique was issued the day after.[16]

Despite a number of minor skirmishes with Israeli authorities, al-Fatah did not emerge as a political force in the Middle East until March 1968, when its military forces attempted to fight off an Israeli

expeditionary attack during the now famous battle of Karamah, which
began on March 21.[17] Although Israeli and Arab accounts differ
widely as to what occurred at Karamah,[18] confirmed reports suggest
that Palestinian forces took the lives of nearly 30 Israeli soldiers and
wounded over 90, although sustaining even heavier losses themselves.[19]
The showing of al-Fatah at Karamah provided a factor desperately desired by the Palestinians after the Six-Day War. Palestinians had
successfully engaged the Israelis in battle. Theirs was a "moral" victory that sent signals throughout the Arab world that a new force was
emerging. After Karamah, the development of al-Fatah began to ac-
celerate. Within two years, al-Fatah became "the biggest, richest,
and most structurally complex"[20] of all the resistance organizations.
In 1969, it in effect took over the PLO.[21]

The PLO represents the second major axis in the Palestinian
resistance movement. It has traditionally been held in dubious esteem
by the Palestinians, however. The PLO was first conceived at the
40th meeting of the Arab League Council, in September 1963, during
which Ahmed Shukeiry was appointed as the representative of Palestine and charged with creating a viable political organization.[22] On
May 28, 1964, nearly 400 Palestinians met in Jerusalem as delegates
to the Palestine National Congress and elected Shukeiry as their chairman. At this meeting, the PLO was formally established, with Shukeiry as chairman of its executive committee.[23] The second Arab
summit meeting, held in Alexandria on September 5-11, 1964, "welcomed the establishment" of the organization. The member states
also specified the forms of support they would bestow upon the new
organization.[24] This raised a new political issue.

A major political argument that divides the various terrorist
organizations is the degree to which the resistance should depend on
any non-Palestinian source of support. Al-Fatah, while successful
in obtaining assistance from a variety of sources, has elevated the
need to remain independent into an ideological principle. In part this
no doubt stems from witnessing the stultifying experience of the PLO
under Ahmed Shukeiry.

It has become commonplace among Arab commentators that,
although the PLO was ostensibly established by the Arab states to provide a central forum for the Palestinians, in fact it was set up as a
vehicle to keep the Palestinians under control. The following example
is typical:

> When the PLO was created, as is often the case with
> such political organizations, it was declared to have
> been established for certain reasons which did not
> really reflect the true motives behind its creation.
> . . . The Arab governments feared losing control

> over the bulk of the Palestinians who favored the small
> rising organizations such as Fateh. . . . Under the cir-
> cumstances, the Arab heads of state, meeting in Cairo,
> recognized the necessity of creating an organization
> which would contain the Palestinians' independent ini-
> tiative, and over which they might retain some control.[25]

Arab commentators generally argue that the PLO was initially a Nas-
serite creation that immediately became discredited in the eyes of the
Palestinians. In early 1965, Nasser accused al-Fatah of being a Central Treaty Organization (CENTO) agency attempting to provoke a military confrontation between Egypt and Israel.[26] Similarly, Arafat was
imprisoned by Syrian authorities during the same year and remained
incarcerated for nearly two months.[27]

During the years between 1965 and 1967, therefore, the PLO
and al-Fatah competed in their attempts to provide a common roof for
the fedayeen groups that were now rapidly forming. As the stature of
al-Fatah increased, particularly after the battle at Karamah, that of
Shukeiry shrank. One non-Arab observer maintains that it was "Shu-
qayri's autocratic style and his complete dependence on Cairo—which
was held accountable among the Palestinians for his opposition to
commando activities against Israel," that elicited demands for his
ouster.[28] Shukeiry was finally replaced by Yahya Hammudah, who
was elected acting chairman of the PLO executive committee at the
fourth Palestinian National Congress (PNC) held in Cairo on July 10,
1968.[29] With the selection of Hammudah, attempts at establishing a
common framework could begin in earnest.

The PLO has contributed nonmilitary resources to the movement over the years, and its importance has been in the areas of propaganda and publicity. As the usefulness of these instruments were
becoming recognized during 1968-69, al-Fatah gradually assumed control over the PLO and thus its nonmilitary institutional resources.
Arafat emerged out of the underground at this time to become the
front-office spokesman of al-Fatah. He began to take a more direct
role in the management of the PLO, which had already built up fund-
raising, publicity, and research staffs that could be important to al-
Fatah and the other fedayeen groups as well. Equally significant was
the fact that the PLO had become, or at least pretended to be, the
parent organization of the Palestine National Assembly (PNA), the
congressional forum that linked, to varying degrees, all Palestinian
organizations, nonmilitary as well as commando. In 1968, therefore,
Arafat and al-Fatah made an effort to dominate the PLO and thereby
control the entire resistance movement by standing over the political
machinery that only the PLO could operate.

On January 5 and 6, 1968, al-Fatah began its campaign to gain
authority over the PLO and the PNA by calling for a "national" con-

ference. In its opening gambit, al-Fatah stressed two major themes
—the need for unity and the primacy of the fedayeen among the entire
Palestinian resistance. It requested that all "active," that is, "fighting," organizations meet "to strengthen the pillars of national unity."[30]
The PLO, correctly perceiving this as a challenge to its future as a
coordinating body, issued its own request on January 15 to all units
in the "armed resistance to co-operate with the PLO in order to unite
this struggle and escalate it."[31] The executive committee of the PLO
announced that it would reconvene the dormant PNA; it also declared
that the assembly would be reduced to 100 seats. The stage was thus
set for a series of altercations that would eventually determine which
of the two bodies, the PLO or al-Fatah, would emerge as the controlling umbrella organization. On January 19, a spokesman for al-
Fatah officially welcomed the resuscitation of the PNA but objected to
"bi-lateral agreements" and the "action of each behind the other's
back" in an obvious reference to the trips to Damascus and Amman
taken by Hammadah at this time to shore up the position of the PLO.[32]

During the following months, al-Fatah derided the capacity of
the PLO to act as the legitimate "mother organization." As one of its
representatives declared, "the PLO is not able to control its own affairs and conflicts, and splits still exist within it. . . . How, then,
can it organize the Fida'i activity in which it does not believe and
which it joined only lately."[33] These points were telling. One observer of the executive meeting between the PLO and al-Fatah reported
in mid-March 1968 that "the PLO recognized that it was not the sole
element to make decisions connected with the 'problems of the Palestinian people'; the PLO was forced to admit that the major fida'iyyun
organizations had a better right than [less active] organizations to
take part in such decision-making."[34] The leadership of the Palestinian people thus began to be turned over to the commando organizations.

The actual transfer of power took place in the context of the PNA.
Through a series of negotiations among the PLO, al-Fatah, and a number of other groups, a formula was devised whereby the fedayeen organizations, including al-Fatah, would hold 50 seats in the new assembly and 50 would go to "unaffiliated individuals who had been active in
Palestinian affairs."[35] Al-Fatah reneged on several occasions during
the next few months, apparently in accordance with a faction that wanted
to hold out for more seats. Such pressures increased after Karamah.
At the end of May 1968, however, a binding agreement was achieved
by which al-Fatah, along with a number of nominal organizations under its control, received 38 seats, the largest single bloc of seats in
the PNA.[36]

When the long-awaited congress finally met in the Arab League
building in Cairo on July 10, 1968, al-Fatah had obtained almost total
control. As one account went, "It was obvious that through its major-

ity in the PNA, al-Fath would be able to carry out its own plans while using the financial, military, and information resources of the PLO."[37] The conference proclaimed a new national charter,[38] revising the one of 1964, and established an 11-man executive committee that would oversee the PNA. Significantly, the members of the assembly would elect the members of the executive committee who would in turn elect their own chairman. According to the Lebanese daily Al-Anwar, all candidates for the chairmanship were from the ranks of al-Fatah.[39]

The primacy of al-Fatah would not come easily, however. The consensus on ruling structures and governing procedures, the achievement of which had been the very purpose of the conference, eventually broke down. Al-Fatah released a statement declaring, "Al-Fath absolutely refuses to allow the principles of the revolution to become a subject of bargaining or bidding. Al-Fath flatly rejects the formation of a lame, disunited and irrational Executive Committee emanating from compromise and haggling. Such a Committee will be as paralyzed as previous committees. . . . Al-Fath wants a rational Executive Committee made up largely of revolutionary leaders who are actually living the revolution."[40] The PNA was forced to adjourn by reelecting the old PLO executive committee.

Al-Fatah was not alone in rejecting the consensus or in making it impossible to form a new governing body. The army of the PLO itself also forced what turned out to be merely a postponement of the July 1968 consensus. Rank and file in the Palestine Liberation Army (PLA), the fighting wing of the PLO and a full-fledged army, objected to being taken over by the irregulars. Moreover, the commando organization of the PLA, the Popular Liberation Forces (PLF), which had been set up in early 1968 to attract some of the glory to the PLA that was being attached to terrorist groups in general, also vehemently objected.[41] The voices of the PLA and the PLF could only delay the al-Fatah takeover, however.

First, both the PLA and the PLF had had the reputation of being the richest and best supplied of the fedayeen, but also the least likely to engage in any serious fighting.[42] Like its parent organization, the PLA had tended to suffer in Palestinian eyes from being too closely associated with non-Palestinian sources of support. In the words of the An-Nahar (Beirut) research staff, for example,

> Since the PLA was formed under the indirect supervision, at least in principle, of the Arab governments which condoned the existence of the PLO, the PLA has been totally dependent on its host states for armament, training, financial support, and even qualified officers. In effect, the various PLA units have been no more than Palestinian contingents of the Syrian and

Iraqi armies and were only controlled nominally by the
PLO. In fact, the host governments went to the trouble
of assuring that the upper echelon officers of these units
were more loyal to the host governments than to the
cause of the PLO. [43]

Second, a debilitating mutiny occurred within the PLA on or about August 1, 1968, over the appointment of Brig. Abd Al-Razzaq Yahya to
replace Brig. Subhi Al-Jabi. [44] This conflict, which brought the governing council of the PLO into conflict with the rank and file of the
PLA, rendered the entire army and its terrorist arm incapable of
serious political or military action until the issue was settled with the
appointment of Brig. Musbah Al-Budayri in December 1968. By the
time the PLA and the PLF regained their disciplinary composure, al-
Fatah had successfully subordinated the PLO.

Victory came to al-Fatah at the fifth congress of the PNA, held
in Cairo on February 1-5, 1969. [45] A new 11-man executive council
of the PLO was formed with Arafat as its chairman. Ostensibly there
existed proportionate representation on the executive council; the
cards, however, were clearly stacked in al-Fatah's favor. An observer wrote:

In February 1969, when Fatah succeeded in seizing
control of the PLO, only two members of the old PLO
executive committee were among the eleven-man body.
Fatah was directly represented by Yasir Arafat,
chairman and head of military affairs, as well as
Khalid al-Hassan, Faruq al-Qaddumi, and Muhammad
Yusif al-Najjar, all members of Fatah's central committee. In addition, Fatah seemed to have the support
of Ibrahim Bakr, deputy chairman, Kamal Nasir, and
Hamid Abu Sittah. [46]

Two axes in the Palestinian resistance had thus come together. Now,
too, the ideological themes of political leadership became unrelievedly
those of the fedayeen—self-sacrifice in battle.

The third axis is the al-Sa'iqah forces that challenged the supremacy of al-Fatah. At the point when al-Fatah seemed to have
forged a common framework for the movement, it became embroiled
in a lethal battle between certain Arab states—Jordan in particular—
on the one hand and a number of other terrorist groups on the other.
Involved were government-sponsored commando organizations, the
most important of which was and still is the al-Sa'iqah forces (of the
Vanguards of the Palestine Popular Liberation War), which was
founded and remains controlled by the Syrian Ba'ath Party. Also in-

cluded were the so-called splinter groups, the terrorist organizations that had sprung up during the 1960s around a particular leader, ideological orientation, or operational strategy. The al-Sa'iqah forces and the list of splinter groups represent the third and fourth axes along which terrorist organizational activity has been structured. Both in their way contributed to the open confrontation between the fedayeen and the Bedouin army of King Hussein that culminated in the disaster for the Palestinians now known as Black September (1970).

Al-Sa'iqah has, as Al-Nahar observers wrote, "presented itself from the start as an alternative for Fateh and has been trying ever since to take the political and military lead from the largest commando organization."[47] Founded by the Ba'ath Party as early as 1958, it started fedayeen activity around September 1967.

The aims, actions, and ideology of al-Sa'iqah have always been molded to promote the political interests of the Ba'ath Party. Indeed, the creation of this terrorist organization resulted from the distinct need of the Syrian government to recapture some of the luster it had lost during the Six-Day War. Also, the terrorist organization has helped the party's leadership to "divert the attention of the young people from domestic to foreign affairs."[48] It appears that the Ba'ath Party has used al-Sa'iqah as a counterbalance against the Syrian army itself and has sponsored programs requiring civilian members of party organizations, student groups, and the like to take training courses with al-Sa'iqah.[49] However, the command of al-Sa'iqah is invariably taken from the upper ranks of the Syrian army, as in the case of Colonels Raif Al-Wani and Mustapha Sa'ad El-Din, who lead it at the present time.

The single major act of terrorism perpetrated by al-Sa'iqah outside the Middle East was organized under the name of the "Eagles of the Palestine Revolution" and occurred in Austria in September 1973. In a widely reported operation, two heavily armed terrorists took over a train compartment of Soviet Jewish immigrants en route to Israel on September 28, 1973. Their main demand was the closing down of several transit facilities used by Soviet Jews upon leaving the Soviet Union. Early in the morning of September 29, Austrian Chancellor Bruno Kreisky agreed to close the Schoenan transit camp run by the Jewish Agency on the grounds that the safety of the Soviet Jews could no longer be guaranteed. The terrorists were later given safe passage to Libya. At a hastily called news conference, they declared: "Our objective is to stop at all costs the emigration of Soviet Jews to Israel."[50] Their purpose also may have been to divert world and Israeli attention from the military build-up in Syria and Egypt that took place prior to the October war.

Al-Sa'iqah's participation in this particular operation becomes comprehensible only in this context. This organization, so completely under the thumb of Syrian President Asad, could not have acted without his explicit orders. He, in turn, was one of the few to know of the imminent war. It is interesting to speculate, furthermore, that the Syrian government must have informed the Soviet Union of its intentions. It is highly unlikely that Syria would have acted so close to Soviet interests and territory without having kept the Soviets fully informed. The Vienna operation, however, represents a departure. Al-Sa'iqah tends to operate within Israel or around it.

Given its close ties to Ba'athist socialism, the ideology of al-Sa'iqah has exalted the role of Arab states surrounding Palestine. Starting from the premise that "the Palestine revolution is an integral part of the Arab revolution," al-Sa'iqah and its parent organization, the Vanguards assert that "the density of Palestine is historically decided along with the future conditions surrounding Palestine," that is, "Palestine is influenced by and influences its neighbors." Al-Sa'iqah also clearly pursues a Socialist philosophy. The "non-Nationalistic nature of the Palestinian-Jordanian bourgeoisie has made it a direct ally of the forces of colonialism and imperialism, hence of the Zionist movement,"[51] it has declared. These principles tend to contradict the precepts of al-Fatah, which generally underscore the nationalist character of the Palestinian struggle—the need for the Palestinians to take their fate into their own hands—and which also emphasize the importance of obtaining the goals of the nationalist struggle before making any ideological commitment to a particular social system.

Yet, al-Sa'iqah, unlike the PLA, is held in high regard by many non-Ba'athist Palestinians. First, there are numbers of Palestinians in it, but, more important, al-Sa'iqah has performed comparatively well in battle. Although never receiving the publicity of some of the other terrorist organizations, al-Sa'iqah has been an important factor in numerous encounters with Israeli Defense Forces (IDF), especially on the southern Lebanese front, often referred to as "Fatahland." Even today, al-Sa'iqah enjoys "a privileged position over the commando groups" in Lebanon.[52] As a Beirut daily wrote in 1970, "it can even be said that the Palestinians themselves are using this organization for their own ends and not for the Syrian ends." This became manifest when on March 21, 1975, the integration of al-Sa'iqah and al-Fatah commandos was announced. Cooperation and affiliation between al-Fatah and al-Sa'iqah have thus tended to diminish earlier patterns of competition.[53]

Cooperation between the two organizations began in 1968. It was al-Sa'iqah that cooperated with al-Fatah after the failure of the July 1968 PNA meeting to produce a consensus on governance, and it was undoubtedly its acceptance of al-Fatah as the predominant organization that led to the agreement over the composition of the executive committee of the PLO in February 1969. Furthermore, when the time came in June 1970 to make another major adjustment in the leadership of the resistance organizations, al-Sa'iqah sided with al-Fatah on the question of the composition of the central committee of the PLO. [54] Perhaps the cooperation shown by al-Sa'iqah toward al-Fatah during 1969 and 1970 stemmed from a Ba'athist interest in the possibility of forming a modus vivendi to destroy the Jordanian regime of Hussein. We know that in 1969 operatives from within al-Sa'iqah began "working to topple the Hussein regime and . . . contracted some Jordanian officers" to achieve this end. [55]

It appears that terrorists in al-Sa'iqah perpetrated one of the earliest clashes between the fedayeen and Hussein in 1968, which culminated in all-out war in 1970. One such event occurred on October 8, 1968, when Hasan al-Atrash, a right-wing politician and a member of a prominent Druse family in Jordan who had served in several Syrian cabinets during the 1950s, was kidnapped by al-Sa'iqah forces. The obvious purpose was to smuggle him back into Syria to bring him to trial for his role in a coup that had unsuccessfully attempted to bring down the Syrian government of Salim Hatum. The kidnapping of al-Atrash seriously embarrassed the Jordanian government. Within a week, desert clashes between the fedayeen and the Bedouin troops were reported. [56]

In the midst of attempts to resolve this crisis, an even more divisive conflict occurred. On November 4, 1968, a terrorist group known as the "Battalions of Victory" under the leadership of Tahir Dablan, who had once led al-Sa'iqah, attacked Jordanian security forces. This led to their widespread arrest by the Jordanians. The significance of this incident and the ensuing hostilities that claimed 33 lives and wounded 82 was that it brought the simmering tensions between the Jordanian government and the fedayeen to the fore. [57] It led to the establishment of Jordanian anti-fedayeen task forces under the leadership of Wasfi Al-Tall, and it pitted the different fedayeen organizations not only against the government but against each other as well. [58]

Al-Fatah deplored these developments by condemning "small organizations" for perpetrating "regrettable events." It criticized the sponsors of these groups with "burdening the revolution with heavy troubles." [59] But there were other groups that, like al-Sa'iqah, wanted to take on Hussein in real battle. Eventually al-Fatah also took a hand in the actions designed to depose Hussein. To understand the conflict between Jordan and the fedayeen, which nearly decimated the ranks of al-Fatah, one must go beyond al-Fatah, al-Sa'iqah, and the PLO to the fourth main axis of terrorist organization and activity. [60] This axis originates with the founding of the Arab Nationalist Movement (ANM) in 1952 and revolves around the career of George Habash.

The history of the internal conflicts among the terrorist organizations represents, in large part, a joint biography of the lives of

Habash and Arafat. The two rarely discuss each other in public, but
their intense rivalry is a well-known fact in the resistance. Both have
had an enormous impact in shaping Palestinian terrorism, but their
styles and opinions differ starkly. Whereas Arafat is generally regarded as an ascetic who neither smokes nor drinks and has never
married, Habash (at least before his heart attack in 1973) smokes two
packs of cigarettes a day, enjoys "political" conversation, and has
two daughters. While Arafat revels in the operational side of terrorist action and deplores intellectuality, Habash is an ideologue. To
Arafat's logistical realism, Habash has counterposed Socialist idealism. Whereas the former tends to the Right in the name of nationalism, the latter tends to the Left in the name of a universalist Marxism-Leninism. Whereas Arafat is a devout Moslem, Habash is a
Christian who rejects religion. Arafat was born into a relatively
well-to-do family and is related to the former grand Mufti of Jerusalem, Haj Amin El-Husseini; Habash is the son of a corn dealer. [61]

Born in 1926 into a Greek Orthodox family, Habash grew up in
Jerusalem in the Jewish and Arab communities. In 1944, Habash entered medical school at the American University in Beirut, and he
left Palestine forever after the 1948 war. During this period, he first
began to be associated with terrorism and is known to have led a group
that attacked British personnel in Damascus during the late 1940s. [62]

In the early 1950s, just as Arafat was beginning to gather around
him the cadre that later emerged as the leadership of al-Fatah, Habash was attempting to establish the ANM. While one organization developed in Cairo, the other evolved in Beirut. Whereas al-Fatah always remained thoroughly Palestinian in membership, the ANM has
allowed its ranks to become diluted. While al-Fatah was almost
completely Moslem, the leaders of the ANM more often than not were
non-Moslem, usually Greek Orthodox, like Habash himself and Wadi
Haddad and Ahmad Al-Yamani. Whereas the stance taken by al-Fatah
with regard to Arab governments has stressed the need for Palestinian independence, the ANM has consistently become involved in the
politics of Arab governments. It actually became a Pan-Arab party
in the mid-1960s with the result that the ANM sided with Nasser
against the terrorists in 1965 when al-Fatah was first emerging. [63]

The success of al-Fatah, and no doubt the recognition it was
beginning to enjoy after Karamah, prompted the ANM to begin supporting terrorist activity, and in late 1966, it announced that it was forming its own commando organization, the "Heroes of the Return."
Based in Lebanon, this group was led by an anti-Shukeiry faction
within the PLO, including Shafiq Al-Hut, who was at the time the head
of the PLO's Beirut office. [64] Some PLO funds were directed to it,
but the Heroes of the Return remained basically an adjunct of the Palestinian section of the ANM. [65]

After the Six-Day War, Habash renounced normal political activity, dropped from the ranks of the ANM, and went underground. Here he formed a terrorist organization of his own, the "Vengeance Youth," that largely absorbed the resources of the so-called Old Front for the Liberation of Palestine, the military arm of the ANM.[66] In late 1967, the Heroes of the Return and the Vengeance Youth combined resources with the PLF. The latter had once been a Syrian-sponsored organization and at the time was under the leadership of Ahmad Jibril, formerly a Palestinian officer in the Syrian army.[67] Together these three groups formed the PFLP.

The PFLP has from its inception tended to be a "front" organization. One of its explicit goals is to provide an institutional framework for a diverse range of terrorist groups. In a major policy statement issued in February 1969, the PFLP stated:

> As regards organization, it likewise was not designed
> that the Front should at that stage of its formation be
> a unified party organization. . . . What was also un-
> derstood was that the Front would for some time con-
> tinue to consist of a group of organizations, each of
> which would maintain its independent existence. How-
> ever there would be a beginning made to planning for
> coordination among these organizations.[68]

This intention to coordinate all the constitutent terrorist organizations, however, never came to fruition. The phrase "popular front," when applied to the PFLP, is a contradiction in terms. The concept of the popular front as introduced by the Stalinist Communist parties of the 1930s involved the coming together of diverse political parties —often representing contrasting ideologies—around the framework of a common political platform and program. To broaden their base of popular support, individual parties tended to accept some compromise in their political programs or ideological appeals and promoted those compromises considered necessary for the maintenance of a common platform. Within the PFLP, there has existed no such willingness. No common political platform, nor even a generally acceptable operational strategy among the various groups, has emerged. Above all else, the factor that most distinguishes the PFLP from al-Fatah is its fractious nature—despite the dominating personality of Habash. This stems in part from the personalities and political styles of its leaders, in part from serious ideological conflict characterized by extremism rather than compromise. Whatever the cause, the result has been an unending series of splits.

The PFLP has since 1968 spawned a terrorist group that has named itself the Popular Front for the Liberation of Palestine General

Command (PFLP-GC), under the leadership of Jibril;[69] this in turn led to a splinter group known as the Organization of Arab Palestine (OAP), led by a former Palestinian colonel in the Jordanian army, Ahmad Za'rur.[70] These two groups are basically militarist and represent fissures on the Right of Habash.

Of late, Jibril's group has been supported largely by the Libyan government, as admitted by Colonel Quaddafi at the time of the May 22, 1972 PFLP-GC attack on an Israeli bus. Quaddafi, parenthetically, deplores the leftist movements in the front and particularly resents Habash's communism.

To the Left of even Habash, and more ideologically oriented, is the Popular Democratic Front for the Liberation of Palestine (PDFLP), under the inspiration of Na'if Hawatima,[71] and the Popular Revolutionary Front for the Liberation of Palestine (PRFLP), formed in 1972 under the leadership of Iraqi-born Ahmad Dalimi, or Abu Shihab.[72]

The sources of the conflicts that have spawned these groups identified with the "front" probably originate with the move to the Left in the early 1960s[73] on the part of certain factions within the ranks of the ANM. A group of young ANM radicals challenged the "centrist" tendencies of the them "moderate" leaders like Habash and Haddad at this time.[74] The Marxist-Leninist faction arose within the ANM and tried on several occasions to wrest control of the ANM away from Habash but always without success. The Six-Day War, however, generated a near total revision of the ideological orientation of the ANM, which became Marxist-Leninist. Habash underwent a personal radicalization as well.

When the PFLP was formed, a vociferous Marxist-Leninist faction within the ANM—the one associated with Hawatima—agreed to join despite the presence of Jibril and his band of terrorists. This uneasy alliance between the Right and the Left within the PFLP was reflected in 1969 by statements that sought to contrast the "progressivism" of the ANM with the eclecticism of the PFLP. "It is evident," declared the PFLP,

> that there is a definite objective distinction between the organization of the Palestinian branch of the Movement [ANM] on the one hand and the Front on the other. The Movement . . . possesses a socialist revolutionary concept through which it views the strategy of the Palestine Liberation struggle, while the Front presents a liberation thought with progressive features. Moreover, the Movement represents a unified party organization preparing to rebuild itself according to a revolutionary organizational strategy, while

> the Front represents a group of organizations which differ in their organizational structure. [75]

The amalgam that held the organizations together did not stick for very long, however; ideology, politics, and personality dissolved it.

For one thing, the Vengeance Youth, the terrorist group that Habash had originally founded, was intently anti-Syrian. Although Jibril was dismissed from the Syrian army in 1958 after the merger of Egypt and Syria, he and his faction were pro-Syrian; indeed, they were supported by the Syrian government. [76] The issues between Jibril and Habash were to some extent ideological in nature but also involved the refusal of the Syrians to permit at this time terrorist acts to be carried out from Syria into the Golan Heights, which Habash wanted. The ANM also wanted Jibril and his men placed under tighter political control, to which he and the Syrian government objected. [77] Thus Habash and Jibril were pitted against each other soon after the PFLP was founded. Habash became increasingly anti-Syrian and was finally arrested by Syrian authorities. He remained imprisoned in Damascus for seven months. [78]

With Habash in prison, whatever cement there had been along the perimeters of the PFLP disappeared. With no one between them, Jibril and Hawatima confronted each other. Each decided to withdraw his terrorist group from the PFLP rather than operate together. [79]

Hawatima, who, like Habash, was born a Christian and educated at the American University of Beirut, became a radical force in Arab politics in his early teens. By 1954, when he was only 23, he came under a death sentence in Iraq for his alleged role in an antigovernment plot. Nine years later he was in fact jailed and tortured and narrowly escaped execution in Iraq for attempting to set up secret ANM cells. From a Jordanian peasant family, Hawatima has become the ideologue of the masses within the resistance movement. In August 1968, while Habash was still in jail, the PFLP held a conference in which the conflicts between Hawatima, Habash, and Jibril clearly emerged, leaving deep wounds on all sides. Hawatima accused Habash of dissembling Marxism-Leninism but of remaining a "fascist demagogue"; Habash later described Hawatima and his followers as a group of "adolescent cafe intellectuals." [80]

The doctrinal disputes at the 1968 meeting, which have been present ever since, centered around the roles to be played in the resistance by the petit bourgeois and the proletarian masses. Habash, who had become even more vehemently Marxist after his prison term, has asserted that the Palestinian national cause needs to maintain relations with "progressive" Arab governments. The national liberation movement has to enlist the help of those Palestinians who are of the petit bourgeois class, since "to alienate and antagonize them would

bring a heavy loss to the national cause." Habash has also argued that
the leading cadres of the resistance, and of the PFLP in particular,
"should be in the hands of those who are committed to the ideology of
the proletariat." In 1970, Habash, in a swipe at both al-Fatah and
the PDFLP, declared, "the Laborers, peasants and lower middle-
classes are the ones who will liberate Palestine. 'Fateh' is middle-
class."[81]

Hawatima and his followers in the PDFLP tend to argue that the
resistance should not create cadres of fedayeen separate from the
masses; on the contrary, the peasants and lower classes should be
educated in true socialism first. They then will carry on the battle.
Implicit in this argument is a basic distrust of Arab governments,
whether "progressive" or "reactionary," as well as a distrust of regular army units of Arab states which, to the members of the PDFLP,
are invariably instruments of capitalist repression. From this perspective, the PDFLP has also seen fit to be critical of al-Fatah and
the PLO, on the grounds that these organizations have become subser-
vient to reactionary forces within the Arab world.[82] The only way the
Palestinian resistance can hope to succeed, the PDFLP has asserted,
is to enlist the latent but powerful resources of the alienated lower
classes throughout the Arab world and even inside Israel:

> Not just the Palestinians but all Arabs have to become
> like the Vietnamese freedom fighters for the cause of
> Palestine. All the means and energy, which is now
> being poured into the rearming of the regulars and the
> training of them, ought to be directed towards achiev-
> ing a real social revolution, which would free the
> workers and peasants to fight their people's war.[83]

One European observer has summarized these arguments by suggesting that, whereas al-Fatah fights against "Zionists" and the PFLP
against "Zionism and world imperialism," the PDFLP fights an enemy
that consists of the "Zionist imperialist upper classes."[84] These
theoretical disputes resulted in bitter conflict between the mainstream
of the PFLP, which continued to identify with the ANM and has remained faithful to Habash.

In December 1968, after Habash had been released from prison,
a conference was scheduled as a follow-up to the calamitous July
meeting. Hawatima and his followers were invited. Hostility had
gone too far, however; agents of the PFLP arrested and beat up several members of the PDFLP whom they far outnumbered.[85] The result was an open war between cadres loyal to Habash and those loyal
to Hawatima. Machine-gun battles raged through the streets of Amman in late February 1969 until stopped by the intervention of other
fedayeen groups and Jordanian forces.[86]

It was in February 1969 that al-Fatah gained control of the PLO. The spectacle of two PFLP factions actually waging war against each other presented a threat to unity within the movement. Al-Fatah representatives undertook to mediate in the conflict and, by way of forcing an end to open hostilities, officially recognized the PDFLP.[87]

During the following few months, al-Fatah continued these efforts to promote greater coordination among the terrorist groups. Beyond the usual reasons there was the "communique war" that had broken out among the groups. It was becoming usual for several organizations to claim responsibility for a terrorist action as soon as it was announced over Kol Israel. As Reuters reported at the time, "two or three organizations had sometimes taken credit for the same operation when it was a major one. On certain occasions this conflict in taking credit caused friction among commando organizations. To avoid this friction Arafat ordered that notices "omit the name of the organization which undertook the operation reported in the communique. Identification of the group would have to come from the executive committee of the PLO."[88] The PLO executive committee, however, proved cumbersome as a coordinating body for the operational units. The result was that in April 1969, the Palestine Armed Struggle Command (PASC) was established outside the framework of the PLO to provide a common coordinating unit for the terrorist campaigns of the various organizations. Still another of its tasks was to act as a police force in Jordan with responsibility over the fedayeen stationed there. The PFLP, remaining as contentious as before, rejected the plan. Al-Fatah, al-Sa'iqah, the PLA, and the PDFLP were among the first members to join; the ALF and the PFLP-GC joined soon thereafter.[89] Only in February 1970 did the PFLP consent to join the PASC, which had by that time evolved into the Unified Command.[90] The reason was that the fedayeen were now engaged in a full-scale civil war against Jordan.

The story of the open conflict between Jordan and the fedayeen has been told many times.[91] It went on for 11 days, from September 16 to 27, pitting the combined resources of the Palestinian resistance organizations, with some assistance from Syria, against the Bedouin army of Hussein. Relations between the Palestinian terrorist groups and the Hussein regime had been tense for years. It was, and remains, an indelible part of al-Fatah's historical record that "one of its first partisans was killed in 1965 by the Jordanian army."[92] Yet special responsibility for igniting the civil war probably rests with the PFLP and to some extent with the PDFLP. It was these two groups that seem to have decided that the time had come to depose the Hashemite throne.[93]

In keeping with their general ideological assertion that the liberation of Palestine must necessarily entail a revolution within the Arab world, the PFLP and the PDFLP mounted an effort to embarrass

the resistance and Jordan in late 1972. The PFLP's hijacking of
three planes to Jordan and one to Cairo on September 6, 1970 was as
much due to this effort as it was to publicize the Palestinian cause.[94]
Some evidence suggests that al-Fatah "resented this tactic"[95] and attempted to avoid an all-out fight with Hussein, again, not for reasons
of sentiment but in the cool calculation that the liberation movement
could not afford this distraction. This argument should not be over-
drawn, however, since al-Fatah resented the Hashemite throne as
passionately as did the other terrorist groups.

The maneuvers of the PFLP at this time, however, placed the
leadership of al-Fatah in a difficult dilemma. Either al-Fatah would
go along with the battle against Hussein or else risk sacrificing its
role, only just recently consolidated, as the vanguard of the resistance;
either al-Fatah would expose itself to the onslaughts of the Bedouins or
else risk losing its credibility among the rank and file of the fedayeen.
It was a choice between accepting the risk of revealing those weaknesses that a terrorist or guerrilla force almost always has in fighting
a regular army or accepting the possibility of losing the partisan support among its rank and file without which a terrorist army cannot
exist. It eventually chose the former. "They [al-Fatah] had started
under the slogan of 'No meddling in Arab affairs,'" wrote one observer, "but was there ever a more complete form of meddling than taking over the government of an Arab state? This was the line Fateh
tried to follow, at least in theory, but in practice the 'revolution' carried them along in its maelstrom. For whenever they tried to bring
it to a halt, their competitors from Sa'eqa, the Popular Front for the
Liberation of Palestine or the Popular Democratic Front denounced
them as 'counterrevolutionaries' and tried to capture their followers."[96]
Events took their course; sporadic fighting became a daily occurrence
during August and September. "All the _fida'iyyun_ groups involved in
it could do was to drift along with it and hope that it would lead them
to victory in the end. But what was victory? The Fateh leaders knew
that they did not want to take over Amman, because that would have
meant the end of guerrilla and terrorist activities against Israel.
For they would have had to settle down to the responsibilities of running a state—and a rather difficult state to run."[97] In the end, it was
Arafat himself who, by breaking off negotiations with the Jordanian
government on September 16, signaled the outbreak of war. Habash
at the time was on a visit to North Korea. When the fighting was over,
2,000 to 3,000 had been killed and 6,000 wounded; it also left the ranks
of the fedayeen decimated, although Hussein's forces stopped short of
wiping them out completely.

In what would be his last accomplishment, Nasser himself
brought about the cessation of hostilities by convening a conference
of the heads of state of Saudi Arabia, Kuwait, Libya, Lebanon, the

Sudan, and Yemen along with Hussein, Arafat, and Bahi Ladgham of
Tunisia. The latter, working closely under Nasser, actually drafted
the terms of the cease-fire. The Cairo Agreement, signed on September 27, 1970, [98] the day before Nasser's death, provided for a cease-
fire that was to be supervised by a commission under the chairmanship of Ladgham. It called for the withdrawal of fedayeen forces from
Amman and stipulated that all persons arrested or detained during the
hostilities be released. Arab governments were to be allowed to intervene in the case of violations. A subsequent arrangement, the Amman Agreement, signed on October 13, 1970, [99] by both Arafat and
Hussein, provided a basis for a more long-range set of undertakings
between the fedayeen and Jordan. This document attests, first, that
Jordan is one and indivisible but constitutes a "fundamental" base for
resistance; and second, that while the freedom of the fedayeen to organize themselves and mobilize their resources is guaranteed, "commando freedom" has to be restricted by the need for discipline.

This agreement applied only to operatives working for al-Fatah,
since Jordan issued a warrant for the arrests of Habash and Hawatima.
Al-Fatah openly rejected the role played by the PFLP in the instigation
of the September 1970 hostilities. In a typical warning to the PFLP,
Kamal Adwan, an authorized spokesman for al-Fatah, declared on
January 16, 1971:

> First—the Palestinian revolution will not allow itself
> to be led astray by vague mottos and out biddings.
> Second—henceforth the revolution must follow a uni-
> fied course; and adventurism will not be tolerated.
> Third—the policy of appeasement within the Pales-
> tinian revolution is over and in our capacity as lead-
> ers, we should be responsible for the survival of our
> movement. We thus allow no one to endanger it even
> if we have to use force. [100]

Adwan and al-As'ifa, the radio voice of al-Fatah, have moreover repeatedly accused the PFLP of direct responsibility for the civil war:

> We begin with the incident of the hijacking of the air-
> liners before September and of blowing them up in
> spite of the undertaking of the Central Committee to
> return them, and of George Habash's approval of the
> decision. The blowing up of the airliners in a dra-
> matic manner played an important role in precipitat-
> ing the massacres of September. [101]

Arafat, for his part, immediately set about to regroup the fedayeen.
He succeeded eventually in reasserting control over the resistance.

Arafat's preeminence has continued to rise as the complexity of
structure and interests represented within the Palestinian liberation
movement has continued to develop. In February 1971, the number
of seats in the PNA, or PNC, as it came to be called, increased from
100 to 150 to accommodate new constituencies such as the West Bank
and the Israeli Arabs. Equally important as a sign of the growing in-
tricacy of the movement is the fact that, as of June 1974, the distribution of seats on the executive committee of the PLO has been increased to 14 with the following distribution: al-Fatah—2, PFLP—1,
PDFLP—1, PFLP-GC—1, al Sa'iqah—1, PLA—1, ALF—1, indepen-
dents—2, and exiles from the West Bank—4. The ties of the PLO to
other major Palestinian organizations would appear to be strengthened
with the result that the PLO is coming to play the role of a representative authority. The PLO is thus acting as if it were a government, or,
as A. Yaniv observed, "in meetings of the Arab League it participates
as if representing the 23rd Arab State." Difficulties with Jordan have
persisted up until the present, however. The PFLP has insisted on
assuming a recalcitrant stance, which the leadership of al-Fatah rejects by taking an even harder line toward it.

The events of September 1970 were important not only in terms
of their impact upon the internal relations of the terrorist organizations but also on the patterns of violence that the fedayeen would pursue. The aim of a terrorist organization, after all, is to generate
terror and to do so from a position of weakness. As noted above, al-
Fatah had made its greatest advances at moments when the rest of
the Arab world appeared weakest, as in 1956 and 1967. At the end of
1970 and for the duration of 1971, the viability of the resistance movement once again came into question. In July 1971, a respected al-
Fatah leader, Abu Ali Iyyad, was killed by Jordanian authorities. The
survival of the fedayeen, it appeared, had once again become an open
question. They had to respond—now or never—and respond they did,
with the formation of the Black September organization, with the assassination of Wasfi Al-Tall, the Jordanian prime minister and arch-
enemy of the fedayeen, and, finally, with a pattern of terrorist violence that assaulted the normal routines of international comity. Their
response would also test the ability of the al-Fatah leadership to engage
in effective verbal strategy.

WHAT TERRORISTS DO AND
HOW THEY JUSTIFY IT

Every resistance movement struggles for recognition. Attention is the lifeblood of its existence. For the terrorist, the path to

legitimacy is through one's reputation for resilience, for self-sacrifice and daring, for brutality, and, above all, for effective discipline over words and actions. The terrorist is his own torch and bomb; he ignites the flames of national passion and, if possible, of political sympathy, and he does it by violating universal human sensibilities. It is the credibility that violence produces whenever it appalls that renders terrorism horrifying yet powerful and, if successful, self-legitimating.

Salah Khalaf, an al-Fatah leader, speaking of the rise of Palestinian terrorism, declared:

> All the people of the world only respect strength.
> And I do not mean by strength the mere possession
> of vast military equipment. I mean the determina-
> tion and resolution of groups of organized people to
> strive for their right at any expense, summoning up
> their inner forces. It is my belief that on the basis
> of this understanding in the last two years we have
> made up for the past 20 years when all of our activ-
> ity and propaganda centered on the wretched refu-
> gees queuing at UNRWA soup kitchens. This pic-
> ture of refugees has been transformed into one of
> fighters carrying arms to win their freedom.[102]

An act of terrorist violence uninformed by discipline or politics stops dead without achieving its aims. For violence to have impact, it can never be its own reward; when effective, terrorism pulls violence out of the realm of war and into the world of politics. But politics has rules, patterns of normative interaction, do's and don't's of legitimate conduct. In the beginning it is the terrorist's task to violate norms of civilized conduct. Yet terrorism is fundamentally a psychological strategy and must point to a way of resolving the conflict. If terrorist violence appears wanton, it threatens to lose the support, or at least the respect, it is seeking to gain. Thus the terrorist irrevocably comes face to face with a torturous self-contradiction: as he becomes more successful, he must become more responsible. He is left to live with the painful tension of responsible violence, that is, calculated, disciplined, and permeated with politics. As he wins recognition through violence, he must place limitations on the use of violence.

This section will analyze Palestinian terrorism from the perspective of politics: it will relate the history, ideology, and interrelationships of the major terrorist organizations to their operational and verbal strategies. Our task will be to determine whether or not a distinct pattern of violence and verbal strategy can be associated with a particular group; in particular, we are interested in relating what

the group is or represents in the resistance movement to what the
group does and what it says it is doing as it terrorizes.

We will begin by asking who or what these groups are, that is,
which factors seem necessary or sufficient to an understanding of the
particular nature of the more important Palestinian terrorist organizations? We have already pointed to the crucial role of ideology in the
formation and maintenance of the PDFLP, for example, and to the
rightist militarism of Jibril's PFLP-GC as well as the important political ties of this group to the governments of first Syria, then Iraq,
and currently Libya. Although not necessarily conclusive, these admittedly partial data do reveal at least a few of the determining forces
operating within these groups. As for the PFLP, moreover, how can
anyone understand it without taking into account the tremendous, if
nihilistic, role played by Habash, and who can trace the psychological
and ideological nihilism of Habash if he has not followed his life as an
atheistic Christian in a Moslem world, as the odd leader out, the person who would wish to be leading the resistance movement, who gave
up family and career to have a chance, but who must now suffer the
fact that his lifelong competitor, Arafat, is instead occupying this
role?

We have devoted much attention to the emergence of al-Fatah as
the organization that has succeeded in providing a certain center of
gravity for the resistance. Although at times it has been forced to
issue open threats to the PFLP to contain the latter's flamboyant
style of terrorism, al-Fatah has tended to insinuate itself into the
role of consolidator of the resistance with, it appears, a minimum of
conflict in relation to the other groups. To some extent this is due to
the substantial resources that al-Fatah has had available to it, especially after it took control of the PLO. It stems from the stature of
Arafat, the leader who seems to be the most successful in centering
in himself the aspirations of the Palestinians. It also derives—and
this returns us to the thrust of our analysis—from the operational
strategy adopted by al-Fatah or, after 1968, by the PLO.

The term "operational strategy" as used here refers to three
interrelated phenomena: the general normative or ideological framework of common faiths or generalized principles that unifies a movement, the actions themselves, and the verbal strategy used to justify
specific actions in the context of broader norms. The different ideological and normative "sets" flowing within the Palestinian terrorist
groups have helped to identify them.

But beyond the range of disagreement there lies a vast reserve
of common commitment among the terrorist organizations. This is
especially true of the first element in the operational strategy, the
category of visionary belief, value construct, or ideological assertion.

In the context of the Palestinian resistance movement, these have been embodied in the assertions of the Palestinian National Covenant, which declares, among other things, that Palestine is the homeland of the Palestinian people, that the homeland existed as "an integral regional unit" at the time of the British mandate over Palestine, and that, therefore, the Palestinians "possess the legal right" to liberate this homeland and exercise their right of self-determination. The 1968 version of the covenant, as revised from that of 1964, substitutes the word "al-watani," referring to nationalism in the narrow sense of patriotism toward a geographically defined and concrete territorial unit, for the word "al-qawmi," or national in the sense of ethnic identity or Pan-Arabism.[103] Given this vision of their rights to a propriety claim over what is now Israel, the Palestinians are, the covenant asserts, legally justified in seeking to "liberate" it. Actions taken in behalf of this aim reflect rights sanctioned by international law to self-defense. As Article 18 of the covenant states, in part: "The liberation of Palestine, from an international viewpoint, is a defensive act necessitated by the requirements of self-defense."[104] There is no disagreement among the resistance groups as to the validity of these ethical, legal, and political presumptions. Nor is there dispute in regard to the fundamental role to be played by the fedayeen in the restoration of Palestinian national rights. Article 10, for example, states:

> Fida'iyyun action forms the nucleus of the popular Palestinian war of liberation. This demands its promotion, extension and protection, and the mobilization of all the masses and scientific capacities of the Palestinians, their organization and involvement in the armed Palestinian revolution and cohesion in the national [watani] struggle among the various groups of the people of Palestine, and between them and the Arab masses, to guarantee the continuation of the revolution, its advancement and victory.[105]

The terrorist organizations are, therefore, "legal representatives" of the Palestinian people who possess the right to promote an active, that is, violent, resistance, and which are solely empowered to act in the name of national liberation. Article 9 declares:

> Armed struggle is the only way to liberate Palestine and is therefore a strategy and not tactics. The Palestinian Arab people affirms its absolute resolution and abiding determination to pursue the armed strug-

gle and to march forward towards the armed popular
revolution, to liberate its homeland.[106]

But there has been, and continues to be, disagreement over certain
other provisions of the covenant centering on Articles 21 and 24. They
point to the meanings of such concepts as "moderate" and "extremist"
in the realm of terrorist action and interaction.

When Article 24 declares, for example, "The Palestinian Arab
people believes in the principles of justice, freedom, sovereignty,
self-determination, human dignity and the right of peoples to exercise
them,"[107] does this preclude acts of international piracy outside the
Middle East, especially those against "neutral" civilians? Some
groups say yes, others no. Or when Article 21 declares,

> The Palestinian Arab people, in expressing itself
> through the armed Palestinian revolution, rejects
> every solution that is a substitute for a complete
> liberation of Palestine, and rejects all plans that
> aim at the settlement of the Palestine issue or its
> internationalization,[108]

does it intend to subordinate all political consideration to military
concerns? Must the movement be forever rooted to a maximalist position, rejecting all compromise and dedicated to the infliction (and
acceptance) of brutal punishment? The positions taken on these questions and the actions that are produced as a result tend to separate
the moderates from the extremists in the Palestinian resistance.

As already stated, it is not that some of the terrorist organizations are less willing than others to employ violence; it is rather that
some impose discipline on where and against whom and are prepared
to disavow or condemn those who do not. Nor is it that some of the
terrorist agencies are more amenable to living with Israel than others;
rather, the question has to do with which organization, if any, has the
courage to make its credibility hostage to a political program that is
less than a military campaign. As Shafiq Al-Hut recently stated:
"Today, it takes more guts to fight on the side of those Palestinians
who want to go to Geneva than it does for Israelis to say their government should recognize us."[109] Differentiating "moderate" from "extremist" in these terms points to the possible evolving role of Arafat,
al-Fatah, and the PLO.

There have been to date four major phases through which the
Palestinian movement has gone. The first is the incipient era between
1965 and 1967. The second is the mobilization period, stretching between two disasters, the Six-Day War and the ten-day war against
Jordan. The third, lasting until the Yom Kippur War, may be de-

scribed as the time of radicalization. The fourth and current phase
is the period of recognition and legitimization. All terrorist organizations have had to adjust to the different political and tactical conditions attendent on these phases. What they did by way of terrorist
activity and what they said by way of justification varies from era to
era.

We have already suggested that, throughout the first phase and,
to a degree, during the second, al-Fatah patterned its terrorist violence as a military organization waging war against the martial infra-
structure of its enemy. There were exceptions, like the August 18,
1968, "night of the grenades," in which al-Fatah claimed responsibility for an operation that injured nine civilians in Jerusalem resulting
from the detonation of three hand grenades left in garbage bins. There
is also the case of the more serious "infernal engine" explosion at
the Mahaneh Yehuda market on November 22, 1968, during which 12
civilians were killed and 52 injured. Al-Fatah readily accepted credit
for the explosions and declared that it had turned Jerusalem into "a
city of horror."[110] Yet, in general, civilian losses inside Israel as
a result of fedayeen activity were less than the losses of military personnel. IDF figures for 1968, for example, reveal that, whereas 47
Israeli civilians lost their lives and 290 were wounded as a result of
terrorist action, 130 IDF personnel were killed and 423 were wounded.
That this targeting on the military was largely an al-Fatah decision
is demonstrated by the fact that, of the casualties incurred by the
fedayeen, 450 were identified as belonging to al-Fatah, whereas 39
were linked to the PFLP and only nine to al-Sa'iqah.[111] Moreover,
al-Fatah did not engage in terrorist operations outside of Israel during
1968 or 1969.

The rejection of terrorist violence outside the Middle East was
a decision of al-Fatah's alone and was not accepted by the groups
emerging out of the front.

The first international hijacking by a Palestinian terrorist organization was carried out by Jibril's group, the PFLP-GC, on July
22-29, 1968, and involved an El Al plane flying from Rome to Tel
Aviv. The PFLP-GC justified this action on the grounds of the close
connection between El Al and the military establishment of Israel.
The verbal strategy used at this time articulated several points that
came to represent the model response used by terrorist groups engaging in similar forms of violence. The attack, the PFLP-GC argued, was to remind everybody of the Palestinian question and "to
demonstrate to the world the standard of efficiency" now achieved by
Palestinian terrorist groups. No Arab government was involved in
the operation; clear instructions had been given to the terrorists not
to harm civilians wherever possible. "This behavior demonstrated
the humane aspect of the Palestinian resistance." The PFLP-GC also

stated that "resistance acts were not directed against Jewish citizens but against the Zionist racialist ruler in occupied Palestine"; that terrorism was designed to warn potential immigrants "not to be deceived by the Zionist call to emigrate to Israel." This is typical of the verbal strategy used to justify Palestinian terrorism outside Israel during this early phase (1969-70).[112] It is relatively moderate in tone. No civilians were to be harmed; terrorist acts were not to be directed against Jewish citizens, and so on. Later, even tourists in Israel were branded as "the enemy." Thus, the nature, tone, and quality of the verbal strategy used by the PFLP and the PFLP-GC to justify hijackings reflects the tendency toward extremism within the front itself. The July 1968 hijacking carried out by Jibril's group occurred just prior to its break from the PFLP as the latter moved to the Left in the ideological spectrum. It appears, therefore, that the verbal strategies of both Jibril's and Habash's groups changed somewhat after their split from more or less conciliatory and normatively oriented ones to increasingly strident, categorical, and ideologically oriented ones. The tendency toward extremism became even more pronounced after 1970.

The second major incident was also perpetrated by the PFLP, but this time by Habash's group. It involved an attack against an El Al airliner at the Athens airport on December 26, 1968, in which one Israeli passenger was killed and several others wounded. Pamphlets distributed by the PFLP at the time described Israel as an "artificial entity." They also stated that El Al was conducting "aggressive military activities." The PFLP declared that it had not intended to kill anyone. The attack was designed as a "Christmas present" for Israel.[113]

The next major terrorist operation involving the hijacking of an airplane was perpetrated in August 1969, also by Habash's group. This was the attack against a TWA airliner involving Leila Khalid, a PFLP operative. Six months later, on February 21, 1970, Jibril's PFLP-GC engineered the explosion of an Israeli-bound Swiss airplane leaving Zurich. All 47 passengers and crew were killed, including 11 Israelis. The PFLP-GC, in announcing its responsibility for the attack, justified it by describing the dead Israelis as "senior officials" and therefore the legitimate targets of military attack.[114]

As already suggested, al-Fatah represented the predominant force within the resistance during the 1967-69 period. We have alluded to the factors contributing to the hegemony of al-Fatah—financial and organizational support from various Arab states, popular recognition, established bases on the West and East banks of the Jordan, and a record of successful military actions against Israel. Indeed, prior to the 1967 war, al-Fatah had had no serious competition. After the Six-Day War, any terrorist organization wishing to emerge had to contend with the supremacy of al-Fatah, a superiority that was being continually manifested in the field of action. The result was the increased use of international hijackings on the part of the PFLP and related groups.

It is perhaps not surprising that a segment of the Palestinian terrorist resistance resorted to this tactic. The lesson in 1969-70 was clear. If a resistance organization were to be credible, it had to prove itself in action. Only through violence could it build a reputation for behavior. Since the home arena was the preserve of al-Fatah, at least for the moment, the most immediate way for the PFLP to establish its credibility was to expand the battlefield and make an impact on the order of al-Fatah at Karamah. The hijacking of aircraft provided the chance.

Yet the PFLP discovered almost instantaneous opposition to these tactics. Within the resistance movement, sneak attacks were criticized for romanticizing terrorist violence and thereby contradicting the principle of the people's right to participate in the fighting. A number of major Communist governments, including the Chinese, North Korean, and Soviet, echoed these sentiments.

Al-Fatah, for its part, adopted a verbal strategy that implied rejection of these forms of international violence. On February 23, 1970, it issued a statement that offered its condolences to the Swiss nation and declared that no person or group associated with these attacks could "belong to the Palestinian revolution."[115] The al-Fatah statement indicated that "such acts could only benefit Israel. Fateh's strategy was to direct military operations against military targets on Palestinian territory and never outside it."[116] It is noteworthy that the PFLP and the PFLP-GC later reversed their verbal strategy by disavowing responsibility for the attack on the Swiss airliner, describing the communique that had linked them to the explosion as "a planted story."[117]

The PFLP under Habash, however, continued its terrorist operations outside the Middle East. February 1970 was the month when al-Fatah was becoming preeminent within the executive committee of the PLO. The PFLP had to compete with al-Fatah by establishing its credibility and by making itself distinct from the larger organization. The desire of the PFLP to become distinguishable from al-Fatah was realized as al-Fatah concentrated on military operations inside Israel while Habash's group and the front's PFLP-GC concentrated not only on targets inside Israel but on international civil aviation as well. This transformed the pattern of Palestinian terrorism: it was a shift from war to piracy, from a struggle for legitimacy to a resort to open criminality.

Habash adopted an unrepentant verbal strategy. Interviewed by the well-known journalist Oriana Fallaci for a mass circulation maga-

zine (a rare opportunity to practice verbal strategy), Habash argued
that, after the injustice done to the Palestinians, they had the right
to attack all Israeli targets, including soldiers, civilians, children,
and women, as well as El Al airplanes, buildings, and so on, inside
or outside of Israel. "El Al planes are a perfectly legitimate military
target," he argued.

> They belong to the enemy; they connect the island of
> Israel with other shores; and they transport troops
> and ammunition. They are flown by reserve officers
> of the Israeli Air Force. In a war it is fair to strike
> the enemy wherever he happens to be, and this rule
> leads us also to the European airfields where El Al
> planes land or take off.[118]

Zionism, Habash declared, was a manifestation of capitalist imperialism; as a result, there were no neutrals except Socialist countries, and
only they would be spared. "Israel is a product of colonialism, colonialism is a product of imperialism, and imperialism is a product of capitalism. Therefore, the only nations we consider friendly, the only
ones whose planes we spare, are the socialist countries."[119] Habash
continued, "The world has been using us and has forgotten us. It is
time they realized we exist, it is time they stopped exploiting us.
Whatever the price, we'll continue our struggle to return home."[120]
Habash justified international acts of terrorism by referring to a "qual-
itative" as opposed to a "quantitative" approach:

> Let me explain: the attacks of the Popular Front are
> based on quality, not quantity. We believe to kill a
> Jew far from the battleground has more of an effect
> than killing 100 of them in battle; it attracts more at-
> tention. And when we set fire to a store in London,
> those few flames are worth the burning down of two
> kibbutzim.[121]

Habash's statements appear to be consistent with his background. A
Christian in a predominantly Moslem world, a physician educated in
Beirut, he would almost naturally expostulate a set of principles that
point beyond the immediacy of the Palestinian nationalist struggle. We
have pointed to certain significant differences between the leadership
of al-Fatah and that of the PFLP. These are contrasts of religion
(Moslem versus Greek Orthodox or Christian), of education (University of Cairo versus the American University of Beirut), and of political training (the Moslem Brotherhood versus the ANM), as well as
differences in socioeconomic class, professional or occupational back-

ground, and so on. These characteristic differences seem to have contributed to the divergent programs and ideologies developed by al-Fatah and the PFLP. The PFLP's excursion into the international arena, its labeling of capitalism and imperialism as "the enemy," is concrete testimony to its social and political origins. In this sense, the PFLP remains true to its parent organization, the Socialist-oriented Pan-Arab ANM, which gradually came to regard the Palestinian revolution as being inextricably linked to the Arab Socialist revolution. Habash represents an internationalist revolutionary outlook in which the success of the "Socialist" revolution in Palestine is regarded as being dependent upon the success of the "Socialist" revolution throughout the world.

Ultimately, however, Habash's extolling of terrorism as a weapon is indicative of a minority perspective. Terrorism for Habash has a function beyond the struggle against Israel. Terrorism is the means through which the PFLP can achieve parity with, and perhaps supremacy over, al-Fatah. The verbal strategy used by Habash, therefore, represents the extremist rhetoric of a leader aware, or at least sensitive, to the political and military weaknesses of his organization.

In contrast, during approximately the same period of time, Arafat was evolving a doctrine of responsible violence. This differentiated so-called disciplined terrorism or moderation from adventurism. Implicit in Arafat's verbal strategy was direct criticism of the position assumed by Habash:

> The overwhelming majority of the masses believe that Fateh is wise and objective. Wisdom means such proper conduct of affairs the attainment of the objective is guaranteed. And if in saying "Fateh is moderate" some people imply that it uses violence with responsibility, this would be a source of pride to us and it would be an honor to us to be dubbed "moderate" in that sense.
>
> We in Fateh believe that hope is one thing and reality another. Our masses cannot anymore tolerate an extremist demagogue who does nothing to change the status quo. That's why Fateh's Command always tackles matters seriously and refuses to embark on adventures. If you followed closely our march since the beginning of our armed struggle, you would note that we never relinquished any of the positions we were able to reach. Nevertheless, while holding to and safeguarding the gains we achieved, we study our next step thoroughly. We are

> a revolution which cannot afford a setback at pres-
> ent.
>
> Some people who want to distinguish themselves
> from us by acting in such a way as to make the peo-
> ple believe that they are extremists, do so while re-
> alizing that mass reaction will be limited. We, on
> the other hand, are responsible for the masses. We
> refuse to drive the masses into positions where they
> cannot secure new mass gains.
>
> We are proud of the fact that despite the world's
> knowledge that force has its basic role on the Arab-
> Palestinian field, we were able to convince the world
> that ours is a human revolution which respects the
> human being, wherever he is. I think it is about
> time to start speaking of responsible violence which
> respects the human being and which is exercised for
> his sake.[122]

Here is the offer of responsibility that a terrorist must adopt as he begins to obtain recognition. Arafat's implicit rejection of Habash's verbal strategy is reflective of the superior position of al-Fatah within
the resistance movement. Al-Fatah, predominantly Moslem, the religion of the vast majority of Palestinians, nationalist in perspective
and thus lacking in universal adherence to ideology, set for itself a
specific objective—to liberate Palestine. The military perspective of
al-Fatah follows from this political orientation. Given this nationalist
perspective, "the enemy" is much more clearly defined and the goals
of the movement become much less determined by international revolutionary ideology or rhetoric. When Arafat proclaims a doctrine of responsible violence, he is practicing the verbal strategy of a leader
who is required to deal with political realities, the need for diplomatic
support, and the dependence upon outside sources of financial and logistical assistance. Despite the dependence this might imply, "responsible violence" in this context represents an expression of strength and
reflects the legitimacy that flows from strength.

Salah Khalaf, second in al-Fatah only to Arafat, also spoke at
this time (June 1969) of the need to integrate political and military
strategies. In terrorist violence, political considerations must always
come first: "On the whole we in Al-Fateh clearly recognize that military action is of no value if it does not serve a political program and
is not a part of a comprehensive political plan."[123] Khalaf continued:

> The first nucleus of Al-Fateh was formed on a politi-
> cal basis which rejected a specific political situation
> and developed its own political beliefs, which they be-

lieved, and still believe, will lead to the accomplishment of their aim. Out of the political attitude of Al-
Fateh emerged the military action of the armed resistance movement as a concrete manifestation of such
a line. Military action follows Al-Fateh's political
orientation. We thus believe that we have placed political action in its right place. We in Al-Fateh struggle in the political and military fields. Either one
of these two fields serves the other within the general
framework of the strategic plan of Al-Fateh. Thus
we do not separate or distinguish between political
and military action. To ensure the implementation of
such a policy we do not admit to the armed struggle
movement of any fighter unless he is recommended
by the political organization.[124]

Khalaf called upon the Israelis not to perceive the resistance movement as uniformly rabid. His verbal strategy included the following
statement:

We feel that the individual in Israel, as far as being
a man is concerned, especially the soldier—if we exclude the leaders who work within the framework of
the Zionist colonialist plan—is not convinced of war
except from the viewpoint of self-defense. If we were
able, through our behavior, to reach the heart of this
individual and convince him that we are truly not
butchers who want to slay him and throw his women
and children into the sea, as Zionism portrays us,
we can make a psychological separation between the
human being and the Zionist, the Jewish soldier and
the military Zionist colonist establishment.[125]

Here again is the commitment to responsibility that many politically
oriented terrorist verbal strategies contain, a commitment to break
away from stereotypes, a promise to move away from political reifica-
tion. Here was a verbal strategy that held out the possibility of relief
from the excesses of terrorism. Within one year of this statement,
however, Khalaf, or Abu Iyad, would lead the most terrifying of all
terrorist organizations—Black September. The Black September movement represents a low point in the development of Al-Fatah and the
resistance movement.[126] It can be understood only in the context of
the strategic situation that had befallen al-Fatah after the civil war
with Jordan in September 1970.

The decisive defeat suffered by the fedayeen at the hands of the Jordanians was an enormous blow to the credibility of the resistance groups, especially al-Fatah. They had fully assumed their ability to destroy Hussein. Moreover, it created serious logistical problems. Without Jordan as a base, the fedayeen could no longer infiltrate the West Bank as easily. This would make it doubly hard to establish an underground network among the "human wood" of Palestinians living in Israel. Israeli security was being intensified along the Jordan River. Finally, the Jordanian government continued to harass the Palestinian terrorists and succeeded in isolating them in a single area—the forests of Jerash and Ajloun. Here, between April and July 1971, Hussein attempted to extirpate the resistance movement from Jordanian soil with combined land and air attacks against the Palestinian terrorists. During this period Abu Ali Iyyad, a fierce fighter whose terrorist feats had made him legendary in al-Fatah, was killed, along with several thousand other al-Fatah operatives. Arafat later indicated that 17,000 fedayeen had been wounded in the Amman, Jerash, and Ajloun massacres.[127]

One other serious threat to al-Fatah existed at this time—the ever-present Habash. The PFLP had demonstrated the "glamour" of international terrorism. Actions within Israel and the Middle East were becoming more difficult, dangerous, and costly. It was becoming increasingly attractive to take the route paved by the PFLP; therefore, al-Fatah faced the possibility of losing many of its members to other organizations.

So the dilemma that the leadership of al-Fatah had faced before the war against Hussein remained after its defeat. Al-Fatah had to show it could "act" in the field or it would lose support among the rank and file of the resistance, perhaps even to the PFLP. Only now it had to prove itself when it was weaker than before and shorn of its most important strategic bases. The result was Black September. It would not be useful, however, to develop an extremist image so inimical to the PLO's political interests. Therefore Black September was set up without any manifest connection to al-Fatah. Khalaf was placed in control of the operation.[128] Its first act was to assassinate the prime minister of Jordan, Wasfi Al-Tall, in Cairo on November 28, 1971. The terrorists who claimed responsibility for the act called themselves "the Abu Ali Iyyad group."

Black September functioned as no fedayeen group had ever functioned before or has functioned since. It made no announcements and admitted to no leadership. It is commonly believed that Black September was composed of 300 to 400 dissident members of al-Fatah who were enraged by Hussein after Jerash and Ajloun.[129] These men, all part of an elite commando corps, set up what one observer called "less a secret army than a revolutionary sect of separate, self-gener-

ating cells."[130] Apparently, a Black September group was formed
each time a specific operation had been decided upon. Once that operation had been executed, the terrorists would disband and "melt" away
into the main body of terrorists.[131] All operatives associated with
Black September were "young men . . . armed with an exalted, self-
sacrificial fanaticism and a growing ruthlessness."[132] The links between al-Fatah and Black September were always a matter of the highest secrecy.

Israeli sources have insisted that the leadership of al-Fatah fostered the Septembrist movement.[133] Other sources, such as David
Hirst, have suggested that it was "a grass roots phenomenon which
the Fatah leadership, unable to beat, decided to join."[134] Writing in
the Manchester Guardian he indicated that al-Fatah "provides some
of the finance, facilities, equipment, and skills. It does so because
it has to. Its own failures have deeply eroded its moral authority over
the guerrilla movement as a whole. The pressure from below is said
to have been laced with threats."[135] Black September was a way for
al-Fatah to work itself out of its July 1971 predicament. It could
maintain its initiative over the terrorist movement but without becloud-
ing its organizational image. Black September, finally, represented
a deviation from al-Fatah's stated policy of "Palestinizing the struggle," meaning that it abjured all terrorist action on foreign territory.[136]

Actions performed by Black September began in November 1971
and continued until April 1973. Practically all were abroad. Its opening fire, as already indicated, was aimed at the Jordanian prime minister, who was primarily responsible for Jerash and Ajloun and for anti-
fedayeen activities inside Jordan since 1968. The second operation
was aimed at Zaid Rifa'i, Jordanian ambassador to London, who
was wounded by gunfire on December 15, 1971, but survived to become
prime minister of his government.[137] Next came the sabotage of a
Dutch gas plant reputedly owned by a corporation refusing to cut ties
with Israel, along with a number of similar operations in Germany and
Italy.[138]

Black September's turning away from sabotage and political assassination occurred on May 8, 1972, with an abortive attempt to hijack a Belgian Sabena airline.[139] Commandeered at Lydda airport
outside of Tel Aviv, the plane was eventually boarded by Israeli security agents disguised as members of the international Red Cross, who
succeeded in shooting the two men hijackers and capturing two women
hijackers.

Perhaps to compete with Black September and angry at this obvious incursion into the realm of international hijacking, the PFLP organized the Japanese Red Army attack at Lydda airport on May 30,
which killed 25 and wounded 78, all of them civilians. "The mere
choice of our occupied territory as a place for tourism is in itself a

bias in favour of the enemy," the PFLP declared in justifying the attack.[140] A PFLP spokesman admitted on May 31 that the primary aim of the operation was "to raise the temperature which he foresaw coming through Israeli reprisals—perhaps successful ones—and the Arab reaction to them."[141] A secondary goal outlined by the PFLP was to boost Palestinian morale:

> Our purpose was to kill as many people as possible
> at the airport. Israelis, of course, but anyone else
> who was there. There is a war going on in Pales-
> tine. People should know that. Why don't they go
> to Saigon . . . ? This operation does affect the or-
> dinary Englishman. He will feel shocked. What hor-
> rible, coldblooded murderers. But he will think
> three times before coming to Israel.[142]

Al-Fatah maintains the policy of never criticizing a terrorist act inside Israel on the grounds that such actions are all military in nature. It has, however, condemned international acts of terrorism especially damaging to the reputation of the Palestinian resistance. On this occasion, al-Fatah adopted a verbal strategy more typical of the PFLP than of it. This action, it declared, "shows that the revolutionaries of the world stand united against Zionism and imperialism."[143] The PLO spokesman, Kamal Adwan, in a news conference on June 13, did offer some modification of the PFLP position in declaring, "We deeply regret the death of the Puerto Rican pilgrims, who were not our targets. We were aiming for Moshe Dayan, who was supposed to be there at the time."[144]

Black September's next operation was against the Israeli Olympics team in Munich. This operation, which culminated in the deaths of 11 members of the Israeli team and four Palestinian terrorists, represents a tragic event in the history of the conflict between Palestinians and Israelis. The verbal strategy released by the terrorists at first tried to emphasize that it was a military operation with specific goals in mind: "We are not highwaymen or thieves. We are not killers or shedders of blood."[145] The Septemberists also stated:

> Our fighters had strict instructions not to harm the
> Zionist hostages unless in self-defense. Our fight-
> ers implemented their instructions precisely. Some
> members of the team tried to provoke and attack
> our fighters in order to wreck the operation. . . .
> The remaining members surrendered. They were
> treated most humanely by our fighters.[146]

Black September's verbal strategy later became more rhetorical: "We are not against any people, but why should our place here be taken by the flag of the occupiers."[147] In a carefully worded statement, the PLO disassociated itself from the action, but without rejecting it. The PLO, it stated, "is not responsible for the actions of the Black September Organization and would like to draw world attention to the fact that the mission in Munich was only aimed at pressuring Israel to release guerrillas detained in Israeli jails."[148]

On September 27, a Black September spokesman vowed in an interview published in a Munich magazine that his organization would obtain the release of the three members detained during the Munich operation. "We have anti-Zionist friends throughout the world and we can act at any moment," he declared.[149] On October 29, a Lufthansa airliner en route from Beirut to Ankara was hijacked for the specific purpose of forcing the release of the Munich operatives. They succeeded, and the Munich assailants were flown to Tripoli on October 30. One of them declared in a hastily called news conference, "We are not savages, terrorists or monsters."[150]

Black September's next two targets were two embassies—the Israeli embassy in Bangkok on December 28, 1972, and the Saudi Arabian embassy in Khartoum on March 1, 1974. "We consider that every Israeli embassy is a Palestinian land and we have the right to practice our rights here . . . ," read the Black September note.[151] Eventually, the Septemberists who perpetrated the attack in Bangkok received safe conduct to Cairo. They did not obtain the release of prisoners, which had been the ostensible object of the raid. However, an even greater disaster awaited the movement with the take-over of the American embassy in Khartoum. Friends of the Palestinian resistance, like the Saudi Arabian government and President Numeiri of the Sudan, were appalled by this assault not only against the United States but against their own diplomatic integrity and political images.

Two American and one Belgian diplomat were brutally killed in this attack. The verbal strategy of Black September, moreover, became excessive, losing some of its former control. The dead diplomats, for example, were described as having taken part in "massacring our people and conspiring against our Arab nation."[152] A Black September statement issued on March 4 justifying the killings declared:

> The strugglers of Black September know no fear . . .
> and will not crawl on their bellies before the American
> imperialists. . . . The Black September Organization
> promises our people to continue the struggle and prom-
> ises our people to continue the struggle and promises
> every prisoner of our people that its war against Zion-
> ism, American imperialism and their hirelings will
> continue.[153]

This statement went on to suggest that the Black September terrorists "had been ordered to surrender to Sudanese authorities and people because of the high esteem we hold for President Numayri. We leave them in trust in his hands. We are confident they will be treated as true revolutionary fighters."[154] However, Numeiri was—initially, at least—outraged.

On March 5, the Sudanese government announced that the eight Khartoum terrorists would be tried for murder. The day before, Numeiri had cabled President Nixon and King Badouin of Belgium to inform them of his personal bereavement over the murders of their representatives, stating that "such ways of resolving problems have always been condemned by us. We in the Sudan are always averse to acts of violence."[155] In the meantime, al-Fatah had attempted to deny any connection with the operation or with Black September. On March 5, the Palestine News Agency quoted an al-Fatah spokesman as saying, "Certain information media have tried to link the recent Khartoum operation and Fateh elements by accusing these elements of taking part in the operation. The Fateh movement affirms that it has no connection at all with this operation."[156] Numeiri was prompted to contradict this openly. In a major address to the nation on March 6, he revealed evidence collected by Sudanese police that showed that, even if al-Fatah had not been formally connected with Black September, the personnel involved in the case were. Numeiri delineated the incriminating evidence:

> The head of the Fateh office in Khartoum—Fawaz Yassin Abder-Rahman (Abu-Marwan)—has been the brains behind this operation as proved by the documents he wrote with his own hand and left behind in his office before fleeing aboard a Libyan plane to Tripoli on the day of the incident. A cable which was found instructed him to be in Tripoli by March 1. The man who implemented the operation was the second man in the Fateh office—Rizq Abu-Kaas (Abu-Salem). . . . The car used for transporting the eight participants in the operation was a car belonging to the organization. . . . What worries me is what was revealed by the numerous documents that have been found. . . . They showed that the Fateh office had initiated a watch on some embassies and even on some state officials and had been following their steps and movements. They had recruited commercial agents to write daily reports about the activities of trade unions, students and farmers in Sudan, not in Israel.[157]

The Sudanese president complained that he was especially disappointed since he had offered unlimited assistance to representatives of al-Fatah in the past, "disregarding all the criticisms made against us by some sister Arab countries."[158] The Sudanese daily Al-Sahafa declared that the Palestinians had chosen Khartoum for their attack "forgetting that it was the Sudanese leader who went to Jordan in 1970 to save their leader Yasser Arafat."[159]

Al-Fatah tried to recoil from this unexpected public denunciation. In response to Numeiri's speech of March 6, a spokesman for al-Fatah stated, "We would have wished very much that President Numayri had waited until our investigations are over and did not make his accusations. He will discover shortly that he has made a serious mistake."[160] The following day Arafat appealed to President Sadat to intervene with Numeiri, who, the al-Fatah leader complained, was "seeking to turn the Khartoum incident . . . against the whole Palestine movement" by means of a "feverish and surprising campaign."[161] Information Minister Omer Haj Musa, replying on behalf of the Sudanese government, stated, "We will give him [Arafat] the facts: it was his men, and a Fateh car and the plans were found in the Fateh's leader's drawer after he fled the country before the attack."[162] Musa added, "In the absense of convincing proof to the contrary we have all rights to assume the Sudan was the target of attack."[163] The Saudis too were angry that it was their embassy that had been selected for attack and they let this be known publicly. What also offended was the fact that the three diplomats were killed without provocation from the police or the army and that the demands of the terrorists—which included the release of Sirhan Sirhan, all Arab women detained in Israel, and the members of the Baader-Meinhoff West German revolutionary organization—were clearly unattainable and in any event unrelated to the Palestinian cause. It was principled self-hostaging at its very worst.

Arafat attempted to justify the operation by adopting a verbal strategy that rendered the Black Septemberists piteous rather than honorable. The acts of Black September "were loud expressions of despair." He added, "Despair will drive the Palestinians increasingly toward the adoption of a policy of consuming the world's tranquility."[164] Arafat suggested that it was virtually impossible to stop the activities of this group. "Let those who are interested in world security or who are disturbed by revolutionary activity stop them," he declared.[165] After this, however, al-Fatah's verbal strategy gradually changed, and as it did, Black September's operations became less frequent.

Two other events, along with the debacle at Khartoum, may have acted as factors in the decision to reduce Black September activities and to alter the verbal strategy attached to them—the arrest by Jordanian authorities of Muhammad Daoud Odeh, known as Abu

Daoud, and the counterterrorist action on the part of the Israelis in
Beirut, which killed three high-ranking al-Fatah officers.

On February 15, 1973, approximately 20 al-Fatah operatives
were arrested by Jordanian security police as they crossed into Jordan from Syria. The leader of this group was Abu Daoud, and their
self-confessed mission was to murder Hussein. Four days after their
capture, Abu Daoud appeared on Amman television indicating that the
operation had been organized by Black September "to disrupt Jordan's
recent rapprochement with other Arab states."[166] Five weeks later,
Abu Daoud appeared on Amman radio, this time to make explicit his
allegations of the Black September-al-Fatah connection. And on March
27, Abu Daoud, interviewed by Peter Snow for British commercial
television, stated simply, "Black September is not an organization
separate from Fateh, it is a group of people from Fateh itself."[167]
These revelations on the part of a leading al-Fatah operative tended
to confirm the evidence released by Numeiri that Black September
constituted an elite corps of al-Fatah. The release of Abu Daoud had
been the one specific demand made at Khartoum. It would be difficult
for Black September to act in the future without involving the reputation or image of al-Fatah.

The Israelis appear to have signaled this fact in their Beirut ex-
pedition of April 10, 1973. Israeli units landing by helicopter and boat
drove in awaiting cars to Rue Khaled ben al-Walid, a small street in
the heart of downtown Beirut, and proceeded to assassinate Muhammad
Yousef Nasser, or Abu Yousef, a deputy leader of al-Fatah and member of the PLO executive committee. Also assassinated were Kamal
Adwan, the al-Fatah information officer, and Kamal Nasir, a PLO
spokesman. The Israelis also destroyed a building that was known to
have housed PFLP activity.[168] The events of March and April, the
disaster at Khartoum, the arrest of Abu Daoud, and the assassination
of the three al-Fatah leaders did not prompt an immediate end to Black
September actions. On April 27, Vitorio Olivares, a Jewish-Italian
working for El Al, was killed by Black September.[169] Earlier in
April, Black September operatives had attacked the Israeli embassy
in Nicosia, Cyprus. Black September also occupied the Saudi Arabian
embassy in Paris on September 5, 1973, and succeeded in comman-
deering a plane to Kuwait. But these actions were among the last in
Black September's terrorist campaign. The verbal strategy announcing the cessation of Black September actions came from Khalaf himself.

As suggested earlier, Khalaf, or Abu Iyad, the second-ranking
official in al-Fatah, had been linked to Black September from its inception. He had been arrested by Jordanian officials at the very beginning of the hostilities between the fedayeen and Bedouin forces in
September 1970, apparently arousing the anger of his long-time asso-

ciate Arafat. He did have one important friend, however, in the person of President Nasser of Egypt. Nasser, an admirer of Khalaf's
political acumen, sent Egyptian War Minister Muhammad Ahmad
Sadeq to Amman in September 1970 to obtain Khalaf's release.[170]
Perhaps as a way to redeem himself in the eyes of Arafat, perhaps as
a way to seek vengeance against Hussein, Khalaf seems to have assumed primary leadership of Black September.

　　Abu Daoud, in his confessions in March 1973, confirmed the alleged leadership role of Abu Iyad in Black September. "Abu Iyad does
not link his operations to Black September," Abu Daoud declared.
"Abu Iyad carries out operations whose quality, not quantity, is accentuated. He plans for big operations like the Munich one and the
abortive attempt to take over the [Jordanian] Premiership's office."[171]
In January 1973, moreover, Khalaf went as far as to hint that al-
Fatah was no longer opposed to international terrorism or to hijackings in particular. He blamed the encirclement policies of some
Arab countries in a clear reference to Jordan:

> When . . . we were fighting in Jordan we attacked
> our comrades in the Popular Front because they hi-
> jacked a plane. . . . However, when we are deprived
> of the honour of fighting from the Arab fronts, when
> some quarters try to make us prisoners of the . . .
> bases from which we proceed to the occupied land,
> when these bases are encircled . . . then there can
> be no fighting. . . . If you encircle us in this manner
> we will follow the enemy everywhere. We will not
> limit our arena to the Palestinian field. . . . We
> will set forth to pursue our enemy in all directions.[172]

Here was Black September speaking; here too was the left wing of al-
Fatah pronouncing a verbal strategy akin to that of the PFLP. But on
July 16, 1973, Khalaf altered his position and condemned international
hijacking.

　　It may have been that the pressure from Arab governments
aroused to anger over Khartoum and Cyprus and the embarrassing
leads of Abu Daoud combined to convince the al-Fatah leadership that
Black September operations could only serve the resistance movement
in a counterproductive way. It may also have been concern over the
escalation signaled by the Israelis in Beirut. Whatever, Khalaf, on
July 16, 1973, announced a change in policy that led to a cessation of
Black September activities. On this occasion, he emphasized that
the resistance had maintained firm disciplinary control over 90 percent of its fedayeen. Abu Iyyad then stated, "But there is another
10 percent. . . . I defy any command in the world to control this 10

percent . . . and prevent them from doing what they want in the world." Khalaf added, "We understand the meaning of Black September as a phenomenon. We understand the motives which prompt these youths to carry out such acts . . . but this does not mean that we are the planners or the financiers."[173] After this July 16, 1973 statement, however, al-Fatah continued to pursue a condemnatory verbal strategy. At each successive act of international terrorism, official spokesmen for al-Fatah denounced it as being contrary to the interests of the Palestinian resistance. The decided shift in verbal strategy forecast not only the end of Black September but also the return of al-Fatah to its operational strategy of rejecting terrorism abroad.

In response to the hijacking of a Japan Air Lines plane on July 24, 1973, for example, the PLO stated, "The hijacking incident harms the reputation and prestige of the Palestinian revolution because it has no patriotic justification and does not therefore serve the goals of the Palestinian revolution." Here was a return to the theme of the primacy of politics.[174]

When two Arab terrorists fired into a crowded transit lounge in the Athens airport on August 5, 1973, killing three people and wounding 55, al-Fatah condemned the attack even though the operation had been carried out by the "Yousef Najar Suicide Squad" of Black September. On August 8, 1973, al-Fatah, taking note of this use of Abu Yousef's name, declared, "Fateh, while denouncing the slander to the martyred leader Yousef Najjar . . . sees the attempt to attach the Athens attack to the name of one of Fateh's leaders as new evidence of the suspicious aims of the Athens incident."[175] Moreover, a reputed member of Black September called the Beirut newspaper Al-Muharrir, edited by PLO representative Shafiq al-Hut, to release a statement disavowing the Athens attack: "We have nothing to do with the Athens Airport attack. We strongly denounce it and we also denounce individualistic terrorism."[176] The verbal strategy of Black September had indeed changed.

When the Saudi embassy in Paris was attacked on September 5, 1973, the PLO hinted that it was an attempt to rupture relations between the mainstream of the Palestinian resistance and King Faisal. Arafat stated in a news conference, "I declare on behalf of the Palestine Liberation Organization that we disclaim all responsibility for this incident and do not know its perpetrators. But I assure you they will be brought to account together with all those who planned it."[177] Palestinian representatives claimed that the agents who participated in the attack were not Palestinian but quite possibly Jordanian. David Hirst in the Manchester Guardian reported that the attack on the Saudi embassy had been masterminded by a disenchanted "middle-echelon Fateh leader with a French wife who planned the operation to stop Arafat from falling into Faisal's munificent embrace."[178] On September 18, 1973, however, it was announced that the raid on the Saudi embassy had been planned by a Palestinian terrorist leader based in Iraq named Abu Nidal. A Kuwait daily reported that Abu Nidal, an "al-Fath left-winger" known for his "hostility to Saudi Arabia and Jordan," had planned the operation without the knowledge of the PLO leadership. It also reported that the PLO would place him on trial.[179]

By the time the October 1973 war broke out the Black September movement had, with a few minor exceptions, ceased action. Certainly, al-Fatah and the PLO were prepared to disavow all terrorist acts endangering the lives of civilians abroad. When the October war broke out, the PLO and al-Fatah had therefore probably already adopted the new policy against the Black September type of terrorism.

The October war marks a watershed in the history of the Arabs and the Israelis. But the war was fought primarily by regular armies, not by fedayeen forces. The war was largely designed to vindicate Arab states, particularly Egypt and Syria. It was designed to validate their claims for the return of land captured by the Israelis in 1967 and to remove the burden of failure that had weighed upon them since the Six-Day War. Although the fedayeen had played a relatively insignificant role in the actual war, they emerged more important after it. As Eric Rouleau wrote, "Paradoxically, Arafat's organization, whose military role in the October war had been entirely marginal, emerged strengthened from the conflict, much to the astonishment of Israeli authorities."[180] The Arab heads of state, meeting in Algiers, hastened to recognize al-Fatah and the PLO as "the only legitimate representative of the Palestinian people" immediately after the war in November 1973. Thus, the Palestinian resistance entered into the current era, which we term a period of recognition and legitimization.

Recognition and legitimization represent important incentives conducive to the disciplined use of terrorism in terms of both action and verbal strategy. The shift in operational strategy that we detect as having occurred as early as July 1973 now emerges more clearly, but it also tends to exacerbate the differences among the groups.

Since the October war, the PLO has experienced the pains of being successful and of being attacked for being successful. On the one hand, it has been legitimized under the auspices of the governments of the Arab states and the United Nations. On the other hand, the PLO has experienced increased divisiveness, and there is talk in some quarters of "a civil war" within the Palestinian resistance. These tensions first appeared in August 1974 but became more salient between September and December. At the beginning of the 1975, the PLO was trying to enhance "its peace seeking image," while certain other "elements," to use Sadat's terms, were attempting to wreck such efforts. There are, consequently, two crosscurrents within the resistance: legitimization and moderation on the one hand and renegade recalcitrance on the other.

These tensions have manifested themselves in a variety of ways.
First they can be seen in a series of terrorist operations outside Israel, then in a set of brutalizing acts inside Israel. Most of these
operations were carried out by the PFLP, the PDFLP, and the PFLP-
GC. Al-Fatah has accepted responsibility for a few, however, such
as the attack at Nahariya. In a few instances it implicitly supported the
actions of the other groups, but for the most part Al-Fatah has condemned them. With the formation of the "rejection front," however,
and the gradual emergence of Abu Nidal and his Iraqi-based "counter-
groups"—in combination with the Rabat resolution and the UN appearance—the PLO and al-Fatah have become more willing to appear "moderate" than ever before. Obviously, this is subject to interpretation
in light of the al-Fatah-sponsored attack in Tel Aviv on March 6, 1975.
But it seemed apparent that, as of mid-1975, the PLO and al-Fatah
appeared ready to adopt a verbal strategy condemning those forms of
terrorist violence that threaten to shatter its "legitimized" image.

The importance of this shift in verbal strategy should not be un-
derestimated, for it may well come to represent a new era in self-
hostaging, which could in turn signify a new, possibly less violent,
range of behavior. At the very least, it could signal the possibility
of political discussions between the Palestinians and Israelis by means
of the Geneva conference or through the intervention of the United
States and the Soviet Union. In any event, the two crosscurrents composed of emerging legitimacy and increased divisiveness within the
movement revealed themselves in the period between October 1973
and February 1974 in three discrete subphases. The first mostly involved terrorist actions outside Israel and lasted until April 1974;
the second lasted only five months and witnessed a number of brutal
operations inside Israel, including the ones at Qiryat Shemona and
Maalot. The third began around August 1974 with the formation of the
rejection front and became accentuated after the events of October-
November 1974.

The period between the Yom Kippur war and the April 1974 attack on Qiryat Shemona was punctuated by international terrorist actions in November and December 1973 and in February 1974. The
first two elicited broad condemnations from PLO and al-Fatah spokesmen, but those in February involved an open break between al-Fatah
and the front.

On November 25, 1973, Arab terrorists identifying themselves
as members of the Organization of Arab Nationalist Youth for the Liberation of Palestine hijacked a KLM Royal Dutch Boeing 747 with 271
passengers and 17 crew members aboard and diverted it from Tokyo
first to Damascus, then to Nicosia, Tripoli, and Malta, and finally
to Dubai. They demanded the release of seven Arabs imprisoned in
Cyprus and the closing of camps in the Netherlands used for Soviet

Jews in transit to Israel. The terrorists eventually released their
hostages without achieving their goals. A PLO executive committee
member, Khaled Hasan, stated that his organization "deplored this
action obviously undertaken by irresponsible persons."[181] The following day, the PLO offices in Beirut declared, "Our people cannot agree
to our struggle being distorted in this manner."[182] In an obvious reference to the diplomatic discussions taking place in the aftermath of
the Yom Kippur war, the PLO underscored the delicacy of the "present
crucial circumstances."[183]

A more serious incident occurred on December 17, 1973, when
five Arab terrorists threw bombs into a Pan American airplane at
Rome's Fiumicino airport, killing 32 persons and wounding 40. Among
the dead were four Moroccan officials. The terrorists eventually commandeered a Lufthansa plane and, with seven Italian policemen as hostages, flew it to Athens, where they demanded the release of the two
Arab terrorists that had attacked the Athens airport the previous August. They shot one of the Italian hostages when the Greek government
hesitated to meet their demand. Eventually they gave themselves up
to Kuwaiti authorities. Arafat declared that the operation represented
"a sabotage and carnage aimed against the Palestinian revolution even
more than against the Italian people."[184] An-Nahar stated that the
killings had placed a "burden on the Arab conscience at a moment
when the plight of the Palestinian people was starting to be a burden
on the conscience of the world."[185] The New York Times reported
that many Arab officials perceived the operation as designed to encourage anti-Arab propaganda; other diplomats saw it as a way of forcing
the cancellation of the Geneva conference on the Palestinian question.[186]
The PLO itself offered condolences to the victims of the "criminal
act."[187] The Palestine News Agency described the act as "a conspiratorial act aimed at distorting the real picture of our people and their
culture."[188] Habash alone seems to have come to their defense when
he declared that the Palestinian resistance should never participate in
the Geneva conference, even if invited.[189]

The rift between the PFLP and al-Fatah seems to have broadened
at this point. Khalaf declared in January 1974—perhaps in response to
Habash—that it had become necessary to analyze political realities.
In an interview published in the January 19, 1974 issue of Le Monde,
Khalaf seems to have returned to the verbal strategy he had used in
June 1969. "We must carefully evaluate our ability to influence events
without fooling ourselves," he declared.[190] Forecasting the probability of a prolonged armed struggle, he admitted that the political situation had changed since the October war. "We must seek realistic answers that do not neglect any immediate gain for our people," he
stated. "Refusals and saying 'no' are not automatically revolutionary
answers. . . . No dialogue is possible if it begins with a 'no.' Any

decision should be taken in 'seriousness and with responsibility' without 'ideological posturing.'"[191] This seems to have signaled his acquiescence to diplomatic efforts being made by the Egyptian government at this time to achieve a modus vivendi with the Israelis.

The divergent operational strategies of the PFLP and al-Fatah emerged again during February 1974, when the PFLP sponsored a number of terrorist actions outside the Middle East.

Between January 31 and February 7, 1973, members of both the PFLP and the Japanese Red Army held eight hostages on a ferry-boat after attacking an oil refinery in Singapore. As the drama on the Singapore ferry was unfolding, five PFLP comrades took over the Japanese embassy in Kuwait. Holding over a dozen hostages, including the Japanese ambassador to Kuwait, they demanded that the terrorists involved in the Singapore operation be given safe passage to Kuwait. The Singapore government consented immediately and the terrorists were safely flown out of Singapore. (Kuwaiti authorities at first refused to allow the plane carrying the Singapore terrorists to land. They eventually conceded when the terrorists inside the Japanese embassy threatened to kill their hostages.) When the plane arrived in Kuwait, it picked up the Arab terrorists. The terrorists, who now numbered nine in all, then flew to Yemen-Aden with a representative of the PLO and two Japanese foreign ministry officials. The terrorists were greeted by the foreign minister of Aden and by the Aden minister of state; cars awaited them and they were released on February 10.[192]

The verbal strategy of the terrorists in Singapore followed the basic pattern used by the PFLP in its justification of international acts of terrorism.

In its initial statement, issued on February 1, 1974, the PFLP declared that it was attacking the oil refinery in Singapore in retaliation for the "aggressive role of oil companies and the government of Singapore against the Arab peoples in general and the Palestinian people in particular."[193] The operation occurred at a time "when international imperialism and its agents were waging a ferocious attack on the Arab peoples to bend them to their will," the PFLP declared. It also stated that the attack "constitutes an implementation of the revolutionary strategy aimed at undermining imperialist interests."[194] On February 8, 1974, the PLO rejected the operation.[195] The following day, the Palestine News Agency declared that the executive committee of the PLO, meeting under the chairmanship of Arafat, had discussed "certain acts by the Popular Front for the Liberation of Palestine. . . . The executive committee expressed regret at this and its rejection of such acts which compromise the Palestinian people's struggle."[196] On February 10, the Palestine News Agency, continuing to represent the official PLO position, declared that such actions as those in Singapore and Kuwait "will harm our struggle."[197]

This gave rise to an open dispute between the PLO and the PFLP. Habash, on February 9, 1974, criticized the position of the PLO and condemned the larger organization for failing to take any steps to ensure the safety of the terrorists trapped on the ferryboat in Singapore.[198] Turning to the larger issue of Palestinian terrorism abroad, the PFLP declared that it was "fully aware . . . of the danger to our cause and revolution that is represented by imperialist—particularly American—moves. It is also aware of the danger of moves by Arab reactionaries and all forces of surrender, including that of Sadat." The PFLP concluded by stating, "The Popular Front, realizing the danger of these policies of our cause, was surprised Saturday morning at the attitude of the executive committee and its condemnation of the operation against an imperialist interest in Singapore and the course we took to rescue our colleagues, who remained for seven days in Singapore without the PLO taking any step to save their lives."[199] The seeds that eventually led to the so-called rejection front in August 1974 had thus been planted.

A new subphase in the tactics and verbal strategy of the Palestinian movement was declared on April 11 with the attack on Qiryat Shemona. This period lasted only five months. It involved, however, some of the most virulent cases of terrorist attacks by the Palestinian resistance. It also witnessed attempts to smooth over the rift between al-Fatah and the PLO and certain elements within the front.

Between April and June 1974, four major terrorist operations took place inside Israel—at Qiryat Shemona, Maalot, Shamir Kibbutz, and in the settlement of Nahariya.

The PFLP-GC initiated the attack on Qiryat Shemona. On April 11, three terrorists in Jibril's organization—the group that had been the first to hijack an airplane—shot their way into an apartment house in this northern settlement. They held out for four hours before blowing themselves up. Eighteen Israelis were killed—eight civilians, eight children, and two soldiers. This time, unlike in the past, the PFLP-GC adopted a verbal strategy that contained a number of political points. First, it rejected all "defeatist compromises." A communique released by the PFLP-GC the day after the attack asserted a maximalist position and implied criticism of the PLO for considering agreements that would obtain for the Palestinians anything less than all:

> There are at the heart of the masses a large number
> who reject these solutions, and this front will stand
> against any settlement of this kind. . . . We carried
> out the operation at Qiryat Shemona to underline that
> our liberation struggle is not limited to the West Bank
> or Gaza but covers all Palestinian territory.[200]

The April 12 communique condemned "attempts to liquidate the Arab
revolutionary movement and its vanguard the Palestinian armed struggle" as well as "the Palestinian leaders who accept a defeatist solution
and the creation of a Palestinian state."[201]

One day later, Abul-Abbas, an official spokesman for the PFLP-
GC, held a news conference. Threatening a new wave of suicidal violence inside Israel, he declared that "this campaign is aimed at blocking an Arab-Israeli peace settlement."[202] The verbal strategy used by
the PFLP-GC emphasized that the three terrorists involved in the attack had all lived inside Israel and had not crossed into Israel from
Lebanon to carry out this attack. To assert that the Palestinian resistance was evolving an intricate and effective network inside Israel represented the second most important feature of the verbal strategy used
by the PFLP-GC at this time. Abul-Abbas underscored this point at
considerable length by noting that the terrorists had actually been working in Israel with forged identity papers.

Al-Fatah avoided direct comment on the attack, although it was
timed to occur on the anniversary of the Israeli operation in Beirut
that killed the three ranking members of the PLO. Only Zuhair Muhsin, a leader of the al-Sa'iqah movement and a member of the PLO
executive, declared support by stating, "We promise the people to undertake more such operations as they express real sacrifice and represent a new stage in guerrilla operations."[203] Muhsin's promise
soon materialized at Maalot.

On May 15, 1974, three terrorists entered a schoolhouse where
90 Israeli schoolchildren on a tour of the Galilee region were spending
the night and held them hostage for 12 hours. They demanded the release of 26 prisoners. For the first time, the Israeli government was
prepared to accede to terrorist demands for the release of certain
prisoners. "We cannot wage war over the heads of our children,"
Prime Minister Golda Meir declared. But the negotiating process between the Israelis and the terrorists broke down over the issue of
when a certain code word would be given to French and Rumanian
mediators.[204] After 12 excruciating hours, and with the deadline
past for receipt of the code word, Israeli soldiers stormed the school
building. The terrorists opened fire. When it was over, 21 children
—19 of them girls—were dead or dying and 74 others were wounded.
The terrorists were killed in the attack.

Several parallels can be drawn between the attacks at Qiryat
Shemona and Maalot. Both operations took place within Israel. Both
involved symbolism. Whereas the first had been timed to coincide
with the assassinations in Beirut, the Maalot terrorist unit called itself the "Kamal Nasir group" in reference to one of the three PLO
leaders killed by the Israelis at that time. Syrian, Iraqi, and Pales-
tinian-born terrorists had carried out the assault at Qiryat Shemona,

and the demand for the release of 26 prisoners was designed to sym-
bolize the 26 years of Israel's existence. More relevant, however, is
the fact that both attacks were organized by extremes within the front,
by the rightist PFLP-GC in the first instance and the leftist PDFLP
at Maalot.

As in the case of the PFLP-GC after its attack at Qiryat Shemona, a news conference was held by the PDFLP after Maalot. Hawatima, its leader, conducted it in Beirut. Surprising to some, Hawatima's major points paralleled those made by Abul-Abbas, namely,
that the overriding purpose of the attack was to defeat the Kissinger
peace drive and to destroy any solution that would leave the Jewish
State of Israel standing.[205] "To put it bluntly," he declared, "we
will spare no effort to foil the Kissinger mission." The disengagement agreement between Egypt and Israel was "detrimental" and the
PDFLP would work to prevent further similar arrangements.[206]
Hawatima, unlike Abul-Abbas, did reiterate the theme of a secular
Jewish-Palestinian state. "Palestinian land is for the Palestinians,"
he declared, "and land from which the Zionists must withdraw . . .
for the purpose of establishing a democratic state for Arabs and Jews
in which there will be no place for imperialism and zionism."[207]
Hawatima also developed the same tactical point that Abul-Abbas had
stressed, namely, that the operation had originated within Israel.
"Dayan knows," he stated, "that the leader of the group that staged
the operation was in Israel two months before the attack took place.
. . . The operation was launched from Safad, inside Israel."[208] Most
of the Israeli children and one of the terrorists had also come from
Safad.

The PFLP-GC next struck at Shamir Kibbutz, where on June
13 four of its operatives entered this northern kibbutz and engaged in
a duel with its members. They blew themselves up when the IDF arrived. Several Israeli civilians were killed. But the major target
of the attack, at least in the verbal strategy used at the time, was
those Palestinians who might be tempted to settle for a partial solution. Alleging, as before, that the attack had come from inside Israel, the PFLP-GC declared, "He who can get to the heart of the
homeland can reach all traitors, deviationists and agents."[209] On
June 5, 1974, a disengagement implementation agreement had been
signed between Israel and Egypt, and both the timing and import of
the warning could not have been more obvious. Now, on June 17, the
PFLP-GC stressed that the attack had been aimed at the "defeatists"
—those who had accepted an "American imposed settlement" on the
Middle East.[210] It had also been timed to coincide with Nixon's visit
to Cairo.

The next and final terrorist action in this series of attacks was
organized by al-Fatah itself. On June 24, 1974, three terrorists

landed on the Israeli coast from Lebanon by boat and proceeded toward
Nahariya. They were quickly identified and eventually killed in battle
by Israeli security forces but not before attacking a residential building. An Israeli woman and two children were killed, and six soldiers
were wounded. An analysis of the verbal strategy used by al-Fatah
reveals that two motives prompted the attack at this time—the fear of
being associated with the "defeatist" elements and serious concern
that the Egyptian signature on the disengagement agreement previewed
a possible sellout of the Palestinians.

The operation at Nahariya had been ordered, al-Fatah declared
on June 25, 1974, when "the U.S. imperialist alliance marches into
our Arab region through its Zionist base . . . and through its capitals
of the Arab reactionaries."[211] This statement, revealing continued
concern over the possibility of losing leadership control of the resistance movement, also indicated that al-Fatah "would always remain
in the vanguard of the revolution in spite of certain groups which have
entered the revolution's structure . . . and have worked by various
means, consciously or unconsciously, to plunge our armed struggle
into pitfalls of compromise."[212] The attack was to demonstrate that
"all the disgraceful defeatist agreements some Arab rulers have
signed with the enemy" will not be permitted to last. This verbal
strategy, so reminiscent of that used by the front, may have been al-
Fatah's maneuver to keep the PLO intact at this time. Ever since April it had acquiesced in the attacks by the PFLP-GC and the PDFLP;
now it was engaging in a similar kind of operation and employing a
similar kind of rhetoric. This attempt to align itself with the diehards,
however, did not succeed. In August the so-called rejection front
was formed and a new subphase began.

During the second week of May 1974, the leaders of the main
contesting groups in the resistance had met in Beirut to discuss possible agreement on a set of major issues. The six-man meeting included
such rivals as Arafat, Habash, Jibril, and Hawatima, along with
Muhsin of the al-Sa'iqah movement and Abdel-Wahab Al-Kayyali of
the Iraqi-supported Arab Liberation Front (ALF). Issues discussed
at that time included such fundamentals as the establishment of a national authority on Palestinian territory, future relations with Jordan,
and the official position on the Geneva conference. So heated did the
deliberations become that the PLO executive committee, through its
news agency, requested that Arab newspapers refrain from reporting
on the meeting to allow debate to take place in a more tranquil atmosphere. Habash issued "a bitter statement attacking newspapers which
published news about the discussions."[213] He also declared that the
PFLP rejected the formation of a Palestinian government. When the
meeting broke up, agreement had been forged on unity among the resistance groups and on the rejection of all attempts to coordinate mili-

tary and political efforts with the Jordanian command. But agreement
on the more delicate matters concerning political interests and diplomatic negotiations could not be forged.[214]

By June, actual fighting broke out near Beirut between Jibril's
group and Hawatima's organization. In August, the rejection front
was formed rejecting the leadership of the PLO. And in September,
the PFLP officially walked out of the PLO. The first of these events
marked a continuation of the feud between members of the PFLP-GC
and those of the PDFLP. On June 28, 1974, as a result of a series
of kidnappings on the part of both sides, an open clash occurred between the PFLP-GC and the PDFLP involving artillery and rockets.
The PASC had to be brought in to settle the situation, but not before
40 terrorists had been killed or wounded. Lethal hostility between
these two groups remains a characteristic of the resistance movement.[215] More serious was the rejection of the PLO by the PFLP
along with the PFLP-GC and the ALF in August 1974.

On August 2, the PFLP, the PFLP-GC, and the ALF, calling
themselves the "rejection front," held a news conference and issued a
joint communique. They denounced all moves toward a negotiated
Middle East settlement and specifically disassociated themselves from
Arafat's August trip to Moscow that seemed to imply eventual recognition of Israel. "The Palestine Liberation Organization in the way it
was formed does not represent the real opinion of the PLO, but only
one particular trend of it," the rejection front declared. Habash,
speaking as chairman of the rejection front, declared, "Soviet pursuit
of a peaceful settlement in the Middle East has weakened the socialist
movement in the Arab World. . . . The Soviet Union wants to see a
national Palestinian authority established on only a part of Palestinian
soil, something we reject."[216] Habash then threatened that the rejection front would leave the PLO if it agreed to participate in the Geneva
conference. "We will be within the PLO," he stated, "in general as
long as the PLO remains outside Geneva."[217]

But it was only a matter of weeks before the PFLP withdrew from
the PLO. On September 27, 1974, the PFLP announced that it had decided to leave the PLO in protest against "the dangerous, gradual deviation" toward surrender taking place within the PLO leadership.[218]
In a press conference held at a Palestinian refugee camp outside Beirut, Abu Maher, himself a PFLP representative on the PLO executive
committee, accused the PLO of entering into "secret contacts with the
United States." He alleged that the PLO was preparing to enter into
a Middle East settlement that "will lead to the expansion of U.S. influence in the area, and will concede the existence of Israel with future guarantees of its security and stability."[219] He also declared,
"We are convinced that for some time now there have been serious
efforts to drag the PLO into becoming a party to this liquidationist

imperialist settlement."[220] The term "liquidationist" became the
code word representing the PFLP's condemnation of the PLO.

The PLO, for its part, reacted in a conciliatory fashion by asking the PFLP to remain and by admitting its regret that the decision
of the PFLP had come at "a time when the PLO is engaged in its greatest political and military struggle against the enemy."[221] It hastened
to deny PFLP allegations concerning contact with the United States or
interest in a settlement that would sell out Palestinian interests. The
PFLP remained unmovable, however; on October 3, 1974, it reiterated
its belief that the PLO was pursuing policies that "smacked of treason,
led by the United States and Arab retrogression."[222]

CONCLUSION

The end of 1974 and early part of 1975 witnessed the rise of the
PLO as the fully authorized representative of the Palestinian people.
The Rabat summit of October 1974 and the Arafat appearance before
the UN General Assembly on November 13, 1974, bestowed a new degree of legitimacy upon the PLO leadership. Yet during the same period, the PLO found itself being attacked with unprecedented vehemence
from within the movement itself. Habash began to sepak of the PLO's
leading "an Arab capitulationist policy."[223] The rejection front solid-
ified its ranks. The PFLP joined forces with Jibril's PFLP-GC. The
Iraq-ALF and other dissident elements supported by Libya and even
groups from within al-Fatah also decided to oppose the PLO at this
time. Legitimacy is a double-edged sword for a terrorist movement,
especially if it devolves prior to (or appears contrary to) the achievement of the goals of the resistance itself.

During the three months between November 1974 and January
1975, the rejection front waged a war of verbal strategy designed to
sever the connection between legitimacy and the willingness to compromise on the part of the PLO. Condemning any partial resolution
of the conflict that left any portion of Palestine in Israeli hands, the rejection front warned the PLO against being tempted by "surrender
solutions" and declared that "a Palestinian civil war" was quickly becoming a "practical inevitability."[224]

This period also witnessed various terrorist actions—cinema
bombings in Tel Aviv, attacks against civilians in Jerusalem—all perpetrated by groups within the rejection front and almost in defiance of
the PLO. The most significant of these actions was the hijacking of a
British DC-10 in Dubai on November 23, 1974, an event that was punctuated by the killing of a West German banker in cold blood after the
plane had been flown to Tunisia. Hundreds of witnesses at Carthage
airport in Tunis saw Gustav Kehl being shot from behind in an open

doorway of the jet, his body falling onto the asphalt.[225] The ostensible purpose of the raid was to obtain the release of the Khartoum terrorists who had killed the American ambassador and who were being held in detention in Cairo.

The breach between the PLO and the rejection front became ever more clearly defined as PLO spokesmen condemned the operation. Muhsin, the al-Sa'iqah leader, declared in an interview in a Soviet publication that the "PLO denounces and deplores acts of terrorism committed by extremist Palestinian groups against civilians and in third countries."[226] The Egyptian government called upon the PLO "to face its responsibilities and retaliate against dissident groups that defame its struggle."[227] The PLO, obviously prepared to accept Sadat's call, condemned the raid. Arafat, on November 24, declared that his organization would weed out those responsible for the "crime for which they shall pay the price."[228] The PLO asked the Tunisian government to turn over the hijackers to it "as an inevitable step to uncover all the ramifications of this operation, and those who stand behind."[229] Two days later, the PLO announced that it had arrested 26 individuals alleged to have been connected with the operation and that it would place them on trial "so everybody will see that the PLO has passed the punishment seen necessary against them."[230] A five-man PLO delegation traveled to Tunis to obtain custody of the terrorists. A spokesman for the group indicated that a trial, "the first ever in Palestinian commando history," would be held with Cairo as its venue, since "it was the first Arab country to welcome the idea."[231]

The Tunisian government did eventually turn over the Palestinians, with their consent, to the PLO. On January 25, 1975, the PLO announced that it had found these men guilty of crimes and had imposed upon them heavy sentences involving long prison terms at hard labor.[232] Four days later, the PLO took a group of Western reporters to a prison camp outside of Damascus as a way of proving that the PLO meant to enforce discipline within its ranks.[233]

Sporadic outbursts of terrorist violence continued throughout early 1975. Several attacks at Orly airport in January seemed specifically designed to embarrass Sadat, who paid a state visit to France beginning on January 27, 1975, prompting the latter to remark of the Palestinians, "Let them go to the devil."[234]

During February and March 1975, U.S. diplomatic initiatives led by Kissinger preempted the attention of all parties in the Middle East. Now the crucial question became whether or not the step-by-step approach would produce an accord, however informal, between Egypt and Israel. With "a separate peace" looming as a real possibility, the PLO, specifically al-Fatah and al-Sa'iqah, formed a rejection front of their own to the moderate stance that Sadat appeared to be assuming. It was one thing for the PLO to ostracize elements that en-

gaged in nonnormative violence; it was quite another for it to become
isolated through the peace initiatives of other parties. On February
21, 1975, it was reported that Arafat had "shunned" several invitations
from Sadat.[235] One week later, it was revealed that Sadat had "refused to invite" a Palestinian delegation to Cairo for a parley on Egypt's
negotiating position.[236] Later, however, a reconciliation between the
two seemed to develop.

The impact of the Kissinger mission in the Middle East during
February and March 1975, despite its failure to obtain a working agreement between the Egyptians and the Israelis, was to hasten the integration of al-Fatah and al-Sa'iqah. On March 21, 1975, the Palestine
Central Council unanimously agreed to accept the offer of President
Hafez Asad to unify the political and military commands of al-Sa'iqah
and al-Fatah.[237] Thus, the two most politically aware and militarily
disciplined organizations within the Palestinian resistance sought to re-
tain their primary role within the movement. The terrorist action
conducted by them on March 6, 1975, within the heart of Tel Aviv in
the midst of the Kissinger shuttle was designed to show that no agreement could work meaningfully without their acceptance or acquiescence.

With the resurgence of calls to convene the Geneva conference
that followed in the wake of Kissinger's failure, the PLO, Arafat,
and the rest of the mainstream of the Palestinian resistance were faced
with the question of how much less than a complete victory would be
acceptable as a political solution. As Arafat declared in Bahrein on
April 3, 1975, "First I must know which Geneva they want me to go
to. Is it the umbrella Geneva, for the step-by-step solution? Is it
the Geneva where I'm supposed to be just a witness? Is it the Geneva
of Resolution 242, which the Palestine National Council, the highest
Palestinian legislative body, rejected, thereby committing the P.L.O.
to reject it?"

One question that Arafat did not raise publicly but that surely
must have been on his mind is what would be the future role of terrorism in the resistance? What forms would the violence assume? How
could they maintain pressure but without becoming productive? How
could they be normative, include offers to the Israelis that the Israelis
could accept, yet without appearing to blunt the thrust of the movement?

That these questions became pertinent again was signified by the
April 7, 1975 announcement of the healing of the rift that had developed
between Arafat and Sadat during the Kissinger shuttle. The relationship of politics to terrorism in the Middle East, therefore, once again
appeared in need of redefinition—offering the hope that is seared with
tragedy—that such an event has always involved.

NOTES

1. For a full account, see the New York Times, November 14, 1974, p. 24.

2. Arab Report and Record (London), no. 20 (1974), p. 465. (Hereafter referred to as Arab Report and Record.)

3. Michael Hudson, "The Palestinian Arab Resistance Movement: Its Significance in the Middle East Crisis," Middle East Journal 23, no. 3 (1969): 297.

4. Ehud Yaari, Strike Terror: The Story of Fatah (New York: Sabra Books, 1970), p. 199.

5. Daniel Dishon, ed., Middle East Record (Tel Aviv: Israel University Press for the Tel Aviv University Shiloah Center for Middle Eastern and African Studies, 1973), vol. 4, 1968, p. 423. (Hereafter referred to as Middle East Record [1968].)

6. William D. Quandt, Fuad Jabber, and Ann Mosely Lesch, The Politics of Palestinian Nationalism (Berkeley: University of California Press, 1973), part 2, William B. Quandt, "Political and Military Dimensions of Contemporary Palestinian Nationalism," p. 55.

7. Middle East Record (1968), p. 400.

8. For a full presentation of the various ideological positions and in particular of the different operational strategies of the main Palestinian resistance organizations, see Leila S. Kadi, ed., Basic Political Documents of the Armed Palestinian Resistance Movement (Beirut: Palestine Liberation Organization Research Center, 1969); of special interest in this connection is "A dialogue between Al-Fateh and Al-Tali'ah: The Resistance, How Does It Think and Act? How Does It Face the Present? How Does It See the Future?" pp. 39-134. (Hereafter referred to as Basic Political Documents of the Armed Palestinian Resistance Movement.) For a full history of the early phase of Palestinian terrorism, see Quandt et al., op. cit., part 1, Ann Mosely Lesch, "The Palestine Arab Nationalist Movement Under the Mandate," pp. 7-42; also, see Basic Political Documents of the Armed Palestinian Resistance Movement, pp. 11-35.

9. For a full account of this period in Arafat's life, see Yaari, op. cit., pp. 9-25. Al-Qadir died in 1948 outside of Jerusalem and his name is revered in al-Fatah songs and literature.

10. Ibid., pp. 15-16.

11. Ibid.

12. Basic Political Documents of the Armed Palestinian Resistance Movement, p. 16.

13. Ibid.

14. See Riad N. El-Rayyes and Dunia Nahas, eds., Guerrillas for Palestine: A Study of the Palestinian Commando Organization (Beirut: An-Nahar Press Services for the An-Nahar Arab Report Re-

search Services, 1974), pp. 249-52. (Hereafter referred to as Guer-rillas for Palestine.)

15. Ibid., p. 246.

16. Emile A. Makhleh, "The Anatomy of Violence: Theoretical Reflections on Palestinian Resistance," Middle East Journal 25, no. 2 (1971): 192.

17. Michael Hudson, "The Palestinian Resistance Movement Since 1967," in The Middle East: Quest for an American Policy, ed. Willard A. Beling (Albany: State University of New York Press, 1973), p. 105.

18. See Middle East Record (1968) for two reports: "The Fight-ing at Karamah and S. of the Dead Sea: The Israeli Account," pp. 365-68; and "The Fighting at Karamah and S. of the Dead Sea: The Arab Accounts," pp. 368-70. Between 1964 and 1968, al-Fatah used the name of its military wing, al-Asifa, "so that, in the event of failure, al-Fath might continue its preparations and its secret activi-ties" (see Basic Political Documents of the Armed Palestinian Re-sistance Movement, p. 18).

19. Karamah was a Palestinian refugee camp and a stronghold of al-Fatah situated on the East Bank of the Jordan River. The Israeli expeditionary force sent out to destroy the military operations at the Karamah camp consisted of approximately 200 Israeli soldiers.

20. Michael Hudson, op. cit., p. 105.

21. Guerrillas for Palestine, p. 10; Quandt et al., op. cit., p. 58.

22. Basic Political Documents of the Armed Palestinian Resis-tance Movement, p. 19.

23. Ibid., p. 20.

24. Ibid., pp. 20-21.

25. Guerrillas for Palestine, p. 72.

26. Basic Political Documents of the Armed Palestinian Resis-tance Movement, p. 17; Guerrillas for Palestine, p. 246.

27. Ibid.

28. Quandt et al., op. cit., p. 68.

29. Guerrillas for Palestine, p. 75; Basic Political Documents of the Armed Palestinian Resistance Movement, p. 25.

30. Middle East Record (1968), p. 423.

31. Ibid., p. 424.

32. Ibid.

33. Ibid., p. 425; citing al-Hayat.

34. Ibid., citing Hurriyya.

35. Ibid.; citing al-Hayat and an-Nahar.

36. Ibid., p. 427.

37. Ibid., p. 428.

38. Ibid., pp. 432-36.

39. Ibid., p. 430; citing al-Anwar.

40. Ibid.

41. Guerrillas for Palestine, p. 76.

42. Ibid., pp. 76-77; the research staff of an-Nahar wrote that
when the PLO "was overshadowed by the various guerrilla organizations after the June 1967 war, the PLA was prompted to get on the
bandwagon of guerrilla warfare in order to avoid being totally left
out of the picture. Thus, in February 1968, the PLA formed its own
commando organization, the Popular Liberation Forces (PLF). However, this group neither had the impetus of the Fateh nor the flair of
the Popular Front for the Liberation of Palestine. They failed to capture the imagination and remained in the background never exceeding
2,000 men, according to the best estimates."

43. Ibid.

44. Middle East Record (1968), pp. 421-22.

45. Basic Political Documents of the Armed Palestinian Resistance Movement, p. 29.

46. Quandt el al., op. cit., pp. 91-92.

47. Guerrillas for Palestine, p. 50.

48. Ibid.

49. Ibid.

50. Daily Star (Beirut), October 1, 1973, p. 1.

51. Guerrillas for Palestine, p. 49.

52. Ibid.

53. Washington Post, March 21, 1975, p. A 23.

54. Quandt et al., op. cit., p. 92.

55. Guerrillas for Palestine, p. 51.

56. Middle East Record (1968), p. 740.

57. Ibid., pp. 592-94.

58. Ibid.

59. Ibid.

60. There is one other major terrorist organization that is closely
tied to a specific Arab country. The so-called Arab Liberation Front
(ALF) was founded in April 1969 by the Iraqi-Arab Ba'ath Socialist
Party. As its name suggests, this organization draws its membership
from non-Palestinian operatives. Since its founding, the ALF has
been alone among the resistance groups in having a majority of its
members come from Arab countries such as Iraq, Lebanon, and Jordan, while including only a minority of Palestinians. One source reveals that the ALF had, as of the end of 1973, from 400 to 500 commandos operating in bases in southern Lebanon. Unlike the Syrian al-
Sa'iqah organization, the ALF is not an important force among commando groups. For that reason it is not given separate treatment in
the text. As Guerrillas for Palestine suggests, the ALF "has won no
military distinction for itself. It has opposed foreign operations, con-

fining its activity to attacks across the border. It has failed to establish any presence within the occupied territories. Its point of strength
and weakness remains the Ba'ath Party of Iraq. Its ups and downs
within the Resistance Movement reflect the degree of commitment—
or lack of commitment—by the Ba'ath Party to the Palestine cause."
Basically, the ALF is the Iraqi answer to the Syrian al-Sa'iqah organization. See Guerrillas for Palestine, pp. 55-58.

61. For a fuller description of Arafat and Habash, see Yaari,
op. cit., p. 211; also see Guerrillas for Palestine, pp. 245-49.

62. Ibid.

63. Ibid., p. 213.

64. Middle East Record (1968), p. 407.

65. Ibid.

66. Ibid.

67. Yaari, op. cit., p. 215. Yaari suggests that "Jibril, a
professional military man far removed from politics, had thought of
joining Fatah, but soon realized that he would be overshadowed by
'Arafat, whereas an alliance with Habash would enable him to preserve
his status as an independent military leader."

68. Popular Front for the Liberation of Palestine, A Strategy
for the Liberation of Palestine, mimeographed (Amman: PFLP Information Department, 1969), p. 34.

69. See Guerrillas for Palestine, pp. 43-44.

70. This terrorist group has not been given separate treatment
since it does not represent an important force (see Yaari, op. cit.,
p. 217.

71. For a general description of Hawatima, see Guerrillas for
Palestine, pp. 265-66.

72. See ibid., pp. 45-58.

73. Middle East Record (1968), p. 407.

74. Ibid.

75. Popular Front for the Liberation of Palestine, op. cit., p.
34.

76. Yaari, op. cit., pp. 216-17; Guerrillas for Palestine, pp.
43-45; Middle East Record (1968), pp. 408-09.

77. Ibid.

78. Ibid.

79. Ibid.

80. Yaari, op. cit., p. 218; Basic Political Documents of the
Armed Palestinian Resistance Movement, p. 32.

81. Ibid.

82. Ibid.

83. Record of the Arab World (Beirut), March 1970, pp. 1893-
94.

84. Ibid. The observer is J. Gaspard.

85. Yaari, op. cit., p. 218; Middle East Record (1968), pp. 408-09.

86. Ibid.

87. Quandt et al., op. cit., p. 71.

88. Record of the Arab World, October-December 1970, pp. 6234-35.

89. Quandt et al., op. cit., pp. 71-72.

90. Ibid.

91. Ibid., chap. 6, "The September 1970 Crisis and Its Aftermath," pp. 124-48.

92. Basic Political Documents of the Armed Palestinian Resistance Movement, p. 17.

93. Quandt et al., op. cit., pp. 124-26.

94. These hijackings are discussed below.

95. William D. Quandt in Quandt et al., op. cit., p. 115.

96. Record of the Arab World, October-December 1970, pp. 6228-29.

97. Ibid.

98. Arab Report and Record, September 16-30, 1970, p. 538.

99. Ibid., October 1-15, 1970, p. 572.

100. Record of the Arab World, January 1971, pp. 274-75.

101. Ibid., p. 280.

102. Basic Political Documents of the Armed Palestinian Resistance Movement, p. 91.

103. The 1964 and 1968 covenants are conveniently found in Middle East Record (1968), pp. 432-36.

104. Ibid. For an elaboration of this point of view, see Ezzeldin Foda, Israeli Belligerent Occupation and Palestinian Armed Resistance in International Law (Beirut: PLO Research Center, 1970).

105. Ibid.

106. Ibid.

107. Ibid.

108. Ibid.

109. From an interview with Paul Jacobs, in IDOC Middle East Quarterly, no. 2 (1974), p. 54.

110. Middle East Record (1968), pp. 384-86.

111. Ibid., p. 352.

112. Ibid., pp. 388-89.

113. Ibid., pp. 393-94.

114. Record of the Arab World, February 1970, pp. 1168-69.

115. Ibid.

116. Ibid.

117. Ibid.

118. Oriana Fallaci, "A Leader of Fedayeen: 'We Want a War Like the Vietnam War': Interview with George Habash," Life, June 12, 1970, pp. 32-34.

119. Ibid.

120. Ibid.

121. Ibid.

122. Record of the Arab World, June 1970, p. 3882.

123. Basic Political Documents of the Armed Palestinian Resistance Movement, p. 62.

124. Ibid.

125. Ibid., p. 98.

126. The Black September movement has recently been given a full but rather journalistic treatment in Christopher Dobson, Black September: Its Short, Violent History (New York: Macmillan Publishing Co., 1974).

127. Free Palestine, April 1, 1974, p. 5. Abu Iyad, or Salah Khalaf, is not to be confused with Abu Ali Iyyad, who died in 1971. The New York Times, October 4, 1971, p. 17, made this mistake in an analysis of the origins of the Black September movement when it reported, "The death of Abu Iyad, whose real name was Salah Khalaf, is said to have inspired the formation of Black September."

128. Guerrillas for Palestine, pp. 63-68.

129. Ibid.

130. Ibid.

131. Ibid.

132. Ibid.

133. A. Yaniv, P.L.O.: A Profile (Jerusalem: Israel Universities Study Group for Middle Eastern Affairs, 1974), p. 19.

134. David Hirst in the Manchester Guardian, October 21, 1972, p. 5.

135. Ibid.

136. Yaniv, op. cit., p. 18.

137. Guerrillas for Palestine, p. 65.

138. Ibid.

139. Arab Report and Record, May 1-15, 1972, p. 245.

140. Ibid., May 16-31, 1972, p. 270.

141. Ibid.

142. Ibid.

143. Ibid.

144. Ibid., June 1-15, 1972, p. 295.

145. Ibid., September 1-15, 1972, p. 438.

146. Ibid.

147. Ibid.

148. Ibid.

149. Ibid., September 16-30, 1972, p. 463.

150. Ibid., October 16-31, 1972, p. 516.

151. Daily Star (Beirut), December 29, 1972, p. 2.

152. Arab Report and Record, March 1-15, 1973, pp. 117-18.

153. Ibid.

154. Ibid.

155. Ibid.

156. Ibid.

157. Ibid.

158. Daily Star (Beirut), March 7, 1973, p. 1.

159. Ibid., March 8, 1973, p. 1.

160. Ibid.

161. Arab Report and Record, March 1-15, 1973, p. 118.

162. Daily Star (Beirut), March 9, 1973, p. 1.

163. Ibid.

164. Ibid., March 15, 1973, p. 1.

165. Ibid.

166. Arab Report and Record, February 15-28, 1973, p. 83.

167. Ibid., March 16-31, 1973, p. 145.

168. See accounts in ibid., April 1-15, 1973, pp. 169-70; Time, April 23, 1973, pp. 19-23.

169. See account in the Daily Star (Beirut), April 28, 1973, p. 1.

170. Guerrillas for Palestine, p. 250.

171. Arab Report and Record, March 16-31, 1973, p. 148. The New York Times, on March 6, 1973, p. 6, and on March 25, 1973, p. 14, revealed reports that Abu Iyad, or Salah Khalaf, was the leader of Black September.

172. Arab Report and Record, January 16-31, 1973, p. 46.

173. Ibid., p. 333.

174. New York Times, July 25, 1973, p. 13.

175. Arab Report and Record, August 1-15, 1973, p. 356. In its statement, al-Fatah accused "terrorist Zionism in complicity with American Central Intelligence" of having murdered Yousef Najjar. See the Daily Star (Beirut), August 9, 1973, p. 1.

176. Ibid.

177. Daily Star (Beirut), September 15, 1973, p. 1.

178. Arab Report and Record, September 1-15, 1973, p. 400.

179. Al-Rai-al-Aam (Kuwait), September 17, 1973, p. 1; also see the Daily Star (Beirut), September 18, 1973, p. 1.

180. Erie Rouleau, "The Palestinian Quest," Foreign Affairs 53, no. 2 (1975), pp. 264-65.

181. Arab Report and Record, November 16-30, 1973, p. 552.

182. Ibid.

183. Ibid.

184. Daily Star (Beirut), December 27, 1973, p. 2.

185. An-Nahar (Beirut), December 17, 1973, p. 1.

186. New York Times, December 18, 1973, p. 18.

187. Arab Report and Record, December 16-31, 1973, p. 593.

188. Ibid.

189. New York Times, December 18, 1973, p. 18.

190. Le Monde, January 19, 1974, p. 1; also see Arab Report and Record, January 16-31, 1974, p. 39.

191. Ibid.

192. Daily Star (Beirut), February 1, 1974, p. 1, and February 7, 1974, p. 1; also see Arab Report and Record, February 1-14, 1974, p. 57.

193. Daily Star (Beirut), February 1, 1974, p. 1.

194. Ibid.

195. Arab Report and Record, February 1-14, 1974, p. 57.

196. Daily Star (Beirut), February 9, 1974, p. 1.

197. Arab Report and Record, February 1-14, 1974, p. 57.

198. Daily Star (Beirut), February 10, 1974, p. 1.

199. Ibid.

200. Arab Report and Record, April 1-15, 1974, pp. 138-39.

201. Ibid.

202. Ibid.

203. Ibid.

204. The code word "al-Aqsa" was supposed to be delivered from Damascus to the intermediaries after the Palestinians had been released and flown to Damascus. Israeli authorities believed that the code word would be conveyed once meaningful negotiations had begun; thus, precious hours were allowed to elapse.

205. For an account of the Maalot raid, see Arab Report and Record, May 1-15, 1974, pp. 185-88; see also Newsweek, May 27, 1974, pp. 36-43. The Times (London), May 19, 1974, also carried a report.

206. Daily Star (Beirut), May 17, 1974, p. 3; also see International Herald Tribune, May 21, 1974, p. 2.

207. Ibid.

208. Ibid.

209. Daily Star (Beirut), June 14, 1974, p. 1.

210. Arab Report and Record, June 16-30, 1974, pp. 266-67.

211. Ibid.

212. Ibid.

213. Daily Star (Beirut), May 12, 1974, p. 1.

214. Ibid.

215. Ibid., June 29, 1974, p. 1.

216. Arab Report and Record, August 1-15, 1974, p. 337. In response, the Soviet press attacked Habash personally for the first time, describing him as a "pseudo-revolutionary" and an "extremist" misled by "Maoist demagogy" into believing that "peace and socialism were not compatible" (ibid.).

217. Ibid.

218. Daily Star (Beirut), September 27, 1974, p. 1.

219. Ibid.

220. Ibid.

221. Ibid.

222. Ibid., October 3, 1974, p. 1.

223. Ibid., October 26, 1974, p. 1.

224. Ibid., October 31, 1974, p. 1; November 30, 1974, p. 12; December 8, 1974, p. 2.

225. New York Times, November 24, 1974, p. 1.

226. Daily Star (Beirut), December 7, 1974, p. 2; the interview was published in Novaya Vremya, December 6, 1974.

227. Daily Star (Beirut), November 25, 1974, pp. 1, 12.

228. Ibid., p. 12.

229. Ibid., November 26, 1974, p. 1.

230. Ibid., November 28, 1974, p. 1. The PLO claimed that Iraq was behind the hijacking.

231. Ibid., November 29, p. 2.

232. New York Times, January 26, 1975, pp. 1, 4.

233. Ibid., January 30, 1975, pp. 1, 3.

234. Ibid., January 26, 1975, p. 4.

235. Ibid., February 21, 1975, p. 4.

236. Ibid., February 28, 1975, p. 8.

237. Washington Post, March 21, 1975, p. A 23.

INTERNATIONAL TERRORISM AND
THE UNITED NATIONS
Seymour Maxwell Finger

The increase in international terrorist activity following World War I prodded nations and criminologists into the first organized international attempts to deal with this problem. A series of meetings held under the auspices of the International Conference for the Unification of Penal Law in the late 1920s and 1930s, attended by delegations representing states and both intergovernmental and private international organizations, served to focus attention on the subject. Another result was the revision of some extradition treaties to exclude certain terrorist acts from the category of "political offenses," thereby making them extraditable.[1]

Following the assassination of King Alexander of Yugoslavia and Foreign Minister Barthoru of France in 1934, the Council of the League of Nations established a committee of experts to study the question of terrorist activity with a view to drawing up a preliminary draft of an international convention to assure the repression of conspiracies or crimes committed with a "political and terrorist" purpose. The committee held three sessions in 1935, 1936, and 1937 and prepared two preliminary draft conventions—one for the prevention and punishment of terrorism and a second for the establishment of an international criminal court. On the basis of these two preliminary drafts, an international conference on the repression of terrorism, convened at Geneva in November 1937, adopted two conventions, neither of which ever entered into force.[2]

The Convention for the Prevention and Punishment of Terrorism was ratified only by India, perhaps because of the approach of war. Also, some states may have been reluctant to ratify the convention because of the breadth of its definition of terrorism. The convention is not now listed among those for which the League was a depositary and with respect to which the United Nations has taken any responsibility; therefore, it may be considered a dead issue.[3]

THE UNITED NATIONS AND
TERRORISM—BACKGROUND

During the first two decades of the United Nations, international terrorism received only tangential attention in the General Assembly and the Security Council.

In its resolution 177(II) of November 21, 1947, the General Assembly entrusted the International Law Commission (ILC) with the task of preparing a draft code of offenses against the peace and security of mankind. This draft code, prepared in 1954 by the ILC pursuant to that resolution, deals mainly with the principles recognized in the charter of the Nuremberg tribunal and the judgment of the tribunal; however, it has one paragraph concerned with international terrorism. Article 2, paragraph 6, defines as an offense against the peace and security of mankind

> the undertaking or encouragement by the authorities
> of a State of terrorist activities in another State, or
> the toleration by the authorities of a State of orga-
> nized activities calculated to carry out terrorist
> acts in another State.[4]

No action has been taken on the draft code to date. In 1957, the General Assembly decided to defer consideration of the question until such time as it again took up the question of defining aggression (GA R. 1186[XII]). Now that the Special Committee on the Question of Defining Aggression has agreed on a definition,[5] the question of a draft code may be raised at the 29th session of the General Assembly; however, from the standpoint of international terrorism, the single paragraph in the code would add nothing to similar provisions in the Declaration on Principles of International Law Concerning Friendly Relations and Cooperation Among States in Accordance with the Charter of the United Nations, which was approved by the General Assembly in Resolution 2625 (XXV) of October 24, 1970. Relevant portions of that resolution are quoted below:

> The General Assembly . . .
> 1. Solemnly proclaims the following Principles:
> The principle that States shall refrain in their in-
> ternational relations from the threat or use of force
> against the territorial integrity or political indepen-
> dence of any State, or in any other manner inconsis-
> tent with the purposes of the United Nations. . . .
> Every State has the duty to refrain from organiz-
> ing, instigating, assisting or participating in acts of

civil strife or terrorist acts in another State or ac-
quiescing in organized activities within its territory
directed towards the commission of such acts, when
the acts referred to in the present paragraph involve
a threat or use of force. . . .

The principle concerning the duty not to intervene
in matters within the domestic jurisdiction of any
State, in accordance with the Charter. . . .

No State may use or encourage the use of economic, political or any other type of measures to coerce another State in order to obtain from it the sub-
ordination of the exercise of its sovereign rights and
to secure from it advantages of any kind. Also, no
State shall organize, assist, foment, finance, incite
or tolerate subversive, terrorist or armed activities
directed toward the violent overthrow of the regime
of another State, or interfere in civil strife in another
State. . . .

2. Declares that:

In their interpretation and application the above
principles are interrelated and each principle should
be construed in the context of the other principles.

. . .

3. Declares further that:

The principles of the Charter which are embodied
in this Declaration constitute basic principles of international law, and consequently appeals to all States
to be guided by these principles in their international
conduct and to develop their mutual relations on the
basis of the strict observance of these principles.

The definition of aggression submitted to the General Assembly
focused on acts of aggression by states rather than by individuals or
nonstate organizations; however, Article 3, paragraph (g) gives the
following definition:

The sending by or on behalf of a State of armed bands,
groups, irregulars or mercenaries, which carry out
acts of armed force against another State of such gravity as to amount to the acts listed above, or its substantial involvement therein.

The application of this provision appears to be restricted, however, by Articles 7 and 8 of the definition, which read:

Nothing in this definition, and in particular article
3, could in any way prejudice the right to self-determination, freedom and independence, as derived
from the Charter, of peoples forcibly deprived of
that right and referred to in the Declaration on
Principles of International Law concerning Friendly
Relations and Co-operation among States in accordance with the Charter of the United Nations, particularly peoples under colonial and racist regimes
or other forms of alien domination; nor the right of
these peoples to struggle to that end and to seek and
receive support, in accordance with the principles
of the Charter and in conformity with the above-men-
tioned Declaration.

In their interpretation and application the above
provisions are interrelated and each provision should
be construed in the context of other provisions.

ACTION BY THE ORGANIZATION
OF AMERICAN STATES

In recent years, the states of the Western Hemisphere in the
Organization of American States (OAS) have come alarmed by the
growing frequency of acts of terrorism, especially kidnappings, for
political or ideological purposes. Following resolutions on the subject
in 1970 by the OAS Permanent Council and its General Assembly,[6]
the third special session of the OAS General Assembly in February
1971 adopted a "Convention to Prevent and Punish the Acts of Terrorism Taking the Form of Crimes Against Persons and Related Extortion That Are of International Significance."[7]

The convention, although establishing in Article 1 a duty for
States parties to cooperate in the prevention or punishment of "acts
of terrorism," does not in fact deal with terrorism as a whole. It
extends only to certain terrorist acts further characterized in Article
2 as common crimes against the life or personal integrity of those
persons to whom the state has the duty to give special protection according to international law, as well as extortion in connection with
those crimes. The convention, which is based on the principle "aut
dedere aut judicare," contains detailed provisions concerning extradition (Articles 3, 5, and 7) and, in those cases in which extradition
will not be granted, it establishes the duty of a state to submit the
case to its competent authorities for the purpose of prosecution as if
the act had been committed in its territory. A specific provision is
included in Article 6 to safeguard the right of asylum and a number

of concrete obligations are set out in Article 8 to effectuate the general duty of cooperation in the prevention and punishment of the crimes covered. Finally, under the terms of Article 9, the convention is open to participation by states other than those that are members of the OAS.[8]

To date only three countries—Costa Rica, Nicaragua, and Venezuela—have ratified the convention. Under its terms, the convention is now in force among those three countries. The fact that so few countries have ratified it after more than three years is not encouraging.

ACTION BY THE INTERNATIONAL CIVIL AVIATION ORGANIZATION

During the past decade, acts endangering international civil aviation have become alarmingly more numerous and widespread. Such acts have been the object of concern by the UN General Assembly in its Resolutions 2551 (XXIV) and 2645 (XXV) and by the Security Council in its Resolution 268 (1970) and its Decision of June 20, 1972. For understandable reasons, the development of conventions in this area has taken place under the auspices of the International Civil Aviation Organization (ICAO), supported and encouraged by the UN General Assembly resolutions mentioned above.

The Convention of Offences and Certain Other Acts Committed on Board Aircraft, signed at Tokyo on September 14, 1963, imposes upon States parties certain obligations concerning the return of a hijacked aircraft and its cargo and the release of the passengers and crew. It is not, however, concerned with the suppression of such acts and offenses, as are the two subsequent conventions.

The Convention for the Suppression of Unlawful Seizure of Aircraft, signed at The Hague on December 16, 1970, obliges States parties to make such offenses punishable by severe penalties (Article 2). Article 7 obliges the State party in the territory of which the alleged offender is found, if it does not extradite him, to submit the case "without exception whatsoever" to its competent authorities for the purpose of prosecution. The system of extradition established by the convention is dealt with in Article 8, which states that the unlawful seizure of aircraft is "deemed to be included" in any extradition treaty existing between States parties and which also obliges States parties to include the offense as an extraditable offense in every extradition treaty to be concluded between them. Last, the convention contains provisions obliging States parties to afford one another judicial assistance in any criminal proceedings brought in respect of the offense (Article 10) and to report to the Council of the ICAO any relevant information in their possession (Article 11).

The Convention for the Suppression of Unlawful Acts Against the Safety of Civil Aviation, signed at Montreal on September 23, 1971, establishes a system of suppression that in outline is the same as that laid down in the 1970 Hague convention. The difference is that the Hague convention is concerned with the aircraft itself when it is in flight and when the offense is committed by a person on board the aircraft; the Montreal convention covers a series of acts, mostly committed on the ground, which are likely to cause the destruction of the aircraft or otherwise endanger the safety of aircraft in flight. It also includes a special provision (Article 10) requiring that "Contracting States shall, in accordance with international and national law, endeavor to take all practicable measures for the purpose of preventing the offenses mentioned."

All three of these ICAO-launched conventions are now in effect. The increasing concern of most governments with hijacking and other threats to civilization is indicated by the pace of ratification. In 1970, after seven years, only 32 countries had ratified the Tokyo convention; by May 1974, the total was 72. The Hague convention of December 1970 had, only three and a half years later, been ratified by 67 states. The Montreal convention of September 1971 had, three and a half years later, been ratified by 53 states.

There must be concern, however, when hijackers can still find santuary in states that have not ratified the conventions. Among the more than 20 Arab countries, only Jordan and Libya have ratified the Montreal convention. Only Iraq, Jordan, and Lebanon have ratified the Hague convention and only Jordan and Libya have ratified the Tokyo convention. Nor has Cuba, for many years a target of hijackers, ratified any of these three instruments, although it has of late taken measures, in cooperation with the United States, to suppress hijacking.

Efforts taken by ICAO in August and September 1973 to strengthen measures against hijackers and nations affording them safe haven have failed; largely because of Arab opposition, the necessary two-thirds vote could not be mustered even for relatively mild proposals.[9]

Occasional threats by the International Federation of Air Line Pilots to boycott safe-haven countries have not been made effective, nor have the giant airlines that carry the bulk of passengers come forward with a boycott. It would appear, therefore, that little further progress can be made on this issue unless there is a major shift of policy in safe-haven states. An even more serious threat to civil aviation might, of course, provoke stronger reactions by pilots, airlines, or governments, but such an increased threat is hardly to be desired.

In sum, the ICAO conventions, while affording some measure of security to international civil aviation, leave significant safe havens for hijackers, and there is no convention in force that deals comprehensively with the protection of human lives from international terrorism.

CONSIDERATION OF INTERNATIONAL
TERRORISM BY THE UN GENERAL
ASSEMBLY, 1972-73

Two weeks before the opening of the 27th session of the UN General Assembly in September 1972, the subject of international terrorism was thrust upon the consciousness of the world community by the murder of 11 Israeli athletes at the Olympic Village in Munich. A host of other terrorist acts had underscored the increasing threat of terrorism. During 1972 alone, acts of terrorism were committed against 30 airlines of 14 countries, killing 140 people and wounding 99. In the preceding few years, 27 diplomats from 11 countries had been kidnapped, and three had been killed. And a new form of terrorism—letter-bombs—was just being unleashed.[10] In the last six months of 1973 alone, the casualty toll from terrorism outside the homeland of the terrorist rose to 268 dead and 571 wounded.[11]

Shocked by the Munich massacre, UN Secretary General Kurt Waldheim decided that the United Nations could not remain a mute spectator to the acts of terrorism plaguing the world. He consulted first with certain middle powers in the hope that they would propose an item for the agenda. That failing, on September 8 he took the unusual and courageous step of proposing the item himself, as an "urgent and important" matter. He was well aware of the opposition his proposal would encounter from the 18 Arab states, which have a strategic position in the Afro-Asian bloc, which in turn includes a majority of the votes in the Assembly. Yet he felt that, given the state of world opinion, it would be better to take the risk of failure than not to try at all.

The item proposed by the secretary general, "Measures to prevent terrorism and other forms of violence which endanger or take human lives or jeopardize fundamental freedoms," cleared its first hurdle, the General Committee, without serious change. By a vote of 15 in favor, 7 against, and 2 abstentions, the General Committee recommended to the General Assembly that the item be inscribed on the agenda. But the fact that the seven negative votes were all African and Asian, along with the arguments advanced by the opponents, portended trouble in the full Assembly.

The main thrust of the opposition in the General Committee was the argument that the inclusion of this item "would constitute yet another attempt to classify the legitimate struggle of peoples under the yoke of colonialism and alien domination as 'terrorism.'" This position, advocated in the General Committee by Libya, Mauritania, and Syria and supported by Guinea, Mauritius, and China was a continuation of the clever and effective Arab tactic of linking the Palestinian cause to the struggle of the black African peoples for independence; it undoubtedly had an impact on many African and Asian delegations. It was also argued that "state terrorism" (suppression of colonial peoples by force) was far more noxious and costly in lives than acts by individuals and guerrilla groups. (The fact that the United Nations had repeatedly taken a stand against colonial repression appeared to have little impact on these opponents.) Further, it was argued that the underlying causes of violence and terrorism were misery, frustration, grievance, and despair; consequently, the only way to deal with terrorism was to deal with these underlying causes.

This last argument took the form of an amendment when the General Assembly considered inscription. Proposed by Saudi Arabia, the amendment adopted by the Assembly added the following to the title of the item: "and study of the underlying causes of those forms of terrorism and acts of violence which lie in misery, frustration, grievance and despair and which cause some people to sacrifice human lives, including their own, in an attempt to effect radical changes." Thus amended, the item was adopted by the Assembly and referred to its Sixth (legal) Committee for consideration.

While no one would deny that the international community must be concerned with causes, the amendment raised a real danger that the net result would be a failure to condemn or take action against terrorism. This danger was signaled in the document prepared by the Secretariat for the Sixth Committee:

> The effort to eliminate those causes should be intense and continuous, as mankind, despite its intellectual powers, has not yet succeeded in creating a social order free from misery, frustration, grievance and despair—in short, an order which will not cause or provoke violence. Yet terrorism threatens, endangers or destroys the lives and fundamental freedoms of the innocent, and it would not be just to leave them to wait for protection until the causes have been remedied and the purposes and principles of the Charter have been given full effect. There is a present need for measures of international co-operation to protect their rights as far as possible. At all times in history, mankind has recognized the unavoidable necessity of repressing some forms of violence which otherwise would threaten the very existence of society as

well as that of man himself. There are some means
of using force, as in every form of human conflict,
which must not be used, even when the use of force
is legally and morally justified, and regardless of the
status of the perpetrator.[12]

Erik Suy, chairman of the Sixth Committee at the 27th session
of the General Assembly and later legal counsel of the United Nations,
made the following observation at a colloquium in March 1973:

But in reality, a simultaneous study of "causes" and
"measures" is a condition impossible to sustain. One
of the most frequent manifestations of acts of violence
is air piracy; yet, measures have been found without
studying the causes. Further, the Commission on International Law has prepared a draft convention on the
protection of diplomats without having first elucidated
the reasons for the acts of violence directed against
them. The demand to consider the question en bloc
was in reality nothing more than a maneuver designed
to reduce terrorism to a simply political question and
to prevent concrete measures from being adopted.[13]

In fact, the majority in the Sixth Committee thrust aside all efforts to condemn terrorism or to take any action against it.

The first concrete proposal was a draft resolution and convention
submitted by the United States, carefully drafted so as to omit any
constraints on wars of national liberation. Secretary of State William
Rogers launched the U.S. proposals in his statement to the General
Assembly on September 25, 1972, referring to the need for "a new
treaty on the export of international terrorism." The draft convention, circulated the same day, dealt only with the most serious criminal threats (unlawful killing, serious bodily harm, and kidnapping)
and only under the following conditions:

1. The act must be committed or take effect outside the territory of a state of which the alleged offender is a national.
2. The act must be committed or take effect outside the territory of the state against which the act is directed.
3. The act must not be committed either by or against a member
of the armed forces of a state in the course of military hostilities.

Thus, the proposed draft convention would clearly not affect the
efforts of African peoples fighting or struggling for independence, nor
would it affect Arab attacks in or against the State of Israel.

Nevertheless, the leaders of the Afro-Asian bloc, with the Arab states carrying on an intensive lobbying campaign, opposed the U.S. draft. The African and Asian states have no major world airlines, few pilots, and relatively few air passengers; hence, the problem of hijacking was not a matter of much direct concern to them. By comparison, the Africans, in particular, were actively interested in the fight against colonialism and apartheid. Since they felt that the United States and other Western powers showed little real concern over those issues, many were not disposed to be accommodating on terrorism. Also, the Arabs, with obvious reference to Vietnam, argued that terrorism by bombing was far worse than the acts of terrorism envisaged in the U.S. draft.

A number of other factors hampered the U.S. effort. First, the draft was introduced by the United States alone. Second, it was presented in a complete form only days after the item had been inscribed and months before the Sixth Committee began discussions, a factor that provoked resentment even among the European friends of the United States. Third, U.S. lobbying at the United Nations and approaches in capitals in the fall of 1972 had as their prime objective the reduction of the assessed U.S. share of the UN budget from 31.5 to 25 percent, an effort that succeeded. While congressional pressure for the reduction made this priority virtually inevitable, the choice did somewhat weaken the amount of effort and influence that could be brought to bear on the issue of international terrorism. Finally, the Arab delegations had their own instruments of influence and pressure, which they used; for example, the Cambodian delegation, faced with a threat to the recognition of its credentials, had little real choice on the terrorism issue.

Conscious that its proposal would not succeed, the United States decided not to press it to a vote in the Sixth Committee. Instead, it supported a compromise proposal (Doc. A/C.6/L.879) sponsored by Australia, Austria, Belgium, Canada, Costa Rica, Guatemala, Honduras, Iran, Japan, Luxembourg, New Zealand, Nicaragua, and the United Kingdom. The sponsor group, while numerous, failed to include any African countries (and the Africans have about one-third of the votes) and had only one Asian developing country—Iran. This situation was not an oversight; it reflected the factors described above.

The draft resolution represented a twofold compromise. First, it slowed down the timetable of the U.S. draft, which called for a conference of plenipotentiaries in 1973 to draft a convention. Instead, a three-stage process was proposed:

1. The Assembly would ask the ILC to draft a convention.
2. This draft would be submitted to the Assembly in the fall of 1973.

3. A special conference would then be convened "as soon as practicable" to adopt a convention.

The second compromise feature was a provision for the president of the General Assembly to appoint an ad hoc committee to study the underlying causes of terrorism.

Shortly after the 14-power draft resolution was submitted, another draft was introduced that reflected the interests and concerns of the Arabs and their black African supporters. Incidental critical references to violence were balanced by a strong affirmation of "the inalienable right to self-determination," support of the "legitimacy" of the national liberation "struggle," and condemnation of "repressive and terrorist acts by colonial, racist, and alien regimes." The draft advanced no concrete proposal for international action to combat terrorism; instead, it merely established a 40-member committee (later, in plenary, changed to a 35-member committee), appointed by the Assembly president, which would study both the underlying causes of terrorism and "proposals" submitted by various countries "for finding an effective solution to the problem." The next session of the Assembly would be given a report by the ad hoc committee.

The new draft was sponsored by 16 powers—Afghanistan, Algeria, Cameroon, Chad, the Congo, Equatorial Guinea, Guinea, Guyana, India, Kenya, Madagascar, Mali, Mauritania, the Sudan, Yugoslavia, and Zambia. Most were African states. The non-African states were ones traditionally linked with Third World aspirations.

Normally, since it was introduced before the 16-power draft, the 14-power Western draft would have been voted on first. But, as the committee is its own parliamentary master, it voted 76 to 43 with 7 abstentions to grant priority to the Afro-Asian draft. That draft was then adopted by a vote of 76 to 34 with 16 abstentions. Had the 14-power resolution been voted upon first, it might very well have received the support of the Soviet Union, since its representative endorsed the idea of the ILC's drafting an international treaty combating terrorism. It is even conceivable that the 14-power draft might have won a majority, but the bloc pattern of voting prevented a test by ballot.

The General Assembly, on December 18, 1972, approved this draft resolution by a similarly lopsided vote, and it became GA Resolution 3034 (XXVII). Under paragraph 9 of the resolution, the president of the General Assembly, after appropriate consultation, appointed the following 35 states to the Ad Hoc Committee on International Terrorism: Algeria, Austria, Barbados, Canada, the Congo, Czechoslovakia, Democratic Yemen, France, Greece, Guinea, Haiti, Hungary, India, Iran, Italy, Japan, Mauritania, Nicaragua, Nigeria, Panama, Sweden, the Syrian Arab Republic, Tunisia, Turkey, the

Ukrainian Soviet Socialist Republic, the Soviet Union, the United Kingdom of Great Britain and Northern Ireland, the United Republic of
Tanzania, the United States, Uruguay, Venezuela, Yemen, Yugoslavia,
Zaire, and Zambia. (Thus, of the 35 members, six were Arab states,
whose combined population represents less than 3 percent of the world's
population.)

Under paragraph 8, the General Assembly requested the secretary general to transmit an analytical study of the observations of
states submitted under paragraph 7 of the same resolution. This was
done in Document A/AC./60/2 of June 22, 1973, which was provided
to the ad hoc committee.

The overwhelming majority of the states that submitted written
observations expressed concern over and opposition to acts of international terrorism; these encompassed all the major economic powers,
including the Soviet Union, which, however, expressed the following
reservation: "It is unacceptable to give a broad interpretation to the
term international terrorism and to extend it to cover national liberation movements, acts committed in resisting an aggressor in territories occupied by the latter and action by workers to secure their
rights against the yoke of exploiters." Interestingly, this reservation
would be fully consistent with the provisions of the U.S. draft convention, tending to substantiate other indications that the Soviets might
have eventually gone along with something like the U.S. draft had the
Afro-Asian group, spearheaded by the Algerians, not blocked a vote
on the 14-power proposal in the Sixth Committee.

Of the 34 written replies, only two—those of Syria and Yemen—
took positions that would constitute a serious obstacle to a workable
convention on terrorism. Syria stated that "official terrorism . . .
contains the most drastic form of savagery and barbarism and the
greatest dangers threatening the security and safety of peoples. Any
consideration that evades coming face to face with terrorism practiced
by the State, as the real source of violence, blackmail, domination
and illegitimate exploitation, would defeat the very purposes and objectives of the Charter it intends to defend." While it is true that violent
acts by states cause far more suffering and loss of life than terrorism
by individuals or groups, the fact is that such state actions against
peoples of other states are already dealt with in the charter, notably
in chapter 7, while terrorism by individuals or groups is not. Also,
as pointed out by a number of representatives to the ad hoc committee,
the Declaration on Friendly Relations amply covered interstate violence, and acts committed by armed forces during military operations
were already the subject of extensive treaty law and were being considered in the context of the protection of human rights in armed conflicts.

Discussion in the ad hoc committee, which met from July 23 to August 11, 1973, substantially reflected the same fundamental divisions that had become apparent in the Sixth Committee discussion in the fall of 1972. First, there was the issue of "state terrorism," as outlined above. Second, there was the argument that, "since the acts of violence described as acts of terrorism were in fact merely the logical outcome of certain situations, it would be a serious mistake, and one fraught with consequences, to seek to eliminate such acts by means of punitive measures before having clearly identified the causes from which they sprang." Other representatives, while acknowledging that analysis of the causes should not be sacrificed to the devising of preventive and punitive measures, observed that the study of the political or socioeconomic causes of international terrorism would necessarily take much time and that the adoption of the necessary protective measures could not be postponed pending completion of that study. In this connection, it was noted that in their domestic legislation, states did not wait for the underlying causes of crime to be identified before enacting penal laws.[14]

The committee members were also divided as to what measures should be taken to deal with the problem. Some representatives emphasized the need for each state to initially take action at the national level. Others stressed the desirability of bilateral agreements, in particular on the subject of extradition.

A number of representatives expressed support for the preparation of multilateral treaty provisions. They stressed the principle that States parties be obliged either to proceed to extradite the alleged offender or to bring him before the competent authorities for the purpose of judicial proceedings (as in the U.S. draft). Some expressed the view, however, that it would be better to draw up several conventions, each dealing with a specific category of acts of terrorism (for example, the taking of hostages or the use of letter-bombs) rather than attempt to draw up a general convention on the subject.

At its meeting on July 31, the ad hoc committee set up three subcommittees of the whole dealing, respectively, with the definition, the underlying causes, and measures for the prevention of international terrorism. In the first subcommittee it soon became evident that there was substantial disagreement as to whether or not a definition was either necessary or desirable. In the second there was a rerun of the debate as to whether measures could be undertaken to restrain terrorism parallel with efforts to deal with underlying causes or whether elimination of the causes must precede such measures. Again, no consensus or compromise was reached.

This same conflict was repeated in the third subcommittee. In addition, there were differences as to whether to aim for a general convention on terrorism or a series of conventions, each related to a specific type of act—for example, the taking of hostages for political extortion, the kidnapping of diplomats, or the sending of letter-bombs. There was also a dispute on whether such conventions should cover state terrorism.[15]

With no consensus or compromise emerging from any of the subcommittees, it is not surprising that the committee's report to the General Assembly was little more than a summary of the divergent views expressed. The draft proposals and suggestions submitted to the various subcommittees are reproduced in the annex to the report. In general, they reflect the divergences described above; however, certain individual state proposals warrant special attention.[16]

For example, the following submission of Nigeria shows that at least one major African country—the largest—has a serious concern with international terrorism:

> The Nigerian delegation is of the opinion that acts
> such as the recent Portuguese massacre, the kid-
> napping of diplomats attending a cocktail party and
> their subsequent murder, hijacking of aircrafts or
> even holding at bay innocent tourists in a hotel lobby
> with the muzzles of sub-machine guns pointing at
> them all constitute some forms of international ter-
> rorism. These acts do not include the activities,
> within their own countries, of those peoples strug-
> gling to liberate themselves from foreign oppression
> and exploitation.

Nigeria also expressed a willingness to consider the U.S. and British proposals as a basis for negotiation, offering reasonable suggestions for modification.

Among the Asian delegations on the committee, Iran was noteworthy for its efforts to achieve a compromise, based on a reference to state terrorism as well as that of individuals and groups. Also, there were indications that Yugoslavia would be interested in constructive action, as it demonstrated at the 28th session, when the Convention on the Prevention and Punishment of Crimes Against Internationally Protected Persons was considered.

In the present world political atmosphere it is doubtful that any of these three important members of the Third World could or would take the lead in the General Assembly toward additional measures against terrorism. Naturally, this forecast could change radically if a settlement is reached on the Palestinians and, as now appears likely, Guinea Bissau, Angola, and Mozambique achieve independence from Portugal.

At its 28th session, in 1973, the General Assembly did not consider the item or the ad hoc committee's report for "lack of time," and it was deferred to the 29th session in 1974. There is no reason to believe that any serious effort will be made at the 29th session.

CONVENTION ON THE PREVENTION AND PUNISHMENT OF CRIMES AGAINST INTERNATIONALLY PROTECTED PERSONS

In contrast with the failure of the General Assembly to deal effectively with the general question of international terrorism at its 27th session, it did succeed at its 28th session in adopting a Convention on the Prevention and Punishment of Crimes Against Internationally Protected Persons Including Diplomatic Agents (Resolution 3166 [XXVIII] of December 14, 1973). Moreover, the adoption in both the Sixth Committee and the Assembly was by consensus.

In view of the numerous similarities between provisions of this convention and the draft convention on terrorism proposed by the United States, it is useful to analyze the reasons why one succeeded and the other failed. This analysis will take the form of examining the history of the 1973 convention, including the steps leading to its preparation and adoption; similarities and differences between that convention and the U.S. proposal; and whether lessons of substance, procedure, and tactics learned from the successful enterprise might usefully be applied to future efforts to negotiate conventions in this area.

The origins of the concern of the ILC with the protection of diplomatic agents is summarized succinctly in two paragraphs of the commission's 1972 report:

> At its twenty-second session, in 1970, the Commission received from the President of the Security Council a letter dated 14 May 1970 transmitting a copy of document S/9789 which reproduced the text of a letter addressed to him by the representative of the Netherlands to the United Nations concerning the need for action to ensure the protection and inviolability of diplomatic agents in view of the increasing number of attacks on them. The Chairman of the Commission replied to the foregoing communication by a letter dated 12 June 1970 which referred to the Commission's past work in this area and stated the Commission would continue to be concerned with the matter.

  At the twenty-third session of the Commission, in
1971, in connection with the adoption of the Commission's agenda, the suggestion was made by Mr. Kearney
(U.S.) that the Commission should consider whether
it would be possible to produce draft articles regarding such crimes as the murder, kidnapping and assaults upon diplomats and other persons entitled to
special protection under international law. The Commission recognized both the importance and the urgency of the matter, but deferred its decision in view
of the priority that had to be given to the completion
of the draft articles on the representation of States
in their relations with international organizations. In
the course of the session it became apparent that there
would not be sufficient time to deal with any additional
subject. In considering its programme of work for
1972, however, the Commission reached the decision
that, if the General Assembly requested it to do so,
it would prepare at its 1972 session a set of draft articles on this important subject with the view to submitting such articles to the twenty-seventh session of
the General Assembly.[17]

Omitted from the above summary is the political and shock effect
produced by the murder of the Yugoslav ambassador in Stockholm on
April 7, 1971, shortly before the commission met. Thus, the strong
interest and motivation of a leading state member of the Third World
was added to the earlier Western concern. At its fall session that
year, the General Assembly adopted Resolution 2780 (XXVI) of December 3, 1971, requesting

  (a) the Secretary General to invite comments from
Member States before 1 April 1972 on the question
of the protection of diplomats and to transmit them
to the International Law Commission at its twenty-fourth session; and (b) the Commission to study as
soon as possible, in the light of the comments of
Member States, the question of the protection and
inviolability of diplomatic agents and other persons
entitled to special protection under international
law, with a view to preparing a set of draft articles
dealing with offences committed against diplomats
and other persons entitled to special protection under international law for submission to the General
Assembly at the earliest date which the Commission
would consider appropriate.

The comments of 26 member states, including a working paper submitted by Denmark, [18] were provided to the ILC at its 24th session, along with a working paper produced by Uruguay and one by Richard Kearney, U.S. member of the ILC. Some ILC members wanted to extend the concern of the convention beyond "specially protected persons" to provide some means of protection against terrorist acts in general. The majority, however, expressed the view that the question of the scope of draft articles on the subject had been determined by Resolution 2780 (XXVI) of the General Assembly. The commission functioned accordingly, producing agreed draft articles on the prevention and punishment of crimes against diplomatic agents and other internationally protected persons. (It finished its work two months before the murder of the 11 Israeli athletes at Munich.)

At the 27th session of the General Assembly, the ILC draft was discussed extensively, and there were still many delegations that had doubts about the wisdom of negotiating a new convention on the subject. Some stressed that existing instruments, notably the Vienna conventions on diplomatic and consular relations and the convention on special missions, gave substantial coverage; draft articles on the representation of states in their relations with international organizations were in an advanced state of preparation; and the ILC was engaged in the elaboration of articles on state responsibility. Some also questioned whether it was wise to protect one group of persons without protecting other victims of international terrorism. Others argued that strict application of existing conventions was the real need rather than a new convention. Finally, there was the same argument that had been raised against the proposal for a convention on international terrorism (considered under another item at the same session); that is, that the right answer was to eliminate the causes of such violent acts.

There was also disagreement over whether a new convention should be treated as an urgent matter and whether negotiations should take place at a special conference or in the Sixth Committee. [19]

Despite these differences over desirability, substance, urgency, and procedures, the General Assembly adopted Resolution (XXVII), in which it decided to include in the provisional agenda of its 28th session an item entitled "draft convention on the prevention and punishment of crimes against diplomatic agents and other internationally protected persons with a view to the final elaboration of such a convention by the General Assembly" (paragraph 3). Meanwhile, states, the specialized agencies, and other interested organizations were invited to submit comments and observations to the secretary general, who would in turn circulate them to member states.

At the 28th session, the Sixth Committee, acting as a negotiating conference, succeeded in negotiating a convention that the General

Assembly adopted by consensus—a notable achievement, considering the many different views expressed during the 27th session and in marked contrast to its failure to act on international terrorism.

A comparison of the convention, adopted in Resolution 3166 (XXVIII), on internationally protected persons and the proposed U.S. draft on international terrorism shows that they are largely parallel; the obvious difference is that the scope of the former, in terms of the acts covered, is wider. Both cite as crimes murder, kidnapping; or other bodily harm, as well as attempts to commit such acts or serving as accomplices. The convention further covers violent attacks "upon the official premises, the private accommodation or the means of transport of an internationally protected person likely to endanger his person or liberty" and threats or attempts to commit such attacks or serving as an accomplice to them (convention Article 2 [1], U.S. draft Article 1).

Both call upon each State party to make the crimes cited punishable by appropriate penalties (convention Article 2 [2], U.S. draft Article 2).

Both call upon each State party to take such measures as may be necessary to establish its jurisdiction (convention Article 3, U.S. draft Article 4).

Both call upon each State party on whose territory the act has been committed, if it has reason to believe an alleged offender has fled from its territory, to communicate to other States all pertinent facts regarding the offense committed and all available information regarding the identity of the alleged offender (convention Article 5, U.S. draft Article 5).

Both call upon the State party in whose territory the alleged offender is present to take appropriate measures under its internal law to insure his presence for prosecution or extradition (convention Article 6, U.S. draft Article 6).

Both provide for extradition or, as an alternative, prosecution in accordance with internal law (convention Articles 7 and 8, U.S. draft Article 7). Thus, both seek to deny safe haven to offenders.

Both call for guarantees of "fair treatment at all stages of the proceedings" (convention Cert. 9, U.S. draft Article 8).

Both call on States parties to afford one another the greatest measure of assistance in connection with criminal proceedings (convention Article 10, U.S. draft Article 2).

Significant differences between the two instruments, other than the fact that the convention covers a wider range of acts against a narrower range of persons, are as follows:

1. Article 12 of the convention stipulates that its provisions "shall not affect the application of the Treaties on Asylum, in force at the date of the adoption of this Convention, as between the States,

which are parties to those Treaties; but a State Party to this Convention may not invoke those Treaties with respect to another State Party to this Convention which is not a party to those Treaties."

This article was introduced as an amendment by Bolivia during the Sixth Committee consideration of the draft convention prepared by the ILC and supported by the Latin Americans in general. (It was adopted by a vote of 50 to 0 with 52 abstentions.) Presumably, given the strong tradition on asylum among Latin Americans, a similar amendment would be introduced with respect to any future conventions in this area (there is a provision on asylum in the OAS Convention of 1971).

2. The U.S. draft (Article 16) provides for the establishment of a three-member Conciliation Commission to deal with disputes between States parties over the interpretation of any of its provisions, with decisions or recommendations to be made by a majority vote. The commission may ask "any organ that is authorized by or in accordance with the Charter of the United Nations to request an advisory opinion from the International Court of Justice to make such a request regarding the interpretation or application of the present articles."

Article 13 of the convention provides that

> 1) Any dispute between two or more States Parties concerning the interpretation or application of this Convention which is not settled by negotiation shall, at the request of one of them, be submitted to arbitration. If within six months from the date of the request for arbitration the parties are unable to agree on the organization of the arbitration, any one of those parties may refer the dispute to the International Court of Justice by request in conformity with the Statute of the Court.
>
> 2) Each State Party may at the time of signature or ratification of this Convention or accession thereto declare that it does not consider itself bound by paragraph 1 of this article. The other States Parties shall not be bound by paragraph 1 of this article with respect to any State Party which has made such a reservation.

It should be noted that the Warsaw Pact countries, which were among the first to sign the convention, have all attached a reservation to Article 13, paragraph 1, indicating their position that a dispute may be submitted to the International Court of Justice for arbitration only with the consent of all States parties to the dispute.[20]

3. On November 15, 1973, a group of 34 African countries in-troduced an amendment to add the following article to the convention: "No provision of the present articles shall be applicable to peoples struggling against colonialism, alien domination, foreign occupation, racial discrimination and <u>apartheid</u> in the exercise of their legitimate rights to self-determination and independence" (GAOR, Doc.A/9407, p. 50).

After extensive consultations by the chairman of the Sixth Com-mittee and negotiations in the Drafting Committee, a compromise pro-posal was submitted on December 6 by the chairman of the Drafting Committee on its behalf. With one minor change, it was adopted that same day by the Sixth Committee and on December 14 by the General Assembly.

The compromise provided for the simultaneous adoption by the Sixth Committee of a resolution and the convention. Also, paragraph 6 of the resolution (GA R. 3166 [XXVIII]) stipulates that "the present resolution, whose provisions are related to the annexed Convention, shall always be published together with it."

The key paragraph of the resolution, on the basis of which 37 Afro-Asian sponsors agreed not to press their amendment to the con-vention itself, reads as follows:

> [The General Assembly] <u>recognizes also</u> that the provisions of the annexed Convention could not in any way prejudice the exercise of the legitimate right to self-determination and independence, in accordance with the purposes and principles of the Charter of the United Nations and the Declaration on Principles of In-ternational Law concerning Friendly Relations and Co-operation among States in accordance with the Charter of the United Nations, by peoples struggling against colonialism, alien domination, foreign oc-cupation, racial discrimination and <u>apartheid.</u>

Obviously, this paragraph could be used by a State party so in-clined to justify exceptions to the provisions of the convention. Yet it is less noxious in this form than if it were in the convention itself, as proposed in the amendment, and evidently those who negotiated the compromise considered it essential to the achievement of consensus. Moreover, if the 37 states and their sympathizers had been outvoted, this fact might have caused a large number of states not to ratify the convention. It would appear better to aim for universal ratification and take the risk of exceptions rather than have a large part of the world not bound at all.

In addition to this compromise, what other factors contributed to the successful negotiation of this convention as contrasted to the failure on terrorism?

First, the scope was limited to "internationally protected persons"; this includes a class of people—diplomats—for whose protection states have traditionally assumed special responsibilities, many of which are the subject of numerous existing conventions.[21]

As the second preambular paragraph of the convention states, "crimes against diplomatic agents and other diplomatically protected persons jeopardizing the safety of those persons create a serious threat to the maintenance of normal international relations which are necessary for co-operation among States." It should also be noted that those negotiating the convention were members of the class to be protected and were well aware of numerous attacks on diplomats in the recent past.

Second, there was the shock caused by the murder of the Yugoslav ambassador to Stockholm on April 7, 1971. Had a South African instead of a Yugoslav ambassador been murdered, there is at least some question as to whether the draft convention for the protection of diplomats would have received the same impetus toward completion. Similarly, if the 11 Olympic athletes murdered at Munich in September 1972 had been African or Arab, the reaction of the Afro-Asian group to a proposed convention on terrorism would certainly have been less antagonistic. To state this, it is not necessary to conclude that a United Nations so strongly influenced by bloc politics is "morally bankrupt," as William Korey does.[22]

All political institutions are responsive to political forces, and an organization composed of sovereign states cannot move against the strong opposition of a substantial group of them. It is therefore more realistic to assess the organization as it is and, in that light, make the best feasible use of it. There is always the danger that a group with a built-in majority will ram through resolutions without a serious attempt to negotiate a consensus, but such resolutions are in general nugatory and of little use to the majority.[23] Thus, such political forces can be more successful at blocking action through the United Nations than achieving it. The chief restraint on such a built-in majority is the realization that such frustration of other members, particularly the rich and powerful ones, will give them further incentive for conducting their serious business outside the United Nations. Playing a game of mutual frustration will not help either side, the United Nations, its states members, or the world's people.

Third, the subject of the prevention and punishment of crimes against internationally protected persons is more precise in definition and less politically and emotionally loaded than the term "international terrorism." While the latter makes good copy for the media, it is bound to be a handicap in negotiating a legal instrument with African and Arab countries in the present political climate, where one side's "terrorists" are the other side's "freedom fighters." It would appear prudent, therefore, to concentrate on criminal actions rather than the labels of those who commit them.

In this connection, the Yugoslav letter of May 5, 1972 on the subject of internationally protected persons is of great interest.[24] Paragraph 2 of that letter states: "Grave offenses and serious crimes should not be treated as political criminal acts even in those cases where motivations for committing such acts are of a political nature." Paragraph 8 states: "If the perpetrators of criminal acts belong to an organization which instigates, organizes, assists or participates in the execution of those criminal acts, each State is obliged, in addition to punishing the culprits, to undertake effective measures and to dissolve such an organization." If the concepts expressed in those two sentences could be incorporated into a convention for the protection of all innocent civilians outside an area of conflict, a substantial step could be taken to prevent or punish those actions commonly called "international terrorism." The convention could thus be conceived in terms of international criminal or humanitarian law.

In summary, those planning future efforts toward conventions designed to curb terrorism might profit by a study of the following factors involved in the negotiation of the successful convention:

1. Early efforts should be made to enlist the support of one or more Third World countries of stature; this might involve compromises on both timing and text, particularly on references to the right to struggle for self-determination and independence. Such efforts must be made before a draft is introduced.

2. It might be better to draft the convention in terms of international criminal and humanitarian law rather than use the emotionally loaded term "terrorism." As Thomas M. Franck and Bert B. Lockwood commented, "terrorism is an historically misleading and politically loaded term which invites conceptual and ideological dissonance."[25]

3. The ILC, which combines professionalism and expertise with broad political representation, should be considered as a vehicle for developing the draft articles.

There should, of course, be no illusion that any combination of tactics will succeed if the international political atmosphere is fundamentally unfavorable. Even when conventions are completed, as in the case of the three ICAO instruments, the failure of a significant number of Arab states to ratify or comply with their provisions makes safe havens readily available. Progress toward solution or alleviation of the Palestinian problem would not only pave the way for additional and more effective international instruments but would, as the Arabs and many Africans argued during consideration of the question, eliminate many acts of terrorism by eliminating the causes.

As the foregoing indicates, dealing with the causes of much terrorism—misery, frustration, and repression—must be a crucial factor in eliminating or substantially reducing such acts. But given the present international situation and the dismal record of human history, what approaches to additional international instruments might be useful?

Here one is again drawn to the Yugoslav logic: "Grave offenses and serious crimes should not be treated as political acts even in those cases where motivations for committing such acts are of a political nature."[26] Next efforts, therefore, might be directed to offenses so grave and crimes so serious that all states, or at least the preponderant majority of states, are prepared to legislate against such acts. Logical candidates for international instruments might be:

1. a convention to prevent the export of violence to countries not parties to a conflict (This might, in substance, be similar to the U.S. draft on terrorism, but a new effort might have a better chance of success by avoiding use of that term; enlisting Third World sponsorship, with appropriate modifications to accommodate their views; and working on a less hurried timetable, thus allowing for drafting by the ILC and a certain cooling-off period after the emotions generated in the fall of 1972.)

2. a convention against the dispatch, through the international postal service, of letter-bombs and other explosive devices

3. a convention against the taking of child hostages or other violent acts against children

The foregoing are illustrative and are by no means exhaustive. In any such moves, the politically loaded term "terrorism" should be avoided, leaving it to polemics and the media. Further, as Franck and Lockwood argue, governments and individuals should be equally enjoined from carrying out such actions.[27]

Of obviously great importance is further action against threats to civil aviation. Such action must include efforts for change in countries that have not ratified and do not apply the three existing ICAO conventions. As long as almost a score of Arab countries afford safe haven to hijackers and other violators of civil air safety and hold an oil weapon over Western Europe and Japan, the acts prohibited in those conventions will continue to jeopardize, maim, and kill international air travelers.

Some amelioration is possible even outside the conventions, as shown by the effectiveness of U.S.-Cuban bilateral agreements against hijacking and other threats to civil aviation. Unfortunately, the Cuban example has not spread to the uncooperative among the Arab countries, nor is such a spread likely unless there is progress toward solving the Palestinian problem.

Many have advocated a convention providing for the suspension of all air service to countries that fail to punish or extradite hijackers or saboteurs of aircraft. But the failure of efforts at the ICAO in August-September 1973 to strengthen measures against hijackers and states affording them safe haven make one pessimistic about efforts toward additional conventions. It was simply not possible to get a convention that bound those who needed to be bound.

With current prospects so dim for any further civil aviation conventions, it may be that international lawyers and scholars can work at perfecting drafts on a stand-by basis, waiting for a new situation to evolve out of events, the passage of time, and the workings of diplomacy. Meanwhile, the problem can be alleviated by continued cooperative efforts by nations interested in the enforcement of the existing ICAO conventions, with particular emphasis on preventive measures.

One area in which scholarly and legal planning might be useful is the prevention of nuclear blackmail. Restraint on states was dealt with in the 1968 treaty banning the proliferation of nuclear weapons beyond the five states that then possessed them. (Although a number of important threshold states have not ratified the treaty and India has conducted a nuclear test, no state outside the "nuclear club" of five has to date declared that it would produce nuclear weapons.) With the use of nuclear energy certain to expand greatly, the possibility of nuclear materials falling into the hands of individual or group terrorists cannot be excluded. Certainly a crucial element in negotiating treaties to ban the positioning of weapons of mass destruction from outer space and the seabeds was the fact that no state had yet taken such actions; consequently, it was not a hot political issue. For similar reasons it might be well to plan for an instrument to prevent nuclear blackmail before any case develops that would arouse strong political and emotional overtones.

NOTES

1. United Nations, General Assembly, Summary Records (A/C.6/418), November 2, 1972, pp. 10-16.

2. Ibid., pp. 22-23. The text of the Convention for the Prevention and Punishment of Terrorism is in Annex I of the same document.

3. Thomas M. Franck and Bert B. Lockwood, "Preliminary Thoughts Towards an International Convention on Terrorism," American Journal of International Law, January 1974, p. 70.

4. United Nations, General Assembly, Report of the International Law Commission on the Work of Its Sixth Session, Suppl. 2 (A/2693).

5. United Nations, General Assembly, Report of the Special Committee on the Question of Defining Aggression, Suppl. 19 (A/9619).

6. OAS/Official Documents; CP/Doc. 19/70 Res. 1, Corr. 1 and AG/Res. 4 (1/70) Res. 1.

7. United Nations, Secretariat, Treaty Series, No. 37 OAS/Ser. A/17. OAS/Official Documents.

8. Summary Records (A/C 6/418), op. cit., p. 39.

9. Franck and Lockwood, op. cit., pp. 70-71.

10. William Korey, "Moral Bankruptcy at the UN," Midstream, February 1973.

11. The Interdependent, March 1974, p. 1.

12. Summary Records (A/C 6/418), op. cit., p. 41.

13. Reflexions sur la Definition et la Repression du Terrorisme (Brussels: Editions de l'Universite de Bruxelles, 1974), pp. 194-96.

14. United Nations, General Assembly, Report of the Ad Hoc Committee on International Terrorism, Suppl. 28 (A/9028), p. 6.

15. Ibid. For a legal analysis of the divergences on key points, see Franck and Lockwood, op. cit., pp. 72-82, and Reflexions sur la Definition et la Repression du Terrorisme, op. cit., pp. 105-97.

16. Report of the Ad Hoc Committee on International Terrorism, op. cit.

17. United Nations, General Assembly, Report of the International Law Commission on the Work of Its 24th Session (A/8710/Res. 1), 1972, p. 88, paragraphs 54 and 55.

18. Ibid., pp. 108-24.

19. United Nations, General Assembly, Report of the Sixth Committee on Agenda Item 85 (A/8892), November 21, 1972, pp. 41-72.

20. Statements submitted by the German Democratic Republic, Poland, the Soviet Union, Byelorussia, the Ukraine, and Bulgaria on signing the convention in May and June 1974.

21. See list in Report of the International Law Commission on the Work of Its 24th Session, op. cit., p. 108.

22. Korey, op. cit.

23. See Seymour M. Finger, "A New Approach to Colonial Problems at the U.N.," International Organization 26, no. 1: 143-53.

24. Report of the International Law Commission on the Work of Its 24th Session, op. cit., p. 124.

25. Franck and Lockwood, op. cit., p. 89.

26. Note also the following paragraph on hijacking, which was worked out at the 1971 session of the Institute of International Law at Zagreb, as quoted in Verzyl, International Law in Historical Perspective (Leyden: SIJTHOF, 1972), vol. 5, p. 309:

> No purpose or objective, whether political or other, can constitute justification for such illegal acts; and . . . every State in whose territory the authors of such acts may be found has the right and the obligation, if it does not extradite such persons, to undertake criminal prosecution against them.

27. Franck and Lockwood, op. cit., p. 90.

BOOKS

Adamic, Louis. Dynamite: The Story of Class Violence in America. New York: Viking Press, 1934.

Adelson, Alan. SDS: A Profile. New York: Charles Scribner's Sons, 1972.

Alexander, Yonah. The Role of Communications in the Middle East Conflict: Ideological and Religious Aspects. New York: Praeger Publishers, 1973.

Alexander, Yonah, and Nicholas N. Kittrie, eds. Crescent and Star: Arab-Israeli Perspectives on the Middle East Conflict. New York: AMS Press, 1972.

Allon, Yigal. Shield of David. New York: Random House, 1970.

Alves, Marcio Moreira. A Grain of Mustard Seed. Garden City, N.Y.: Doubleday Anchor Press, 1973.

Andics, Hellmut. Rule of Terror. New York: Holt, Rinehart and Winston, 1969.

Antonius, George. The Arab Awakening. Beirut: Khayat, 1955.

Arendt, Hannah. On Revolution. New York: Viking Press, 1963.

_____. The Origins of Totalitarianism. New York: Harcourt, Brace and World, 1966.

Arey, James A. The Sky Pirates. New York: Charles Scribner's Sons, 1972.

Ariel, Dan. Explosion! Tel Aviv: Olive Books, 1972.

Avineri, Shlomo, ed. Israel and the Palestinians: Reflections on the
Clash of Two National Movements. New York: St. Martin's
Press, 1971.

Avner [pseud.]. Memoirs of an Assassin. New York: Yoseloff, 1959.

Avriel, Ehud. Open the Gates! The Dramatic Personal Story of
"Illegal" Immigration to Israel. London: Weidenfeld and Nicolson, 1975.

Azad, Abul Kalam. India Wins Freedom. Calcutta: Orient Longmans,
1959.

Bain, Chester A. Vietnam—The Roots of Conflict. Englewood Cliffs,
N.J.: Prentice-Hall, 1967.

Barron, John. KGB: The Secret Work of Soviet Secret Agents. New
York: Reader's Digest Press, 1974.

Baudovin, Jean. Terrorisme et Justice. Montreal: Editions du Jour,
1970.

Baumann, Carol Edler. The Diplomatic Kidnappings: A Revolutionary Tactic of Urban Terrorism. The Hague: Martinus Nijhoff,
1973.

Bayo, Alberto. 150 Questions to a Guerrilla. Translated by R. I.
Madigan and Angel de Lumus Medina. Montgomery, Ala.: Air
University, n.d.

Bell, J. Bowyer. The Long War: Israel and the Arabs Since 1946.
Englewood Cliffs, N.J.: Prentice-Hall, 1969.

_____. The Myth of the Guerrilla: Revolutionary Theory and Mal-
practice. New York: Knopf, 1971.

_____. The Secret Army: The IRA 1916-1974. Cambridge: Massa-
chusetts Institute of Technology Press, 1974.

Bennett, Richard Lawrence. The Black and Tans. Boston: Houghton
Mifflin Co., 1959.

Berkman, Alexander. Now and After: The ABC of Communist Anarchism. New York: Vanguard Press, 1929.

_____. Prison Memoirs of an Anarchist. New York: Schocken Books, 1970.

Berkowitz, Leonard. A Social Psychological Analysis. New York: McGraw-Hill, 1962.

Bern, Major H. von Dach. Total Resistance. Boulder, Colo.: Panther Publications, 1965.

Bettleheim, Bruno. The Informed Heart. New York: Free Press, 1960.

Black, Cyril E., and Thomas P. Thornton. Communism and Revolution. Princeton: Princeton University Press, 1964.

Bocca, Geoffrey. The Secret Army. Englewood Cliffs, N.J.: Prentice-Hall, 1968.

Borisov, J. Palestine Underground: The Story of Jewish Resistance. New York: Judea Publishing Co., 1947.

Brinton, Crane. The Anatomy of a Revolution. Englewood Cliffs, N.J.: Prentice-Hall, 1965.

Broehl, Wayne G. The Molly Maguires. Cambridge: Harvard University Press, 1964.

Browne, Malcolm W. The New Face of War. Indianapolis: Bobbs-Merrill Co., 1965.

Chailand, Gerard. The Palestinian Resistance. Baltimore: Penguin, 1972.

Clark, Michael K. Algeria in Turmoil. New York: Praeger Publishers, 1959.

Collier, Richard. The Great Indian Mutiny. New York: Dutton, 1964.

Conquest, Robert. The Great Terror. New York: Macmillan, 1968.

_____. The Soviet Police System. New York: Praeger Publishers, 1968.

Coogan, Tim Patrick. The I.R.A. New York: Praeger Publishers, 1970.

Cross, James Eliot. Conflict in the Shadows. New York: Doubleday & Co., 1963.

Crotty, William J. Assassination and the Political Order. New York: Harper & Row, 1971.

Crozier, Brian. South-East Asia in Turmoil. Baltimore: Penguin Books, 1965.

Curtis, Michael, et al., eds. The Palestinians: People, History, Politics. Edison, N.J.: Transaction Books, 1975.

Dallin, Alexander, and George W. Breslauer. Political Terror in Communist Systems. Stanford: Stanford University Press, 1970.

Davies, James C., ed. When Men Revolt and Why. New York: Free Press, 1971.

Davis, Jack. Political Violence in Latin America. London: International Institute for Strategic Studies, 1972.

Davison, W. Phillips. International Political Communication. New York: Praeger Publishers, 1965.

Dekel, Ephraim (Krasner). Shai: Historical Exploits of Haganah Intelligence. New York: Yoseloff, 1959.

Dillon, Martin, and Denis Lehane. Political Murder in Northern Ireland. Baltimore: Penguin Books, 1974.

Dishon, Daniel, ed. Middle East Record, vol. 4 (1968). Tel Aviv: Israel Universities Press, 1973.

Dobson, Christopher. Black September: Its Short, Violent History. New York: Macmillan, 1974.

Dror, Yehezkel. Crazy States: A Counterconventional Strategic Problem. (Hebrew) Tel Aviv: Department of Defense, 1973.

Dubois, Jules. Fidel Castro. Indianapolis: New Bobbs-Merrill Co., 1959.

Eckstein, Harry, ed. Internal War. New York: Free Press, 1964.

Edwardes, Michael. Red Year: The Indian Rebellion of 1857. London: Hamish Hamilton, 1973.

Efrat, Edgar S., ed. Introduction to Sub-Saharan Africa. Lexington/Toronto: Xerox College Publishing Co., 1973.

Einaudi, Luigi R., ed. Beyond Cuba: Latin America Takes Charge of Its Future. New York: Crane, Russak and Co., 1974.

Ellis, Albert, and John Gullo. Murder and Assassination. New York: Stuart Lyle, 1971.

Fanon, Franz. The Wretched of the Earth. New York: Grove Press, 1968.

Feierabend, Ivo, R. L. Feierabend, and T. R. Gurr, eds. Anger, Violence, and Politics: Theories and Research. Englewood Cliffs, N.J.: Prentice-Hall, 1972.

Feraoun, Mouloud. Journal 1955-1962. Paris: Seuil, 1962.

Frank, Gerold. The Deed. New York: Simon & Schuster, 1963.

Freedman, Robert Owen. Soviet Policy Toward the Middle East Since Nasser. New York: Praeger Publishers, 1975.

Gablonski, Edward. Terror from the Sky: Airwar. Garden City, N.Y.: Doubleday, 1971.

Garcia-Mara, Manuel R. International Responsibility for Hostile Acts of Private Persons Against Foreign States. The Hague: Martinus Nijhoff, 1962.

Gaucher, Roland. The Terrorists: From Tsarist Russia to the
    O.A.S. Translated by P. Spurlin. London: Secker & Warburg,
    1968.

Giap, Vo Nguyen. The South Vietnam People Will Win. Hanoi: For-
    eign Languages Publishing House, 1965.

Gilio, Maria Esther. The Tupamaros. London: Secker and Warburg,
    1972.

Gitlin, Jan. The Conquest of Acre Fortress. Tel Aviv: Hadar Pub-
    lishing House, 1962.

Glubb, John Bagot. A Soldier with the Arabs. London: Hodder and
    Stoughton, 1957.

Gott, Richard. Guerrilla Movements in Latin America. London:
    Thomas Nelson and Sons, 1970.

Greene, T. N., ed. The Guerrilla—And How to Fight Him. New
    York: Praeger Publishers, 1962.

Grimshaw, Allen. Racial Violence in the United States. Chicago:
    Aldine, 1970.

Grundy, Kenneth W. Guerrilla Struggle in Africa: An Analysis and
    Preview. New York: Grossman, 1971.

Guillen, Abraham. Philosophy of the Urban Guerrilla. Translated
    by D. C. Hodges. New York: Morrow, 1973.

Gurion, Itzhak. Triumph on the Gallows. New York: Brit Trumpeldor
    of America, 1950.

Gurr, Ted Robert. Why Men Rebel. Princeton: Princeton Univer-
    sity Press, 1970.

Guzman, Campos et al. La Violencia en Colombia. Bogota: Ediciones
    Tercer Mundo, 1963.

Hachey, Thomas, ed. The Problem of Partition: Peril to World
    Peace. New York: Rand McNally, 1972.

_____. Voices of Revolution: Rebels and Rhetoric. Dryden Press,
    1973.

Harkabi, Yehoshafat. The Arabs' Position in Their Conflict with Israel. Jerusalem: Israel Universities Press, 1972.

Harris, John. The Indian Mutiny. London: Hart-Davis MacGibbon, 1973.

Hastings, Adrian. Wiriyamu. London: Search Press, 1974.

Heilbrunn, Otto. Partisan Warfare. New York: Praeger Publishers, 1962.

Hillquist, Morris. Loose Leaves from a Busy Life. New York: Macmillan Co., 1934.

Hodges, Donald Clark. National Liberation Fronts: 1960-1970. New York: Morrow, 1972.

_____. Philosophy of the Urban Guerrilla. New York: Marrow, 1973.

Horn, Carl von. Soldiering for Peace. New York: McKay, 1967.

Horn, F. Stanley. Invisible Empire: The Story of the Ku Klux Klan, 1866-1871. Boston: Houghton Mifflin Co., 1939.

Horrowitz, Irving Louis, ed. The Anarchists. New York: Dell Publishing Co., 1964.

_____. The Struggle Is the Message: The Organization and Ideology of the Anti-War Movement. Berkeley: Glendessary Press, 1970.

Hosmer, Stephen T. Viet Cong Repression and Its Implications for the Future. Lexington: Heath Lexington Books, 1970.

Hudson, M. O., ed. International Legislation, vol. 7. Washington, D.C.: Carnegie Endowment for International Peace, 1931-1950.

Hugh, Davis Graham, and Ted Robert Gurr, eds. Violence in America: Historical and Comparative Perspectives. New York: Bantam Books, 1970.

Hurewitz, Jacob C. The Struggle for Palestine. New York: Greenwood, 1968.

Hyde, Douglas Arnold. The Roots of Guerrilla Warfare. Chester
    Springs, Pa.: Dufour Editions, 1968.

Jenkins, Brian Michael. The Five Stages of Urban Guerrilla War-
    fare. Santa Monica, Calif.: Rand, 1971.

Joll, James. The Anarchists. New York: Grossett and Dunlop, 1964.

Kautsky, Karl. Terrorism and Communism: A Contribution to the
    Natural History of Revolution. Translated by W. H. Kerridge.
    London: George Allen & Unwin, 1920.

Kimche, David. The Secret Roads. New York: Farrar, Straus, and
    Cudahy, 1955.

Kitson, Frank. Low Intensity Operations: Subversion, Insurgency,
    Peace-Keeping. London: Faber Publishers, 1972.

Knohl, Dov. Siege in the Hills of Hebron: The Battle of the Etzion
    Bloc. New York: Yoseloff, 1958.

Laffin, John. Fedayeen. New York: Macmillan, 1973.

Lambrick, H. T. The Terrorist. London: Rowman, 1972.

Leiden, Carl, and Karl M. Schmitt, eds. The Politics of Violence.
    Englewood Cliffs, N.J.: Prentice-Hall, 1968.

Lejeune, Anthony, comp. The Case for South West Africa. London:
    Tom Stacey, 1971.

Lesch, Mosely. The Politics of Palestinian Nationalism. Los Ange-
    les: University of California Press, 1973.

Lifton, Robert Jay. History and Human Survival. New York: Ran-
    dom House, 1970.

Lorch, Netanel. The Edge of the Sword: Israel's War of Indepen-
    dence 1947-1949. New York: Putnam, 1961.

Lum, Dyer D. A Concise History of the Great Trial of the Chicago
    Anarchists. Chicago: Socialistic Publishing Co., 1887.

MacCarthy, J. M., ed. Limerick's Fighting Story. Tralee, Ireland:
    Anvil Books, 1966.

Mallin, Jay. Terror in Viet Nam. Princeton, N.J.: D. Van Nostrand
        Co., 1966.

_____, ed. Terror and Urban Guerrillas: A Study of Tactics and
Documents. Coral Gables, Fla.: University of Miami Press,
1971.

Mao Tse-tung. Basic Tactics. New York: Praeger Publishers, 1966.

_____. On Guerrilla Warfare. New York: Praeger Publishers, 1961.

Mardor, Munya. Haganah. New York: New American Library, 1966.

_____. Strictly Illegal. London: Robert Hale, 1964.

Marighella, Carlos. For the Liberation of Brazil. Harmondsworth:
        Penguin, 1972.

_____. Minimanual of the Urban Guerrilla. Havana: Tricontinental,
n.d.

Marx, Karl. Capital. New York: International Publishers Co., 1967.

Mathur, L. P. Indian Revolutionary Movement in the United States
        of America. Delhi: S. Chand, 1970.

Max, Alphonse. Guerrillas in Latin America. The Hague: Interna-
        tional Documentation and Information Centre, 1971.

McWhinney, E. W., ed. Aerial Piracy and International Law. Lei-
        den: A. W. Sijthoff, 1971.

Mendel, Arthur P., ed. Essential Works of Marxism. New York:
        Bantam Books, 1965.

Meridor, Yaacov. Long Road to Freedom. New York: United Zion-
        ists Revisionists, 1961.

Merleau-Ponty, Maurice. Humanism and Terror: An Essay on the
        Communist Problem. Boston: Beacon Press, 1969.

Moody, T. W., and F. Y. Martin, eds. The Course of Irish History.
        New York: Weybright and Talley, 1967.

Morris, Michael. Terrorism. Cape Town: Howard Timmins, 1971.

Morton, Marian J. Terrors of Ideological Politics. Cleveland: Case Western Reserve, 1972.

Moss, Robert. Urban Guerrillas. London: Temple Smith, 1972.

_____. The War for the Cities. New York: Coward, 1972.

Mphahlele, Ezekiel. The African Image. Rev. ed. New York: Praeger Publishers, 1974.

Mukherjee, Uma. Two Great Indian Revolutionaries. Calcutta: Firma K. L. Mukhopadhyay, 1966.

Mydans, Carl, and Shelley Mydans. The Violent Peace. New York: Atheneum, 1968.

Nasution, Abdul Haris. Fundamentals of Guerrilla Warfare. New York: Praeger Publishers, 1965.

Nkrumah, Kwame. Handbook of Revolutionary Warfare. New York: International Publishers, 1972.

Nolin, Thierry. La Haganah: L'Armee Secrete d'Israel. Paris: Ballard, 1971.

O'Ballance, Edgar. The Indo-China War, 1945–1954: A Study in Guerrilla Warfare. London: Faber and Faber, 1964.

O'Brion, Leon. Dublin Castle and the 1916 Rising. New York: New York University Press, 1971.

O'Farrell, Patrick. Ireland's English Question. London: Batsford, 1971.

O'Flaherty, Liam. The Terrorist. London: E. Archer, 1926.

Oppenheimer, Martin. The Urban Guerrilla. Chicago: Quadrangle Books, 1969.

Osanka, Franklin Mark. Modern Guerrilla Warfare: Fighting Communist Guerrilla Movements 1941–1961. New York: Free Press, 1962.

Panikkar, Sardar K. M. Asia and Western Dominance. London: George Allen and Unwin, 1959.

Payne, Pierre Stephen Robert. The Terrorists: The Story of the Forerunners of Stalin. New York: Funk & Wagnalls, 1957.

_____. Zero: The Story of Terrorism. New York: Day, 1950.

Peres, Shimon. David's Sling. New York: Random House, 1970.

Phillips, R. Hart. Cuba—Island of Paradox. New York: McDowell, Obolensky, 1959.

Pomeroy, William J. Guerrilla Warfare and Marxism. New York: International Publishers, 1968.

Possony, Stefan T., ed. The Lenin Reader. Chicago: Regenery, 1966.

Powers, Thomas. Diana: The Making of a Terrorist. Boston, 1971.

Pranger, Robert J. American Policy for Peace in the Middle East, 1969-1971. Washington, D.C.: American Enterprise Institute, 1971.

Pryce-Jones, David. The Face of Defeat. New York: Holt, Rinehart & Winston, 1973.

Quandt, William D., Fuad Jabber, and Ann Mosely Lesch. The Politics of Palestinian Nationalism. Berkeley: University of California Press, 1973.

Rapoport, David C. Assassination and Terrorism. Toronto: Canadian Broadcasting System, 1971.

Reed, David. 111 Days in Stanleyville. New York: Harper & Row, 1965.

Richardson, Lewis Fry. Statistics of Deadly Quarrels. Edited by Quincy Wright and C. C. Lienau. Pittsburgh: Boxwood Press, 1960.

Robinson, Donald B. The Dirty Wars. New York: Delacorte Press, 1968.

Rosenberg, Milton J., ed. Beyond Conflict and Containment: Critical Studies of Military and Foreign Policy. New Brunswick, N.J.: Transaction Books, 1972.

Sale, Kirkpatrick. SDS. New York: Random House, 1973.

Schechtman, Joseph B. The Mufti and the Fuehrer. London: Thomas Yoseloff, 1965.

Schiff, Zeev, and Raphael Rothstein. Fedayeen: Guerrillas Against Israel. New York: David McKay, 1972.

Shay, R. The Silent War. Salisbury: Galaxy Press, 1971.

Shulman, Alix K. Red Emma Speaks. New York: Random House, 1972.

Sinclair, Andrew. Guevara. London: William Collins & Sons, 1970.

Singh, Khushwant, and Satindra Singh. Ghadar 1915: India's First Armed Revolution. New Delhi: R. K. Publishing House, 1966.

Skobnick, Jerome, ed. The Politics of Protest. New York: Ballantine Books, 1969.

Solzhenitsyn, Alexander. The Gulag Archipelago. New York: Harper & Row, 1973.

Stewart, Anthony Terence Quincey. The Ulster Crisis. London: Faber, 1967.

Suchlicki, Jaime. University Students and Revolution in Cuba, 1920-1968. Coral Gables: University of Miami Press, 1969.

Taber, Robert. The War of the Flea. New York: Lyle Stuart, 1965.

Tanham, George Kilpatrick. Communist Revolutionary Warfare. New York: Praeger Publishers, 1961.

Teixeira, Bernardo. The Fabric of Terror—Three Days in Angola. New York: Devin-Adair, 1965.

Trelease, Allen W. White Terror: The Ku Klux Klan Conspiracy and Southern Reconstruction. New York: Harper & Row, 1971.

Trotsky, Leon. Stalin. New York: Harper & Brothers, 1941.

Tuker, Francis. While Memory Serves. London: Cassells & Co., 1950.

Venter, Al J. _Africa at War_. Old Greenwich, Conn.: Devin-Adair, 1974.

_____. _The Terror Fighters_. Capetown and Johannesburg: Purnell, 1969.

Walter, Eugene Victor. _Terror and Resistance: A Study of Political Violence_. New York: Oxford University Press, 1969.

Whelton, Charles. _Skyjack!_ New York: Tower Publications, 1970.

Wolfe, Bertram D. _Three Who Made a Revolution_. New York: Dial Press, 1961.

Wolin, Simon, and Robert M. Slusser, eds. _The Soviet Secret Police_. New York: Praeger Publishers, 1957.

Woodstock, George. _Anarchism_. New York: World Publishing Co., 1971.

Yaari, Ehud. _Strike Terror_. New York: Sabra Books, 1970.

Zaar, Isaac. _Rescue and Liberation_. New York: Bloch, 1954.

ARTICLES

Aggarwala, Narinder. "Political Aspects of Hijacking." _International Conciliation_, no. 585 (1971), pp. 7-27.

Ahmad, Eqbal. "The Theory and Fallacy of Counterinsurgency." _Nation_ 213 (1971): 70-85.

"Airport Security Searches and the Fourth Amendment." _Columbia Law Review_ 71 (1971): 1039-58.

Alsina, Geronimo. "The War and the Tupamaros." _Bulletin Tricontinental_, August 1972, pp. 29-42.

Alves, M. M. "Kidnapped Diplomats: Greek Tragedy on a Latin Stage." _Commonweal_ 92 (1970); 311-14.

"Anarcho-Nihilism." _Economist_ 237, no. 6635 (1970): 2-33.

"Anti-Soviet Zionist Terrorism in the U.S." _Current Digest of the Soviet Press_ 23 (1971): 6-8.

"Arab Terrorism." Jewish Frontier 36 (1969): 13-16.

Archinard, Andre. "La Suisse et les Infractions Non Aeriennes Com-
mises a Bord des Aeronefs Civils." ASDA Bulletin SVIR, no.
3 (1968), pp. 3-9; no. 1 (1969), pp. 2-10; no. 2 (1969), pp. 1-12.

Arendt, H. "Reflections on Violence." Journal of International Affairs 23, no. 1 (1969): 1-35.

"Argentina: Revolutions Within the Revolution." Latin America 5,
no. 54 (1971): 337-38.

Ashab, Naim. "To Overcome the Crisis of the Palestinian Resistance."
World Marxist Review 15, no. 5 (1972): 71-78.

Baccelli, Guido Rinaldi. "Pirateria Aerea: Realta Effettiva e Dis-
ciplina Giuridica." Diritto Aereo 9, no. 35 (1970): 150-60.

Barner, Don. "PLO at U.N., What Now?" New Outlook 17, no. 9
(1974): 62-66.

Barrie, G. N. "Crimes Committed Aboard Aircraft." South African
Law Journal 83 (1968): 203-08.

Beaton, L. "Crisis in Quebec." Round Table, no. 241 (1971), pp.
147-52.

Beckett, J. C. "Northern Ireland." Journal of Contemporary History 6, no. 1 (1971): 121-34.

Bell, J. Bowyer. "Assassination in International Politics: Lord
Moyne, Count Bernadotte, and the Lehi." International Studies
Quarterly, no. 1 (1972), pp. 59-82.

Bennett, R. K. "Brotherhood of the Bomb." Readers Digest, December 1970, pp. 102-06.

_____. "Terrorists Among Us: An Intelligence Report." Readers
Digest, October 1971, pp. 115-20.

Besedin, Alexander. "Against Air Piracy." New Times, November
2, 1970, pp. 24-25.

Boyle, Robert P. "International Action to Combat Aircraft Hijacking."
Lawyer of the Americas 4 (1972): 460-73.

Brach, Richard S. "The Inter-American Convention on the Kidnapping of Diplomats." Columbia Journal of Transnational Law 10 (1971): 392-412.

Bradford, A. L. "Legal Ramifications of Hijacking Ariplanes." American Bar Association Journal 48 (1962): 1034-39.

Brandon, Henry. "Were We Masterful. . . . " Foreign Policy, no. 10 (1973), pp. 158-70.

Bravo, Navarro M. "Apoderamiento Ilicito de Aeronaves en Vuelo." Revista Espanola de Derecho Internacional 22 (1969): 788-809.

Breton, J. M. "Piraterie Aerienne et Droit International Public." Revue Generale de Droit International Public 75 (1971): 392-445.

Burki, S. J. "Social and Economic Determinants of Political Violence: A Case Study of the Punjab." Middle East Journal 25 (1971): 465-80.

Callanan, Edward F. "Terror in Venezuela." Military Review 49 (1969): 49-56.

Caloyanni, M. A. "Le Terrorisme et la Creation d'Une Cour Repressive Internationale." Revue de Droit International 15 (1935): 46-71.

Chaturvedi, S. C. "Hijacking and the Law." Indian Journal of International Law 11 (1971): 89-105.

Clark, Dennis. "Which Way the I.R.A. ?" Commonweal, no. 13 (1973), pp. 294-97.

Clark, Lorne S. "The Struggle to Cure Hijacking." International Perspectives, January-February 1973, pp. 47-51.

Cobo, Juan. "The Roots of 'Violencia.'" New Times, August 5, 1970, pp. 25-27.

Cooley, John K. "China and the Palestinians." Journal of Palestinian Studies 1, no. 2 (1972): 19-34.

_____. "Moscow Faces a Palestinian Dilemma." Mid East 11, no. 3 (1970): 32-35.

Corning, Peter A., and C. H. Corning. "Toward a General Theory of Violent Aggression." Social Science Information 11, nos. 3, 4 (1972): 7-35.

Craig, Alexander. "Urban Guerrillas in Latin America." Survey 17, no. 3 (1971): 112-28.

Crozier, Brian. "Anatomy of Terrorism." Nation 188 (1959): 250-52.

Dadrian, V. "Factors of Anger and Aggression in Genocide." Journal of Human Relations 19 (1971): 394-417.

Dasgupta, S. "Violence—Development and Tensions." International Journal of Group Tensions 1 (1971): 114-29.

Davies, James C. "Toward a Theory of Revolution." American Sociological Review 27 (1962): 5-14.

Denaro, J. M. "In-Flight Crimes, the Tokyo Convention, and Federal Judicial Jurisdiction." Journal of Air Law and Commerce 35 (1969): 171-203.

Dershowitz, Alan M. "Terrorism and Preventive Detention: The Case of Israel." A Commentary Report (1970), pp. 3-14.

Dinstein, Yoram. "Criminal Jurisdiction over Aircraft Hijacking." Israel Law Review 7 (1972): 195-206.

_____. "Terrorism and Wars of Liberation Applied to the Arab-Israeli Conflict: An Israeli Perspective." Israel Yearbook on Human Rights 3 (1973): 78.

"Dir Yassin." West Asia Affairs, Summer 1969, pp. 27-30.

"Document on Terror." News from Behind the Iron Curtain 1 (1952): 44-57.

Donnedieu de Vabres, H. "La Repression Internationale du Terrorisme; les Conventions de Geneve." Revue de Droit International et de Legislation Comparee 19 (1938): 37-74.

Dugard, John. "International Terrorism." International Affairs 50, no. 1 (1974): 67-81.

_____. "Towards the Definition of International Terrorism." American Journal of International Law 67, no. 5 (1973): 94-100.

Eave, L. "Political Terrorism: Hysteria on the Left." New York Times Magazine, April 12, 1970, pp. 25-27.

Eustathiades, C. "La Cour Penale Internationale pour la Repression du Terrorisme et le Probleme de la Responsabilite Internationale des Etats." Revue Generale de Droit International Public 43 (1936): 384-415.

Evans, Alona E. "Aircraft Hijacking: Its Cause and Cure." American Journal of International Law 63 (1969): 695-710.

_____. "A Proposed Method of Control." Journal of Air Law and Commerce 37 (1971): 171-81.

_____. "Aircraft Hijacking: What Is to Be Done?" American Journal of International Law 66 (1972): 819-22.

Falk, Richard A. "Terror, Liberation Movements, and the Processes of Social Change." American Journal of International Law 63 (1969): 423-27.

Fallaci, Oriana. "A Leader of Fedayeen: 'We Want a War Like the Vietnam War': Interview with George Habash." Life, June 12, 1970, pp. 32-34.

Fawcett, J. E. S. "Kidnappings Versus Government Protection." World Today 26 (1970): 359-62.

Feller, S. Z. "Comment on Criminal Jurisdiction over Aircraft Hijacking." Israel Law Review 7 (1972): 207-14.

Fenello, Michael J. "Technical Prevention of Air Piracy." International Conciliation, no. 585 (1971), pp. 28-41.

Fenwick, C. G. "'Piracy' in the Caribbean." American Journal of International Law 55 (1961): 426-28.

FitzGerald, G. F. "Development of International Rules Concerning Offences and Certain Other Acts Committed on Board Aircraft." Canadian Yearbook of International Law 1 (1963): 230-51.

_____. "Offences and Certain Other Acts Committed on Board Air-
        craft: The Tokyo Convention of 1963." Canadian Yearbook of
        International Law 2 (1964): 191-204.

_____. "Toward Legal Suppression of Acts Against Civil Aviation."
        International Conciliation, no. 585 (1971), pp. 42-78.

Franjeck, S. "How Revolutionary Is the Palestinian Resistance: A
        Marxist Interpretation." Journal of Palestine Studies 1, no. 2
        (1972): 52-60.

Frank, Gerold. "The Moyne Case: A Tragic History." Commentary,
        December 1945, pp. 64-71.

Franck, Thomas M., and Bert B. Lockwood. "Preliminary Thoughts
        Towards an International Convention on Terrorism." American
        Journal of International Law 68 (1974): 4.

Friedman, W. "Some Impacts of Social Organization on International
        Law." American Journal of International Law 50 (1956): 475-
        513.

Fromkin, David. "The Strategy of Terrorism." Foreign Affairs 53,
        no. 4 (1975): 683-98.

Gerassi, Marysa N. "Uruguay's Urban Guerrillas." Nation 209, no.
        10 (1969): 306-10.

Gervasi, Frank. "Terror in Palestine." Colliers, August 11, 1945,
        pp. 64-65.

"Getting Away with Murder." Economist, November 4, 1972, pp.
        15-16.

Goodsell, James N. "Terrorism in Latin America." Commentator,
        March 1966, pp. 9-11.

Gott, Richard. "Latin American Guerrillas." Listener 84 (1970):
        437-40.

de Gramont, Sanche. "Moslem Terrorists in a New Job." New York
        Herald Tribune, July 9, 1962, pp. 1-2.

Hakman, Nathan. "Political Trials in the Legal Order: A Political
        Science Prospect." Journal of Public Law 21, no. 1 (1972):
        73-127.

Hannay, William A. "International Terrorism: The Need for a Fresh Perspective." International Lawyer 8, no. 2 (1974): 268-84.

Hirano, R. "Convention on Offences and Certain Other Acts Committed on Board Aircraft of 1963." Japanese Annual of International Law, no. 8 (1964), pp. 44-52.

Hirsch, Arthur I., and David Otis. "Aircraft Piracy and Extradition." New York Law Forum 16 (1970): 392-419.

Horlick, Gary N. "The Developing Law of Air Hijacking." Harvard International Law Journal 12 (1971): 33-70.

Hubbard, D. G. "Bringing Skyjackers Down to Earth: Views of a Psychiatrist." Time, October 4, 1971, pp. 64-65.

Hudson, Michael C. "The Palestinian Arab Resistance Movement: Its Significance in the Middle East Crisis." Middle East Journal 23 (1969): 291-301.

Hudson, M. O. "The Proposed International Criminal Court." American Journal of International Law 32 (1938): 549-54.

Hutchinson, Marta Crenshaw. "The Concept of Revolutionary Terrorism." Journal of Conflict Resolution 16, no. 3 (1972): 383-95.

Jabber, F. "The Arab Regimes and the Palestinian Revolution, 1967-71." Journal of Palestinian Studies 2, no. 2 (1973): 79-101.

Jack, H. A. "Terrorism: Another U.N. Failure." America, October 20, 1973, pp. 282-85.

Jacobson, Peter M. "From Piracy on the High Seas to Piracy in the High Skies: A Study of Aircraft Hijacking." Cornell International Law Journal 5 (1972): 161-87.

Jay, M. "Politics of Terror," Partisan Review 38 (1971): 72.

Khan, Rahmatullah. "Hijacking and International Law." Africa Quarterly 10 (1971): 398-403.

"Kidnapping Incidents." Bulletin of the International Commission of Jurists, December 1967, pp. 24-33.

Kornilov, Y. "Meetings with the Fedayeen." New Times, no. 42 (1972), pp. 24-25.

Krieger, David. "Terrorists and Nuclear Technology." Bulletin of the Atomic Scientists 31, no. 6 (1975): 28–34.

Kuroda, Yasumasa. "Young Palestinian Commandos in Political Socialization Perspective." Middle East Journal 26 (1972): 253–70.

Lador-Lederer, J. J. "A Legal Approach to International Terrorism." Israel Law Review 9 (1974): 194–220.

"Latin America and Revolution." Christian Century, November 17, 1965, pp. 1409–12.

"Latin America in Revolution." America, April 27, 1968, pp. 562–87.

"Latin America: Revolution Without Revolutionaries." Nation, August 22, 1966, pp. 145–49.

Legum, C. "How to Curb International Terrorism." Current History 147 (1973): 3–9.

Little, Tom. "The Nature of the Palestinian Resistance Movement." Asian Affairs 57 (1970): 157–69.

Lissitzyn, Oliver J. "International Control of Aerial Hijacking: The Role of Values and Interests." Proceedings of the American Society of International Law, 1971, pp. 80–86.

Lopez Gutierrez, Juan J. "Should the Tokyo Convention of 1963 Be Ratified?" Journal of Air Law and Commerce 31 (1965): 1–21.

Loy, Frank E. "Some International Approaches to Dealing with Hijacking of Aircraft." International Lawyer 4 (1970): 444–52.

Lupsha, Peter. "Explanation of Political Violence: Some Psychological Theories." Politics and Society 2 (1971): 88–104.

Malawer, Stuart S. "United States Foreign Policy and International Law: The Jordanian Civil War and Air Piracy." International Problems 10 (1971): 31–40.

Malik, Sushman. "Legal Aspects of the Problem of Unlawful Seizure of Aircraft." Indian Journal of International Law 9 (1969): 61–71.

Mallin, Jay. "Terrorism as a Political Weapon." Air University Review 22 (1971): 45–52.

Malmborg, K. E. "New Developments in the Law of International Aviation: The Control of Aerial Hijacking." Proceedings of the American Society of International Law, 1971, pp. 75-80.

Mankiewicz, R. H. "The 1970 Hague Convention." Journal of Air Law and Commerce 37 (1971): 195-210.

Martin, Bill. "The Politics of Violence—The Urban Guerrilla in Brazil." Ramparts, October 1970, p. 35.

Martinez, Codo Enrique. "Continental Defense and Counterinsurgency." Military Review 50, no. 4 (1970): 71-74.

_____. "The Urban Guerrilla." Military Review 51, no. 8 (1971): 3-10.

McMahon, John P. "Air Hijacking: Extradition as a Deterrent." Georgetown Law Journal 58 (1970): 1135-52.

Medzini, Roni. "China and the Palestinians." The New Middle East, no. 32 (1971), pp. 34-40.

Melo, Artemio Luis. "La Inviolabilidad Diplomatica y el Caso del Embajador Von Spreti." Revista de Derecho Internacional y Ciencias Diplomaticas 19, nos. 37-38 (1970): 147-56.

Mendelsohn, A. I. "In-Flight Crime: The International and Domestic Picture Under the Tokyo Convention." Virginia Law Review 53 (1967): 509-63.

Meron, Theodor. "Some Legal Aspects of Arab Terrorists' Claim to Privileged Combatancy." Nordisk Tidaskrift for International Ret 40, nos. 1-4 (1970): 47-85.

Moss, Robert. "International Terrorism and Western Societies." International Journal 28, no. 3 (1973): 418-30.

_____. "Urban Guerrillas in Uruguay." Problems of Communism 20, no. 5 (1971): 14-23.

Nekhleh, E. A. "Anatomy of Violence: Theoretical Reflections on Palestinian Resistance." Middle East Journal 25 (1971): 180-200.

O'Mara, Richard. "New Terror in Latin America: Snatching the Diplomats." Nation 210, no. 17 (1970): 518-19.

Panhuys, Haro F. van. "Aircraft Hijacking and International Law."
Columbia Journal of Transnational Law 9 (1970): 1-22.

Paust, Jordan J. "Some Thoughts on 'Preliminary Thoughts' on Terrorism." American Journal of International Law 68 (1974):
502-03.

Pella, Vespasian V. "La Repression des Crimes Contre la Person-
nalite de l'Etat." Recueil des Cours de l'Academie de Droit
International de la Haye 3 (1930): 677-831.

Pepitone, Albert. "The Social Psychology of Violence." International
Journal of Group Tensions 2 (1972): 19-32.

Peters, R. "Terrorists at Work: Report from Argentina." National
Review, July 28, 1964, p. 63.

Peterson, Edward A. "Jurisdiction-Construction of Statute-Aircraft
Piracy." Journal of Air Law and Commerce 30 (1964): 292-95.

Poulantzas, Nicholas M. "The Hague Convention for the Suppression
of Unlawful Seizure of Aircraft (December 16, 1970)." Nederlands Tijdschrift voor Internationaal Recht 18, no. 1 (1971):
25-75.

_____. "Hijacking or Air Piracy?" Nederlands Juristenblad, no. 20
(1970): 566-74.

_____. "Hijacking v. Piracy: A Substantial Misunderstanding Not a
Quarrel over Semantics." Revue Hellenique de Droit International 23, nos. 1-4 (1970): 80-90.

_____. "Some Problems of International Law Connected with Urban
Guerrilla Warfare: The Kidnapping of Members of Diplomatic
Missions, Consular Offices and Other Foreign Personnel." An-
nales d'Etudes Internationales 3 (1972): 137-67.

Pulsifer, Roy, and Robert Boyle. "The Tokyo Convention on Offences
and Certain Other Acts Committed on Board Aircraft." Journal
of Air Law and Commerce 20 (1964): 305-54.

Rafat, Amir. "Control of Aircraft Hijacking: The Law of International Civil Aviation." World Affairs 134 (1971): 143-56.

Rein, Bert. "A Government Perspective." Journal of Air Law and Commerce 37 (1971): 183-93.

"The Role of International Law in Combating Terrorism." Current Foreign Policy, January 1973, pp. 1-7.

Roux, J. A. "Le Projet de Convention Internationale pour la Repression des Crimes Presentant un Danger Public." Revue International de Droit Penal 12 (1935): 99-130.

Ruppenthal, Kare M. "World Law and the Hijackers." Nation, February 3, 1969, pp. 144-46.

Russell, Charles A., and Robert E. Hildner. "Urban Insurgency in Latin America: Its Implications for the Future." Air University Review 22, no. 6 (1971): 55-64.

Saldana, I. "Le Terrorisme." Revue International de Droit Penal 13 (1936): 26-37.

Samuels, Alec. "Crimes Committed on Board Aircraft: Tokyo Convention Act, 1967." British Yearbook of International Law 42 (1967): 271-77.

_____. "The Legal Problems: An Introduction." Journal of Air Law and Commerce 37 (1971): 163-70.

Schwarzenberger, Georg. "Terrorists, Hijackers, Guerrilleros and Mercenaries." Current Legal Problems 24 (1971): 257-82.

"Scope and Limit of a Fedayeen Consensus." Wiener Library Bulletin, 1970/71, pp. 1-8.

Segre, Dan, and J. H. Adler. "The Ecology of Terrorism." Encounter 40 (1973): 17-24.

Shaffer, Helen B. "Political Terrorism." Editorial Research Reports 1 (1970): 341-60.

Sheehan, William M. "Hijacking and World Law." World Federalist: U.S. Edition 16 (1970): 14-15, 19.

Shepard, Ira M. "Air Piracy: The Role of the International Federation of Airline Pilots Associations." Cornell International Law Journal 3 (1970): 79-91.

Shubber, Sami. "Is Hijacking of Aircraft Piracy in International Law?" British Yearbook of International Law 43 (1968-69): 193-204.

Silver, Isidore. "Toward a Theory of the Political Defense." Catholic Lawyer 18, no. 3 (1972): 206-36.

Silverman, Jerry M., and Peter M. Jackson. "Terror in Insurgency Warfare." Military Review 50 (1970): 61-70.

Simp, Howard R. "Terror." U.S. Naval Institute Proceedings 96 (1970): 64-69.

Smith, C. L. "Probable Necessity of an International Prison in Solving Aircraft Hijacking." International Lawyer 5 (1971): 269-78.

Smith, D. "Scenario Reality: A New Brand of Terrorism." Nation, March 30, 1974, pp. 392-94.

Smith McKeithen, R. N. "Prospects for the Prevention of Aircraft Hijacking Through Law." Columbia Journal of Transnational Law 9 (1970): 60-80.

Sottile, A. "Le Terrorisme International." Recueil des Cours de l'Academie de Droit International de la Haye 3 (1938): 87-184.

"Soviet Airliner Hijacked to Turkey." Current Digest of the Soviet Press 22 (1970): 6-7.

Sponsler, T. H. "International Kidnapping." International Lawyer 5 (1971): 27.

Stechel, Ira. "Terrorist Kidnapping of Diplomatic Personnel." Cornell International Law Journal 5 (1972): 189-217.

Stephen, J. E. "Going South—Air Piracy and Unlawful Interference with Air Commerce." International Lawyer 4 (1970): 433-43.

Strafford, David. "Anarchists in Britain Today." Government and Opposition 6, no. 3 (1971): 345-53.

Stupack, Ronald J., and D. C. Booher. "Guerrilla Warfare: A Strategic Analysis in the Superpower Context." Journal of Southeast Asia and the Far East, November 2, 1970, pp. 181-96.

Sundberg, J. W. F. "The Case for an International Criminal Court." Journal of Air Law and Commerce 37 (1971): 211-27.

Syrkin, Marie. "Political Terrorism." Midstream 18, no. 9 (1972): 3-11.

Terekhov, Vladimir. "International Terrorism and the Fight Against It." New Times, no. 11 (1974), pp. 20-22.

"Terror Through the Mails." Economist, September 23, 1972, pp. 15-16.

"The Terrorism Act of South Africa." Bulletin of the International Commission of Jurists, June 1968, pp. 28-34.

"Terrorism in Latin America." Atlas 20, no. 10 (1971): 18-21.

"Trail of the Basque Separatists." America, December 19, 1970, p. 532.

Tran, Tam. "Terrorisme et le Droit Penal International Contemporain." Revue de Droit International de Sciences Diplomatiques et Politiques 45 (1967): 11-25.

Tuckerman, A. "U.N.: New Look for 1972—Debate on Terrorism." Nation, October 2, 1972, p. 258.

Vayrynen, Raimo. "Some Aspects of Theory and Strategy of Kidnapping." Instant Research on Peace and Violence, no. 1 (1971), pp. 3-21.

Volsky, Dmitry. "The Beirut Crime." New Times, no. 16 (1973), pp. 12-13.

Vucinic, Milan. "The Responsibility of States for Acts of International Terrorism." Review of International Affairs 23, nos. 536-37 (1972): 11-12.

Wahl, Jonathan. "Responses to Terrorism: Self-Defense or Reprisal?" International Problems 5, nos. 1-2 (1973): 28-33.

Weller, Jac. "Guerrilla Warfare." National Guardsman 24 (1970):
    2-8.

"What Makes a Skyjacker?" Science Digest 71 (1972): 21-22.

"Which Way the IRA?" Commonweal, January 5, 1973, pp. 294-97.

White, Gillian M. E. "The Hague Convention for the Suppression of
    Unlawful Seizure of Aircraft." International Commission of
    Jurists Review, no. 6 (1971), pp. 38-45.

Wilkinson, Paul. "Three Questions on Terrorism." Government and
    Opposition 8, no. 3 (1973): 290-312.

Winegarten, R. "Literary Terrorism." Commentary, March 1974,
    pp. 58-65.

Wohl, Paul. "New Soviet Revolutionary Stance in the Middle East."
    Radio Liberty Dispatch, May 25, 1970, p. 2.

Wolf, Michael. "Cheerleader for the Revolution." New York Times
    Magazine, July 21, 1974, pp. 11-20.

Yaari, Ehud. "The Decline of Al-Fatah." Midstream, May 1971,
    pp. 3-12.

Yamamoto, Soji. "The Japanese Enactment for the Suppression of
    Unlawful Seizure of Aircraft and International Law." Japanese
    Annual of International Law, no. 15 (1971), pp. 70-80.

Zahn, G. C. "Terrorism for Peace and Justice." Commonweal, Oc-
    tober 23, 1970, pp. 84-85.

Zotiades, George B. "The International Criminal Prosecution of
    Persons Charged with an Unlawful Seizure of Aircraft." Revue
    Hellenique de Droit International 23, nos. 1-4 (1970), 12-37.

MONOGRAPHS AND OTHER PUBLICATIONS

The "Activities" of the Hagana, Irgun and Stern Bands. New York:
    Palestine Liberation Organization, n.d.

"Agreement Concerning Mutual Defense Against Undesirable Foreign-
    ers." (Quito, August 10, 1935) Edited by M. O. Hudson. Inter-

national Legislation, vol. 7. Washington, D.C.: Carnegie Endow-
     ment for International Peace, 1931-1950, pp. 166-67.

Aines, Ronald C. "The Jewish Underground Against the British Man-
     date in Palestine." Thesis, Union College, 1973.

Assassination and Political Violence (A Task Force of the National
     Commission on the Causes and Prevention of Violence). Wash-
     ington, D.C.: U.S. Government Printing Office, 1969.

"Brazilian Hijacking Law (October 20, 1969): Decree-law 975 of 20
     October 1969 Defining Crimes of Smuggling and Transportation
     of Terrorists and Subversives in Aircraft." International
     Legal Materials 9 (1970): 180-84.

Caloyanni, M. "The Proposals of M. Laval to the League of Nations
     for the Establishment of an International Permanent Tribunal in
     Criminal Matters." Transactions of the Crotius Society 21
     (1936): 77-91.

Centre de Recherche et d'Information Socio-Politiques. Repression,
     Violence et Terreur: Rebellions au Congo. Brussels, 1969.

Civil Violence and the International System. 2 vols. London: Inter-
     national Institute for Strategic Studies, 1971.

"Convention Entre les Delegues des Polices de Buenos Aires et de la
     Plata (Republique Argentine), Rio de Janeiro (Bresil), Santiago
     (Chile) et Montevideo (Uruguay) pour l'Echange des Antecedents
     des Individus Dangereux pour la Societe." Buenos Aires, 20
     Octobre 1905. Recueil International des Traites du XX^C Siecle,
     Public par Descamps et L. Renault. Paris: Rousseau [1904]-
     1921. 1905, 1945.

"Convention for the Creation of an International Criminal Court.
     Geneva: November 16, 1937." League of Nations Doc. C.94.M.
     47.1938.V., pp. 18-33.

"The Convention for the Prevention and Punishment of Terrorism."
     British Yearbook of International Law 19 (1938): 214-16.

"Convention for the Prevention and Punishment of Terrorism." Gene-
     va, November 16, 1937." League of Nations Doc. C.94.M.47.
     1938.V., pp. 5-17.

"Convention on Extradition. Montevideo, December 26, 1933." Edited by M. O. Hudson. International Legislation 6. Washington, D.C.: Carnegie Endowment for International Peace, 1931-1950: 597-606.

"Convention to Prevent and Punish the Acts of Terrorism Taking the Form of Crimes Against Persons and Related Extortion That Are of International Significance." Pan American Union. Serie Sobre Tratados 37. Washington, D.C., February 2, 1971.

"Cuban Hijacking Law (September 16, 1969)." International Legal Materials 8 (1969): 1175-77.

Davison, W. Phillips. "Some Observations on Viet Cong Operations in the Villages." Rand Abstracts, RM 5367-2 (September 1968).

Dinstein, Yoram. "Terrorism and Wars of Liberation Applied to the Arab-Israeli Conflict: An Israeli Perspective." Israel Yearbook on Human Rights 3 (1973): 78.

"Draft Code of Offences Against the Peace and Security of Mankind." Paris, 1954. U.N. Doc.A/2693 (GACR, 9. sess., Suppl. 9), chap. 3.

"Efforts Continue to Check Arab Terrorism." Washington, D.C.: Embassy of Israel, 1973.

El-Rayyes, Riad N., and Dunia Nahas, eds. Guerrillas for Palestine: A Study of the Palestinian Commando Organization. Beirut: An-Nahar Press Services, 1974.

ESCO Foundation for Palestine. Palestine: A Study of Jewish, Arab and British Policies 1. New Haven, Conn.: Yale University Press, 1947.

FitzGerald, G. F. "The London Draft Convention on Acts of Unlawful Interference Against International Civil Aviation." Edited E. W. McWhinney. Aerial Piracy and International Law. Leiden, A. W.: Sijthoff, 1971, pp. 36-54.

Foda, Ezzeldin. Israeli Belligerent Occupation and Palestinian Armed Resistance in International Law. Beirut: Palestine Liberation Organization Research Center, 1970.

Gall, Norman. "The Only Logical Answer." Hanover, N.H., 1971. American Universities Field Staff Reports 6, no. 1.

Gist, Francis J. "The Aircraft Hijacker and International Law." Thesis, McGill University, 1968.

Goldberg, Yona. "Haganah or Terror." New York: Hechalutz, 1947.

Green, L. C. "International Terrorism." Address delivered to the Edmonton branch of the Canadian Institute of International Affairs, March 20, 1973.

_____. "The Nature and Control of International Terrorism." University of Alberta, Department of Political Science, Occasional Paper No. 1, 1974.

Horrell, Muriel. "Terrorism in Southern Africa." Johannesburg: South African Institute of Race Relations, 1968.

The Human Cost of Communism in Vietnam. Washington, D.C.: U.S. Government Printing Office, 1972.

The ICAO and Arab Terrorist Operations: A Record of Resolutions. Jerusalem: Ministry for Foreign Affairs, 1973.

Inter-American Juridical Committee. "Documentos Preparados por el Comite Juridico Interamericano Sobre los Actos de Terrorismo y en Particular el Secuestro, la Extorsion y Otros Atentados Contra las Personas." Washington, D.C.: Union Panamericana, November 4, 1970. OEA/Ser. G (CP/Doc. 54 Rev. 1).

_____. "Draft Convention on Terrorism and Kidnapping of Persons for Purposes of Extortion [September 26, 1970]; Statement of Reasons for the Draft Convention on Terrorism and Kidnapping [October 5, 1970]." International Legal Materials 9 (1970): 1177-82, 1250-73.

"International Conference on Air Law Approves Convention on Aircraft Hijacking." Department of State Bulletin 64 (1971): 50-55.

International Terrorism. Proceedings of the Third Annual Conference of the Canadian Council on International Law held at the University of Ottawa, October 18-19, 1974.

"Interrogation Procedures: Lord Gardiner's Report." Review of the International Commission of Jurists 8 (1972): 17-22.

Kadi, Leila S., ed. Basic Political Documents of the Armed Palestinian Resistance Movement. Beirut: Palestine Liberation Organization Research Center, 1969.

Khaleque, Abdul. "Terrorism's Menace: How to Combat It." Jalpaiguri: A. Wadubat Jalpaiguri Kohinoor Prtg. Works, 1932.

Knauth, Arnold W. "Status of Aircraft with Reference to Criminal Law for Aircraft." International Law Association. Report of the Forty-Eighth Conference, New York, 1958. London, 1958, pp. 277-305.

League of Nations. "Draft Convention for the Prevention and Punishment of Terrorism." "Draft Convention for the Creation of an International Criminal Court" and "Observations by Governments." L.O.N. 1936. Vol. 2, pp. 3-16.

Loy, Frank E. "Department [of Transportation] Reviews Problem of Aircraft Hijacking and Proposals for International Action." Department of State Bulletin 60 (1969): 212-14.

"Measures to Prevent International Terrorism. . . . " Study prepared by the Secretariat in accordance with the decision taken by the Sixth Committee at its 1314th meeting on September 27, 1972. UN Doc. A/C.6/418, November 2, 1972, pp. 10-16.

Meron, Theodor. Some Legal Aspects of Arab Terrorists' Claims to Privileged Combatancy. New York: Sabra Books, 1970.

Miller, Linda B. "Cyprus: The Law and Politics of Civil Strife." Occasional Papers in International Affairs, no. 19 (1968).

Moss, Robert. Urban Guerrilla Warfare. London: International Institute for Strategic Studies Adelphi Paper no. 79, 1971.

Most, Johann. Science of Revolutionary War: Manual for Instruction in the Use and Preparation of Nitro-Glycerine, Dynamite, Gun-Cotton, Fulminating Mercury, Bombs, Fuses, and Poisons, etc., etc. New York: International Zeitung Verein [1884].

Most, John [Johann J.]. The Beast of Property. New Haven, Conn.: International Workingman's Association Group [1883].

Nasser Terror Gangs: The Story of the Fedayun. Jerusalem: Ministry for Foreign Affairs, 1956.

"The Origins and Fundamental Causes of International Terrorism." United Nations, General Assembly, Doc. A/C.6/418 (November 2, 1972), pp. 6-9.

Pella, V. V. "La Repression du Terrorisme et la Creation d'Une Cour Internationale." Nouvelle Revue de Droit International Prive 5 (1938): 785-810; 6 (1939): 120-38.

Pike, Douglas. The Viet-Cong Strategy of Terror. Saigon: U.S. Mission, Viet-Nam, 1970.

"Piracy: Sea and Air." International Law Association. Report of the Fifty-Fourth Conference, The Hague, August 23-29, 1970. London, 1971, pp. 706-54.

Poulantaas, Nicholas M. "Some Problems of International Law Connected with Urban Guerrilla Warfare: The Kidnapping of Members of Diplomatic Missions, Consular Offices and Other Foreign Personnel." Annales d'Etudes Internationales 3 (1972). Geneva: Association des Anciens Etudiants de l'Institut Universitaire des Hautes Etudes Internationales, 1972: 137-67.

"Protocol Concerning Measures to Be Taken Against the Anarchist Movement. St. Petersburg, March 1-14, 1904." Georg Friedrich von Martens. Nouveau Recueil General de Traites et Autres Actes Relatifs aux Rapports de Droit International. 3 ser. Leipzig: Dieterien, 1909-39, vol. 10, p. 81.

Report of the Ad Hoc Committee on International Terrorism. General Assembly Official Records, 28th Sess., Suppl. 28, UN Doc. A/9028.

Report of the National Advisory Commission on Civil Disorders. New York: Bantam Books, 1968.

Riots, Civil and Criminal Disorders—Hearings Before the Permanent Sub-Committee on Investigations of the Committee on Government Operations, United States Senate. Washington, D.C.: U.S. Government Printing Office, 1970.

Romaniecki, Leon. The Arab Terrorists in the Middle East and the Soviet Union. Jerusalem: Soviet and East European Research Center of the Hebrew University of Jerusalem, 1973.

The Savage Kinship: A Chronology of the Use of Violence for Political Ends in Arab Countries. Jerusalem: Carta, 1973.

Sedition Committee, 1918, Report. Calcutta: Superintendent Government Printing, 1918.

"South American Police Convention. Buenos Aires, February 29, 1920." M. O. Hudsdon, ed. International Legislation. Washington, D.C.: Carnegie Endowment for International Peace, 1931-50, 1: 448-51.

Stevenson, John R. "Department Urges Senate Advice and Consent to Ratification of Hijacking Convention Statement Made Before the Committee on Foreign Relations, U.S. Senate, June 7, 1971." Department of State Bulletin 65 (1971): 84-88.

Stokke, O., and C. Widstrand. Southern Africa: The UN-OAY Conference 2 (Papers and Documents). Uppsala: Scandinavian Institute of African Studies, 1973.

A Strategy for the Liberation of Palestine. Mimeographed. Amman: P.F.L.P. Information Department, 1969.

A Study: Viet Cong Use of Terror. Saigon: U.S. Mission in Viet Nam, 1967.

Sundberg, M. Jacob. "Piracy: Sea and Air." International Law Association. Report of the Fifty-Fourth Conference (The Hague, August 23-29, 1970). London, 1971, pp. 755-71.

"Symposium on the Unlawful Seizure of Aircraft: Approaches to the Legal Problems." (The Legal Problems: An Introduction, A. Samuels. A Proposed Method of Control, A. E. Evans. A Government Perspective, B. Rein. The 1970 Hague Convention, R. H. Mankiewicz. The Case for an International Criminal Court, J. W. F. Sundberg). Journal of Air Law and Commerce 37 (1971): 162-233.

"Task Force on Kidnapping." [Transcript of an interview by the editors of Canada Today with Claude Roquet and Allen Rowe on the operations of the special Task Force created by the Canadian

Department of External Affairs following the kidnapping of James Cross, senior British Trade Commissioner in Montreal, by French Canadian extremists]. External Affairs 23 (1971): 6-11.

Terror in East Pakistan. Karachi Publications, 1971.

Terrorism. A Staff Study prepared by the Committee on Internal Security of the U.S. House of Representatives. Washington, D.C.: U.S. Government Printing Office, 1974.

Terrorism in Cyprus: The Captured Documents. Transcribed extracts issued by authority of the Secretary of State for the Colonies. London: H. M. Stationery Office, 1956.

To Establish Justice, to Insure Domestic Tranquility. Final Report of the National Commission on Causes and Prevention of Violence. New York: Bantam Books, 1970.

"Tokyo Convention." International Criminal Police Review 186 (1965): 81-86.

"Treaty on Extradition and Protection Against Anarchism. Mexico City, January 28, 1902." Georg Friedrich von Martens. Nouveau Recueil General de Traites et Autres Actes Relatifs aux Rapports de Droit International. 3d. ser. Leipzig: Dieterich, 1909-39, vol. 6, p. 185.

"Tribunal de Apelaciones en lo Penal y Juzgado de Crimen de 3er Turno, Extradicion. Delitos Politicos. Terrorismo. Tratado de Derecho Penal Internacional de Montevideo de 1889. Delitos Contra la Seguridad del Estado. Concepto de Delito Conexo." Anuario Uruguayo de Derecho Internacional, 1962. Montevideo: Republica Oriental del Uruguay, 1962, pp. 269-323.

A Trust Betrayed: Namibia. New York: UN Office of Public Information, 1974.

U.K. Commission on Legal Procedures to Deal with Terrorist Activities in Northern Ireland. Report to the Commission to Consider Legal Procedures to Deal with Terrorist Activities in Northern Ireland. HMSO, 1972.

"Unlawful Interference with Aircraft." International Law Association. Report of the Fifty-Fourth Conference, The Hague, August 23-29, 1970. London, 1971, pp. 336-404.

U.S. Congress. House. Committee on Foreign Affairs. "Aircraft
Hijacking." Hearings before the Committee on Resolutions referred to the Committee Concerning Aircraft Hijacking and Related Matters, September 17, 22, 23, and 30, 1970. Washington, D.C., 1970. (U.S. 91. Cong., 2. sess.)

_____. Subcommittee on Inter-American Affairs. "Air Piracy in the
Caribbean Area." Report of the Subcommittee pursuant to H.R.
179 authorizing the Committee to conduct thorough studies and investigations of all matters coming within the jurisdictions of the
Committee. Washington, D.C., 1968. (U.S. 90. Cong., 2.
sess. Committee print.)

_____. "Safety of U.S. Diplomats." Hearings, April 27, 1970.
Washington, D.C., 1971. (U.s. 91. Cong., 2 sess.)

U.S. Congress. House. Committee on Interstate and Foreign Commerce. "Aircraft Piracy." Preliminary report, March 11,
1969. (U.S. 91. Cong., 1. sess. House. Report, 91-33.)

_____. Subcommittee on Transportation and Aeronautics. "Imple-
mentation of Tokyo Convention." Hearing, November 4, 1969,
on H.R. 14301, a bill to implement the Convention on Offenses
and Certain Other Acts Committed on Board Aircrafts, and for
other purposes. Washington, D.C., 1969. (U.S. 91. Cong., 1.
sess. Serial no. 91-26.)

U.S. Congress. Senate. Committee on Finance. "Skyjacking."
Hearing on H.R. 19444, October 6, 1970. Washington, D.C.,
1970. (U.S. 91. Cong., 2. sess.)

U.S. Congress. Senate. Committee on Foreign Relations. "Aircraft Hijacking Convention: The Convention for the Suppression
of Unlawful Seizure of Aircraft, signed at The Hague, December 16, 1970." Hearings before the Committee on Executive A,
92d Congress, 1st session, June 7 and July 20, 1971. Washington, D.C., 1971. (U.S. 92. Cong., 1. sess.)

U.S. Department of Justice. Terrorism: Statistics and Techniques—
An FBI Special Study, January 12, 1973.

Valladao, H. "Piracy: Sea and Air." International Law Association. Report of the Fifty-Fourth Conference (The Hague, August 23-29, 1970). London, 1971, pp. 735-54.

Viet Cong Directive on "Repression." Saigon: Joint U.S. Public Affairs Office, n.d.

Viet Cong Terror Tactics in South Viet Nam. Washington, D.C.: Department of State, July 1967.

Violence and Dialogue in the Middle East: The Palestine Entity and Other Case Studies. A summary record [of] the 24th annual conference of the Middle East Institute, Washington, D.C., October 2-3, 1970.

Weigert, Gideon. Whose Killeth a Believer. Jerusalem: Israel Communications, 1971.

Yahalom, Dan. File on Arab Terrorism. Jerusalem: Carta, 1973.

Yahalom, Yivtah. Arab Terror. Tel Aviv: World Labour Zionist Movement, 1969.

Yaniv, A. P.L.O.: A Profile. Jerusalem: Israel Universities Study Group for Middle East Affairs, 1974.

ABOUT THE EDITOR AND CONTRIBUTORS

YONAH ALEXANDER is Professor of International and Area Studies at State University of New York (College at Oneonta); Senior Fellow, the American University (Institute for Studies in Justice and Social Behavior); and Research Associate, Columbia University (Graduate School of Journalism).

Educated at Columbia (Ph.D.) and the University of Chicago (M.A.), Professor Alexander has studied, taught, and done research in North and South America, Europe, Asia, Africa, and the Middle East. Among his books are The Role of Communications in the Middle East Conflict: Ideological and Religious Aspects, International Technical Assistance Experts: A Case Study of the U.N. Experience (both Praeger), Israel, Crescent and Star: Arab and Israeli Perspectives on the Middle East Conflict (coeditor with N. N. Kittrie), and War and Peace in the Middle East: Psychological Warfare and Propaganda (forthcoming).

J. BOWYER BELL is Research Associate, Columbia University (Institute for War and Peace Studies). He is the author of The Myth of the Guerrilla: Revolutionary Theory and Malpractice, The Secret Army: The IRA 1916-1974, The Long War: Israel and the Arabs Since 1946, Besieged: Seven Cities Under Attack, and On Revolt: Strategies of National Liberation (forthcoming).

ROSS BUTLER is President of Permavest International. He is a former Professor of Latin American Affairs at the University of Oregon, University of Arizona, and University of Victoria. Dr. Butler has also studied, taught, and done research in Latin America.

EDGAR EFRAT is Professor of Political Science at the University of Victoria. Previously he taught at the University of Texas and University of Washington. Among his numerous publications is Introduction to Sub-Saharan Africa.

SEYMOUR M. FINGER is Professor of Political Science at Staten Island Community College and the Graduate School of the City University of New York; Director of the Ralph Bunche Institute on the United Nations; President of the Institute for Mediterranean Affairs; and member of the Council on Foreign Relations. Previously he was Ambassador and Senior Adviser to the Permanent U.S. Representative to the United Nations, and Special Consultant to the Brookings Institution.

ROBERT O. FREEDMAN is Associate Professor of Political Science and Dean, Graduate School, Baltimore Hebrew College. He is author of Soviet Policy Toward the Middle East Since Nasser, and Economic Warfare in the Communist Bloc: A Study of Soviet Economic Pressure Against Yugoslavia, Albania, and Communist China (both Praeger).

LESLIE C. GREEN is University Professor, University of Alberta, and Academic in Residence, Legal Bureau, Department of External Affairs, Canada. Formerly Dean, Faculty of Law, University of Singapore, he is author of International Law Through the Cases (3rd ed.), and Law and Society.

THOMAS E. HACHEY is Associate Professor of History at Marquette University. He is author of The Problem of Partition: Peril to World Peace, editor of Anglo-Vatican Relations, 1914-1939: Confidential Annual Reports of the British Minister to the Holy See and Confidential Dispatches: Analyses of America by the British Ambassador, 1939-1945, and co-editor with Ralph Weber of Voices of Revolution: Rebels and Rhetoric.

BERNARD K. JOHNPOLL is Professor of Political Science at State University of New York (Albany). Formerly a newspaper reporter and editor, he is the author of Pacifist's Progress, The Politics of Futility, The Impossible Dream, and History of Radicalism in the U.S., 1826-Present (forthcoming).

SALEEM QURESHI is Professor of Political Science at the University of Alberta. He is currently conducting research on "Institutional Policies and Political Integration" at the Centre for South Asian Studies, Nehru University in New Delhi.

DAMIR ROGULY is a Research Assistant at State University of New York at Binghamton, where he received his B.A. and M.A. degrees. He is currently engaged in research on Eastern Europe.

EDWARD WEISBAND is Associate Professor of Political Science and Director of International Studies of State University of New York at Binghamton. He is author of Turkish Foreign Policy 1943-1945: Small State Diplomacy and Great Power Politics and The Ideology of American Policy: A Paradigm of Lockian Liberalism, and co-author (with Thomas M. Franck) of Resignation in Protest: Political and Ethical Choices Between Loyalty to Team and Loyalty to Conscience in American Public Life and World Politics: Verbal Strategy Among the Superpowers, as well as co-editor of Secrecy and Foreign Policy and A Free Trade Association.

RELATED TITLES
Published by
Praeger Special Studies

CIVIL WARS AND THE POLITICS OF INTERNATIONAL
RELIEF: Africa, South Asia, and the Caribbean
edited by
Morris Davis

CRIMES AGAINST INTERNATIONALLY PROTECTED
PERSONS: PREVENTION AND PUNISHMENT: An Analysis
of the UN Convention
Louis M. Bloomfield
Gerald F. Fitzgerald

NONSTATE NATIONS IN INTERNATIONAL POLITICS:
Comparative System Analyses
edited by
Judy S. Bertelsen

*PLANNING ALTERNATIVE WORLD FUTURES: Values,
Methods, and Models
edited by
Louis Rene Beres
Harry R. Targ

THE POLITICS OF DIVISION, PARTITION, AND
UNIFICATION
edited by
Ray Edward Johnston

SMALL STATES AND SEGMENTED SOCIETIES: National
Political Integration in a Global Environment
edited by
Stephanie G. Neuman

*Also available in paperback as a PSS Student Edition.